THE VIRGINIA CONSERVATIVES
1867–1879

THE VIRGINIA CONSERVATIVES

1867–1879

A STUDY IN RECONSTRUCTION POLITICS

by Jack P. Maddex, Jr.

THE UNIVERSITY OF NORTH CAROLINA PRESS
Chapel Hill

To Ellen

"But I reckon I got to light out for the territory ahead of the rest, because Aunt Sally she's going to adopt me and sivilize me, and I can't stand it. I been there before."

Contents

By Way of Introduction

The Conservative party that governed Virginia between 1870 and 1879 deserves a great deal of attention in discussions of Southern conservatism during and after the Reconstruction period. Winning control of its state early in the Reconstruction process, it provided a model of "redemption" for other Southern states. It educated such young men as John W. Daniel, William Mahone, Thomas M. Logan, and Jabez L. M. Curry for later leadership in pioneering a "New South." The Conservative party's history, between its inception in 1867 and its division in 1879, developed many of the general tendencies of Southern conservatism between 1865 and 1900.

Recent discussion of the post-Reconstruction South has centered on its relationship to antebellum Southern society. One interpretation, long popular, has been the tradition of "Bourbon" continuity—the belief that the dominant elite of the slavery era recovered its ascendancy after Reconstruction, restoring its traditional policies and most of its social institutions. Many Southerners have used that viewpoint as a defense mechanism, adapting to "Yankee" ways but insulating their minds from stark recognition of the transformation. Virginians, especially, have often posited a changeless tradition extending, with only a few sporadic interruptions, from the William Byrds of Westover to the Harry Byrds of Winchester. A number of scholars, emphasizing the less unique features of the earlier South and the more traditional features of the later, have found elements of validity in the popular impression of a "Bourbon" restoration.

The principal alternative interpretation has been the one that C. Vann Woodward has stated. "Even though a few of the old names were prominent among the new leaders," Woodward wrote in 1951, "Redemption was not a return of an old system nor the restoration of an old ruling class. It was rather a new phase of the revolutionary process begun in 1865."[1] The conservative "redeemers," he contended , had sought to bring their region into conformity with contemporary industrial capitalism. Woodward's interpretation accords with Charles A. Beard's description of the conflict of the 1860's as "the Second American Revolution," and Barrington Moore, Jr.,'s, as "the Last Capitalist Revolution."

In the present study, in spite of many disagreements with Woodward on lesser matters, I have concluded that the Virginia Conservatives fit very well his general model of "redeemer" leadership. They united a number of schools of thought, but their effective leaders were, indeed, a new elite, agents of adaptation instead of restoration. Working to integrate their homeland into the structure of the contemporary United States, they adopted "Yankee" institutions and ideas: industrial capitalism, American nationalism, Gilded-Age political practices, and a system of race relations that made the Negro a freeman and officially a citizen but not an equal. They looked forward to a new South modeled in many respects on the pattern of the conquering North.

The conservatives of Virginia manifested the adaptive tendency more consistently than those of most other Southern states. Proponents of a "New South" were frustrated by their region's economic retardation, its dependent role in the national economy, the smallness of its urban middle class, and the persistent hold of Southern tradition on many minds.[2] These obstacles were less imposing in Virginia than in the Lower South, and the Conservatives of Virginia, consequently, were readier to adapt than conservatives of most Southern states. Even so, they underestimated the impediments—many, of their own making—that doomed their expectation of rapid social change to decades of painful postponement. Virginia's "redeemers," therefore, are an extremely significant case for the study of Southern conservatism after 1865—distinctive mainly in that conditions in their state gave freer rein to modernizing forces than in many other parts of the South.[3]

In all parts of this book, the reader should keep in mind the im-

1. C. Vann Woodward, *Origins of the New South, 1877–1913* (Baton Rouge: Louisiana State University Press, 1951), pp. 21–22 (hereafter cited as *Origins*).

2. For the obstacles that inherited southern traditions, even in their vestigial twentieth-century forms, impose on capitalist development, see William H. Nicholls, *Southern Tradition and Regional Progress* (Chapel Hill: University of North Carolina Press, 1960), pp. 157–63.

3. I have less of a controversy than one might expect, therefore, with William J. Cooper, Jr., in his *The Conservative Regime: South Carolina, 1877–1890* ("Johns

pact for change of the War of 1861–65—the armed phase of "the Last Capitalist Revolution"—and of its attendant events. This is largely a study of what happens to people defeated by revolutionary wars. Some withdraw; some drift with the tide, unable to chart a course; some fume and fuss, deprived of a social base from which to continue effective resistance. But others adapt, finding their way to leadership positions in the new order by conforming to its terms. They thereby become participants in the mopping-up phases of the movement that has engulfed them.

A NOTE ON NOMENCLATURE

Many writers have referred to the conservative "redeemers" as "Bourbons." That name presupposes the opinion that the conservatives were an antebellum elite who returned to power having "learned nothing and forgotten nothing." The "redeemers" themselves used the term "Bourbon" principally as a pejorative epithet for irreconcilables, usually powerless, who refused to conform to the post-Confederate world. In this study, I have avoided the word "Bourbon," using the official name "Conservative" for the party and its leaders generally and "traditionalist" for the unreconstructed.

Some twentieth-century readers, imposing their customary nomenclature on a past era, may read into the name "Conservative" a general adherence to inherited ways and resistance to social change. In the political vocabulary of the 1870's, as a matter of fact, the terms "conservative" and "liberal," innocent of the meanings with which the twentieth century would invest them, functioned more often as synonyms than as antonyms.

The name "conservative," as the Southern redeemers used it, was largely negative in content. It stood not for intransigent traditionalism but for a union of all the elements opposing "Radical" Republicanism. The traditionalist Henry A. Wise called the name a "lucus a non lucendo," indicating that it failed to describe the principles of the "Omnium gatherum combination" to which it referred.[4] To contemporaries, the word "conservatism" connoted moderation.

Hopkins University Studies in Historical and Political Science," 86th Series, No. 1 [Baltimore: The Johns Hopkins Press, 1968]). It seems reasonable to suppose, however, that if I had chosen to write on South Carolina and Cooper on Virginia, the resulting books would differ significantly in findings from those we have in fact written.

4. James A. Bear, Jr., ed., "Henry A. Wise and the Campaign of 1873: Some Letters from the Papers of James Lawson Kemper," *Virginia Magazine of History and Biography*, LXII (July, 1954), 330. Republican Congressman James H. Platt, Jr., of Vir-

Governor Francis H. Pierpont, during presidential Reconstruction, expressed his intention "to get the conservative white men in the state to form a party against the radical rebels."[5]

In Virginia as in other Southern states, former members of the Whig party—relatively moderate, nationalist, and economically innovative—preferred the party name "Conservative" in order to avoid identification with the Democratic party.[6] The first Virginians to assume the party name "Conservative" had been the business-oriented followers of William Cabell Rives. Breaking from the Democratic party in 1837, Rives's Conservatives had, after several years as an independent party, found their way into the Whig ranks. During the 1850's, Whigs in Virginia had sometimes called themselves the "Conservative Opposition."[7] "The leading principle of the Whig party," the Whig leader Alexander H. H. Stuart wrote in 1856, "was conservatism."[8] In national politics during the Reconstruction period, the name "conservative" was commonly adopted by Republicans and Unionists who had broken with the Radical Republicans and by alliances between those "conservatives" and Democrats.[9]

Traditionalist Democrats sometimes objected to the Conservative party's name and attempted to substitute the name "Democratic."[10] The federal government, one of them asserted, "cannot be admin-

ginia also accused the Conservatives of evasion in their nomenclature. A "Conservative," Platt declared, was "a man who is a democrat, but is ashamed to acknowledge it." *Congressional Globe*, 42 Congress, 2 Session, *Appendix*, 197 (1872).

5. Quoted in Charles H. Ambler, *Francis H. Pierpont: Union War Governor of Virginia and Father of West Virginia* (Chapel Hill: University of North Carolina Press, 1937), pp. 295–96. See the similar usage in Richmond *Evening State Journal*, unidentified clipping on Senator John W. Johnston, 1870, in Johnston-McMullen Papers, Duke University.

6. John S. Wise, *The Lion's Skin: A Historical Novel and a Novel History* (New York: Doubleday, Page, and Company, 1905), p. 244; see Woodward, *Origins*, pp. 2–3, and Thomas Benjamin Alexander, "Persistent Whiggery in the Confederate South, 1861–1877," *Journal of Southern History*, XXVII (August, 1961), 313, 321, 323.

7. Richmond *Daily Whig*, April 25, 1860.

8. Alexander F. Robertson, *Alexander Hugh Holmes Stuart, 1807–1891: A Biography* (Richmond: William Byrd Press, 1925), p. 63.

9. The most extreme Democrats were suspicious of such "Conservatives." See H. H. Young, "Democrats and 'Conservatives,'" *The Old Guard*, V (July, 1867), 543–45; [C. Chauncey Burr], "Dialogue between a Democrat and a 'Conservative,'" *The Old Guard*, VIII (April, 1870), 257–63.

10. Alvin Arthur Fahrner, "The Public Career of 'Extra Billy' Smith" (Ph.D. dissertation, University of North Carolina, 1955), p. 320. See Willie D. Halsell, "The Bourbon Period in Mississippi Politics, 1875–1890," *Journal of Southern History*, XI (November, 1945), 521–22.

istered upon any other principles but the old Democratic platform. As to Conservatism [, that] is all *claptrap*, and effects nothing."[11] Some other Conservatives, on the other hand, felt that the party's name did not adequately reflect its receptivity to innovation. In 1869, when the Conservatives won control of the state government, Governor-elect Gilbert C. Walker stated that his party should properly be called "Liberal Republican."[12] Congressional candidate Joseph E. Segar preferred the name "Reconstruction party," and the Louisville *Journal* believed that the name "Liberal" would best describe the movement.[13] As late as 1873, an occasional Conservative would propose to rename the party "Liberal" in order to describe its policies more accurately.[14]

If the Conservatives themselves could not all agree on a single-word definition of their role and policy, neither can the present-day reader learn much about them from the exegesis of a single word. The many words in this volume constitute an extended definition of the "Conservative" movement in post-1865 Virginia—and no definition of publishable length can suffice to explore all the significant facets and varieties of its meaning.

11. S. B. Major to James Lawson Kemper, May 24, 1876, James Lawson Kemper Papers, University of Virginia.

12. Richmond *Daily Whig*, July 16, 1869.

13. *Ibid.*, August 25, 1869; [Joseph Segar], *Letter of the Hon. Joseph Segar, on the Late Elections in Virginia* (n.p., [1869]), p. 3.

14. C. B. Raine to William Mahone, August 1, 1873, William Mahone Papers, Duke University.

Acknowledgments

I wish to acknowledge the encouragement and advice that a number of persons have extended to me in the course of this work. It was Professor Edward Younger of the University of Virginia who convinced me, years ago, of the absurd proposition that I might carry out a study of the Virginia Conservatives within the scope of an undergraduate thesis. He has assisted and encouraged me at a number of other points in the ensuing years. I began the task under the supervision, successively, of Professors Arthur S. Link of Princeton University and Robert P. Sharkey now of the George Washington University. It is hard to find words to express my obligation to Professor George B. Tindall of the University of North Carolina at Chapel Hill, who guided the work in dissertation form. I cannot imagine how an advisor could offer more intelligent co-operation than he afforded. I wish also to express gratitude to the other members of my dissertation committee, Professors Frank W. Klingberg, Hugh T. Lefler, George V. Taylor, and Guy B. Johnson.

Professors Robert F. Durden of Duke University, Robert R. Jones of the University of Southwestern Louisiana, and F. Nash Boney of the University of Georgia have assisted me in various ways during the course of the project. Professor Thomas P. Govan of the University of Oregon read and criticized the manuscript, and Calvin M. Jensen and Terry J. Gould did the same for parts of it. Mr. Henry P. McGill granted me permission to examine the William Mahone Papers, deposited at Duke University, which are in his ownership. At one point, the Smith Fund at the University of North Carolina at Chapel Hill gave me a small grant to assist in the project. I owe thanks to Mrs. Leland Stilwell of Eugene, Oregon, for typing the manuscript and to The University of North Carolina Press for its consideration and co-operation. The two anonymous critics who at different times reviewed versions of the manuscript for the Press have been especially helpful. Finally, I want to express heartfelt thanks to my wife, Ellen, for putting up with me while I've been at work on this task.

Voices

Revolutions are the grand occasions of history—grand Quarterdays on which the transactions of preceding periods of work and steady labor are audited and balanced. . . .

We are on the unspent wave of a mighty revolution; and this revolution shall fulfill no man's delineations; it shall accomplish no man's prophecies; it shall flatter no man's prescience; it shall culminate in no man's ideals.

It is the MASTER-SPIRIT who is touching the springs; who is convulsing the firm earth; who is dashing its mountains together; who is turning its streams into new channels: when the storm lulls; when the thunders are hushed; when the seams in the clouds are closed; when the mist rises:—we do not know what we shall see—but a stratification which nobody expected to see.

—Richmond *Enquirer and Examiner*, 1869

It would be great folly for any one belonging to our generation to be twitting his neighbor on inconsistency of opinion in regard to public affairs during the last twenty years. . . .

—WILLIAM HENRY RUFFNER, 1875

Virginia Conservatism is the outgrowth of that public safety which is the supreme law. . . . The essential condition is that every possible concession and compromise must be freely made for the common good, and in every hour of its history it has vindicated this principle. In its very birth it accepted the fellowship of a party alien to it in name and principle, and sacrificed some of its worthiest citizens, sweeping into the highest office in the Commonwealth . . . a stranger in birth and associations. It placed Republicans who entered its ranks in both branches of assembly. . . . It supported for the presidency the bitterest and most consistent political enemy Virginia ever knew. In a word, it crystallized, in abundant practical

[*xix*]

forms, its purpose to merge every other consideration that could be merged in this one aspiration and resolve—to regenerate the State.

—ARMSTRONG M. KEILEY, 1876

The revolution by arms ended with Lee's surrender, but . . . *the* revolution goes on year by year—nay, day by day. How, where and when it will cease, God only knows.

—JUDGE EDWARD C. BURKS, 1873

[A] northern fort has been established in our political citadel bearing our old flag which it is not entitled to carry & seeking to place Virginia under the control of northern men & I fear northern principles.

—ROBERT M. T. HUNTER, 1874

Trade killed Chivalry and now sits in the throne. It was Trade that hatched the Jacquerie in the 14th century: it was Trade that hatched John Brown, and broke the saintly heart of Robert Lee, in the 19th.

—SIDNEY LANIER, 1872[1]

1. Sources of quotations: Richmond *Enquirer-Examiner*, March 13, 1869; William Henry Ruffner in Richmond *Enquirer*, April 6, 1875; Armstrong M. Keiley, speech in Richmond, reported in Richmond *Dispatch*, May 25, 1876; Edward C. Burks to Wyndham Robertson, October 4, 1873, Wyndham Robertson Papers, University of Chicago; Robert M. T. Hunter to Lewis E. Harvie (copy), January 17, 1874, Hunter-Garnett Papers, University of Virginia; *The Works of Sidney Lanier*, edited by Charles R. Anderson and Aubrey H. Starke (Baltimore: The Johns Hopkins Press, 1945), VIII, 224.

THE VIRGINIA CONSERVATIVES
1867–1879

I.

A Long Time Dead

It was with a "painful intensity" of emotion, in 1873, that Henry A. Wise considered a letter from his old friend James Lawson Kemper, asking him to support Kemper as the Conservative candidate for governor of Virginia.

In former days, Wise himself had been one of the giants of Virginia politics—successively congressman, governor, and brigadier general in the Army of Northern Virginia. The Southern Confederacy's collapse had decisively terminated his political career. Refusing to apply for recovery of his political rights, he had held no public position since 1865 except as a member of the commission to determine the boundary between Maryland and Virginia. His fellow citizens, puzzled and amused by his occasional pronouncements on current events, regarded him as a relic of a departed era. Kemper, like Wise, had been a Democratic politician and a Confederate general—but eight years of bitter experience had taught the elder statesman that a great gulf separated most of his former associates from himself in outlook.

His lesson began at the time of Lee's surrender. Since the Freedmen's Bureau was occupying his plantation, Wise wandered about Virginia, isolated, for months. Coming to rest in Richmond, he was startled to discover that many of his Confederate comrades-in-arms, including General Robert E. Lee, had applied to President Andrew Johnson for amnesty for their Confederate service. Old Governor Wise could not understand their eagerness to confess, implicitly, that in defending the constitutional right of secession they had committed treason.[1]

---

1. James A. Bear, Jr., ed., "Henry A. Wise and the Campaign of 1873: Some Letters from the Papers of James Lawson Kemper," *Virginia Magazine of History and Biography*, LXII (July, 1945), pp. 326–28 (hereafter cited as "Wise and 1873 Campaign"); all citations from this source refer to Wise's letter of August 18, 1873, to Kemper.

Wise's hopes rallied in 1867, when conservative Virginians united to resist the congressional Reconstruction policy as an assault on their traditions. The year 1869, however, brought the most crushing disappointment of all. Nine Conservatives journeyed to Washington to offer federal authorities a settlement in which the Conservatives would accept enfranchisement of Negroes, the most hated Northern imposition. At first, it appeared that the "Committee of Nine" represented only itself; but in the ensuing months, the Conservative party dramatically reversed its policy. Withdrawing its candidates for state office, it endorsed instead a Republican faction's ticket, headed by a "carpetbagger" intruder. The Conservative organization also endorsed the Radical-dictated proposed state constitution, opposing only the separate clauses to deprive erstwhile Confederates of political rights. Accepting Negro suffrage, it held biracial election gatherings and appealed to Negroes for their votes. After winning its election, the Conservative legislature promptly ratified the Fourteenth and Fifteenth Amendments to the federal Constitution and subserviently petitioned Congress to restore the state to the status to which, Wise insisted, it was unconditionally entitled.[2]

After the surrender of 1869, Wise could not credit the Conservatives' credentials as redeemers from Radicalism and guardians of white supremacy. Their subsequent support of the antislavery reformer Horace Greeley, "that Harlequin of wickedness and folly," for president of the United States redoubled his disgust. The Conservatives seemed to him unprincipled opportunists, "out-carpetbagging the Carpet Baggers & out-scallawagging the Scallawaggers." Although he might vote for Kemper for governor, the old man made up his mind, he could not "touch, taste, handle or sort with the Conservative party or its ticket."[3]

In Henry A. Wise's eyes, the Virginia of the 1870's was in fact and law a different realm from the Old Dominion that had honored him before the war, and the Conservative party was related to no important political force in that other, antebellum, Virginia. Like many another disaffected traditionalist, the old governor could say with Benét's Clay Wingate, "The world I knew is a long time dead."[4]

2. *Ibid.*, pp. 328–31.
3. *Ibid.*, pp. 331–33, 336–37.
4. Stephen Vincent Benét, *John Brown's Body* (New York: Rinehart and Company, 1928), p. 318.

2.

Old Virginia

The Virginia Conservatives' education began in the period before 1861. Nearly all reared in a society characterized by slave labor, they later spent many years adjusting to one organized on a different basis. Insofar as the need to adjust resulted from external—not internal—events, men used to the Old South found it difficult to adjust to the New. Antebellum Virginia was not, however, a world to itself. In some respect distinctively "Southern," in others it participated in the common life of the American Union. With vestiges of precapitalist traditional societies—slavery and its social concomitants—it combined elements of nineteenth-century liberal capitalism. Although it was external force that overthrew slavery in the 1860's, the factors tending to its extinction were present in muted form within Virginia as well. Before the free-soil Republicans won control of the federal government, those factors were already educating some Virginians for the world in which they would live after 1865.

SOCIETY

During the 1850's, the Commonwealth of Virginia occupied a topographically symmetrical area centering in the Shenandoah Valley. The Blue Ridge bounded the Valley on the east and the Appalachian plateau, on the west. Eastward from the Blue Ridge, rivers made their way past Piedmont hills and Tidewater plain to the Chesapeake Bay. Westward from the Appalachians other streams wended through more rugged country toward the Ohio and Tennessee Rivers. In general, eastern Virginia was a land of slave-labor plantations and farms, dotted with a few small cities; western Virginia was a smallholder's free-labor frontier.

Of the 1,596,318 inhabitants of Virginia in 1860, 1,219,630 lived in the counties that would compose Virginia after 1865.[1] Five-twelfths of the latter number were Negro slaves, and only the 140,000 white adult males were able to qualify as voters. About 50,000 voters were slaveowning agriculturists, about half of whom owned more than five slaves each. About 13,000 voters were merchants or professional men, most of them small-scale slaveowners. The remainder of the electorate consisted of three groups about equal in numbers: farmers who owned land but no slaves, "mechanics," and propertyless "poor whites." These groups exercised very slight political power.[2]

In every part of the state, agriculture was the principal economic activity. Land was concentrated in large estates or in parcels belonging to the powerful families who also, ordinarily, owned the largest numbers of slaves and provided most of the political leadership.[3] "Previous to 1860," a southwest Virginia school superintendent later recalled with some exaggeration, "five great families held nearly the entire fertile portion of our county. They divided society into two classes, Virginia gentlemen and slaves, the poor dependent whites occupying a position like the grain between two millstones."[4]

Of the 490,865 slaves within Virginia's 1860 boundaries, 428,351 lived east of the Blue Ridge. In that politically dominant region, they were a majority of the population; in the remainder of the state, a small minority. In fifty-six of the sixty-four eastern counties, more than two-fifths of the free families owned slaves; in only one western county, a county later included in West Virginia, did the proportion of slaveowners reach that figure. In thirteen eastern counties, more than three-fifths of the inhabitants were slaves; in

1. U.S. Bureau of the Census, *Historical Statistics of the United States, Colonial Times to 1957* (Washington: Government Printing Office, 1960), p. 13 (hereafter cited as *Historical Statistics*). The postwar state of West Virginia included trans-Appalachian Virginia except for sixteen southwestern counties, plus six northern counties of the Valley.

2. George M. McFarland, "The Extension of Democracy in Virginia, 1850–1895" (Ph.D. dissertation, Princeton University, 1925), pp. 1–3 (hereafter cited as "Extension of Democracy").

3. For remarkably contrasting calculations of the distribution of land ownership, compare *ibid.*, pp. 36–37, and Appendix, Table X, with Emmett B. Fields, "The Agricultural Population of Virginia, 1850–1860" (Ph. D. dissertation, Vanderbilt University, 1953), pp. 122–23 (hereafter cited as "Agricultural Population"). McFarland finds a planter monopoly of land; Fields, an equitable distribution. Similar in sources and method, the studies differ in conceptual definitions.

4. Quoted in Amory D. Mayo, "Education in Southwestern Virginia," in *Report of the* [United States] *Commissioner of Education, 1890–1891* (Washington: Government Printing Office, 1891), p. 904 (hereafter cited as "Education").

sixteen, more than three-fifths of the free families owned slaves.[5]

The geographic distribution of slaves corresponded strikingly to that of the tobacco crop. Both, by 1860, concentrated most heavily in the southern Piedmont, extending with decreasing incidence eastward and northward.[6] That region most completely realized the ideal of the plantation system. Working slaves in gangs with close supervision, planters devoted as much land as possible to tobacco—or, if their land has ceased to support tobacco, to another "money crop" such as wheat. Many planters, in addition to managing their estates, practiced law or medicine and participated in county courts and political gatherings. Long-established planters lived by a well-defined code of proper behavior, respectful to social equals and paternalistic to inferiors. Leisurely and aristocratic, they did not understand the Yankee cult of money-grubbing efficiency and did not like its social manifestations. They prized above all a proud independence that expressed itself at best in self-discipline, at worst in eccentric irascibility.[7]

The traditional specialization in tobacco, by the 1820's, had ruinously exhausted the soil of the old tobacco lands of the Tidewater. The tobacco belt, consequently, moved westward across the southern Piedmont, and eastern planters turned to wheat and corn as alternative staple crops that they could send to Northern cities in the form of flour.[8] Many planters talked about improved methods of cultivation, but few practiced them before Edmund Ruffin's experiments with marl in the 1830's. Thereafter, especially in the tobacco-gutted Tidewater, real improvement occurred. Fertilization, superior implements, and crop diversification and rotation began to appear.[9]

5. Henry T. Shanks, *The Secession Movement in Virginia, 1847–1861* (Richmond: Garrett and Massie, 1934), pp. 5, 7, 10 (hereafter cited as *Secession Movement*); Fields, "Agricultural Population," p. 132.

6. Fields, "Agricultural Population," pp. 70–71, 131–32, 164–65, 168.

7. See Ulrich B. Phillips, *Life and Labor in the Old South* (Boston: Little, Brown and Company, 1929), pp. 112–15, 131–39, 188–251 (hereafter cited as *Life and Labor*); and George W. Bagby, *The Old Virginia Gentleman and Other Sketches*, edited by Ellen M. Bagby (4th ed.; Richmond: Dietz Press, 1943), pp. 1–30, 179–95 (hereafter cited as *Old Virginia Gentleman*).

8. Avery O. Craven, *Soil Exhaustion as a Factor in the Agricultural History of Virginia and Maryland, 1606–1860* ("University of Illinois Studies in Social Sciences," XIII, No. 1 [Urbana: University of Illinois Press, 1925]), 32, 35–36, 64, 66, 97–98 (hereafter cited as *Soil Exhaustion*); Shanks, *Secession Movement*, pp. 3, 5–7; Phillips *Life and Labor*, pp. 127, 138, 230, 231, 236, 238–49, 310–16.

9. Craven, *Soil Exhaustion*, pp. 122–61; McFarland, "Extension of Democracy," pp.

Simultaneously, slave labor began to disappear. As plantation agriculture expanded in the Deep South, some planters migrated with slaves and others sold economically redundant slaves southward and westward. In Virginia, the export of slaves increased efficiency, simplified the managerial task, and provided capital for agricultural experimentation. Between 1830 and 1860, slaves declined from 39.2 per cent of Virginia's population to 30.1 per cent. Counties in which farming practices progressed often reduced their proportions of slaves greatly, while the southern Piedmont greatly increased its proportion.[10] These facts posed a dilemma for planters: by selling slaves they could stabilize their agriculture, but by depleting Virginia's slave population they might undermine the system of slavery there.[11]

Agricultural reform also eroded faith in the economic benefits of slavery. Alert Virginians began to reflect on their slaves' inefficiency, and a few slaveowners converted to free-labor farming as more productive. In 1852, the Virginia State Agricultural Society adopted a statement calling attention to Virginia's agricultural backwardness in comparison with several Northern states; the members later rescinded the document for fear that it would supply ammunition for antislavery writers.[12] In some areas, principally Fairfax County, diversification attracted Northern settlers who pioneered in scientific farming.[13] The immigrants were another channel by which economic modernization might introduce social subversion. In 1860, Fairfax and adjoining counties distinguished by Northern immigration accounted for almost all of the votes that Abraham Lincoln, the "Black Republican" presidential candidate, received in the post-1865 area of Virginia.[14]

9–12. From postbellum complaints about Virginia farmland and planting practices, it appears that Craven overstates the reformers' success in restoring soil fertility.

10. Eugene D. Genovese, *The Political Economy of Slavery: Studies in the Economy and Society of the Slave South* (New York: Pantheon Books, 1965), pp. 88–105, 143–44, 152–53 (hereafter cited as *Political Economy*); Shanks, *Secession Movement*, p. 11; Fields, "Agricultural Population," p. 133.

11. Genovese, *Political Economy*, p. 139; see John C. Rutherfoord to William Cabell Rives, April 11, 1860, William Cabell Rives Papers, Library of Congress.

12. Frederick Law Olmsted, *The Cotton Kingdom: A Traveller's Observations on Cotton and Slavery in the American Slave States, Based upon Three Former Volumes of Journeys and Investigations by the Same Author*, edited, with an introduction, by Arthur M. Schlesinger (New York: Alfred A. Knopf, 1953), pp. 47–48, 72–109, 587–90, 601–5 (hereafter cited as *Cotton Kingdom*).

13. Clement Eaton, *Freedom of Thought in the Old South* (Durham: Duke University Press, 1940), pp. 238–39 (hereafter cited as *Freedom of Thought*).

14. Richard G. Lowe, "Republicans, Rebellion, and Reconstruction: The Repub-

Food crops, the family farm, and efficient cultivation characterized agriculture in western Virginia, where slavery and the plantation system penetrated only to a small extent. In the northwestern
Appalachian region, slavery never won a firm foothold and antislavery sentiment found open expression. Elsewhere in western Virginia, free-labor farming flourished and slaves enjoyed working
conditions approximating those of free laborers. C. C. Baldwin of
Rockbridge County attributed his farm's prosperity to his unortho-
dox policy of "no domestic restraints" on his slaves, who lived and
worked as hired hands would, ate as much as they chose, and even
carried keys to everything on the farm.[15]

From the great rural sea of Old Virginia, a few commercial cities
stood out as islands. As a rule, influential gentlemen lived on country estates rather than in towns. The principal business of the cities
and large towns, concentrated in the Tidewater area accessible to
seagoing ships, was to exchange the staple crops for goods planters
purchased. Only in such cities as Richmond, Petersburg, and Norfolk did a self-conscious business class exert much influence. The
Branches, Haxalls, Macfarlands, Crenshaws, and other Richmond
commercial families made themselves conspicuous as directors of
banks and mercantile houses, promoters of transportation projects,
and leaders of the Whig party. The merchants and urban professional men were few in number, depended on the planters economically, shared many of their values, and often aspired to become
country gentlemen. Nevertheless, their business interests, their relations with northern capitalists, and their desire for civil peace led
them to try to increase their share of the profits from staple agriculture, to promote economic rationality and diversification, and to
support the Whig policies of Henry Clay.[16]

The business interest was commercial and financial rather than
industrial. Virginia's 26,000 "mechanics" produced fifty million
dollars worth of goods in 1860, putting her far ahead of any other
Southern state in manufacturing but still in a very modest position
by Northern standards. Industry in the Old Dominion consisted primarily of domestic and local manufactures in the western free-labor

---

lican Party in Virginia, 1856–1870" (Ph.D. dissertation, University of Virginia, 1968),
p. 68n; Patricia P. Hickin, "Antislavery in Virginia, 1831–1861" (Ph.D. dissertation,
University of Virginia, 1968), p. 747.

15. Genovese, *Political Economy*, pp. 140–41.

16. The antebellum files of the Richmond *Whig* afford a good insight into the business community's activities and outlook.

region and of processing of staple crops in the eastern counties. During the 1850's the revival of agriculture provided an attractive channel for investment, and railroad transportation enabled Northern manufacturers to capture markets Virginians had previously commanded. In 1850, 3 per cent of the Americans engaged in "manufacturing" worked in Virginia; in 1860, only 2 per cent.[17]

Although businessmen expressed only the mildest criticism of the slave-plantation economy, their work-a-day activities nibbled at the peculiar institution's fringes. Slavery did not flourish in the cities. In 1840, slaves comprised 34 per cent of Richmond's population and 37.3 per cent of Norfolk's. In 1860, they were only 22.5 per cent of the population in Richmond, and 30.9 per cent in Norfolk. In addition, urban life increased the slave's experience and responsibility and decreased the master's immediate supervision. Richmond slaves destined for sale asked their master to sell them within the city because they had "acquired town habits."[18] Industry also exposed the dilemma of economic progress within Old Virginia's social framework. The tobacco and iron factories of Richmond and Petersburg employed large numbers of slaves, hiring them from planters on a yearly basis. These industrial slaves worked for regular work-days of eleven or twelve hours, received additional pay for overtime, went where they pleased except when at work, and spent their pocket-money freely. Some enjoyed the privileges of choosing their employers and of securing their own board and lodgings. Slaves whose working conditions resembled those of wage laborers threatened social stability. In 1853, the Richmond *Dispatch* pronounced the factory slaves a nuisance to public order and social stability. In spite of prohibitory laws, the "board-money" practice persisted. In 1860, the Richmond census listed four hundred slaves with the ominous notation, "owner unknown."[19]

By the standards of the Old South, Virginia exhibited much economic diversity. On the perimeter of the traditional system of plantation slavery other social sectors grew, resembling the northern states' free-labor capitalism: subsistence farming, scientific agriculture, urban commerce, and industry. These sectors stabilized the plantation system by diversification, but there were disturbing

17. McFarland, "Extension of Democracy," pp. 12–13.
18. Richard C. Wade, *Slavery in the Cities: The South, 1820–1860* (New York: Oxford University Press, 1964), pp. 18–22, 246, 327.
19. *Ibid.*, pp. 33–36, 51; Kathleen Bruce, *Virginia Iron Manufacture in the Slave Era* (New York and London: Century Company for American Historical Association, 1931), pp. 231–58; Genovese, *Political Economy*, p. 225.

signs that their continued growth might someday endanger its foundation. The sections of the state characterized by economic growth were those in which free labor predominated.[20] Farmers and businessmen did not draw the conclusion that there was an "irrepressible conflict" between their interests and the plantation system. Instead, they worked for their short-term interests by playing subordinate roles within the established economy. They were not insurgents. Nevertheless, their everyday experience was quietly preparing them for social leadership in an unforeseen future in which external intervention would reduce the plantation economy to a shambles, its ruling class to a curiosity, and its peculiar institution to a memory.

Some northern businessmen and economists indulged the hope that Virginia slaveowners would allow gradual economic change to bury their social system. In 1856, Eli Thayer, the Massachusetts businessman whose New England Emigrant Aid Company was helping win Kansas Territory for free labor, joined with John C. Underwood, an antislavery resident of Virginia, to incorporate the North American Emigrant Aid and Homestead Company. The incorporators hoped to hasten slavery's demise by fostering free-labor economic development in Virginia. The company founded the colony of Ceredo in congenial northwestern Virginia but, after some hesitation, the press and politicians of the Commonwealth closed ranks against the "Black Republican" scheme for subversion through investment. Finding the door closed to free-labor conquest by gradual economic penetration, Underwood concluded that Republican control of the federal government would be necessary to bring about the peaceful victory of free labor over slavery in Virginia.[21] Many proslavery Virginians, concurring, prepared for secession in that event.

GOVERNMENT

The planters and their allies held a firm rein on political power. In each house of the legislature elected in 1859, and in the Secession Convention of 1861, the great majority of the members

20. See Olmsted, *Cotton Kingdom*, pp. 88–89.
21. George Winston Smith, "Ante-Bellum Attempts of Northern Business Interests to 'Redeem' the Upper South," *Journal of Southern History*, XI (May, 1945), 177–213; Patricia Hickin, "John C. Underwood and the Antislavery Movement in Virginia, 1847–1860," *Virginia Magazine of History and Biography*, LXXIII (April, 1965), 161–65.

belonged to the slaveowning minority of white Virginians, and most of them owned more than five slaves each.[22] Not until 1851 were all white men entitled to vote in the Old Dominion. Planters ordinarily managed the small, poorly publicized meetings in which the political parties selected their candidates for local office and delegates to their state conventions. The political system did not insure officials' responsibility to the voters' desires. Legislators did not vote along party lines, election campaigns provided spectacles and rhetoric rather than political education, and the press editorialized on federal rather than state issues.[23] Most Virginians were satisfied to defer to one or another element of the established political leadership. All the functions of local government reposed in the "county court," an assembly of local squires who held office indefinitely and replenished their own ranks. The Constitution of 1851 created a few elective county offices and granted the justices monetary compensation for their services. Otherwise, the system functioned as it had in the colonial era.[24]

Public policy showed the planters' guiding hand. Fidelity to "the peculiar institution" of slavery became the principal test of candidates' fitness for office, and partisans diligently scrutinized their opponents' records for suggestions of "unsound" opinions on the question. Southern politics in the 1850's, a Virginia editor later recalled, "could all have been reduced to the simple question of, How can we save the institution of slavery? That was the substratum of our society, its very life and soul, and it must be saved at all hazards." Plantation agriculture benefited from a fiscal policy that drew a third of the state revenue from head and commercial taxes and imposed a property tax of only three mills on the dollar. Since slaves under the age of ten were tax-exempt, and no slave might be taxed at a higher valuation than three hundred dollars, masters paid taxes on barely a quarter of their slaves' market value. The capitation, or head, tax was the only county tax. The state contributed to elementary education only by providing inadequate schools for children of indigents and by supplementing the efforts of the few cities and counties that supported public elementary schools. For higher edu-

22. McFarland "Extension of Democracy," pp. 38–40.

23. *Ibid.*, pp. 15–19.

24. Lester J. Cappon, "The Evolution of County Government in Virginia," in Historical Records Survey Division of the Division of the Women's and Professional Projects, Works Progress Administration, *Inventory of the County Archives of Virginia*, No. 21: *Chesterfield County* (Charlottesville: University of Virginia Press, 1938), pp. 14–27 (hereafter cited as "County Government").

cation, on the other hand, the Commonwealth maintained the University of Virginia and the Virginia Military Institute, attended chiefly by sons of wealthy families.[25]

Before 1851, the principal themes of Virginia politics were sectionalism and democratization. During the 1820's western Virginians demanding increased representation in the General Assembly made common cause with an eastern democratic movement opposing the freehold qualification for suffrage. In the state Constitutional Convention of 1829, both democrats and westerners won some of their demands. The convention made taxpaying the qualification for voting and apportioned the House of Delegates by white population and the state Senate by white population plus three-fifths of the black population. The trans-Appalachian counties, still disaffected, voted in vain against ratifying the Constitution of 1830, but most of the Valley folk were satisfied with the compromise.[26] In 1832, after Nat Turner's slave insurrection, western Virginia's legislators took their most important stand against the eastern planters by proposing gradual, compensated emancipation and colonization of slaves. Soon afterward, prominent Virginians ceased to consider the dangerous question debatable.[27]

One result of the sectional controversy within Virginia was state investment in transportation projects. In 1816, the Commonwealth had set up a Fund for Internal Improvements and created a Board of Public Works to invest the fund in transportation enterprises. During the 1830's the mixed-enterprise policy flowered: the state floated large bond issues to assist railroad and canal companies—especially the James River and Kanawha Company, which hoped to connect the Mississippi Valley by canal with the Atlantic Ocean. The Board of Public Works, investing haphazardly in railroad projects by the 1850's, fell short of the ideal of central planning. There were no railroads in the Valley, none connecting the northwest with eastern Virginia, and no direct line between Richmond and Washington. The state greatly stimulated railroad construction,

25. McFarland, "Extension of Democracy," pp. 27–35; Charles H. Ambler, *Francis H. Pierpont: Union War Governor of Virginia and Father of West Virginia* (Chapel Hill: University of North Carolina Press, 1937), p. 201 (hereafter cited as *Pierpont*); Richmond *Enquirer*, June 26, 1872.

26. Charles H. Ambler, *Sectionalism in Virginia from 1776 to 1861* (Chicago: University of Chicago Press, 1910), pp. 137–74 (hereafter cited as *Sectionalism*); Richard Orr Curry, *A House Divided: A Study of Statehood Politics and the Copperhead Movement in West Virginia* (Pittsburgh: University of Pittsburgh Press, 1964), pp. 16–21 (hereafter cited as *House Divided*).

27. Ambler, *Sectionalism*, pp. 185–202.

nevertheless, and the board provided a measure of public regulation. By 1860 the railroads occupied the principal trade routes with the exceptions mentioned above, in a rational pattern.[28] Extension of rail and canal connections to southwest Virginia during the 1850's helped bind that section to eastern Virginia politically.[29]

During the Jacksonian era, political alignments underwent a transformation. The Whig party emerged as a coalition of opposition groups, including disciples both of John C. Calhoun's proslavery particularism and of Henry Clay's commercial nationalism. Uniting planter aristocrats and city merchants, the Whigs considered themselves the party of wealth and culture.[30]

The late 1830's and early 1840's brought Clay Whigs into conflict with Calhoun Whigs. The Panic of 1837 raised divisive issues and the Whigs, finding themselves in command of both state and federal governments, fell out in formulating their programs. William Cabell Rives led his business-minded "Conservatives" from the Democratic to the Whig party. Robert M. T. Hunter led his State-Rights planters, and Henry A. Wise his State-Rights yeomen, from the Whig camp to the Democratic.[31] After 1844, Clay's adherents held the reins of the Whig party in Virginia. Thereafter, the Whigs became the permanent minority party, unable ever to carry the state in an election. The plantation counties voted Democratic, the cities voted Whig, and the other regions divided in accordance with complex allegiances.[32]

Such Whig spokesmen as Alexander H. H. Stuart of Staunton preached not proslavery doctrine but a timid commercialism. Stuart supported Clay's American System and advocated state aid to internal improvements. In President Millard Fillmore's administration, he served as secretary of the interior, a department that State-Rights

28. McFarland, "Extension of Democracy," pp. 5–6, 28–29; Carter Goodrich, "The Virginia System of Mixed Enterprise: A Study of State Planning of Internal Improvements," *Political Science Quarterly*, LXIV (September, 1949), 355–87 (hereafter cited as "Mixed Enterprise").

29. Curry, *House Divided*, pp. 21–22.

30. Ambler, *Sectionalism*, pp. 219–24; John Herbert Claiborne, *Seventy-Five Years in Old Virginia: with Some Account of the Life of the Author and Some History of the People among Whom His Lot Was Cast—Their Character, Their Condition, and Their Conduct before the War, during the War and after the War* (New York and Washington: Neale Publishing Company, 1904), pp. 132–33 (hereafter cited as *Seventy-Five Years*). See also John S. Wise, *The Lion's Skin: A Historical Novel and a Novel History* (New York: Doubleday, Page, and Company, 1905), pp. 83–84.

31. Ambler, *Sectionalism*, pp. 228–33.

32. Charles Grier Sellers, Jr., "Who Were the Southern Whigs?" *American Historical Review*, LIX (January, 1954), 342–44.

men disliked as an instrument of centralization. To Northern audiences, Stuart praised the bourgeoisie who had supplanted feudalism with capitalism and defended the tariff in terms of free-labor economics. To Virginians, he proposed commercial and industrial development to cure agricultural stagnation. Stuart did not, however, go so far as to advocate a free-labor industrial economy for Virginia. The planting South and the commerical North, he thought, played complementary roles in the Union for their mutual benefit. Accepting the primacy of the agricultural interest in Virginia, he argued for diversification in order to stabilize the economic system.[33]

In the late 1840's, western sectionalism and agrarian democracy again built up pressure for constitutional reform. Westerners wanted reapportionment, public schools, and railroad connections.[34] Some threatened to organize an independent state. The Reverend Henry Ruffner of Lexington contributed to this agitation an *Address to the People of Western Virginia*, attacking slavery on economic grounds and proposing gradual emancipation in western Virginia. Only beyond the Appalachians did approving echoes greet the "Ruffner pamphlet"; the Valley's recognized spokesmen joined eastern Virginia's in denouncing it. Shunned as a pariah, Ruffner found it necessary to resign the presidency of Washington College and seek a new home. Western sectionalists such as John Letcher of Lexington, who had co-operated with Ruffner up to a certain point. became increasingly "sound" on slavery.[35] Their allies in reform, the yeoman democrats, were also quite orthodox on the subject. Henry A. Wise, an eastern planter and fiery State-Rights man, led the movement for white manhood suffrage partly in order to unite all white men against Northern antislavery aggression.[36]

The Constitutional Convention of 1850, meeting in an atmosphere of uneasiness about the stability of slavery, responded to the democratic pressures. It enfranchised all white men and made elective the offices of governor and judge, the members of the Board of

33. Alexander F. Robertson, *Alexander Hugh Holmes Stuart, 1807–1891: A Biography* (Richmond: William Byrd Press, 1925), pp. 21–24, 26–29, 31–33, 35–38, 41, 43–53, 163–66 (hereafter cited as *Stuart*).

34. Ambler, *Sectionalism*, pp. 251–58.

35. William G. Bean, "The Ruffner Pamphlet of 1847: An Antislavery Aspect of Virginia Sectionalism," *Virginia Magazine of History and Biography*, LXI (July, 1953), 259–82; F. N. Boney, *John Letcher of Virginia: The Story of Virginia's Civil War Governor* (University, Ala.: University of Alabama Press, 1966), pp. 38–39, 46–47, 53, 76 (hereafter cited as *Letcher*).

36. Chilton Williamson, *American Suffrage from Property to Democracy, 1760–1860* (Princeton: Princeton University Press, 1960), pp. 239–41.

Public Works, and some county offices. It made legislative apportionment more equitable and provided for a referendum to be held
in 1865 to determine the future basis of apportionment. On the
other hand, it kept taxation of slave property to a minimal level.[37]
In the Constitution that went into effect in 1851, Old Virginia accepted political democracy without sacrificing the social power of
planters and their allies.[38] Henry A. Wise had accomplished his
desire. The internal battle to enfranchise all white men was completed; the external battle to defend "Southern Rights" against
Northern encroachment was beginning.

CRISIS

By the 1850's, Virginians could not ignore the statistical
evidence that the Old Dominion, and the South generally, were de-
clining in relative influence within the federal union. The Northern section was outstripping the Southern in population and pro-
ductivity and, consequently, in political power. In 1790, Virginia
had been the most populous state; in 1860, four northern states
exceeded her in population. By 1851, Virginians outside the northwestern region ordinarily accepted plantation slavery as a "given,"
and they could not be indifferent to their social system's relative
decline. In the 1830's, when Nathaniel Beverley Tucker had predicted a sectional civil war over the slavery question, few Virginians
had heeded his call for Southern solidarity.[39] In the 1850's, however,
current events seemed increasingly to fulfill Tucker's prophecies.

Throughout the world, slavery was evidently receding. It had
passed away in one after another nation of Latin America. In Dela-
ware, Maryland, and Missouri, the free-labor sectors of the economy
were growing rapidly at the expense of the slave-labor sector. Those
states were increasingly manifesting social phenomena Southerners
associated with the Northern states—including antislavery movements.[40] Virginia shared, to a lesser degree, the border states' diversity. Might not her own mountain region, free-labor farms, commercial cities, and embryonic industries become centers of subversion
that might someday undermine plantation slavery? Seward's "irre-

37. Ambler, *Sectionalism*, pp. 259–71; Boney, *Letcher*, pp. 44–50.
38. Whigs occasionally regretted the effects of mass democracy. See Richmond *Daily
Whig*, January 20, 1860.
39. Shanks, *Secession Movement*, pp. 67–69.
40. Allan Nevins, *The Emergence of Lincoln* (New York: Charles Scribner's Sons,
1950), II, 132–42, 149–51, 163–66, 168–69.

pressible conflict" between slave labor and free labor might soon manifest itself within Virginia.[41] A scion of a planter family could not contemplate indifferently the downfall of a way of life which, to his mind, contained unique virtues. Yet, as the free states increased their representation in Congress, the antislavery movement was becoming influential in their politics. A federal administration prejudiced against slavery might find peaceful, constitutional means to convert Virginia gradually into a free state. "The ruin and degradation of Virginia," the Richmond *Enquirer* warned, "will be as fully and fatally accomplished as though bloodshed and rapine ravished the land."[42] Already, a few Virginians east of the Appalachians voiced skepticism and even hostility to slavery.[43]

As national events grew ominous, many spokesmen for the planter interest joined the "Southern Rights" movement to defend southern institutions against Northern attack. Exalting slavery as a positive good, "Southrons" found it necessary to deplore the direction of nineteenth-century progress. George Fitzhugh of Caroline County carried his defense of precapitalist institutions as far as to declare war on capitalism, democracy, and middle-class liberalism. Southern Rights men came to the conclusion that Northern society was fundamentally antagonistic to their own and that coexistence within the Union had injured the South for decades and would eventually destroy its social system. The only remedy, they argued, would be for the slave states to withdraw from the Union. The University of Virginia and the *Southern Literary Messenger* of Richmond became active centers of proslavery and Southern Rights cultural progaganda.[44]

Most Virginians were slow to take the Southern Rights creed seriously. In the state election of 1851, both parties endorsed the Compromise of 1850 as the final settlement of the sectional tension concerning slavery. The Whigs, under the nationalist influence of Richmond's former Congressman John Minor Botts, denied that a

41. See John C. Rutherfoord to William Cabell Rives, April 11, 1860, Rives Papers.

42. Richmond *Enquirer*, July 10, 1860, reprinted in Dwight L. Dumond, ed., *Southern Editorials on Secession* (New York and London: Century Company for American Historical Association, 1931), p. 141. See also Edmund Ruffin, *Anticipations of the Future, To Serve as Lessons for the Present Time, in the Form of Extracts of Letters from an English Resident in the United States, to the London Times, from 1864 to 1870, with an Appendix, on the Causes and Consequences of the Independence of the South* (Richmond: J. W. Randolph, 1860), pp. 1–82, 103–8.

43. Eaton, *Freedom of Thought*, pp. 133–36, 179, 181–82, 245, 257–63, 270–71, 274, 275.

44. Shanks, *Secession Movement*, pp. 69–79.

state could constitutionally secede and ran George W. Summers, a nationalist who had criticized slavery twenty years before, for governor. The Democratic candidate, Joseph Johnston, carried the state by a wide margin. Most Whig leaders, perhaps seeking to recover their losses, broke with Botts in 1854 to support the Kansas-Nebraska Act.[45] In 1855, they opportunistically reorganized as part of the nativist American (Know-Nothing) party, which opposed sectional discord. The Virginia Know-Nothings, recruiting hardly any Democrats, operated as the Whig party had rather than as a secret society. In 1855, they nominated Thomas S. Flournoy for governor.[46]

Among the Democrats, Henry A. Wise for a time resisted the extreme sectionalism of R. M. T. Hunter's Southern Rights faction. In the party convention at Staunton in November, 1854, Wise's followers, abolishing the customary two-thirds rule, nominated their hero for governor.[47] Breaking with tradition, the oracle of the small-scale farmers took to the stump, not only to scourge Know-Nothingism, but also to expound a progressive program. In language no abolitionist could surpass, he blamed the planters for Virginia's economic stagnation. The politicians, he charged, had neglected the Commonwealth's needs to engage in demagogy in national politics. Wise proposed to co-ordinate the state public works into a unified system and to establish a free public school system and a number of technical schools. Politicians of both parties, embarrassed, ignored the Democratic candidate's insurgence. The press censored accounts of his speeches. The Richmond *Whig*, organ of the opposition, described Wise as "a reckless visionary" and condemned his "agrarian notion of compelling the rich to pay for the education of the poor."[48]

Wise decisively defeated Flournoy, but no revolution in state policy ensued. The governor recommended reform measures to the General Assembly, but Hunter's lieutenants, controlling the principal senate committees, prevented their enactment. Wise's own commitment to reform weakened. Frustrated at home and tempted by the presidency, he involved himself in federal politics, which in 1855 he had called the "curse" of Virginia statesmen. Wise at-

45. *Ibid.*, pp. 48–51.
46. W. Darrell Overdyke, *The Know-Nothing Party in the South* (Baton Rouge: Louisiana State University Press, 1950), pp. 54–56, 64–66, 75–76, 91–95.
47. Shanks, *Secession Movement*, p. 48.
48. McFarland, "Extension of Democracy," pp. 19–24.

tempted to ride simultaneously the horse of democratization and economic reform in Virginia and also the horse of resistance to the democratic and economically progressive antislavery forces in national politics. In 1856, he united with the Hunter Democrats in threatening secession if the Republican candidate John C. Frémont should become president.[49] In 1857 and 1858, though, Governor Wise again deviated from the Southern Rights movement in the interest of yeoman democracy. Standing by the "popular sovereignty" doctrine, he endorsed Senator Stephen A. Douglas' battle against the proslavery Lecompton Constitution for Kansas that was unrepresentative of the settlers' desires. The Buchanan administration and the Southern Rights movement combined in a war against Douglas. Wise remained loyal to the Illinois senator, but the deviation decreased his popularity.[50]

The gubernatorial election of 1859 showed how far the Wise Democrats and Whigs had, by degrees, capitulated to the growing Southern Rights feeling. The Hunter Democrats tried to broaden their appeal by supporting the candidacy of John Letcher, a westerner and a recent recruit to their faction. Wise's organ, the Richmond *Enquirer,* attacked Letcher as a sponsor of the "Ruffner pamphlet" of 1847 and, therefore, "unsound" on slavery—although he had repudiated the pamphlet after its publication. Letcher won the Democratic nomination, in spite of the opposition of Wise's followers and some desertions from Hunter's. The Whigs then showed how well they had learned the Southern Rights game. Nominating William L. Goggin, a Whig "sound" on slavery and State Rights, they took up the slander campaign against the "unsound" Letcher. Gaining Southern Rights votes in southern and eastern Virginia, but losing Unionist and free-labor votes in the northwest, they went down as usual to defeat.[51]

If anything remained of Wise's former moderation in defense of Southern Rights, it disappeared on October 17, 1859. On that day John Brown's abolitionist band occupied the federal arsenal at Harper's Ferry as the first stage of a projected slave revolt. After

49. *Ibid.,* pp. 25–26; Clement Eaton, *The Mind of the Old South* (rev. ed.; Baton Rouge: Louisiana State University Press, 1967), pp. 98–99, 102 (hereafter cited as *Mind of the Old South*); Shanks, *Secession Movement,* pp. 52–54.

50. Shanks, *Secession Movement,* pp. 56–58; Eaton, *Mind of the Old South,* pp. 99–100.

51. Shanks, *Secession Movement,* pp. 57–62; Boney, *Letcher,* pp. 74–90; William G. Bean, "John Letcher and the Slavery Issue in Virginia's Gubernatorial Contest of 1858–1859," *Journal of Southern History,* XX (February, 1954), 22–49.

the suppression of the attempt, Governor Wise and others inter-
viewed Brown, whose cool determination to conduct guerilla war-
far against their social institutions shook them emotionally. Before
Brown's execution, it became clear that many Northerners, including prominent intellectuals and Republican officeholders, sympa-
thized to some extent with the prisoner. Many a moderate Virginian
suddenly perceived the antislavery movement as an immediate
threat, no longer distant and abstract, and joined the Southern
Rights camp. Rumors of slave insurrection swept the Commonwealth.[52]

The General Assembly session that began in December, 1859,
marked the crisis of the Whig party, the only element outside the
northwest not yet fully committed to the Southern Rights trend.
Frustrated by repeated defeat, isolated by their party's dissolution in
the North, and plagued by wholesale desertions to the Democrats,
the Whig leaders had drifted progressively closer to the politics of
the dominant party, itself taking an increasingly sectional course.
For awhile after the 1859 election, the Whigs returned to moderation, hoping for a coalition of all opposition elements except the
abolitionists for the forthcoming national election, with John Minor
Botts as a possible presidential candidate. After John Brown's raid,
however, they repudiated the idea of fusion with "Black Republicans."[53]

Southern Rights Democrats now realized that to prepare for disunion would entail measures for military preparedness and economic self-sufficiency. They therefore began to advocate home industry.[54] This policy could benefit from the Whigs' business acumen
and might attach them to the Southern Rights cause. Consequently,
the Democratic legislature chose Alexander H. H. Stuart, the Whig
advocate of industrialization, to chair its joint committee on the
Harper's Ferry incident. The Whigs swallowed the bait. Stuart's
committee proposed measures to encourage economic diversification, boycott northern products, and equip the state militia for combat.[55] The Richmond *Whig* crowed triumphantly that the Demo-

52. Shanks, *Secession Movement*, pp, 64–66; Louis Ruchames, ed., *A John Brown Reader* (London and New York: Abelard-Schuman, 1959), pp 117–25; Eaton, *Mind of the Old South*, pp. 100–102.
53. Shanks, *Secession Movement*, pp. 62, 64–65, 91; Richmond *Whig and Public Advertiser*, September 24, October 5, and November 29, 1859.
54. See Richmond *Whig and Public Advertiser*, January 6, 1860.
55. Robertson, *Stuart*, pp. 168, 405.

crats had embraced home industry, "the sum and substance of the Whig platform."[56] The General Assembly adopted a program of military preparedness.[57]

The parting of the ways had come for John Minor Botts. An unconditional Unionist who disliked slavery, Botts had long been suspect as a heretic. "There is scarcely a shade's difference," a Georgia newspaper stated, "between Mr. Botts' position and that of the Republicans."[58] In January, 1870, twenty-seven Whig legislators asked him to publish his opinions on the political situation. Botts replied with a blistering attack on the defense and diversification measures, in which the Whigs were collaborating, as steps to disunion.[59] Almost all his twenty-seven admirers quickly disavowed his nationalist precepts. "To render Virginia commercially and socially independent of the Northern States," one of them insisted, "will in no way injuriously affect the Union."[60] Acquiescing in preparedness measures, the Whigs unconsciously cast in their lot with the secessionists.

When the Democratic party divided in 1860, almost all Virginia's Democratic leaders supported Vice-President John C. Breckinridge, the Southern Rights faction's presidential candidate. All the parties paid lip-service to the Union, but none clearly defined their "Unionism." The Democratic party split gave the Whigs their first statewide election victory in nearly twenty years. John Bell, their candidate, won a plurality of 74,681 votes against Breckinridge's 74,323 and Douglas' 16,290; Abraham Lincoln, the victorious Republican candidate, received only 1,929 votes in Virginia, almost all from the northwest. Bell's plurality revealed that many voters feared the drift to disunion.[61]

After the states of the Lower South seceded from the Union, Virginians pondered their alternatives. The Southern Rights leaders called for immediate secession. Conditional Unionists, on the other hand, asserted that only an overt governmental act to undermine slavery or coerce the seceding states would justify Virginia in seceding. The General Assembly, predominantly secessionist, called a state convention to consider the subject. The immediate secessionists, to their embarrassment, elected only about 30 of the 152 mem-

56. Richmond *Daily Whig*, January 14, 1860.
57. Shanks, *Secession Movement*, pp. 93–96.
58. Eaton, *Freedom of Thought*, pp. 262–63; Columbus (Ga.) *Times*, in Richmond *Semi-Weekly Enquirer*, March 22, 1859.
59. Richmond *Daily Whig*, January 19, 1860.
60. *Ibid.*, January 24 and 27, 1860.
61. Shanks, *Secession Movement*, pp. 103–19.

bers of the convention. A very few unconditional Unionists won election from the northwest. Almost all the other members had promised to vote for secession in the event, all too probable, of a federal attempt to coerce the seceding states. The secessionist members came principally from counties heavily populated by slaves; the Unionists, from counties in which slavery played a relatively minor role.[62]

The convention deliberated for two months, trying to restore the Union by compromise but awaiting anxiously to see whether compromise, peaceful secession, or civil war would break the impasse.[63] On April 12, the Southern Confederacy's forces bombarded Fort Sumter. A committee from the Virginia convention visited President Lincoln in a final attempt to avert war. After April 15, when the president asked all loyal states for troops to suppress the Confederacy, most convention members united to resist his effort. On April 17, the body voted, by eighty-eight votes to fifty-five, to secede because of Lincoln's "coercion." Only twenty-two members, nearly all from the northwest, failed to sign the Ordinance of Secession. Almost immediately the Old Dominion also joined the Confederate States of America.[64]

Slaveowning planters and their labor system had provided the impetus for secession. The representatives of the farmers and businessmen, in defining their interests, had long accepted the limits that the preservation of slavery imposed. Step by step, they had capitulated to increasingly desperate measures to protect "the peculiar institution." Now, at last, they found themselves committed to a war they had hoped to avert, to protect a society in which they played a subordinate role from one in which their kind played the dominant role. Their situation was ironic, but even more ironic was their own part in bringing it about.

62. *Ibid.*, pp. 120–57; Ralph A. Wooster, *The Secession Conventions of the South* (Princeton: Princeton University Press, 1962), pp. 145, 149, 151, 153–54, 260–62, 264–66.

63. John Minor Botts claimed that President Lincoln had promised John B. Baldwin, a Unionist member of the convention, that he would evacuate Fort Sumter if the convention would adjourn. Baldwin denied the story. Probably few of the conditional Unionist members would have accepted such an offer. See Shanks, *Secession Movement*, pp. 192–95.

64. *Ibid.*, pp. 196–208.

3.

The Confederate Crucible

It was not only the North's victory over the South that made the War of 1861–65 a "Second American Revolution." Within each of the contending sections, the war effort exerted a strong influence toward national consolidation and industrial capitalism. Wartime experience, therefore, helped to transform the state of mind that had prompted Virginia's rulers of 1861 to secede into the one that led her rulers of the 1870's to reunite with the northern victors.

GOVERNMENT IN CONFEDERATE VIRGINIA

After voting to join the Confederate States, the Secession Convention appointed a committee, under Stuart's chairmanship, to propose amendments to the state constitution. Since the convention consisted mainly of Whigs skeptical of democracy and of Southern Rights Democrats disillusioned with it, the time seemed ripe to undo some of the 1851 constitution's democratic innovations. Presenting his committee's recommendations in November, Stuart pointed to the Northern states as examples of the deplorable effects of universal suffrage. The convention approved amendments to make several previously elective offices appointive, to extend judges' terms of service, and to have the legislature select the governor if no candidate should win a majority in the popular election. The convention also submitted to the voters, separately from the other amendments, a proposal to restore the taxpaying qualification for suffrage. In March, 1862, the few voters who went to the polls gave the suffrage restriction a majority but narrowly rejected the package of amendments, on the ratification of which the suffrage restriction was conditional.[1] Perhaps the need to unite Virginians against invasion discouraged encroachments on democracy.

1. Henry T. Shanks, "Conservative Constitutional Tendencies of the Virginia Secession Convention," in Fletcher M. Green, ed., *Essays in Southern History Presented*

The Confederate States government, which established its capital at Richmond, disappointed many Virginians. Leading an underdeveloped nation in resisting a more advanced adversary, Jefferson Davis' administration found itself adopting its enemy's weapons. Gradually and reluctantly, it diversified agriculture and fostered manufacturing, centralized governmental power, entrusted authority to men of military and business experience instead of aristocrats and Southern Rights theorists, and, as a last desperate measure to win independence, considered emancipating the slaves. Some Southern Rights men, by 1864, found the Confederate government almost as intolerable as the Union had been in 1861; many other Confederates, on the other hand, criticized their government's actions as too little and too late. Consequently, every important war measure increased the new nation's internal dissension.

Revolutionary though these measures seemed to State Rights men, they did not go far enough to solve the Confederacy's logistical problems. Railroad warfare in Virginia was a case in point. Since the government pre-empted all iron manufacture for direct military purposes, railroad companies had to tear up minor lines to repair major ones. By diminishing the potential supply area, this attrition wore down the efficiency of General Lee's army. The federal government, on the contrary, established an agency—the United States Military Railroads—to operate and repair lines in Union-occupied districts. During the siege of Petersburg in 1864, Union commander Ulysses S. Grant concentrated his efforts on destroying and capturing the Confederates' railroad supply lines. The Army of Northern Virginia outlived the last of those lines by only a week.[2] Lessons such as these were not lost on the Confederates who later began to build the New South.

The Confederacy's dilemma divided Virginians. Virginia's generals pressed the government for emergency action. Her Confederate congressmen stood out for their support of administration war policies.[3] Governor Letcher tried to co-operate with the central government but often opposed its actions on State-Rights grounds.[4]

to *Joseph Gregoire de Roulhac Hamilton, Ph.D., LL.D., by His Former Students at the University of North Carolina* ("The James Sprunt Studies in History and Political Science," XXXI [Chapel Hill: University of North Carolina Press, 1949]) , 29–48.

2. Angus James Johnston II, *Virginia Railroads in the Civil War* (Chapel Hill: University of North Carolina Press, 1959), pp. v–vi (hereafter cited as *Virginia Railroads*).

3. W. B. Yearns, *The Confederate Congress* (Athens, Ga.: University of Georgia Press, 1960), pp. 53–54.

4. Boney, *Letcher*, p. 200.

Edward A. Pollard, a Southern Rights writer for the Richmond *Examiner*, found Jefferson Davis' Richmond "a Chinese copy of Washington, with all its stripes of 'red tape'."[5] Both the *Examiner* and the *Whig* began in 1862 to criticize the administration. Their criticism rose by 1864 to a virulent crescendo of opposition that hastened the erosion of Confederate morale.[6]

On the surface, party lines disappeared. The *Whig* soon discovered, nevertheless, that President Davis' remarks about ignoring parties meant only that he ignored the Whigs in allotting patronage and formulating policy.[7] In 1863, correspondents of the *Whig* pressed the names of former Whig leaders as candidates for governor.[8] Shortly before the election William L. Goggin withdrew as a candidate, probably to unite the Whig voters behind Thomas S. Flournoy. Only by a very small margin did Democrats William "Extra Billy" Smith and Samuel Price win the offices, respectively, of governor and lieutenant governor. Flournoy won a plurality of the *civilian* vote for governor, and General John D. Imboden, a Whig, led the military vote for lieutenant governor. John B. Baldwin, one of the state's most important Whig leaders, defeated Governor Letcher, who had never before lost an election, for the Valley's seat in Congress. Voters disillusioned with secessionist preachments by the harsh reality of war were turning to the former Whigs for leadership.[9]

Loyalty to the Confederacy and wartime submergence of partisanship put the opposition party and its organ in a difficult policy position. Before secession, the *Whig*'s publishers had dismissed its editor, Robert Ridgway, as too uncompromising a Unionist, and appointed Alexander Moseley, a former editor, in his place.[10] Henry Hotze, Confederate propagandist in Britain, explained the *Whig*'s perplexity: it found that its enemies were in power, and that it was

5. Edward A. Pollard, *The Lost Cause Regained* (New York: G. W. Carleton and Company, 1868), pp. 27–28 (hereatfer cited as *Lost Cause Regained*).

6. Harrison A. Trexler, "The Davis Administration and the Richmond Press," *Journal of Southern History*, XVI (May, 1950), 178–91.

7. *Ibid.*, p. 186.

8. "If party would be mischievous," one wrote, "the works of party are mischievous. . . . One of these mischiefs is the occupancy of nearly all offices by men of one side in the old division." Richmond *Whig and Public Advertiser*, May 21, 1863.

9. *Ibid.*, June 5 and 9, 1863; Boney, *Letcher*, pp. 192–93; see Thomas Benjamin Alexander, "Persistent Whiggery in the Confederate South, 1861–1877," *Journal of Southern History*, XXVII (August, 1961), 308–9 (hereafter cited as "Persistent Whiggery").

10. Anonymous sketch (written after 1890) of Moseley, William Henry Ruffner Papers, Historical Foundation of the Presbyterian and Reformed Churches.

committed to their principles.[11] Shifting, with the mercantile interests, from state intervention to *laissez faire*, the paper opposed wartime price controls. Unlike the Democratic papers, it retained respect for conservative Northern Democrats and conservative Whigs.[12] The *Whig* bided its time, hoping that events would somehow enhance the postwar role of those for whom it spoke.

UNIONIST VIRGINIA

While the Richmond government wrestled with its problems, a rival government claiming sovereignty over Virginia sprang up in the Unionist northwestern counties. Northwestern Virginians, largely natives of the North, enjoyed communication with Northern states by the Ohio River and the Baltimore and Ohio Railroad, but were isolated from eastern Virginia. They lived not by plantation agriculture but by subsistence farming and domestic industry. In politics, they had stood for democracy, economic nationalism, and sectional demands for public works and banks.[13] Only here, in Virginia, were unconditional Unionists a majority and antislavery men a significant minority.

The news of Virginia's secession touched off local meetings in the northwest to protest the action and organize a new, Unionist state. The movement's leaders were mostly economic individualists new to political leadership. In a convention at Wheeling, they set up the "Restored Government of Virginia"—ostensibly a government for the entire state but in the intentions of many a steppingstone to a separate Appalachian state.[14]

As governor of "restored" Virginia, the Wheeling convention chose Francis Harrison Pierpont, a man representative of his movement. A "self-made man," Pierpont was an attorney for the Baltimore and Ohio Railroad and also operated a coal mine, a tannery, and a firebrick business.[15] "In the last fifteen years," he boasted to a slaveowner, "I have superintended the tanning and selling of more good leather than *you* and all your '*niggers*' that run *off*, are worth."[16] Disliking slavery for moral and economic reasons, Pierpont blamed the planters' influence in Richmond for retarding

11. London *Index*, November 27, 1862, pp. 75–76.
12. Richmond *Whig and Public Advertiser*, March 6, 1863.
13. Curry, *House Divided*, pp. 23–25.
14. *Ibid.*, pp. 34–35; Ambler, *Pierpont*, pp. 81, 89, 162.
15. Ambler, *Pierpont*, pp. 27–32.
16. Quoted in *ibid.*, p. 32.

northwestern Virginia's economic growth. An unconditional Unionist Whig, he had disavowed his party's campaign against Letcher in 1859. He attacked the Democratic party in the south as "the 'nigger' party" and the great enemy of the manufacturing interest.[17]

The restored government established its rule with assistance from Northerners and the federal government. Pierpont made his administration a striking financial success through borrowing, federal assistance, seizing state property in the northwest, and railroad lawyer Peter G. Van Winkle's business contacts. General George B. McClellan's Ohio troops assured Union military supremacy in the northwestern counties.[18] Outside that region, the restored government ruled only a few Union-occupied enclaves.

Separatists, pointing out northwestern Virginia's Northern and western ties and the Richmond legislature's neglect of that region, proposed to divide the Commonwealth into two states. Two years of complex political conflict ensued before the new state of West Virginia came into being in 1863. The fast-growing Republican party won its demand for abolition of slavery. Conservative Unionists managed, on the other hand, to enlarge the new state's boundaries to twice the area the restored government actually controlled so that, after the War, former Confederates might join them to overcome the Republican majority in the northwest. West Virginia also absorbed several counties of the Valley, to keep the Baltimore and Ohio route within its friendly jurisdiction.[19]

The restored government then moved to Alexandria, to administer the Union-controlled parts of Virginia's reduced area. Many of the Alexandria personnel were Northerners and West Virginians, but they attempted, when practicable, to assimilate Confederate local officials as more counties came under Union authority. The restored government's small officialdom included such future Republican leaders in Virginia as John C. Underwood, the Reverend James W. Hunnicutt, John W. Hawxhurst, Lewis McKenzie, and Joseph E. Segar.[20]

In Alexandria, Pierpont advocated emancipation, both to create equality among white men and to fulfill "God's plan" as events

17. *Ibid.*, pp. 35–50, 55–58, 63, 65–68, 70–71.

18. *Ibid.*, pp. 104–7, 212; Curry, *House Divided*, pp. 55–66.

19. Ambler, *Pierpont*, pp. 129–31, 167–69, 207–8; Curry, *House Divided*, pp. 79–130, 136–40.

20. Ambler, *Pierpont*, pp. 220–23, 227–28. Hunnicutt, Hawxhurst, McKenzie, and Segar participated in Virginia's "redemption" in 1869 by entering a coalition with the Conservative party.

were revealing it. Emancipation, he predicted, would redound to Virginia's economic benefit. In 1864, a Unionist convention drafted a new state constitution that abolished slavery, reduced the residence requirement for voters from three years to one, disfranchised Confederate officeholders, and required voters to swear allegiance to the United States and the restored government. The Alexandria legislature ratified the Thirteenth Amendment, but it did not permit Negroes to testify in courts. Nor did it establish a free-school system, as the new constitution authorized it to.[21]

Governor Pierpont's most trying task was to assert his authority over the city of Norfolk, which, occupied by Union forces since May of 1862, was gaining a head start in postwar economic recovery. Trade with the North resumed, the new "greenback" currency appeared, and Northern entrepreneurs—one of whom would occupy the governor's chair five years later—settled. General Benjamin F. Butler, the Union military commander, ignored Pierpont's government and regulated the city's business for his own profit and that of his frends. Pierpont and Butler quarreled until February, 1865, when President Lincoln removed Butler from his command.[22] The Reconstruction contest for economic spoils had begun.

THE CONFEDERATE MILITARY EXPERIENCE

The Conservatives of the 1870's inherited the governmental experience of both the Richmond and Alexandria governments. Most of the later Conservative leaders, though, spent the War not as politicians but as officers in the Confederate Army. Their military experience helped to prepare them for leadership in the industrial nation against whose supremacy they were contending in vain.

The Confederacy's military leaders were rarely devotees of Southern Rights. Among the high officers from Virginia, a large-scale slaveowner or an original secessionist was a rarity. The skills that warfare demanded would be at least as functional in the New South as in the Old. Engineering and logistics, essential to the contemporary science of war, were readily transferable to industrial pursuits. William Mahone had received his training in engineering at the Virginia Military Institute; he employed it, first in railroading (becoming president by 1860 of the Norfolk and Petersburg Railroad), then as a brigadier general in Lee's army, and finally as Virginia's

21. *Ibid.*, pp. 217–27.
22. *Ibid.*, pp. 231–43.

great railroad entrepreneur of the Reconstruction years.[23] The Confederate Army selected and trained men who would be qualified to lead the South onto innovative paths. It also adapted its members to the world that was intruding on their own, by breaking down local provincialisms, disciplining aristocratic individualism, and democratizing social life.[24]

The Confederacy's logistical crises produced severe civil-military tensions. The inadequacy of the government's supply services and economic mobilization inspired lasting bitterness among the troops. Such young officers as John Sergeant Wise and William L. Royall learned both to admire their comrades-in-arms and to despise the civil government at Richmond.[25] Often, their disillusionment with the government reflected disillusionment with the Southern traditions that tied its hands.

The protracted, grueling discouragement of army life helped to erode the abstractions and romanticism of Southern Rights. Confederate soldiers typically experienced gradual demoralization from an initial flood of enthusiasm to an equilibrium of despair, stoicism, or apathetic withdrawal.[26] The humorist George W. Bagby was willing to die for the South, "but not by freezing, or, worse still, by filth." He found that "the filth, the disease, the privation, the suffering, the mutilation and, above all, the debasement of public and private morals, leave to war scarcely a redeeming feature."[27] The ugly experiences of the War would leave on the heart of the New South a permanent, conditioning scar—a hardened attitude, pragmatic and sometimes cynical, toward inherited traditions.

The Confederate experience might have influenced impressionable Southerners quite differently had it not ended in decisive military defeat. Many soldiers foresaw the outcome by the end of 1863, and General Lee let pessimism creep into his dispatches by August,

23. Nelson M. Blake, *William Mahone of Virginia: Soldier and Political Insurgent* (Richmond: Garrett and Massie, 1935), pp. 12–16, 19, 22, 26, 32, 39–43, 45, 67–68, 72–73 (hereafter cited as *Mahone*).

24. Frank E. Vandiver, "The Confederacy and the American Tradition," *Journal of Southern History*, XXVIII (August, 1962), 283–85.

25. John S. Wise, *The End of an Era* (Boston and New York: Houghton, Mifflin and Company, 1899), pp. 404, 461 (hereafter cited as *End of an Era*); William L. Royall, *Some Reminiscences* (New York and Washington: Neale Publishing Company, 1909), pp. 40–41 (hereafter cited as *Reminiscences*).

26. Bell I. Wiley, *The Life of Johnny Reb: The Common Soldier of the Confederacy* (Indianapolis and New York: Bobbs-Merrill Company, 1943), pp. 124–25, 127–32 (hereafter cited as *Johnny Reb*).

27. Bagby, *Old Virginia Gentleman*, p. 215.

1864.[28] The Confederacy's civil officials, on the contrary, were loath until the very end to admit the accuracy of the discouraging reports from the army.[29] Confederate soldiers became increasingly estranged from their government. During the winter of 1864–65, secessionist orators came from Richmond to exhort the ragged, underfed soldiers at Petersburg to die in the last ditch. General Jubal A. Early, refusing to attend their lectures, heckled from his hut, to the delight of privates who joined in the heckling.[30]

Civilian morale also decayed during the final year of the War. Alexander Moseley, believing Davis' policies would lead to defeat, resigned as editor of the *Whig*, which was now openly calling for a revival of party lines.[31] Three Richmond merchants tainted with Unionist connections ran for city offices, apparently hoping to organize Unionist, defeatist, and disaffected voters. One almost won a seat in the City Council, and another, in the Board of Aldermen.[32] Some concluded that surrender would be a wiser tactic than futile resistance. In March, 1865, William Cabell Rives drafted for the Confederate Congress a resolution admitting that the South could not win independence and advising the administration to negotiate with the Union government for terms of reunion. Rives did not attend the Congress' last session, and Senator William Alexander Graham of North Carolina declined to introduce his fellow Whig's resolution.[33]

On April 2, General Grant's army occupied Petersburg. The Confederate government evacuated Richmond, so hastily that its destruction of official property kindled an uncontrolled fire that further embittered many Richmonders against their recent rulers.[34]

28. Wiley, *Johnny Reb*, pp. 130, 131–32; Douglas Southall Freeman, *R. E. Lee: A Biography* (New York and London: Charles Scribner's Sons, 1934), III, 499 (hereafter cited as *Lee*).

29. Wise, *End of an Era*, pp. 445–46.

30. *Ibid.*, pp. 395–96.

31. Anonymous sketch of Moseley, Ruffner Papers; E. Merton Coulter, *The Confederate States of America, 1861–1865* (Baton Rouge: Louisiana State University Press, 1950), p. 115 (hereafter cited as *Confederate States of America*).

32. Meriwether Stuart, "Colonel Uuric Dahlgren and Richmond's Union Underground, April, 1864," *Virginia Magazine of History and Biography*, LXXII (April, 1964), 190–94. The mayoral candidate, Martin Meredith Lipscomb, was later active in the Conservative party. Richmond *Dispatch*, May 25, 1876.

33. John A. Campbell, *Reminiscences and Documents Relating to the Civil War during the Year 1865* (Baltimore: John Murphy and Company, 1887), pp. 33–34.

34. Coulter, *Confederate States of America*, p. 559; John Townsend Trowbridge, *The South: A Tour of Its Battle-Fields and Ruined Cities, A Journey through the Desolated States and Talks with the People* . . . (Hartford, Conn.: L. Stebbins, 1866), pp. 147–48.

The city's moderates quickly made their peace with the occupying forces. On April 8, the *Whig* resumed publication. Resuming its former Unionism, the paper boasted that the "Flag of the Union," insulted "under Confederate occupation," again flew over the *Whig* building.[35] Ironically, the military authorities' only condition, in permitting the *Whig* to resume publication, was that editor Robert Ridgway, dismissed in 1861 for his Unionism, write no more editorials.[36]

Meanwhile, Lee's army retreated westward as far as Appomattox Courthouse, where its commander surrendered on April 9. The traumatic impact of the surrender haunted many Confederates for the rest of their lives. Some experienced a sort of psychic death, dazed as though the world itself had ended.[37] Others experienced not only death to the Old South but rebirth to the New. Feeling that he was "dead," Lieutenant John Wise seriously prepared a will and testament for his former, Confederate self. Expressing the bewilderment many young Virginians felt, Wise concluded the document: "And now . . . having experienced death to Confederate ideas and a new birth unto allegiance to the Union, I depart, with a vague but not definite hope of a joyful resurrection, and of a new life, on lines somewhat different from those of the last eighteen years. I see what has been pulled down very clearly. What is to be built up in its place I know not. It is a mystery; but death is always mysterious. AMEN"[38]

Colonel Robert E. Withers underwent a similar transformation of identity on noticing a dried codfish before a Yankee sutler's door in Danville. Although he had never tasted cod, Withers reflected that his people must now "turn Yankee" and might as well begin by learning to eat Yankee food. He, therefore, instructed his wife to serve a codfish for breakfast the following morning.[39]

Former Union Whigs, less traditional in outlook than other Virginians, led in translating psychic reorientation into political acceptance. Only three weeks after Lee's surrender, Confederate General

35. Richmond *Evening Whig*, April 8, 1865.

36. John Tyler, Jr., to John D. Imboden, January 6, 1876, John Daniel Imboden Papers, University of Virginia.

37. See A. G. Bradley, *Other Days: Recollections of Rural England and Old Virginia, 1860–1880* (London: Constable and Company, 1913), p. 293 (hereafter cited as *Other Days*).

38. Wise, *End of an Era*, pp. 461–62.

39. Robert E. Withers, *The Autobiography of an Octogenarian* (Roanoke, Va.: Stone Printing and Manufacturing Company, 1907), p. 227 (hereafter cited as *Autobiography*). This experiment in Reconstruction turned out disastrously.

Williams C. Wickham, a former Whig politician, aligned himself with the Republican party and corresponded with wartime Unionists for co-operation in Reconstruction. Wickham now frankly spoke of the Confederacy as a rebellion against lawful authority, conceived by self-seeking schemers and coercing a reluctant people.[40] At the beginning of May, in a more moderate step toward reunion, Alexander H. H. Stuart and other Augusta County leaders held an assembly of citizens to renew their allegiance to the Union and petition the federal government for lenient Reconstruction terms. Confederate Governor "Extra Billy" Smith, who had been in hiding, appeared in Staunton in an attempt to head off the meeting. Smith insisted that he alone was constitutionally entitled to discuss peace terms with federal authorities. The local politicians simply replied that federal officials would not recognize Smith, and proceeded with their plans. Their meeting inspired similar ones in other counties.[41]

During the following years, the Confederacy's downfall exerted a lasting influence on conservative Virginians' political thought. Firstly, it suggested that, whatever might have been the case in the past, Union victory had forever buried the secessionist concept of State Rights. Although traditionalists scouted the idea that combat might determine a question of law or right, most Conservatives accepted the idea that the "tribunal of arms" had decided the antebellum constitutional debate in the North's favor.[42] William Henry Fitzhugh Lee, son of the Confederate commander, stated the case thus: One man had pronounced the word "calf" as "caaf"; another, as "caffe." They had settled the question by a fair fight. "States rights are gone; we must adopt the other pronunciation."[43]

Secondly, defeat stimulated inquiry into the sources—particularly the economic sources—of the North's military superiority. General Joseph E. Johnston blamed defeat mainly on the Confederacy's lo-

---

40. Williams C. Wickham to Franklin Stearns, April 28, 1865, in Richmond *Whig*, September 28, 1880, clipping in Frank Gildart Ruffin Scrapbook, Virginia State Library, I, 51.

41. Robertson, *Stuart*, pp. 220–35, 407–16.

42. See "W.C.E." letter in Richmond *Daily Whig*, December 28, 1865; Albert Taylor Bledsoe, *Is Davis a Traitor*[?]; *or Was Secession a Constitutional Right Previous to the War of 1861?* (Baltimore: Innes and Company, 1866), p. v; Freeman, *Lee*, IV, 238–39, 304; Edward M. Daniel, ed., *Speeches and Orations of John Warwick Daniel* (Lynchburg: J. P. Bell Company, 1911), pp. 145–46 (hereafter cited as *Daniel Speeches*).

43. Wilbur D. Jones, ed., "A British Report on Postwar Virginia," *Virginia Magazine of History and Biography*, LXIX (July, 1961), 348 (hereafter cited as "British Report").

gistical failure.[44] Edward A. Pollard eventually concluded that the Confederacy had lost largely because of "a characteristic infirmity of the South . . . the want of business talent."[45] George W. Bagby held that Southerners had erred in supposing that war meant simply fighting; in reality, nine-tenths of war was prosaic, humdrum "business." It was by business activity that the North had prevailed. Diversification and industry, Bagby concluded, would therefore be the South's means to recovery.[46]

In 1877, Major John W. Daniel of Lynchburg eloquently expounded the reasons why the Union had won:

It was because the North had cultivated the conquering ideas of the world. . . . It was because she had shown herself our superior in finance, in literature, in arts, commerce, and manufactures.

. . . the Southern soldier carried an old-fashioned musket or sportsman's shotgun; and was shot down by repeating rifles before he got close enough to fire back with his short-range weapon. . . . While our ports were hermetically sealed, our currency being carried to market in baskets for what might be brought back in the hand, our people living on what Lazarus would have despised, the North was sweeping the seas and guarding our harbors with iron-clad monitors . . . was upholding paper money to an approximate equality with gold; was affluent, opulent, and unrestrained. And while we could not build a sixty-mile military railroad between Danville and Lynchburg, the North was laying its iron rails across the mighty stretch of the Western plains, climbing the Rocky Mountains, and connecting its splendid highway with the golden gates of the Pacific. These are the facts; thus it is that we were conquered.[47]

Virginians of Daniel's generation profited by the lesson of their defeat. They, too, made peace with "the commanding ideas of the world" in the age of the industrial revolution. Like many other leaders of underdeveloped regions, conquered by industrial adversaries, the Virginia Conservatives reacted by substituting their conquerors' social patterns for their traditional institutions.

In the spring of 1865, many Virginians vaguely understood that Union victory would bring drastic changes, difficult to comprehend,

44. Joseph E. Johnston, *Narrative of Military Operations Directed during the Late War between the States* (New York: D. Appleton and Company, 1874), pp. 421–25.
45. Edward A. Pollard, "New Virginia," *Old and New*, V (March, 1872), 283–84 (hereafter cited as "New Virginia").
46. Bagby, *Old Virginia Gentleman*, pp. 295, 300–301.
47. Daniel, ed., *Daniel Speeches*, pp. 300–301.

in their way of life. They could be sure of only the elementary facts that slavery and secession had passed away and that economic re-building was the primary task ahead of them. They could not even learn from a divided North on what terms their Commonwealth might rejoin the Union. It would take the conservatives four years to discover how to obtain and exercise government power under postwar conditions. As they groped for the way to a New South, their experience of nineteenth-century warfare predisposed them toward nationalist and entrepreneurial solutions.

4.

The Pierpont Government,
1865–1867

For almost two years after Confederate military resistance ended, Northern factions' contests for control of the federal government left the terms of the South's "reconstruction" in doubt. In that interval conservative Virginians made their first attempt to participate in postwar national affairs. Assimilated into the Unionist Pierpont government and dominating its legislative branch, they took conscientious, if misguided, steps to reorganize the Commonwealth and restore it to the Union. In the spring of 1867, Congress, for understandable reasons, rejected their work as unacceptable. The preceding two years had, nevertheless, advanced the conservatives somewhat in coming to terms with new realities.

STABILIZATION

After the Confederate surrender, Virginians "accepted the situation" with amazing rapidity. Harvey M. Watterson of Kentucky, after talking in June with "the most respectable and intelligent" Virginians, concluded that "one of the most remarkable revolutions known in the history of human opinion" had erased all vestiges of rebellion.[1] At the end of the year, the British diplomat Sir Frederick W. A. Bruce made the same discovery. Slavery, Watterson and Bruce found, had become unpopular; many Virginians now declared that it had been unprofitable.[2] Virginia Unionists agreed that immediately after the surrender former Confederates generally acquiesced, even if grudgingly, in the new order.[3]

1. Martin Abbott, ed., "A Southerner Views the South, 1865: Letters of Harvey M. Watterson," *Virginia Magazine of History and Biography,* LXVIII (October, 1960), 479–83.
2. *Ibid.,* p. 482; Jones, ed., "British Report," pp. 350–51.
3. Testimony of John Minor Botts and the Reverend Robert McCurdy before the

"It is impossible," a Unionist clergyman stated, "to make their physical humiliation more complete than it is."[4] The specter of military destruction would haunt the Old Dominion for more than fifteen years. In 1877, a committee of the legislature would calculate Virginia's direct economic losses from the War, including the value of slaves freed, at $457,000,000.[5] In 1865, the loss appeared not as a statistic but as ubiquitous, visible, tangible devastation. Railroads and canals had been rendered useless, the banks had collapsed, and many towns and cities had been sacked. Plantation houses stood deserted, and fields had become wastelands or graveyards. General Philip Sheridan's operations had stripped the Valley of its agricultural resources and left it desolate.[6]

Amid these depressing surroundings, Virginians began to reintegrate themselves into the Union. Many political leaders excluded from general amnesty conformed to the new order, minimally at least, by applying to President Johnson to recover their rights. Henry A. Wise's scorn for men who implicitly admitted treason to obtain "pardons" did not stem the tide of applications. Unionist connections and records of political moderation stood petitioners in good stead.[7] Some renewed their antebellum friendships with influential Northerners and interceded for friends who lacked that resource.[8] Governor Pierpont assisted some petitioners, and a Richmond businessman opined that President John W. Garrett of the Baltimore and Ohio Railroad would be an especially influential advocate.[9] Rumor ascribed special influence in Washington to former Whig leaders William Cabell Rives, Alexander H. H. Stuart,

---

Joint Committee on Reconstruction, *Report of the Joint Committee on Reconstruction*, 39 Cong., 1 Sess., Part II, pp. 92, 120 (hereafter cited as *Reconstruction Committee Report*).

4. *Ibid.*, p. 92.

5. Charles C. Pearson, *The Readjuster Movement in Virginia* (New Haven: Yale University Press, 1917), p. 7n (hereafter cited as *Readjuster Movement*).

6. Ambler, *Pierpont*, pp. 261–62; *Reconstruction Committee Report*, II, 68.

7. Robert R. Jones, "Conservative Virginian: The Post-War Career of Governor James Lawson Kemper" (Ph.D. dissertation, University of Virginia, 1964), pp. 26–27 (hereafter cited as "Conservative Virginian").

8. L. Quinton Washington to Robert M. T. Hunter, August 7, 1865; Washington to Hunter, November 9, 1865; Washington to Mrs. R. M. T. Hunter, August 15, 1865, all in Hunter-Garnett Papers, University of Virginia.

9. Francis H. Pierpont to Robert M. T. Hunter, May 29, 1865, and Lewis D. Crenshaw to Hunter, May 29, 1865, both in *ibid.*

and John B. Baldwin.[10] The traffic in influence between Virginia and the national capital created new careers for some Virginians. Brigadier Generals Patrick T. Moore and James Lawson Kemper exploited their comrades' misfortunes as "pardon-brokers," using their legal talents and personal connections to expedite the amnesty procedure for paying clients.[11] The journalist L. Q. Washington established himself at the seat of government as a lobbyist for Southern interests.[12]

On May 26, Francis H. Pierpont came to Richmond as chief executive of the "restored" Commonwealth which President Johnson had officially recognized. Local dignitaries enthusiastically welcomed the Unionist governor. Addressing his new constituents several days later, Pierpont called for sectional reconciliation and economic recovery. He predicted that, if planters would adjust to free-labor cultivation by selling their lands in small farms, unprecedented prosperity would result. In the same message, however, Pierpont announced that he was closing the state banks, insolvent because the Confederacy's fall had rendered many of their assets valueless and the prohibitive federal tax on notes of state-chartered banks had had the same effect on their notes.[13]

Union victory altered control of railroads as well as finance. By early summer, the United States Military Railroads restored the railroad lines to their managers or to the Board of Public Works. In two instances, the board's new Unionist members used the state stock to unseat executives identified with the old order. They removed Colonel Lewis E. Harvie, a secessionist and spokesman for planter interests, from the presidency of the Richmond and Danville Railroad. The board later joined a faction of private stockholders to unseat Colonel Edmund Fontaine, a wealthy planter, as president of the Virginia Central Railroad and install in his place General Wickham, the wartime Unionists' new ally.[14]

10. John B. Baldwin to Hunter, n.d. [1865] and L. Q. Washington to Hunter, September 2, 1865, both in *ibid.*; John H. McCue to John Cochran, September 8, 1865, William Cabell Rives Papers, Library of Congress. Rives had a voice in federal patronage. F. H. Burch to Rives, September 27, 1865, Rives Papers.

11. Jones, "Conservative Virginian," p. 32.

12. L. Q. Washington to Robert M. T. Hunter, December 12, 1865, Hunter-Garnett Papers.

13. Ambler, *Pierpont*, pp. 263–64, 268–72.

14. Johnston, *Virginia Railroads*, pp. 17, 252. The federal administration also harassed Harvie, by delaying action on his application for amnesty. "I alone of all the R[ail] Road men," he complained, "have been put aside [,] ignored [,] & repudiated by

THE REVIVAL OF POLITICS

In June, a special session of the legislature, on the Governor's recommendation, legalized Negroes' marriages, extended political rights to Confederates taking the amnesty oath, provided for elections, and increased the property tax. The General Assembly rejected Pierpont's advice to increase the interest rate and enacted a law to stay collection of debts for four years. At the end of the session, the speaker of the House of Delegates declared that the legislature, by adjusting the statutes to post-emancipation conditions, had precluded the federal government from trying to impose Negro suffrage on Virginia.[15]

The legislature had provided for a general election to occur in October, 1865. The principal issue was whether to elect only congressional candidates able to take the federal test oath or to elect former Confederates in the hope that Congress would waive the requirement. Charles L. Mosby of Lynchburg argued that the oath was unconstitutional and, in any case, inapplicable to congressmen.[16] Stuart ran for Congress, even though he could not take the oath as he interpreted it. He argued that he had assisted the Confederacy no more than his opponent had, that the requirement was unconstitutional, and that Northern moderates would welcome his election.[17] On the other hand, Armstrong M. Keiley of Petersburg withdrew his candidacy lest the Republican majority deprive Virginia of a seat in the House on his account.[18] The voters chose eight representatives, six of whom could take the oath. Four had been active Whigs before the war; the others had not been prominent in politics. The legislature had chosen the Unionists Joseph Segar and John C. Underwood as senators. Congress declined, however, to seat any members from the former Confederate states. At the October election, the voters also ratified an amendment to delete all political disabilities from the Alexandria Constitution and elected

---

both Gover[n]ments." Lewis E. Harvie to Robert M. T. Hunter, September 21, 1865, Hunter-Garnett Papers.

15. Ambler, *Pierpont*, pp. 272–75; James Douglas Smith, "Virginia during Reconstruction, 1865–1870: A Political, Economic, and Social Study" (Ph.D. dissertation, University of Virginia, 1955), pp. 12–14 (hereafter cited as "Virginia during Reconstruction").

16. Charles L. Mosby, *Congressional Test Act Examined in Two Letters in Which Are Considered, First the Constitutionality of the Act, and Second, Its Proper Construction and Application* (Lynchburg: *Virginian* Power-Press Printing Office, 1865), pp. 1–23.

17. Robertson, *Stuart*, pp. 239–50.

18. Richmond *Whig and Public Advertiser*, September 12, 1865.

a legislature that consisted overwhelmingly of former Whigs and included no Radical Republican or prominent secessionist.[19]

This General Assembly—popularly called the "Baldwin legislature" after Speaker of the House John B. Baldwin—represented the element in antebellum politics best prepared to lead Virginia into harmony with the Northern states. Not even the Whigs, however, comprehended the demands of the new era that the United States was entering. Institutions and ideas that had grown to maturity in the North now penetrated the South by invasion and became the standard by which Northern congressmen measured the South's readiness for reunion. Only vaguely familiar with the new standards, the members of the legislature were not ready to take the forward strides that postwar conditions required and that an impatient North, in the vanguard of world progress, expected from the defeated, dependent South.

When the legislature convened in December, Governor Pierpont called its attention to the urgent economic and social crisis that prevailed. He recommended that the General Assembly provide for paying the state debt, tax the oyster business, consolidate the railroads into a few efficient systems, establish free schools, grant relief to widows and orphans impoverished by repudiation of Confederate bonds, and provide generously for public institutions. In his program, Pierpont, if anything, underestimated the current emergency. He erroneously expected that the national banks would provide adequate currency and that employers' enlightened self-interest would protect the freedmen.[20]

Almost ignoring the problems Pierpont pointed out, the legislature repealed the act consenting to West Virginia's creation, asked Congress to repeal the federal test oath, asked the president to release Jefferson Davis from prison, and hinted that the president should make General Lee governor in place of Pierpont. The legislators repealed the old slave code, making punishments equal for members of both races, but legalized Negroes' testimony only in cases in which Negroes were parties. They enacted a harsh vagrancy law whose enforcement Major General Alfred H. Terry forbade as "slavery in all but its name." They guaranteed payment of the entire antebellum state debt including wartime interest and appropriated money for the university and military institute—but none

19. Ambler, *Pierpont*, p. 280; Smith, "Virginia during Reconstruction," p. 16. Smith erroneously states that the Fifth District elected Colonel Robert E. Withers to Congress; in fact, the Reverend B. A. Davis was elected.

20. Ambler, *Pierpont*, p. 280.

for common schools. Several Virginia newspapers, including the Richmond *Whig* and Rockingham *Register*, criticized the legislature for its traditionalist course.[21]

While the Baldwin legislature resisted innovation, the Republican majority of Congress solidified in opposition to President Johnson's conservative Reconstruction policy. During 1866, Northern moderates organized the National Union Convention at Philadelphia to express support for the president. Virginians showed little interest in the gathering until six weeks before its convening date. Then, on July 2, a public meeting in Albemarle County proposed that Virginia send representatives and that, for want of time to hold a state convention, the members of the Bell, Douglas, and Breckinridge party committees meet to select the delegates. Others endorsed the Albemarle County suggestion. Late in July, some of the committee members met in Richmond on a call appearing in the *Whig* and announced that the entire body would convene on August 7. Breckinridge Chairman John C. Rutherfoord and Bell Chairman William H. Macfarland, both Richmond businessmen, dominated the August meeting. The members rejected suggestions to instruct the delegates and appointed the delegates named by a nine-member nominating committee.[22]

From the Albemarle County meeting onward, former Whigs took the lead in this, Virginia's first postwar participation in national conservative politics. The method for selecting delegates gave Whigs an advantage: the Bell committee, larger than the other two combined, had consisted solely of Richmond residents, but the Breckinridge and Douglas committee members had been dispersed throughout the antebellum area of Virginia.[23] The *Whig* augmented its faction's advantage by calling the July meeting on only three days' notice. At the August meeting, the advocates of instructing delegates were former Breckinridge Democrats; the opponents were former Whigs. The nine-member nominating committee included five Whigs, until one resigned in favor of a Douglas Democrat to afford more equal representation. The committee chose more prom-

21. *Ibid.*, pp. 282–83; Hamilton J. Eckenrode, "History of Virginia since 1865" (typescript in Hamilton James Eckenrode Papers, University of Virginia), pp. 8–9, 74–76 (hereafter cited as "Virginia since 1865"); McFarland, "Extension of Democracy," pp. 41–46; Richmond *Whig and Public Advertiser*, February 27, 1866; James E. Sefton, Jr., *The United States Army and Reconstruction, 1865–1877* (Baton Rouge: Louisiana State University Press, 1967), pp. 71–72 (hereafter cited as *U.S. Army*).

22. Richmond *Whig and Public Advertiser*, July 6, 13, 20, and 27, and August 3, 1866.

23. *Ibid.*, July 12 and 17, 1866.

inent Whigs than prominent Democrats to go to Philadelphia, and the Richmond *Examiner*, the most intransigent of the city's papers, pronounced the selections unfortunate.[24] The episode illustrated the readiness and ability of former Whigs to seize the initiative in conservative organization.

THE WIDENING POLITICAL CHASM

Governor Pierpont sought to steer a moderate course through the turbulent waters of Reconstruction politics. He hoped to gather about himself a moderate, Whiggish party, distinct from both Johnson Democrats and Radical Republicans, on a platform of equal rights, free schools, and public works. During 1865, he enjoyed a measure of success, winning the support of influential figures inside and outside Virginia.[25]

During 1866, Pierpont's dream of a Whiggish consensus faded. The legislature and the press bore witness that Southern traditionalism was organizing as a political force. Observing these manifestations, wartime Unionists—who sometimes mistook misunderstanding for rejection of the new era's requirements—concluded that the former Confederates who had returned to prominence were "disloyal." They did not, John Minor Botts admitted, appear "disloyal" in everyday contacts, but their public statements and policies clearly contradicted loyalty as he understood it.[26]

The Radicals responded by organizing their own movement, uniting Unionists who criticized the enfranchisement of Confederates with Negroes who sought admission to civil rights. In May, 1866, sixty Unionists met at Alexandria to found the Union Republican party of Virginia. They advocated at least temporary disfranchisement of former Confederates, enfranchisement of "all Union men, without distinction of color," and a free-school system.[27] The new party appealed to Northerners to prompt Congress to intervene in Virginia politics. Federal Judge John C. Underwood even wanted Northern Republicans to have Phineas T. Barnum exhibit in the North a Negro child branded by racists, to increase the Republican vote for Congress in 1866.[28]

24. See list *ibid.*, August 3, 1866; Richmond *Daily Examiner*, August 2 and 7, 1866.
25. Ambler, *Pierpont*, p. 288.
26. *Reconstruction Committee Report*, II, 120.
27. *Ibid.*, I, 230–31; Alrutheus A. Taylor, *The Negro in the Reconstruction of Virginia* (Washington: Association for the Study of Negro Life and History, 1926), p. 24 (hereafter cited as *Negro in Reconstruction*).
28. E. Merton Coulter, *The South during Reconstruction, 1865–1877* (Baton Rouge:

Pierpont had hoped to reunite such Confederate Whigs as John B. Baldwin with such Unionist Whigs as John Minor Botts. In 1866, however, he found Baldwin trying to exclude Unionists from office, and Botts asking Congress to overthrow the restored government. The governor would now have to take sides, however reluctantly, or suffer political isolation. He could not align himself with the backward-looking legislature. Landowners' labor policies had refuted his naïve assumption that freedmen needed no positive protective legislation. He began to find signs of "rebellion" everywhere. Seeing no early prospect of a party of "the conservative white men," Pierpont finally embraced the more moderate wing of the Republican party—"the mean white man's party."[29]

The governor still tried to bind up Virginia's political wounds by diverting public attention to the relatively nonpartisan cause of economic development. He advocated a coal tariff for the mining interest and accepted the presidency of a company that moderate Republicans had formed to attract immigrants to Virginia.[30] Even as a promoter, Pierpont found, he must take sides. General William Mahone, president of both the Norfolk and Petersburg and the South Side railroads, had devised the grand design of consolidating his lines with the Virginia and Tennessee (from Lynchburg to Bristol) into one railroad that would span southern Virginia and connect with trunk lines to the west.[31] Opposing Mahone were John S. Barbour's Orange and Alexandria Railroad—principally owned by the Baltimore and Ohio and a rival for southwest Virginia's trade— and Richmond interests afraid that trade would by-pass their city. During the winter of 1866–67, railroad consolidation displaced national politics in public attention. The governor espoused Mahone's cause. In March, 1867, during the Baldwin legislature's last days, he warned the general that he "had better spend ten thousand dollars than to let this legislature fail to pass [*sic*] without securing consolidation." "Commerce and money," he added appropriately, "have no conscience when great commercial interest[s] are to be obtained."[32]

Louisiana State University Press, 1947), pp. 116–17 (hereafter cited as *South during Reconstruction*).

29. Ambler, *Pierpont*, 285–88, 295–98, 307, 314–15.

30. *Ibid.*, pp. 303–5.

31. Blake, *Mahone*, pp. 72–81; Ambler, *Pierpont*, pp. 301–2; Richmond *Whig and Public Advertiser*, October 5, 1866.

32. Quoted in Blake, *Mahone*, pp. 82–83.

THE PASSING OF THE RESTORED GOVERNMENT

The last regular session of the Baldwin legislature convened in December, 1866. Governor Pierpont advised the members to ratify the Fourteenth Amendment to the federal Constitution. By ratifying, he believed, they could persuade Congress to restore Virginia to her full privileges in the Union. There was no other way to recover that status; in the North, the support of the wealthy and educated middle classes guaranteed a long Republican ascendancy, and only the urban lower classes upheld the president.[33]

Pierpont's appeal fell on deaf ears. Conservative Virginians were not yet prepared to take the Fourteenth Amendment seriously, since its first section would assert Federal jurisdiction over civil rights and its second would at least raise the question of enfranchising Negroes. Already the Baldwin legislature had greatly reduced the volume of legislation discriminating against Negroes; the most conspicuous remaining example, besides suffrage, was the prohibition on Negro testimony in cases involving only white litigants. Even laws actually intended to restrict freedmen's freedom of contract had not expressed racial discrimination *in their texts*.[34] Speaker Baldwin assured Congress' Joint Committee on Reconstruction that the trend of Virginia legislation was toward racial equality before the law, but he insisted that circumstances precluded more than a slow, gradual approach toward the goal.[35] The General Assembly had extended passive, civil rights—but active, political rights were another matter. The Richmond *Whig* and the Lynchburg *Republican* advised their readers to accept at least limited Negro suffrage as an unavoidable nuisance, but the great majority of conservatives resolutely opposed enfranchising any Negro.[36]

Nor did conservative leaders trust Congress to readmit their state even if the legislature should ratify the unacceptable amendment. During the War, they argued, the federal government had asked the Southern states only to cease hostilities and resume their customary roles in the Union. After the surrender, however, President John-

---

33. Ambler, *Pierpont*, pp. 289–92.

34. John Preston McConnell, *Negroes and Their Treatment in Virginia from 1865 to 1867* (Pulaski, Va.: B. D. Smith & Brothers, 1910), pp. 49–53, 56–62, 80, 82, 100–101, 104 (hereafter cited as *Negroes and Treatment*).

35. *Reconstruction Committee Report*, II, 108.

36. Smith, "Virginia during Reconstruction," p. 34; McConnell, *Negroes and Treatment*, pp. 87–90.

son had recognized the Alexandria government instead of the Richmond one and required it to meet certain conditions for recognition. Now, Congress was presenting yet another, more stringent, set of terms. How, conservatives asked, could they trust the federal government—which they perceived as a monolith—to keep faith, and not impose even more humiliating conditions in the future?[37] Having accepted Andrew Johnson's word, in 1865, that he represented Northern public opinion, they now became confused about, and suspicious of, federal policy.[38] Northern observers attributed Virginia's rejection of the Fourteenth Amendment to Johnson's personal influence on the legislators.[39]

In the two houses of the legislature, only one member voted to ratify the amendment. The legislators, expecting no adverse consequence from rejecting the measure, lived in a fool's paradise. A year late, they at last attended to the prevalent economic distress. They extended the stay law, exempted homesteads up to 160 acres and $1,200 from judicial sales, paid only 4 per cent interest on the state debt for the following year, and let subscribers to public-works projects pay in land.[40] Ignoring the crisis in federal relations, the legislators politicked in avid anticipation of the forthcoming gubernatorial election. They divided along prewar party lines. Baldwin and his Whig friends had wanted to nominate General Lee, but Lee had declined for fear of increasing Congress' hostility to Virginia. The Whig majority of the General Assembly preferred Baldwin, or perhaps Flournoy or Wyndham Robertson; the Democrats inclined toward General James Lawson Kemper.[41] Speculation in the press featured a host of other candidates, including the conspicuously unreconstructed General Jubal A. Early, then in Canadian exile.[42] After inconclusive caucusing about such subjects, the legislators adjourned their session.

37. See Richmond *Enquirer*, January 13, 1869, and William Smith to (?), October 28, 1867, in John W. Bell, *Memoirs of Governor William Smith of Virginia: His Political, Military, and Personal History* (New York: Moss Engraving Company, 1891), pp. 261–62 (hereafter cited as *Smith*).

38. See Eric L. McKitrick, *Andrew Johnson and Reconstruction* (Chicago: University of Chicago Press, 1960), pp. 186–213, 467–73.

39. *Ibid.*, p. 454.

40. Smith, "Virginia during Reconstruction," pp. 29–31.

41. A. W. Graves to James Lawson Kemper, January 30, 1867, James Lawson Kemper Papers, University of Virginia; Freeman, *Lee*, IV, 310–11; F. B. Deane, Jr., to Wyndham Robertson, February 10, 1867, Wyndham Robertson Papers, University of Chicago; Jones, "Conservative Virginian," pp. 91–94.

42. Richmond *Whig and Public Advertiser*, January 8 and 22, and February 1, 1867.

On March 2, 1867, Congress passed the First Reconstruction Act, requiring the former Confederate states to hold constitutional conventions, whose members would be elected by biracial suffrage, and to organize new state governments whose legislatures would ratify the Fourteenth Amendment. A few days later, fourteen hundred Negroes, in an unprecedented show of militance, attempted to vote in a municipal election in Alexandria.[43] Reconvening the General Assembly, Pierpont warned it that Negro suffrage was now inevitable; the legislators might still moderate its effects by initiating action under the Reconstruction Act. Seeing the alternatives more clearly than ever before, the members relaxed their uncompromising position. The Senate voted, by twenty-seven votes to four, to call a convention to frame a constitution under the act's provisions, but the House procrastinated for two more weeks. On March 23, Congress settled the question by passing the Supplemental Reconstruction Act, which directed the military commanders in the South to initiate the reconstruction process.[44] Four weeks later the legislature, in a futile gesture of repentance for its inflexibility, finally recognized Negroes' full rights to testify in courts.[45]

The moderate former Whigs of the Baldwin legislature, more than any other antebellum political grouping, understood that the outcome of the War would require important changes in Virginia's institutions and policies. In responding to the postwar situation, nevertheless, they did too little and acted too late. Virginia would have to move not only in the direction of the old Whig program, but far beyond it, either to satisfy the Northern Congress or to adjust to postwar social conditions. The legislators' failure was largely one of comprehension. Governor Pierpont was one of very few persons who understood both Congress and the General Assembly well enough to comprehend the gaping cleavage between their viewpoints. The members of the Baldwin legislature learned much in sixteen months, but they did not learn rapidly enough to head off the Reconstruction Acts. The ensuing military Reconstruction served as a "shock treatment" to accelerate conservative Virginians' education in, and accommodation to, the revolutionary ways of Yankeedom.

43. McConnell, *Negroes and Treatment*, p. 110.
44. Ambler, *Pierpont*, pp. 293–95; [Joseph Segar], *Letter of the Hon. Joseph Segar, on the Late Elections in Virginia* (n.p., [1869]), pp. 4–5 (hereafter cited as *Segar Letter, 1869*); see A. W. Graves to James L. Kemper, March 6, 1867, Kemper Papers, University of Virginia.
45. McConnell, *Negroes and Treatment*, p. 85.

5.

Conservatives during
Military Reconstruction, 1867–1868

The Reconstruction Acts ushered in the decisive phase in the origin of Virginia Conservatism. During the years of military Reconstruction, conservatives organized as a party and, in the course of repeated experiments, gradually formulated their policies and their political strategy and tactics. These all took on, and later retained, the impress of the conditions under which they came into being. The resulting Conservative party was a significant contribution to the variety of political organisms that sprang from the fertile soil of national Reconstruction.

RECONSTRUCTION IN VIRGINIA

"Since our last meeting," Judge John T. Harris told his Rockingham County grand jury in May, 1867, "a very material and important change has taken place in our State and National relations. . . . Where once existed legal and political distinctions so broad, positive and marked, that it was thought nothing but Providence could remove them, now are seen the entire obliteration of those distinctions and all before the law are placed in a great measure upon an equal footing." The judge admonished his jurors not to disturb the political situation further by animosity but to acquiesce in the Reconstruction edicts, administer justice impartially, respect differing opinions, try to overcome traditional prejudices, and accept Congress' terms of Reconstruction as the only ones obtainable.[1] General Lee, now the president of Washington College, also advised acquiescence, hoping by a tranquil Reconstruction to minimize social dislocation.[2]

1. John W. Wayland, *A History of Rockingham County, Virginia* (Dayton, Va.: Raebush-Elkins Company, 1912), pp. 161–62 (hereafter cited as *Rockingham County*).
2. Freeman, *Lee*, IV, 220–21, 310–11, 313–14.

In general, the following years realized Harris' and Lee's hopes. The course of Virginia's Reconstruction was "a study in moderation."[3] " Outside of the newspaper circle," the *Whig* observed in 1867, "there seems to be little political excitement in Virginia. . . . The people seem bent upon their business affairs, and surely their time and attention could be devoted to nothing more important."[4] John S. Wise, who spent the Reconstruction years as a Richmond attorney, later denied that there had been "any period in which negroes or alien and degenerate whites were in a position to oppress the gallant people of Virginia."[5] Traditionalists of the Deep South complained that conservatives in Virginia took military Reconstruction too quiescently.[6]

The Reconstruction that conservatives feared was the prospect of a Radical civil government, not the existing military regime. The editor of the Petersburg *Index* later recalled that, under commanding generals John McA. Schofield and George Stoneman, "Virginia knew none of the dreaded 'horrors of military despotism.' "[7] At the Conservative party's founding convention, Alexander H. H. Stuart and R. M. T. Hunter agreed that military rule was preferable to Negro domination.[8] The Richmond *Whig* often commended the military authorities.[9] When Judge Underwood ordered the release of a Negro woman convicted in a military trial, the *Whig* denounced him as a rebel against General Stoneman's authority and against the Reconstruction Acts. The paper greatly preferred "United States troops under United States officers" to "such characters as are now marauding Arkansas."[10] The more traditionalist Richmond *En-*

---

3. Smith, "Virginia during Reconstruction," p. 462.

4. Richmond *Whig and Public Advertiser*, September 17, 1867.

5. John S. Wise, *The Lion's Skin: A Historical Novel and a Novel History* (New York: Doubleday, Page, and Company, 1905), pp. 195–96 (hereafter cited as *Lion's Skin*).

6. William M. Semple to George W. Bagby, July 15, 1867, George William Bagby Papers, Virginia Historical Society.

7. William E. Cameron, *Some Interior Phases of Reconstruction: How Virginia Got Back into the Union; Glimpses of Some Great Men North and South* (broadside, n.p., n.d.; copies in Harrison Holt Riddleberger Papers, College of William and Mary) (hereafter cited as *Interior Phases*).

8. Richmond *Daily Whig*, December 13, 1867; Hamilton J. Eckenrode, *The Political History of Virginia during the Reconstruction* ("Johns Hopkins University Studies in Historical and Political Science," XXII, Nos. 6–8 [Baltimore: The Johns Hopkins Press, 1904]), pp. 85–86 (hereafter cited as *Political History*).

9. See Richmond *Daily Whig*, March 2, April 14, 25, 28, June 1, 2, December 22, 23, 24, 1868; January 29, February 8, March 12, April 20, 1869.

10. Richmond *Daily Whig*, December 15, 1868.

quirer expressed hostility to military government, but it, too, exploited clashes between troops and Negroes.[11]

General Schofield, who commanded Military District Number One—Virginia—longer than any other officer, adhered to a conservative Reconstruction policy. In 1865, he had opposed Negro suffrage. In 1866, he had criticized the Fourteenth Amendment, especially its disability provisions, but had advised Virginians to ratify it for fear of greater impositions. Schofield rarely intervened in government except to moderate Radical officials' actions. His successor, General George Stoneman, a Democrat, followed a similar policy. Military courts showed less leniency to Negroes than did Republican civil officials. The officers often co-operated with conservatives; in fact, Schofield complained that conservatives were constantly asking him to settle their petty differences summarily, by-passing the courts. The general especially disapproved of measures to make the "Iron Clad Oath" of past loyalty a condition of office-holding.[12]

One conservative, General Mahone, found military government especially helpful to his business projects. Soon after Stoneman became commanding general, Mahone's Richmond banker, James R. Branch, sounded him and found him in favor of railroad consolidation. Stoneman declared that he would not permit the Board of Public Works to interfere with the policies of the roads and that he would remove the governor and state treasurer, if necessary, to prevent them from interfering. In sending the good news to Mahone, Branch advised him to meet personally with Stoneman.[13] General Schofield also used his influence for Mahone, even after becoming secretary of war in 1868.[14] Many Republican civil officials assisted the Confederate general, receiving railroad passes from Richard F. Walker, his spy in the state administration. The administration let Mahone select the proxies to represent the state on his companies' boards but sometimes required that he choose Republicans.[15]

11. Richmond *Enquirer-Examiner*, January 6 and 9 and March 30, 1869.

12. Sefton, *U.S. Army*, pp. 14–15, 18, 21, 102–3, 121, 138, 145, 194–95, 197; John McAllister Schofield, *Forty-Six Years in the Army* (New York: Century Company, 1897), pp. 397–99, 403–4 (hereafter cited as *Forty-Six Years*); F. H. Hill to James L. Kemper, March 15, 1869, James Lawson Kemper Papers, University of Virginia.

13. [James R. Branch] to William Mahone, September 1, 1868, William Mahone Papers, Duke University.

14. H. H. Walker to Mahone, October 25, 1868, *ibid.*

15. Richard F. Walker to Mahone, October 6, 1868; Walker to Mahone, November 4, 1868; Walker to Mahone, November 13, 1868; Walker to Mahone, November 20, 1868; Walker to Mahone, December 10, 1868; and Walker to Mahone, January 29, 1869, *ibid.*

Although the conservatives could not complain of oppression under military rule, the mushrooming Radical or Republican party within the Commonwealth challenged them seriously. Although the Virginia Radicals occupied an insecure position and depended on Northern assistance, they represented about half the population, drafted the state's Reconstruction constitution, and expected to control the government after military rule should end.

The Radicals suffered from internal divisions. The party's right wing consisted of Whig Unionists such as John Minor Botts and of business and professional men. These, like the most progressive of the conservatives, were primarily interested in capitalist development. Many were indifferent to Negroes' welfare. The party's center, characterized by Judge Underwood and Governor Henry H. Wells, concerned itself principally with administering the party and the state. Little concerned with political philosophy, it attracted some opportunists and corruptionists.

It was the Radicals' left wing that terrified conservatives. That faction drew its support from the Negroes—five out of every twelve Virginians—and from white men with only a minimal stake in the social *status quo*. Although inadequately represented in the party's leadership, the Negroes provided the bulk of its votes and could often determine which faction would control its policy. Recently "property" themselves, the freedmen were not obsessed by bourgeois property concepts.[16] Many had expected land redistribution in 1865, and some still hoped the federal government would confiscate land and donate it to them. In several places in southeastern Virginia, Negroes occupied plantations or remained encamped on them after the Freedmen's Bureau relinquished control.[17] Also subversive of social order were bands of extralegal Negro "militia," under carpetbagger leadership, in southside counties such as Brunswick.[18]

The Reverend James W. Hunnicutt, a Southern Unionist and

16. See Withers, *Autobiography*, pp. 229–30; [Mary Allan-Olney], *The New Virginians* (Edinburgh and London: William Blackwood and Sons, 1880), I, 55 (hereafter cited as *New Virginians*).

17. Taylor, *Negro in Reconstruction*, p. 35; S. G. Cooke to B. Johnson Barbour, February 8, 1870, B. Johnson Barbour Papers, University of Virginia; Governor's Message, December 7, 1870, Virginia *Senate Journal* (1870–71), pp. 18, 21 (hereafter cited as *Senate Journal*).

18. Myrta Lockett Avary, *Dixie after the War: An Exposition of Social Conditions Existing in the South, during the Twelve Years Succeeding the Fall of Richmond* (New York: Doubleday, Page and Company, 1906), pp. 326–50 (hereafter cited as *Dixie after the War*).

editor of the Richmond *New Nation,* led the left wing. In April, 1867, his black followers, some of whom advocated land confiscation, dominated the Republican State Convention at Richmond. In its platform, the convention placed equalitarian demands for racial equality, free schools, and equitable taxation ahead of capitalist demands for a higher interest rate and encouragement to internal improvements and immigration. It committed the party to represent the interests of the laboring classes regardless of race, to restrain the arrogant and lift up the downtrodden and to promote the greatest good for the greatest number.[19]

The poor, uneducated black masses could not alone insure the continued radicalism of a party that depended also on Northern Republican support. Northern politicians usually played a moderating role in Virginia's Republican politics.[20] Soon after the April convention, Horace Greeley, Thurlow Weed, and Senator Henry Wilson expressed disapproval of Hunnicutt's leadership.[21] The plebeian specter nevertheless menaced Virginia conservatives, impelling them to adjust to the Northern status quo as the surest barrier against social upheaval.

BIRTH OF THE CONSERVATIVE MOVEMENT

In the chaos into which the Reconstruction Acts hurled conservative Virginians, three alternative tactical policies took form.

One policy, most popular among unreconstructed traditionalists, was to abstain from participation in Reconstruction politics. For some traditionalists, abstention sprang from a mood of fatalistic resignation. Others considered it a moral duty not to co-operate in what they considered their degradation. "Extra Billy" Smith was willing to acquiesce in a military regime but wanted to make it clear that *"it would be the act of power, not our own."*[22] More practical abstentionists simply saw no way to influence the course of events at that time. Southerners, one conservative wrote, should "let matters alone in which they have no part & can have none until the

19. Taylor, *Negro in Reconstruction,* pp. 209–12; for text of platform, see James S. Allen, *Reconstruction: The Battle for Democracy, 1865–1877* (New York: International Publishers, 1937), pp. 230–32 (hereafter cited as *Reconstruction*).

20. See quotation from John Hawxhurst in Smith, "Virginia during Reconstruction," p. 127. For Senator Henry Wilson's role, see Ambler, *Pierpont,* p. 288, and below, p. 53.

21. Taylor, *Negro in Reconstruction,* pp. 212–13.

22. Bell, *Smith,* p. 262.

venom of Yankeedom has run its course."[23] Stuart, at first, counseled abstention to "retain our self-respect and avoid entangling commitments" until Northern public opinion should become more favorable.[24] The *Whig*, industrial in outlook, hoped Virginians would direct "the ambition and energy hitherto wasted in politics" to economic development.[25]

This last group of abstentionists assumed that Northerners before long would abandon the policy of the Reconstruction Acts. Conservatives eagerly scanned news from the North for signs of the expected reaction.[26] Edward A. Pollard, the zealot for the "Lost Cause," staked his hopes on the racial sympathies of white Northerners.[27] Business-minded conservatives knew that, on the contrary, the way to a Yankee's heart lay through his wallet. "It is idle," the Petersburg *Index* concluded, "to tell them that our liberty is gone and that we are oppressed by the very lees and refuse of the Northern invasion. But it may not be idle to tell them of the money we lose."[28] Virginia businessmen believed that Reconstruction conditions were depressing business activity,[29] and conservative spokesmen unceasingly preached that conviction to Northerners.[30] Two nationalist Whigs—the Republican Botts and the conservative Stuart—warned Northern Republicans that Negroes, if enfranchised, would eventually vote, as poor whites did, for Democratic demagogues, free trade, and repudiation of public debts.[31] Northern industry would never enjoy a prosperous Southern market, the *Whig* argued, as long as Radicalism spread discontent among laborers and frightened investors away.[32]

23. John A. Harman to James L. Kemper, February 3, 1867, Kemper Papers, University of Virginia.
24. Quoted in Smith, "Virginia during Reconstruction," p. 37.
25. Richmond *Whig and Public Advertiser*, February 5, 1867.
26. Pollard, *Lost Cause Regained*, pp. 133–34, 163n; L. Q. Washington to Robert M. T. Hunter, October 9, 1867, Hunter-Garnett Papers, University of Virginia; William Bell to William Cabell Rives, December 21, 1867, William Cabell Rives Papers, Library of Congress.
27. Pollard, *Lost Cause Regained*, p. 165.
28. *Daily Petersburg Index*, November 17, 1871. Radicals remained in office in Petersburg until 1874.
29. Jones, "Conservative Virginian," pp. 45–46, 53–54.
30. See, e.g., Richmond *Enquirer*, January 21, 1868, quoted in *ibid.*, p. 110n; Robert M. T. Hunter, manuscript Conservative plea to Congress, 1868; L. Q. Washington to Hunter, November 17, 1866; and Washington to Hunter, December 7, 1867, all in Hunter-Garnett Papers.
31. Eckenrode, *Political History*, p. 54; Richmond *Daily Whig*, February 15, 1868.
32. Richmond *Whig and Public Advertiser*, January 11, 1867.

Although most conservatives continued to look for a reaction in Northern public opinion, only the uncompromising traditionalists boycotted politics through the Reconstruction years. The stakes of Reconstruction politics were too high for most conservatives to abandon the field to the Radicals. A Radical state government, subject to Negro and plebeian influence, would shake the social structure. A Republican constitutional convention might, by disfranchising former Confederates, perpetuate its party's control. Republicans' reputation for high taxes, corruption, and partisan exploitation of economic resources brought some conservatives to calculate the cost of abstention in dollars and cents.[33] Many who advocated inaction at the beginning of military Reconstruction, including Smith and Stuart, soon changed their minds.

Wartime Unionists and former nationalist Whigs formulated a *second* conservative policy: to work for moderation within the Republican party. In their "Petersburg Platform" of April, 1867, these men accepted Congress' terms for readmission, advocated civil and political equality of the races, and pledged themselves to co-operate with all organizations supporting that program—that is, with the Radicals. The "co-operation" men adhered to Botts's moderate wing of the Republican party.[34] An argument by Joseph Segar articulated the Whig and Unionist lineage of "co-operation." Almost overlooking the race question, Segar thought that Negro suffrage would only increase Virginia's representation in Congress. Condemning the record of the Democratic party and the State-Rights school, he called for "a new political organization." Envisioning an industrial future, he would support the Republican party because it stood for the old Whig policies of protective tariffs and internal improvements.[35]

The Richmond *Whig* at first hoped to unite former Confederates, wartime Unionists, and moderate Negroes in a conservative coalition, but as the Unionists and Negroes ranged themselves in the Republican camp the *Whig* took up the cause of "co-operation."[36] The paper presented a simple case for supporting the Republican party: only the Republicans, with their majority in Congress, had the power to readmit Virginia to the privileges of statehood, and

33. See Andrew G. Grinnan to James L. Kemper, June 24, 1867, Kemper Papers, University of Virginia, and Eckenrode, "Virginia since 1865," p. 49.

34. Richmond *Whig and Public Advertiser*, April 23, 1867; Eckenrode, *Political History*, pp. 70–72.

35. Richmond *Whig and Public Advertiser*, April 23, 1867.

36. *Ibid.*, April 5 and July 5, 1867.

they had implicitly promised to do so under specified conditions. The Democrats, even if willing to readmit Virginia at once, lacked the power.[37] Principled traditionalists saw rank opportunism in that argument, but many conservatives were learning to appreciate it. "We have no rights," one of them asserted, "except they be given us by 'the powers that be,' and what is required of us is *loyalty to these existing, controlling powers.*"[38]

The "co-operation" movement failed to persuade a significant number of conservatives to associate themselves with the Republican party. Other conservatives greeted its proposals with abuse.[39] The handful of co-operationists could do very little to keep the Republican organization moderate. Hunnicutt's decisive victory at the April, 1867, Republican Convention might have killed "co-operation" at once if Northern Republicans had not stepped in to temper their Virginia allies' militance. Senator Henry Wilson of Massachusetts conferred with leaders of all the factions in an effort to create a moderate Republican party under Whig-Unionist leadership. After moderates issued a call for a new party convention, the Union Leagues of New York, Philadelphia, and Boston intervened and persuaded the Virginia factions to hold another convention at Richmond in August. Seizing on the new opportunity, conservative "co-operation" men held meetings in at least ten cities and counties to send delegates to the conclave. Again, however, the left controlled the convention, refusing admission to conservatives.[40] Thereafter, the "co-operation" movement fizzled out.

It left in the Republican party a residue of "respectable," conservative former Whigs who, unable to control their party, worked to restrain its activity. During the winter of 1867–68, several of them infiltrated the powerful Union Leagues of Richmond, and precipitated a faction fight that effectively "wrecked" the organization.[41] Most of the conservative Republicans later allied with the Conserv-

37. Richmond *Daily Whig*, April 22, 1867, quoted in Eckenrode, *Political History*, p. 71n.

38. "Plain Dealer" in Charlottesville *Chronicle*, September 19, 1867, clipping in William Henry Ruffner Papers, Historical Foundation of the Presbyterian and Reformed Churches.

39. See Richmond *Whig and Public Advertiser*, April 12, 16, 25, 1867; Andrew S. Fulton to Wyndham Robertson, June 20, 1867, Wyndham Robertson Papers, University of Chicago.

40. Taylor, *Negro in Reconstruction*, pp. 212–13, 218–21; Smith, "Virginia during Reconstruction," pp. 43–49; Eckenrode, *Political History*, pp. 72–76.

41. John W. Lewellen to Gilbert C. Walker, February 20, 1870, "Eastern State Lunatic Asylum" packet, Box 4, Gilbert Carlton Walker Executive Correspondence, Virginia State Library.

ative party in the "new movement" of 1869; others led the Republican party to a moderate course during the 1870's.

Most conservatives rejected both "inaction" and "co-operation" in 1867 for a *third* policy of organizing to control the election for the constitutional convention. They thought the prospects favorable. Zephaniah Turner, Jr., of Rappahannock County estimated that, excluding Confederates disfranchised under the Fourteenth Amendment, white voters would outnumber black ones by 45,000.[42] The pre-election registration of voters showed Turner's calculation fallacious; Negroes flocked to register, but traditionalist advocates of "inaction" stayed home. The registration yielded a white majority of about 14,000—but it revealed black majorities in districts electing fifty-nine members, and white majorities in districts electing only forty-six.[43] The *Whig* still saw a prospect of conservative victory. Was there any white Virginian, it asked, "who would not be ashamed to own that he cannot influence at least one colored man to vote as interest and duty require that he shall vote?"[44]

Conservatives, then, began to present their case to black voters. Their Richmond leaders had taken the first step in April, when sympathetic Negroes had arranged a meeting for prominent white men, mostly former Whigs, to advise freedmen on the responsibilities of citizenship. The lawyer Raleigh T. Daniel warned the audience that bloc voting and secret societies violated the only *true* freedom—the freedom of the mind—and the banker William H. Macfarland preached the principles of economic self-help.[45] In the election for the constitutional convention, conservatives repeated those paternalistic counsels. Norfolk conservatives addressed to freedmen the slogan, "Don't quarrel with your bread and butter."[46] The Richmond *Enquirer*, to make the economic argument more persuasive, advised employers to discharge Negroes who voted the Radical ticket.[47]

As the election approached, conservatives found traditionalist apathy a more formidable obstacle than Negro bloc voting. Many white men had not registered, and many registrants ignored the

42. Richmond *Whig and Public Advertiser*, June 7, 1867.
43. *Ibid.*, October 8, 1867; Smith, "Virginia during Reconstruction," pp. 52–53.
44. Quoted in Smith, "Virginia during Reconstruction," pp. 51–52.
45. Richmond *Whig and Public Advertiser*, April 16, 1867.
46. Audrey Marie Cahill, "Gilbert Carleton [sic] Walker, Virginia's Redeemer Governor" (M.A. thesis, University of Virginia 1956), pp. 23–27 (hereafter cited as "Walker").
47. Taylor, *Negro in Reconstruction*, pp. 222–23.

election. In predominantly black Petersburg, a newspaper correspondent found, the pre-Reconstruction voters completely relinquished the field to the Radicals.[48]

The election of October 18–21 disappointed conservatives deeply.
While 93,145 Negroes (seven-eighths of those registered) voted, only
76,084 white men (five-eighths of the registrants) did. Of the whites,
14,835 voted to call the convention, and only 638 Negroes voted not
to. Seventy-three Republicans and thirty-two conservatives won
seats in the convention.[49] Most conservatives excused the Negroes as
misguided, but they bitterly excoriated the traditionalists who had
boycotted the polls.[50] The *Whig* warned Northern Republicans that
it was not their party that had won the election. The moderates had
tried to organize a Republican party in Virginia, but the Negroes
and demagogues had overpowered them. "After that there was nothing but a wild, furious, agrarian Radicalism." The *Whig* asked the
respectable Republicans of the North to repudiate the Virginia
Radicals.[51]

The election showed the need for what some had long suggested—
an organized, statewide conservative party.[52] Early in November,
the available members of the old parties' state committees of 1860,
meeting in Richmond as the "Executive Committee of the Conservative Party," called a state convention to assemble at the capital city
on December 11.[53]

Almost all the prewar political leaders attended the Conservative
party's founding convention. Stuart, unanimously chosen its president, announced that the Conservatives, forgetting all former differences, had united to appeal to Northerners to spare them the
disgrace of Negro rule.[54] Former Senator Hunter expressed paternalistic benevolence toward Negroes but insisted they should not

48. Smith, "Virginia during Reconstruction," p. 53.
49. *Ibid.*, pp. 57–59; Eckenrode, *Political History*, p. 84.
50. See Bell, *Smith*, p. 264.
51. Richmond *Whig and Public Advertiser*, October 29, 1867.
52. Jones, "Conservative Virginian," pp. 97–99, 103.
53. *Ibid.*, p. 106; Richmond *Whig and Public Advertiser*, November 8, 1867. Henry
K. Ellyson, publisher of the Richmond *Dispatch*, served as the committee's chairman,
and James R. Branch, of the banking house of Thomas Branch and Sons, as its secretary. Ellyson and Branch were former Whigs, although Branch had become a Douglas
Democrat by 1860. Since all thirty-five members of the Bell state committee had lived
in Richmond, but only one member each of the Breckinridge and Douglas committees
had, the Whigs must have predominated in the "Executive Committee." On the other
hand, since Branch had not been a party committeeman in 1860, the group must have
co-opted additional members.
54. Eckenrode, *Political History*, pp. 85–86.

govern. He hoped, resignedly, that the current transformation would "prove a new seed of progress" for Virginia as the French Revolution had for France. He rejoiced in the younger generation's activism and in the mining and manufacturing projects.[55] The convention approved resolutions that slavery was extinct and the Union indissoluble; that Virginians must receive their constitutional privileges; that the party regarded Negroes favorably but thought only whites should govern; and that it hoped harmony would return throughout the nation.[56] L. Q. Washington saw in the gathering a spirit recalling the united Republic of Virginia Dynasty days.[57]

The convention adopted a complex organizational plan, allegedly of Baldwin's authorship. Combining Whig and Democratic practices, it provided for a Central Committee of nine Richmonders and an Executive Committee consisting of these nine plus three "consulting members" from each congressional district. In each county, selected local leaders were to call a meeting that would elect a county committee. That body would choose a county superintendent, who would divide the registered Conservative voters into units of fifty and ten, with a chief to organize each unit. The plan, designed to maintain strict discipline, did not actually go into effect at the local level.[58]

Stuart appointed the Whig patriarch William Cabell Rives chairman of a post-convention committee to draft an address to Congress. He implored Rives to write the document himself, but Rives, shortly before his death, declined on personal and tactical grounds. Stuart then delegated the task to another former Whig, William H. Macfarland, but Macfarland devolved it to Hunter. Stuart never published Hunter's address; according to rumor, he suppressed it out of jealousy of the old State-Rights faction.[59] Whiggery and De-

55. Richmond *Daily Whig*, December 13, 1867.

56. Smith, "Virginia during Reconstruction," p. 120.

57. Washington *National Intelligencer*, clipping enclosed in L. Q. Washington to Robert M. T. Hunter, December 29, 1867, Hunter-Garnett Papers.

58. *Ibid.*; Eckenrode, *Political History*, p. 86; Richmond *Whig and Public Advertiser*, December 17, 1867; Conservative Executive Committee Circular No. 1, December 23, 1867, copy in James Lawson Kemper Executive Correspondence and Letter-Books, Virginia State Library.

59. B. H. Magruder to William Cabell Rives, December 15, 1867; Alexander H. H. Stuart to Rives, January 4, 1868; Rives to Stuart (copy), January 7, 1868; Stuart to Rives, January 28, 1868, all in William Cabell Rives Papers; Rives to J. Randolph Tucker, January 8, 1868, and Raleigh T. Daniel to Tucker, January 20, 1868, both in Tucker Family Papers, Southern Historical Collection, University of North Carolina at Chapel Hill; William H. Macfarland to Robert M. T. Hunter, February 13, 1868,

mocracy had not lost their identities, but they had formed a common organization against Radicalism.

THE UNDERWOOD CONVENTION AND CONSTITUTION

A few days before the Conservative Convention, the Constitutional Convention had assembled in Richmond and elected Judge Underwood its president. Of the seventy-three Radical members, twenty-four were Negroes, and thirty-three were white men of Northern or foreign birth.[60] Whatever else Conservatives might dislike in the Republican party, they saw it principally as an instrument of Negro rule and alien rule.

The thirty-two Conservative members were mostly young Confederate veterans without experience in public office; Old Virginia's solons were absent. The Conservatives represented the northern and western counties with considerable white majorities, excluding the environs of Washington and parts of the Southwest. The planter class, largely traditionalist, was unrepresented, because the predominantly black plantation counties had elected Radicals. The homogeneous Conservative delegation always voted as a bloc.[61]

The "Conservatives" were not unreconstructed traditionalists; they nominated the Reverend Norval Wilson, a prewar critic of slavery, for president of the convention.[62] They were not genteel "Virginia gentlemen"; Eustace Gibson offered to fist-fight a Union officer.[63] They were not State-Rights Democrats; rejecting the term "Democrat" for his party, James C. Southall insisted that most members of his caucus had been Union Whigs before secession. He added that the majority was, properly, not the "Republican" but the "Negro" party.[64] The Conservative members did have rigid attitudes on matters of principle and prestige and barred no holds in parliamentary combat. They confused black members with points of procedure, employed ludicrous tactics to protest the convention's inviting General Benjamin F. Butler "the Beast" to address it, and tried to impeach President Underwood.[65] "The opinion is often

---

and L. Q. Washington to Hunter, September 25, 1868, and manuscript Conservative plea to Congress, 1868, all in Hunter-Garnett Papers.

60. Smith, "Virginia during Reconstruction," pp. 58–59.
61. *Ibid.*, pp. 63–64; Eckenrode, *Political History*, pp. 87–88.
62. Smith, "Virginia during Reconstruction," pp. 65–66.
63. *Ibid.*, p. 84.
64. *Ibid.*, p. 87.
65. *Ibid.*, pp. 77–78. A document prepared for General Schofield described nineteen

expressed here," one of them recorded, "that there is too much speaking on their side of the house. The impulsiveness and impudence of some of these gentlemen, it is thought, injure the cause they seek to maintain."[66]

The Radical members of the convention performed the positive work of drafting the constitution, while the Conservatives amended, obstructed, and criticized.[67] By that tactic, the Conservatives took advantage of racial tension within the Radical bloc. Black members annoyed white Radicals by their long, flamboyant speeches and their advanced demands for equal rights. "I have a suspicion," Conservative member Joseph A. Waddell remarked, "that some of the white Radicals are getting sick of their black allies."[68] Negroes wanted to enumerate the rights to vote and serve on juries among the natural rights the constitution listed, but white Republicans feared that enumeration would imperil their measures to disfranchise former Confederates.[69] White Republicans opposed the Negroes' demand for racial integration in the proposed public schools. The Negro leaders Lewis Lindsay and Willis A. Hodges threatened to split the party over the issue.[70] The Conservative press encouraged, and exploited, the cleavages in the Radicals' ranks.[71]

In stating their own position, the Conservative members shifted their ground significantly. The Conservative members of the Committee on Suffrage, in their minority report, persisted in pronouncing the Reconstruction Acts, and the convention itself, unconstitutional. They opposed enfranchisement of Negroes, disfranchisement of Confederates, Negro eligibility for juries and offices, the ballot system, and the requirement that officeholders take an oath accepting racial equality. They proposed to confine the suffrage to taxpayers.[72] In debates on the floor, however, the Conservatives singled

---

Convention members as "unreconstructed" and only thirteen as "conservative," Manuscript on members of Virginia Constitutional Convention, 1868, John McAllister Schofield Papers, Library of Congress.

66. Joseph A. Waddell, *Annals of Augusta County, Virginia, with Reminiscences Illustrative of Its Pioneer Settlers; Biographical Sketches of Citizens Locally Prominent, and of Those Who Have Founded Families in the Southern and Western States; a Diary of the War, 1861–'5, and a Chapter on Reconstruction* (Richmond: William Ellis Jones, 1886), p. 350 (hereafter cited as *Augusta County*).

67. Eckenrode, *Political History*, p. 88.

68. Waddell, *Augusta County*, p. 352.

69. Eckenrode, "Virginia since 1865," pp. 44–45.

70. Eckenrode, *Political History*, p. 94; Richmond *Whig and Public Advertiser*, April 9, 1868.

71. See, e.g., Richmond *Whig and Public Advertiser*, March 20, 1868.

72. Smith, "Virginia during Reconstruction," pp. 86–87.

out the test oath and disfranchisement clauses for their fiercest attacks.[73] These clauses limited eligibility for office and jury service to those who could take the "Iron Clad Oath" and disfranchised those who had held civil or military office under the Confederacy. Conservatives claimed that the former provision would exclude nineteen-twentieths of the white men and that the latter would disfranchise ten or fifteen thousand voters.[74]

On April 20, three days after the convention adjourned, the Conservative members addressed to the voters a plea for rejection of the proposed constitution. In this document they modified their original position significantly. They still poured scorn on the Convention's proceedings, but no longer questioned its constitutionality. They would now grudgingly accept Negro suffrage on the conditions that, to prevent Negro supremacy, the test oath and disfranchisement clauses should be deleted and additional, nonracial suffrage qualifications added. They objected to the emphasis on property taxes in the constitution's fiscal provisions. They predicted that the constitution's innovations would quadruple the tax burden and that the document would integrate the races in all public institutions and places. William L. Owen of Halifax, elected to the convention as a Republican, joined the Conservatives in their appeal for rejection of the "Negro Constitution."[75]

The test oath and disfranchisement clauses of the constitution would never go into effect. The remainder, with several amendments, would constitute Virginia's organic law during the Conservative party's ascendancy.[76] The constitution created a public free-school system and dedicated the revenue from the state's Literary Fund, capitation taxes, and optional local property taxes to school support. The convention reduced the residence qualification for governor from twenty years in the United States to ten, and from five years in Virginia to three. The governor received the veto power, and his pardoning power, previously shared with the legisla-

73. *Ibid.*, p. 88.

74. Robertson, *Stuart*, p. 437.

75. Smith, "Virginia during Reconstruction," pp. 107–11. Nine Republicans had voted against adopting the draft Constitution. *Ibid.*, p. 104.

76. Text in Francis Newton Thorpe, ed., *The Federal and State Constitutions, Colonial Charters, and Other Organic Laws of the States, Territories, and Colonies Now or Hereafter Forming the United States of America, Compiled and Edited under Act of Congress of June 30, 1906*, 7 volumes. *House Document No. 357, 59 Cong., 1 Sess.* (Washington: Government Printing Office, 1909), VII, 3871–900 (hereafter cited as *Constitutions*). See also exposition in Smith, "Virginia during Reconstruction," pp. 93–103.

ture, became exclusive. The constitution imported the New England township system to overthrow local oligarchies, empowered the legislature to elect judges, and gerrymandered several legislative districts to the Radicals' advantage.

Under the new constitution, the tax on landed property would provide most of the state revenue. A prohibition on state investment in internal-improvements stocks ended the antebellum public-works policy. The Commonwealth could not incur additional public debt, and a sinking fund would gradually retire the current debt. To attract capital, the constitution permitted a maximum interest rate of 12 per cent, twice the current statutory maximum. To relieve debtors, it guaranteed to each householder a two-thousand dollar homestead exemption from collection of debts. Until the end of 1868 acceptance of the Underwood constitution, with its many striking innovations, remained the principal issue that defined the difference between the Radical and Conservative parties.

THE CAMPAIGNS OF 1868

General Schofield, who had shown impatience with the Underwood convention, warned it before adjournment that the test oath would make it impossible in many counties to secure competent personnel for local offices. The convention ignored his address.[77] Schofield had already moved to temper the radicalism of Virginia Republicanism. At the end of Pierpont's term as governor, the commanding general passed over the "scalawag" aspirants, Hunnicutt and John Hawxhurst, to appoint his friend Henry H. Wells, a Union brigadier general from Michigan who had settled in Richmond to practice law. Schofield apparently saw in Wells a middle-of-the-road Republican who could unite the party, restrain its left, and attract a considerable number of white voters in the approaching election.[78] Wells used his incumbency and Northern and military contacts to win the allegiance of the black politicians who had until then supported Hunnicutt. In the Republican State Convention of May, 1868, Wells, with the Negro delegates' support, won the nomination to succeed himself. Hunnicutt, drawn swiftly into the whirlpool of disillusionment, threatened to oppose the ticket.[79]

The Conservative party also held its State Convention at Rich-

77. Smith, "Virginia during Reconstruction," pp. 92–93.
78. John McA. Schofield to Ulysses S. Grant (copy), April 6, 1868, John McAllister Schofield Papers; see Eckenrode, "Virginia since 1865," p. 51.
79. Richmond *Daily Whig*, May 7 and 8, 1868.

mond early in May. General Mahone and his business associates, more interested in railroad consolidation than in conservatism or white supremacy, accomplished little in their first foray into convention politics. A Conservative who cultivated both parties for business advantage, Mahone expected Wells to support his interests and thought that hostility to the "foreign" Baltimore and Ohio would enable "the consolidation party" to defeat any candidate, "no matter on what ticket he may run." John Goode of Norfolk suggested that Mahone's men work in the Conservative Convention to nominate "a consolidationist who can be inaugurated under the act of Congress."[80]

Most of the delegates cared little about railroad issues. Opposing the proposed constitution, they nominated candidates they hoped would never take office under it. Most preferred John B. Baldwin for governor. Opposing his own candidacy because he was technically disqualified under the Fourteenth Amendment, Baldwin nevertheless came within two votes of winning the nomination. The convention nominated Colonel Robert E. Withers of Lynchburg for governor, John L. Marye, Jr., of Fredericksburg for lieutenant governor, General James A. Walker of Pulaski County for attorney general, and Marmaduke Johnson of Richmond for congressman-at-large. It also appointed delegates to the "Conservative" (Democratic) National Convention.[81]

Withers, Marye, and Johnson had been Whigs and conditional Unionists before the War. Walker, the lone Democrat, derived from an Augusta County Whig family, had married a damsel who took her Whiggery seriously and had studied law with Baldwin. Withers, a physician unable because of war wounds to resume his practice, edited the Lynchburg *News*. Since he opposed Mahone's railroad project, the general secretly hoped Wells would defeat him. Marye, a lawyer, had served during the War both in the Confederate Army and in the House of Delegates and had been a Conservative member of the Underwood convention. General Walker had worked on an engineering party surveying the Covington and Ohio Railroad's route before settling as a lawyer in Pulaski County. A veteran of the Stonewall Brigade, he was slowly recouping his fortune by legal

80. Smith, "Virginia during Reconstruction," pp. 123–27; Blake, *Mahone,* pp. 99–100.

81. Richmond *Daily Whig,* May 9, 1868; Washington *National Intelligencer,* n.d., clipping in L. Q. Washington to Robert M. T. Hunter, May 14, 1868, Hunter-Garnett Papers.

services to corporations acquiring southwest Virginia land for mining and railroad routes. Walker was a director of the Virginia and Tennessee Railroad, which he was working to enlist in Mahone's consolidation plan.[82]

The candidates faced a spirited election campaign whose outcome might greatly influence the structure of postwar Virginia society. The Radicals claimed to speak for the "laboring classes," and the proposed constitution's homestead exemption might well attract white debtors to their ticket.[83] The Conservatives by no means underestimated their opponents' radicalism. L. Q. Washington informed the *National Intelligencer*'s well-to-do Northern readers that the Conservatives represented "the intelligence, character, genius, and property of the State" and that the Radical movement was a "Plot against Property." The freedmen, Washington wrote, had been re-enslaved to carpetbaggers "who, having failed in the keen competition at the North to make a living by honest industry, or too lazy to work, have come down . . . here to . . . [drive] a sharp trade in 'humanity and justice.'" Under a Radical government, hard-working white men and their property would be "at the mercy of these men who do not own one dollar in a hundred of the property of the State."[84] Propertied Northern Republicans would think twice before endorsing the movement Washington described.

Needing the votes of lower-class white men, Conservative leaders decided to oppose the issue of race to the Radicals' issue of class. In the first campaign strategy conference, Colonel Withers rejected proposals to appeal to black voters. Sure that Negroes were incurably Radical, he thought that a racial appeal would win the poor whites and Unionists of western Virginia to the Conservative cause. On the stump, Withers declared that he wanted no Negro's vote.[85] He asked white voters—whether Whigs or Democrats, Unionists or

82. Smith, "Virginia during Reconstruction," p. 129; Withers, *Autobiography*, pp. 57–58, 111, 113–17, 126–27, 236–39, 242–44; George W. Rogers, *Officers of the Senate of Virginia, 1776–1956* (Richmond: Garrett and Massie, 1959), pp. 54, 57; Willie Walker Caldwell, "Life of General James A. Walker" (typescript in James Alexander Walker Papers, Southern Historical Collection, University of North Carolina at Chapel Hill), pp. 21–22, 24, 201–3, 224–25, 231–32 (hereafter cited as "Walker"); Sallie Poage to James A. Walker, April 6, 1857, James Alexander Walker Papers; Blake, *Mahone*, pp. 85n [misprint "H." for "A."], 119.

83. See Robert Hudgin to Robert M. T. Hunter, April 27, 1868, Hunter-Garnett Papers.

84. Washington *National Intelligencer*, n.d., clipping in L. Q. Washington to Hunter, May 14, 1868, *ibid.*

85. Withers, *Autobiography*, pp. 248–49.

Secessionists—to "show by their votes that they are white men . . . in driving back the horde of blacks and their Carpet Bag allies."[86]

The color line became the keynote of the Conservative campaign. Party leaders knew that the statewide white majority of voters was increasing, as white men who had previously avoided Reconstruction politics now registered to vote.[87] The State Committee reminded its speakers, selected for their "known opposition to negro suffrage," that Radical victory would "forever degrade the white men of Virginia, and reduce the government to the domination of the negro."[88] In some districts, nevertheless, Conservatives dissenting from the racist strategy did solicit Negroes' votes.[89]

Expecting the election to occur in the middle of August, the Conservatives waged a vigorous three-month campaign. However, General Schofield, convinced that the constitution would render good government impossible, refused to finance the election with the state funds at his disposal. Congress hesitated to appropriate funds for the purpose, since many Republican congressmen found the constitution an embarrassment and since the proposed bill would endanger the Radicals by reopening registration of voters. General Schofield, therefore, postponed the balloting indefinitely. Conservatives attributed the postponement to their campaign, believing that Schofield expected rejection of the constitution and subsequent reprisals by Congress.[90]

To turn the party stalemate into a victory, the Conservatives would need sympathy from Congress. They relied, therefore, on the hope that the elections of 1868 would manifest the expected "reaction" in the Northern states.

The Conservative party's delegates to the Democratic National Convention in New York expressed uncertainty about their relationship to the national party. Some trusted the Northern Democrats; others wanted to organize the Southern delegates into a bloc to maximize the region's bargaining power; still others would en-

---

86. *Ibid.,* p. 260.

87. See Raleigh T. Daniel ("Chief Director," Conservative State Committee), form letter, March 8, 1868, copy in Kemper Executive Correspondence and Letter-Books, Virginia State Library.

88. R. T. Lance (Clerk, Conservative State Committee) form letter, February 22, 1868, copy in *ibid.*

89. Taylor, *Negro in Reconstruction,* p. 246.

90. John McA. Schofield to Ulysses S. Grant (copy), April 18, 1868, and Schofield, printed order, April 24, 1868, both in Schofield Papers; Schofield, *Forty-Six Years,* pp. 400–403; Smith, "Virginia during Reconstruction," pp. 128–30; Withers, *Autobiography,* pp. 262–63.

dorse the national ticket only if the convention would adopt the Southern position on Reconstruction; and some did not want to attend the convention at all.[91] At the convention, the Virginians voted, in succession, for a number of presidential candidates, before they—and all the other delegations—rallied on the twenty-second ballot to Horatio Seymour of New York.[92] By mid-summer, all Conservative factions had united to support Seymour. The *Whig*, hoping for an alliance with conservative Republican businessmen, held out until after both national conventions before endorsing the Democrats.[93]

The most fervent devotees of the "Lost Cause" wondered why they should support *any* Northern party. Edward A. Pollard, whose writings in defense of the Confederacy had given him good traditionalist credentials, reinterpreted Confederate history to answer the question. In the book *The Lost Cause Regained,* Pollard identified the cause with white supremacy and constitutional limitations, instead of slavery and Southern independence. Southerners could yet win the more modest objectives, he wrote, by supporting the Democratic party. Pollard explicitly recanted the scorn that, as a Southern Rights spokesman, he had once heaped on the Northern Democrats. He now discovered that they had, during the War, defined the proper ground for conservatives of both regions in the Reconstruction political conflict.[94]

Union General William S. Rosecrans, a manager of the national Democratic campaign, inspired another Virginia contribution to the contest. Rosecrans asked General Lee to write an open letter attesting white Southerners' loyalty and their respect for Negroes' rights. Lee had Stuart draft the "White Sulphur Letter," but he and many other prominent former Confederates signed it. Rosecrans circulated the letter as a campaign document in the North.[95]

91. Jones, "Conservative Virginian," p. 117; James Barbour to James L. Kemper, June 24, 1868; Charles S. Botts to Kemper, June 24, 1868; Thomas S. Bocock to Kemper, June 25, 1868, all in Kemper Papers, University of Virginia; William D. Coleman to William T. Sutherlin, May 12, 1868, William Thomas Sutherlin Papers, Southern Historical Collection, University of North Carolina at Chapel Hill.

92. *Official Proceedings of the National Democratic Convention Held at New York, July 4–9, 1868* (Boston: Rockwell and Rollins, 1868), pp. 77–161. Several Richmonders appeared to lobby for Chief Justice Salmon P. Chase, apparently without influencing the state delegation. L. Q. Washington to Robert M. T. Hunter, August 2, 1868, Hunter-Garnett Papers.

93. Richmond *Daily Whig*, March 2, May 21, June 13, 16, 19, July 14, 1868.

94. Pollard, *Lost Cause Regained*, pp. 13–14, 103–5, 185–88, 207.

95. Freeman, *Lee*, IV, 374–78; Robertson, *Stuart*, pp. 260–64; William S. Rose-

A few Conservatives contemplated more direct political action. L. Q. Washington and J. Randolph Tucker, consulting with former postmaster general Montgomery Blair of Maryland, devised a plan to hold an extralegal presidential election in Virginia, in hope that a national Democratic victory would bring the Senate to recognize Virginia returns. They dropped the plan after early state elections showed a Republican trend.[96] Washington blamed the bad news on widely publicized traditionalist statements by South Carolina's Wade Hampton and other Southerners.[97]

The November election returns did not bear out the prophecy of a Northern reaction against Radicalism. Although General Grant, the Republican candidate, won only a slight majority of the popular vote, he received 214 electoral votes against Seymour's 80. The Democrats carried only three Northern states, and the Republicans won overwhelming majorities in both houses of Congress. All was not lost for the Conservatives. Baldwin, Washington, and Moseley of the *Whig* had for years considered Grant a potential ally; Washington and Moseley had retained that opinion even while supporting Seymour.[98] On the other hand, Conservatives could not count on a federal government friendly to their current political position. Some drew the conclusion that, to win control of their Commonwealth and readmission to representation in Congress, they must abandon positions that their party had resolved never to surrender.

For a few, the abandonment meant joining the Republican party. Colonel Samuel Chapman Armstrong of the Freedmen's Bureau commented scornfully on the swarms of newly converted Republicans who appeared immediately after the election.[99] Larger numbers of Conservatives reconsidered their opposition to Negro suffrage. The principal businessmen and lawyers of Richmond, L. Q. Washington found, would now accept either universal suffrage, or impartial suffrage with nonracial qualifications. Conserv-

crans to Alexander H. H. Stuart, September 6, 1868, Alexander Hugh Holmes Stuart Papers, University of Virginia.

96. L. Q. Washington to J. Randolph Tucker, July 31, 1868, and Washington to Tucker, September 25, 1868, Tucker Family Papers.

97. Washington to Tucker, September 25, 1868, *ibid.*; Washington to Robert M. T. Hunter, September 25, 1868, Hunter-Garnett Papers.

98. Washington to Hunter, September 23, 1866; Washington to Hunter, September 25, 1868; Washington to Hunter, November 4, 1868, all in Hunter-Garnett Papers; Richmond *Whig and Public Advertiser*, May 8, 1866; Richmond *Daily Whig*, May 25, July 30, October 21, 1868.

99. Edith A. Talbot, *Samuel Chapman Armstrong: A Biographical Study* (New York: Doubleday, Page and Company, 1904), p. 144n (hereafter cited as *Armstrong*).

ative advocates of universal suffrage included Conservative Central Committee member Robert Ould; James L. Carrington, proprietor of the Exchange Hotel; and Confederate Secretary of War James A. Seddon, who was about to join a Richmond business firm. Washington and some others were coming to think that Virginia could attain home rule only under some version of the Underwood constitution.[100]

The Republican party maintained a surface harmony in support of the proposed constitution without amendments, but at the end of 1868 the Wells administration committed two indiscreet acts that revived factionalism. Word circulated that the governor was planning to sell the state's stock in the Virginia and Tennessee Railroad to Northern interests. The news outraged many Virginians and revealed to General Mahone that Wells was in fact his enemy. About the same time, the Richmond *State Journal,* the governor's organ, published a letter from the anti-Wells Republican W. H. Samuel to the Radical leader Edgar "Yankee" Allan of Farmville. Allan accused Wells and other Republican officials of abstracting the missive from the mails. These events created hard feelings within the party and did its election prospects no good.[101]

Thus matters stood in December, 1868. The Conservative party officially opposed Negro suffrage and insisted on rejection of the Underwood constitution, and the Republican party officially endorsed the entire constitution and the Wells administration. Each party contained a compact group of moderates, largely businessmen and promoters of Whig antecedents. The moderate groups were groping toward a common program: to ratify a modified version of the proposed constitution that would enfranchise Negroes without disqualifying former Confederates and to elect an administration directed by their own kind. This "center" grouping, divided between the two parties, was less numerous than either the Radical Republicans or the traditionalist Conservatives—but it might be better able than either of those groups to organize a government acceptable to the federal government and to the most powerful and dynamic social interests in Virginia. Through the convergence of many events, the most opportune moment had arrived for the moderates to unite and make their bid for power.

100. L. Q. Washington to Robert M. T. Hunter, December 2, 1868, Hunter-Garnett Papers.
101. Eckenrode, *Political History,* pp. 108, 117–18.

6.

1869: The Conservatives
Come to Power

The year 1869 inaugurated an era in the history of Virginia. In the first place, the Old Dominion during that year completed all but the final formalities of restoration to the Union under the terms of the Reconstruction Acts. Secondly—contrary to the experience of the other reconstructed states—the Conservatives wrested control of the government through the reconstruction process itself. Thirdly, in doing so, the Conservative party underwent a marked reorientation of policy, burning many of its traditionalist bridges to the antebellum past. These events left their stamp on the regime of the succeeding ten years.

THE COMMITTEE OF NINE

The origins of the "new movement" of 1869 were complex.[1] Since the "co-operation" movement of 1867, small groups in both the Conservative and the Republican parties had wanted a moderate, conservative government resting on an electorate that would include both Negroes and prominent Confederates.[2] By the end of 1868, these groups seemed ready to assert themselves. General Ma-

1. The most complete account by a participant is Alexander H. H. Stuart's "A Narrative of the Leading Incidents of the Organization of the First Popular Movement in Virginia in 1865 to Re-establish Peaceful Relations between the Northern and Southern States, and of the Subsequent Efforts of the 'Committee of Nine,' in 1869, to Secure the Restoration of Virginia to the Union," which makes up pp. 406–61 of Robertson, *Stuart*. Stuart, as many Conservatives resentfully pointed out, exaggerated his role. See John C. Shields to William Mahone, February 2, 1874, William Mahone Papers, Duke University, and clippings from Richmond newspapers, October 1880, in Frank Gildart Ruffin Scrapbook, Virginia State Library, I, 50–52.
2. See G. K. Gilmer in Richmond *Dispatch*, October 5, 1880, and Franklin Stearns in Richmond *Whig*, October 6, 1880, both clippings in Frank Gildart Ruffin Scrapbook, I, 51–52.

hone, and his business associates Gilbert C. Walker and George W. Bolling, were then laying plans to ask the federal government to delete the political disqualifications from the Underwood constitution.[3]

It was Alexander H. H. Stuart who, on December 19, 1868, first mustered the courage to draft a public statement for a settlement on the basis of "universal suffrage and universal amnesty," enfranchising Negroes without disfranchising former Confederates. In an open letter over the signature "Senex," Stuart called on the Conservative Executive Committee to draft an organic law on the basis of the constitution of 1850 and the rejected undemocratic amendments of 1861, deleting racial qualifications, and to submit it to Congress for approval.[4] Parsimonious though Stuart was with his concessions, his friend General John Echols could not at first persuade Richmond's Conservative newspapers to publish the "Senex" letter. Fortunately, while in Richmond, Echols encountered Colonel William T. Sutherlin, a prominent Danville tobacco merchant and manufacturer, who was attempting to organize a similar movement. Sutherlin persuaded his fellow Whigs, editors Alexander Moseley of the *Whig* and Henry K. Ellyson of the *Dispatch*, to print the letter on December 25. The *Enquirer* still refused. Meanwhile, Echols returned to Staunton to enlist Stuart in Sutherlin's plans.[5]

A torrent of traditionalist abuse greeted the "Senex" letter. The proposal did, however, inspire some seconding voices. The *Whig* suggested that Judge Alexander Rives, a moderate Republican, and his colleagues on the Court of Appeals draft a constitution acceptable to Congress, and veteran Democrat Robert H. Glass of Lynchburg even proposed that the Conservatives withdraw their state ticket, accepting Wells as governor for another term.[6] Most members of the Conservative Central Committee were unprepared for a major change of policy.[7] Their attitude precluded Stuart's original strategy, but Sutherlin's and Stuart's forces were already organizing

3. Cahill, "Walker," pp. 40–41.
4. Text in Robertson, *Stuart*, pp. 420–23.
5. *Ibid.*, pp. 423–25; Frank G. Ruffin in Richmond *Dispatch*, October 3, 1880, clipping in Ruffin Scrapbook, I, 50. These accounts are irreconcilable in chronology; I have followed Stuart's in that respect.
6. Richmond *Daily Whig*, December 25, 1868; "R.H.G." in *ibid.*, December 31, 1868; see Richmond *Enquirer-Examiner*, January 30, 1869.
7. Richmond *Enquirer-Examiner*, December 31, 1868; Robertson, *Stuart*, p. 418; Richmond *Enquirer-Examiner*, January 8 and 21, 1869.

independently of the party organs. A meeting in Staunton on December 25 invited many prominent Virginians to assemble at the Exchange Hotel in Richmond six days later. The twenty-eight who gathered on December 31 appointed a Committee of Nine to negotiate with federal officials for readmission with universal suffrage and universal amnesty.[8] The committee, like the meeting that organized it, operated almost as a clandestine clique. Henry A. Wise referred to it as "Nine gentlemen, who had no . . . call from any body of the people, except themselves."[9] Stuart, as a member of the committee later observed, instinctively preferred devious, conspiratorial tactics.[10] He controlled the movement tightly, perhaps intending, as L. Q. Washington surmised, to conclude a pact between former Whigs and Republicans to the exclusion of former State-Rights men.[11]

The members of the Committee of Nine mostly lived in western Virginia and included a disproportionate number of city-dwellers. Stuart, the chairman, recruited his brother-in-law John B. Baldwin as a member. These two men, champions of commerce and industry, led the former Whig clique that dominated Augusta County's politics.[12] John L. Marye, Jr., the Conservative candidate for lieutenant governor, was another of the nine. Former Governor Wyndham Robertson, a dabbler in business enterprises and promoter of the James River and Kanawha Canal, had been a conditional Unionist during the secession crisis. During the War, as a legislator from Richmond, he had opposed imposing price controls on food. The leaders of the nine were assisting Robertson in his financial difficulties. Robertson had moved from Richmond to Washington County since the War.[13] James Neeson, the committee's only former Democrat, had taken the opposite direction, leaving southwest Virginia

8. Robertson, *Stuart*, pp. 425–29; Smith, "Virginia during Reconstruction," p. 134.
9. Bear, ed., "Wise and 1873 Campaign," p. 329.
10. Wyndham Robertson to Lewis E. Harvie, December [n.d.] 1876, Lewis Evarts Harvie Papers, Virginia State Library.
11. L. Q. Washington to Robert M. T. Hunter, January 9, 1868 [1869], Hunter-Garnett Papers, University of Virginia; see also Washington to Hunter, September 25, 1868, *ibid.*
12. Robertson, *Stuart*, pp. 428–30; Lyon G. Tyler, ed., *Encyclopedia of Virginia Biography* (New York: Lewis Historical Publishing Company, 1915), III, 38 (hereafter cited as *Virginia Biography*); J. B. Dorman to William Mahone, February 5, 1870, Mahone Papers.
13. Tyler, ed., *Virginia Biography*, II, 52; entry on Robertson in Samuel Bassett French Papers, Virginia State Library; John B. Baldwin to Wyndham Robertson, March 14, 1869, Wyndham Robertson Papers, University of Chicago.

for Richmond. Henry A. Wise claimed that Neeson had become a convert to conciliation to protect his Richmond real-estate holdings from confiscation.[14] Colonel Sutherlin, another member, operated one of Virginia's largest tobacco factories and engaged in banking and railroad enterprises as well as in promoting scientific agriculture.[15] James F. Slaughter of Lynchburg was one of Mahone's railroad allies and would later be a bank executive.[16] William L. Owen, a wealthy merchant of Halifax County, had served in the Underwood convention as a Republican, but had signed the Conservative members' address to the voters.[17] James F. Johnston of Bedford County completed the committee's membership. Frank G. Ruffin, whose agricultural concerns would have helped to balance the membership, declined to serve in the committee. Northern officials, he feared, would suspect a committee that included a kinsman of the "fire-eater" Edmund Ruffin.[18]

The Committee of Nine began work in Washington on January 9. Stuart secured the endorsement of Horace Greeley, who was turning to a more moderate Reconstruction policy to further Northern business investment in the South. Marye enlisted Mahone's associates Gilbert C. Walker and George W. Bolling to assist the nine through their Washington "connections." L. Q. Washington, who controlled the *National Intelligencer*'s Southern policy and wrote for even Republican papers, also helped the committee, although some members distrusted him as a former State-Rights Democrat.[19] Assistance appeared also from the conservative Republicans. While the nine were in Washington, two rival delegations of Virginia Republicans appeared to testify before congressional committees. Governor Wells's adherents insisted on the unexpurgated Underwood constitution, but Franklin Stearns's moderate faction felt that most property-owning Virginians were "reconstructed" and that only a

14. Bear, ed., "Wise and 1873 Campaign," p. 329.
15. Tyler, ed., *Virginia Biography*, III, 277; entry on Sutherlin in French Papers.
16. Blake, *Mahone*, p. 119; letterhead on Charles Statham to William Mahone, January 2, 1877, Mahone Papers.
17. Smith, "Virginia during Reconstruction," p. 111n; Wirt Johnson Carrington, *A History of Halifax County (Virginia)* (Richmond: Appeals Press, 1924), pp. 231–32.
18. Ruffin in Richmond *Dispatch*, October 3, 1880, clipping in Ruffin Scrapbook, I, 50.
19. Robertson, *Stuart*, pp. 431–33; L. Q. Washington to Robert M. T. Hunter, January 9, 1868 [1869]; Washington to Hunter, May 6, 1869, both in Hunter-Garnett Papers; see William B. Hesseltine, "Economic Factors in the Abandonment of Reconstruction," *Mississippi Valley Historical Review*, XXII (September, 1935), 196–200 (hereafter cited as "Economic Factors").

modified constitution could receive the voters' approval. Stearns's group co-operated with the nine.[20]

The committee submitted a memorandum asking the Senate Judiciary Committee to amend the Underwood constitution—not, as Stuart had originally intended, to substitute another document. Specifically, it asked the committee to delete the test oath and disfranchisement clauses; church property provisions injurious to Southern denominations; the township system, which would give Negro majorities control of many localities; and the homestead exemption. The nine asked that the maximum local school tax be one mill on the dollar instead of two mills on the dollar and unofficially requested deletion of the limitation on interest rates. The objectionable clauses, the committee argued, would cripple Virginia economically, making her a burden rather than an asset to the Union.[21] Stuart's committee had two interviews with President-elect Grant, who, without committing himself to its policy, agreed that the disfranchisement, test oath, and township clauses would have harmful effects.[22]

Some Northern Republican newspapers now expressed approval of the "new movement" in Virginia, and the *Whig* claimed that the committee had convinced Grant and many Radical congressmen.[23] The delegation's actual accomplishments were less impressive. Its adherents assured Virginians that it was "doing a great deal of good," but traditionalists derided it as a pleasure excursion. Several Virginians in Washington concluded that it had achieved little. Baldwin, months afterward, confessed himself uncertain about federal officials' intentions, although confident of Grant's beneficence. In fact, the Committee of Nine was only one of several Virginia groups pursuing the same task at the same time. The moderate Republicans probably changed more minds than did the nine, who did, nevertheless, win the confidence of a few very influential individuals, including apparently the president-elect.[24]

The committee also brought the proposal for "universal suffrage

20. Robertson, *Stuart*, pp. 433–35; Smith, "Virginia during Reconstruction," pp. 135–40.
21. Robertson, *Stuart*, pp. 435–41.
22. *Ibid.*, pp. 441–43.
23. Richmond *Daily Whig*, January 20 and 26, 1869.
24. Richmond *Enquirer-Examiner*, January 18, February 18, March 4, and April 7, 1869; Smith "Virginia during Reconstruction," pp. 141–42; Cahill, "Walker," p. 41; Frank Ruffin in Richmond *Dispatch*, October 3, 1880, clipping in Ruffin Scrapbook, I, 50; John B. Baldwin to Wyndham Robertson, March 14, 1869, Robertson Papers; Richard F. Walker to William Mahone, January 29, 1869, Mahone Papers.

and universal amnesty" forcefully to the attention of all Conservatives in Virginia. In the ensuing discussion, the traditionalist critics appeared at first to have the upper hand. Many considered the committee heretical in policy, as well as unauthorized and ineffective. Negro suffrage and Negro eligibility to office, the Richmond *Enquirer* contended, were in themselves as intolerable as the less important provisions the nine wanted to delete from the proposed constitution.[25] The Conservative newspapers divided about evenly in their attitudes to the "new movement." Only three of the nine members of the Conservative Central Committee supported the Committee of Nine; Chairman Raleigh T. Daniel publicly opposed it. The "new movement" proved most popular in the cities and the Southwest, areas of economic progress whose Conservatives were relatively free of racial fears.[26]

Although traditionalists effectively exposed the "new movements'" disloyalty to previous Conservative policies, they did not present a convincing alternative, short of an eventual reversal of federal policy. Henry A. Wise, considering a decade of federal interference in Virginia's government void, proposed extralegal elections to organize a government under the Constitution of 1850. He admitted, though, that his plan presupposed even more trust in Northern opinion and the federal courts than his opponents showed.[27] Most traditionalists were at a loss for alternatives. To the question "What shall we do?" former Congressman John Robertson replied; ". . . any thing; nothing, take the chances; something may turn up; God knows what or when. *N'importe*; let it come. Thank God nothing that I can imagine can be worse."[28] Such men hoped that the Conservative movement, unable to prevent Negro suffrage, at least would not stain its honor by "accepting" it.[29]

General Jubal Early likened the Committee of Nine to a whist player in the nine hole, relying on *tricks* when he could not win by

25. Richmond *Enquirer-Examiner*, January 18 and 20, 1869.

26. Richmond *Enquirer-Examiner*, January 21 and February 2, 1869; Richmond *Daily Whig*, February 3, 1869; L. Q. Washington to Robert M. T. Hunter, January 31, 1869, Hunter-Garnett Papers.

27. Richmond *Enquirer-Examiner*, January 18, 20, 21, 22, and 23, 1869. For excerpts from this series, see Barton Haxall Wise, *The Life of Henry A. Wise of Virginia, 1806–1876* (New York: Macmillan Company, 1899), pp. 393–95 (hereafter cited as *Wise*).

28. John Robertson to Wyndham Robertson, November 19, 1869, Robertson Papers.

29. T. B. Robertson to Wyndham Robertson, February 4, 1869, *ibid.*; Wise, *Wise*, p. 395; J. C. Walker, quoted in Smith, "Virginia during Reconstruction," p. 140.

honors.[30] Other Conservatives, less principled, sought to get out of the nine hole by any possible means. Restoration of home rule, they felt, could not wait on future changes in Northern policy. In February, Congress confirmed their sense of urgency by vacating all offices in Virginia whose incumbents could not take the "iron clad oath." The military authorities conducted painstaking investigations in filling the vacancies, giving much weight to Conservative leaders' recommendations. On March 21, General Stoneman reported that he had appointed 1,972 officials but that, for want of "qualified" persons able to take the oath, there remained 2,613 vacancies and 329 ineligible incumbents.[31] Conservatives had to count the cost of continued rule by Congress. "The hotheads," L. Q. Washington wrote, "if allowed their way, will ruin all. They have no counter plan save endurance and suffering for some indefinite period. But we need settlement imperatively. Under this state of things people are forced to sell their lands at a nominal price & thus the real estate of Virginia is passing to strangers. A year more of this business & where will our people be?"[32]

THE WALKER TICKET

Supporters of the "new movement" remained in doubt about tactics. General Schofield, now secretary of war, wanted to summon under the Alexandria constitution a legislature to amend that document in accordance with the Reconstruction Acts.[33] Most of the movement's adherents, however, were now willing to settle for an amended version of the Underwood constitution. Some "new movement" Conservatives were discussing with "liberal Republicans" the prospect of a coalition.[34] By February 18, L. Q. Washington saw that the Republican party was on the verge of splitting.[35]

30. Wise, *Wise*, p. 395.

31. Sefton, *U.S. Army*, pp. 195, 197; *American Annual Cyclopaedia and Register of Important Events, 1869* (New York: D. Appleton and Company, 1870), p. 710 (hereafter cited as *Annual Cyclopaedia*); F. H. Hill to James L. Kemper, March 15, 1869, James Lawson Kemper Papers, University of Virginia. Military sources agree only approximately in their figures.

32. L. Q. Washington to Robert M. T. Hunter, January 31, 1869, Hunter-Garnett Papers.

33. *Ibid.*

34. Robertson, *Stuart*, pp. 446–47; Cahill, "Walker," pp. 47–50.

35. L. Q. Washington to William T. Sutherlin, February 18, 1869, William Thomas Sutherlin Papers, Southern Historical Collection, University of North Carolina at Chapel Hill.

General Mahone stood to gain much from a Republican split. As a businessman, he wished to minimize turbulence in the readmission process. A conservative Republican governor might accomplish this better than Wells or Withers could. In the interest of his own enterprise, the General feared both Wells and Withers as hostile to his consolidation design.[36] Mahone had many allies among the conservative Republicans, who shared his industrial orientation. He, therefore, co-operated in their attempt to wrest leadership of their party from the governor.

On March 9, a Republican State Convention met at Mahone's home city of Petersburg. After almost riotous scenes of disorder, Wells's supporters secured his renomination and dropped from the ticket his moderate running mates of 1868.[37] Unable to prevent Wells' renomination, Mahone and the conservative Republicans undermined his prospects for election. The carpetbagger Edgar "Yankee" Allan, popular among Negroes in spite of his opposition to Wells, supported Dr. J. D. Harris, a Negro, for lieutenant governor against Wells's candidate, the Confederate surgeon Dr. W. W. C. Douglas. The Negroes and moderates combined to nominate Harris.[38] Running on a biracial ticket, Wells would receive few white men's votes.

After the convention adjourned, eight conservative Republicans met in Petersburg with General Mahone to nominate a "True Republican" ticket: Gilbert C. Walker for governor, John F. Lewis for lieutenant governor, and James C. Taylor for attorney general. Another group of conservative Republican convention delegates, meeting at Franklin Stearns's home in Richmond, was already organizing an independent movement and took up the Walker ticket.[39]

Gilbert C. Walker, thirty-seven years old, had practiced law in his native New York state and in Chicago. Politically, he had been

36. William F. Gordon, quoted in Jones, "Conservative Virginian," p. 121; Blake, *Mahone*, pp. 99–101.

37. Eckenrode, *Political History*, pp. 118–19; *Annual Cyclopaedia, 1869*, pp. 711–12. "General Mahone is here," the *Enquirer's* correspondent reported, "and is said to be using his influence for [James H.] Clements." "Does this mean that General Mahone has become a convert to Radicalism?" Mahone's enemy Withers ironically asked in his Lynchburg *News*; "We can scarcely credit the statement of the *Enquirer's* correspondent." Both quoted in Richmond *Enquirer-Examiner*, March 10, 1869.

38. Eckenrode, *Political History*, pp. 118–19.

39. *Ibid.*, pp. 119–20; *Annual Cyclopaedia, 1869*, p. 712; G. K. Gilmer in Richmond *Dispatch*, October 5, 1880, and Franklin Stearns in Richmond *Whig*, October 6, 1880, both clippings in Ruffin Scrapbook, I, 51–52.

a Douglas Democrat. In 1864, he had settled in Union-occupied Norfolk, where he became a prominent banker and iron manufacturer. Allying himself with Mahone, he had become a director of the General's Norfolk and Petersburg Railroad. After running as a Conservative for a seat in the Underwood convention, he had joined the Republicans, on the grounds that only the Republican Congress could set the terms for Virginia's readmission. According to one account Mahone had, at that early date, envisioned Walker as the leader of a new moderate political movement. As president of the Select Council of Norfolk, Walker had initiated a program to fund the city's debt and had tried to promote direct trade with Europe. He possessed the charm and handsome visage one might expect in a governor of Virginia. His appearance, one follower thought, would convince voters that "he was not a *Yanky*; he don't look like one."[40] Walker's running mates were natives of western Virginia. John F. Lewis had become one of the wealthiest farmers in Rockingham County by introducing advanced agricultural methods, especially by breeding livestock. A nationalist Whig, he had sat in the Secession Convention; he alone, among the delegates from Virginia's post-1865 territory, had refused to sign the ordinance or recognize the Confederate government. For general amnesty in 1865, he had later testified against the restored government before the Joint Committee on Reconstruction. James C. Taylor, also a former Whig and Republican, was a Confederate veteran and a lawyer in Montgomery County.[41]

The Walker ticket came as a surprise to almost all Conservatives outside Mahone's circle, including the members of the Committee of Nine.[42] For Conservatives who did not understand the difference between the Republican factions, the *Whig*, under Mahone's influence, explained:

The Wellsites came here . . . to prey upon the substance of the people.

40. Cahill, "Walker," pp. 2–6, 8–19, 23–31, 56–57; Frank Ruffin in Richmond *Dispatch*, October 3, 1880, clipping in Ruffin Scrapbook, I, 50; James W. Walker to William Mahone, April 11, 1869, Mahone Papers.

41. Entry on Lewis in Samuel Bassett French Papers; William C. Pendleton, *Political History of Appalachian Virginia, 1776–1927* (Dayton, Va.: Shenandoah Press, 1927), pp. 285–86 (hereafter cited as *Appalachian Virginia*); Wayland, *Rockingham County*, p. 371; Eckenrode, *Political History*, p. 46; Richmond *Daily Whig*, July 1, 1868. Although Taylor, like many other Whigs, had joined the Democratic party by 1860, contemporaries characterized him as a former Whig.

42. John B. Baldwin to Wyndham Robertson, March 14, 1869, Robertson Papers.

The Walkerites . . . seek their own interest by promoting the general welfare. They have something, and, by honest industry, hope to have more; they, therefore, favor wise legislation and honest administration. . . . The Wellsites are our enemies; the Walkerites are our *friends*.

As to principles, we know nothing of them—we thought they were all extinct. *Measures and men*—practical expedients for the evils of the day—are all that we are privileged to consider now.[43]

Although three tickets were in the field, federal authorities still had not provided for an election, and their intentions remained a subject of speculation. On March 27, General Stoneman removed Governor Wells from office, apparently as part of an agreement with Mahone's friends to appoint Franklin Stearns governor. President Grant promptly removed Stoneman from his command, and the interim commanding general, Alexander S. Webb, reinstated Wells. Walker men began to doubt Grant's sympathy with their cause.[44] They renewed their optimism on April 7, when the president asked Congress for authority to submit the constitution for ratification, leaving to his discretion the time and the possibility of submitting certain clauses for separate ratification.[45]

"New movement" Conservatives soon began calling on their party's candidates to withdraw from the field. It was expedient, they argued, for anti-Radical voters to unite on a gubernatorial candidate whom Congress would be willing to recognize—not "a red-handed Confederate colonel" like Withers.[46] Walker Conservatives met resistance from "the old Democratic politicians (who are determined to rule or ruin)."[47] A member of the Committee of Nine intimated to Colonel Withers that Grant would permit a separate vote on the obnoxious clauses only if the Conservative candidates would withdraw. Withers agreed to withdraw if his running-mates should do so and a party convention should grant its consent.[48] Marye and General Walker, dedicated to Mahone's consolidation scheme, withdrew their candidacies. Unless Walker should become

43. Richmond *Daily Whig*, March 19, 1869; see *ibid.*, March 16, 1869. On Mahone's relation to the *Whig*, see Pearson, *Readjuster Movement*, p. 29n.

44. Blake, *Mahone*, p. 103; *Annual Cyclopaedia, 1869*, p. 710; Richard F. Walker to William Mahone, April 2, 1869, and Walker to Mahone, April 9, 1869, both in Mahone Papers.

45. Robertson, *Stuart*, pp. 448–50.

46. See *ibid.*, p. 447; Richmond *Daily Whig*, March 22 and April 28, 1869.

47. James W. Walker to William Mahone, March 21, 1869, Mahone Papers.

48. Withers, *Autobiography*, pp. 275–76.

governor, Mahone warned his associates, the Baltimore and Ohio would take over the Virginia railroads.[49]

In view of the changed circumstances, the Conservative Central Committee assembled the Executive Committee members and county superintendents in Richmond for a party conference on April 28. Of the gathering's committee on policy, eight recommended withdrawing Withers and opposing only the clauses of the constitution to be submitted separately; three recommended running Withers and opposing the entire constitution. "The clauses of the Underwood constitution proposed to be submitted to a separate vote," the committee's minority believed, "are immaterial and insignificant compared to the leading features of that instrument: universal negro suffrage, negro eligibility to office."[50]

L. Q. Washington was pleased to find many of his former State-Rights associates willing to accept Walker. Only days before, Chairman Daniel, Robert Ould, and the Richmond *Enquirer* had reconciled themselves to supporting him. Colonel Lewis Harvie (the *Enquirer*'s publisher) and James A. Seddon, still unconvinced, kept their opinions to themselves. "The soul of the opposition," Washington observed, "came from [John Strode] Barbour who is the organ of the Balt[imore] and Ohio Rail Road interest. Wells and Withers are both pledged to that corporation so that if Withers were kept on the track they were secure & could have all as they wanted."[51] General Mahone attended to persuade delegates to unite with "the Walker Republicans who are right upon the great question which involves our material interests," i.e., consolidation of the southside railroads. Mahone's bloc showed that it had learned much about convention politics during the preceding year.[52] "Extra Billy" Smith, struggling to keep the Conservatives a white man's party, accused the consolidation men and the "new movement" of trying to split the party. The convention, rejecting Smith's entreaties, voted to withdraw the Conservative state ticket and oppose only those clauses of the constitution which the president would submit for a separate vote.[53]

49. See William Mahone to John L. Marye, Jr. (copy), May 4, 1869, and Mahone to Abram Fulkerson (copy), May 20, 1869, both in Letter-Books, Mahone Papers.

50. Richmond *Daily Whig*, April 29, 1869; *Annual Cyclopaedia, 1869*, pp. 712–13.

51. L. Q. Washington to Robert M. T. Hunter, May 6, 1869, Hunter-Garnett Papers.

52. William Mahone to Abram Fulkerson (copy), May 3, 1869; Mahone to Fulkerson (copy), May 30, 1869, Letter-Books, Mahone Papers.

53. Richmond *Daily Whig*, April 29 and 30, 1869; Robertson, *Stuart*, p. 456.

This last decision was even more remarkable than the withdrawal of the party's candidates, since, at the time it occurred, President Grant had neither ordered an election nor indicated which, if any, clauses he would submit separately. Virginians again turned their eyes toward Washington for signs of the president's plans. "New movement" men trusted Grant, on the basis of accounts of his interviews with the nine, to submit at least the test oath, disfranchisement, and township provisions separately. On May 14, the president appointed July 6 as the election day, but provided for separate action only on the test oath and disfranchisement clauses. Grant's failure to include the township provision perplexed many Conservatives and drew accusations of betrayal from some. Stuart later heard that Cabinet members had dissuaded Grant from submitting that provision, warning that its defeat would stifle the proposed free-school system at birth.[54]

In the five months since Stuart had written the "Senex" letter, the "new movement" had taken control of the Conservative party and implicitly committed it to accept a modified Underwood constitution and a "True Republican" slate of state officials—positions that even Stuart had not suggested in December. The sweeping change of policy left a residue of hard feelings. "Extra Billy" Smith thought that the Conservatives, without conceding anything, could and should have defeated the constitution and sat tight until the federal government might come to its senses. The Committee of Nine, in his eyes, were renegades who had deserted their party in January, then in April had taken over its "convention" by parliamentary chicanery, reversed its policy, withdrawn its candidates, disorganized its structure, and—adding insult to injury—bound its members by a loyalty resolution similar to the one they had themselves violated. In consequence, Conservatives found themselves with only the choice between two carpetbag Republicans for governor and two versions of the Underwood constitution for their organic law. Smith nevertheless participated in the campaign. He defined his priorities as the defeat of the separate clauses, the election of Conservative legislators, and the election of Walker, in that order. He would vote against the constitution but had no doubt that the majority would ratify it. Knowing little about Walker, he would take others' word that he was abler and more conservative than the notorious Wells. A Walker victory, Smith thought, would give Vir-

54. Robertson, *Stuart*, pp. 450–52; William Mahone to Abram Fulkerson (copy), May 20, 1869, Letter-Books, Mahone Papers.

ginia a bad governor and constitution, but it would also give her home rule for the future. The former governor hoped his countrymen would use that advantage to remove the perpetrators of the "new movement" from all positions of responsibility.[55]

THE CAMPAIGN OF 1869

President Grant's proclamation of May 14 allowed the parties seven and a half weeks for their election campaign. Uncertainty clouded their prospects. One could safely assume that most Negroes would vote for Wells and most white men for Walker. Walker soon recognized two predominantly white regions as "unsafe": southwest Virginia, where wartime Unionists were numerous, and the northern Piedmont route of the Orange and Alexandria Railroad, where Barbour was giving Walker, at best, lukewarm support.[56] The Conservative Central Committee, concerned about the Southwest's polarization between Radicals and "do-nothing" traditionalists, tried to fill urgent requests for speakers there, and General Mahone put his "consolidation" men to work campaigning.[57] He and his associates suspected that the Orange and Alexandria officers, ostensibly State-Rights Democrats, secretly wanted Wells to win.[58] In Madison County, the Mahoneites put up an independent candidate for the legislature, to defeat Barbour's State-Rights Conservative even at the risk of electing a Radical.[59] Republicans in northern Virginia represented the Walker ticket as a front for Mahone's railroad interest.[60]

The Walker forces threw themselves heart and soul into the campaign. Mahone wrote that he could foresee, if Wells should win, no future opportunity to "emancipate" Virginia from "oppression."[61] Not to vote in this election, a Leesburg editor warned,

---

55. William Smith to R. M. [sic] Collier, May 19, 1868, in Bell, *Smith*, pp. 269–75; see also Smith to R. R. Collier, June 22, 1869, in *ibid.*, pp. 264–65.

56. Blake, *Mahone*, pp. 107–8.

57. James R. Branch to William T. Sutherlin, June 9, 1869, and James W. Lewellen to Sutherlin, June 23, 1869, both in Sutherlin Papers; William Mahone to Abram Fulkerson (copy), May 30, 1869, Mahone Papers.

58. Blake, *Mahone*, pp. 106–8; Pearson, *Readjuster Movement*, p. 22n; Cahill, "Walker," pp. 54–55; Richard F. Walker to Mahone, May [n.d.] 1869, Mahone Papers. These suspicions, which applied also to the Richmond and Danville Railroad, were difficult to verify and, in any case, exaggerated.

59. Jones, "Conservative Virginian," pp. 125–26; James W. Walker to Mahone, May 8, 1869, Mahone Papers.

60. Cahill, "Walker," pp. 59–60.

61. Quoted in Jones, "Conservative Virginian," p. 105.

would be equivalent to helping the Radicals impose their "odious" constitution on the Commonwealth.[62] Although the Conservative party conference had simply withdrawn Withers, the Conservative Central Committee endorsed Walker in June. Making up for its hesitation to join the "new movement," the committee, with funds and advice from Mahone, managed the Walker campaign. It sent Stuart, Hunter, Withers, and other speakers around the state on passes from sympathetic railroad companies. Walker himself crossed the southside on Mahone's lines, then continued down the Valley, through the northern Piedmont, and back to Norfolk.[63] Conservative businessmen such as Mahone and Sutherlin supplied large sums of money, which canvassers considered *"equivalent to votes."* Some used the money to persuade Negroes to vote Conservative or stay home, Negro leaders to endorse Walker, and apathetic white men to turn out in force to vote.[64]

The Conservatives directed their appeal to a broad base of potential supporters. The *Whig* rebutted Northern references to Walker men as "Democrats," emphasized the ticket's Whig and Republican origins, and claimed that Northern Republican leaders privately preferred Walker to Wells.[65] The Walker congressional candidates, all wartime Unionists and "True Republicans," included Hunnicutt, the frustrated Radical, and William Milnes, Jr., a Union veteran and iron manufacturer. Almost all candidates for the General Assembly were eligible under the Fourteenth Amendment, and most promised to vote to ratify the Fifteenth. Congressional candidate Joseph Segar represented the Walker movement as a grand coalition of Unionists, secessionists, and reluctant Confederates, "old line Whigs, old-fogy Democrats and moderate Republicans."[66] Pittsylvania Conservatives, adopting the Radical candidate for delegate after he endorsed Walker, were embarrassed by the number of Radicals flocking to join their ranks.[67]

Even more shocking to traditionalists than coalition with Repub-

---

62. Quoted in Smith, "Virginia during Reconstruction," pp. 154–55.
63. Cahill, "Walker," pp. 56–57.
64. J. M. Hudgin to William Mahone, May 31, 1869, Mahone Papers; Walter Coles to William T. Sutherlin, June 12, 1869, Sutherlin Papers; Jones, "Conservative Virginian," p. 126; Smith, "Virginia during Reconstruction," pp. 152–53.
65. Richmond *Daily Whig,* July 1, 1869.
66. *Segar Letter, 1869,* pp. 2, 8–9; see also Richmond *Daily Whig,* July 5, 1869.
67. Walter Coles to William T. Sutherlin, June 12, 1869, and Coles to Sutherlin, June 15, 1869, both in Sutherlin Papers.

licans was the Conservatives' eager appeal to Negro voters.[68] Local
Conservative committees sponsored biracial barbecues. Conservative employers cajoled black employees, exposed them to canvassers,
and threatened to discharge those who would vote the Radical ticket.[69] Conservatives enlisted Negro "leaders" in the Walker campaign. One persuaded "Dr." Thomas Bayne, previously a butt of
Conservative ridicule, to speak for the consideration of a hundred
dollars a month and a promise to give "the damned old wretch . . .
an office after the campaign somewhere about the wash woods in the
lower part of Princess Anne Co."[70] Several Negroes, including the
shoemaker-politician Frederick Norton, ran for the legislature as
Conservatives in predominantly black counties. Under the title
"Whites and Blacks Shoulder to Shoulder!" the *Whig* proposed that
Conservatives endorse Negroes for Congress in five of the ten districts.[71] The *Whig* inconsistently commended white Radicals for
scratching Dr. Harris' name but scolded Wells for shunning his
running-mate.[72] The appeal to Negroes was marred by a tragedy
immediately before the election, when Conservative Central Committee member James R. Branch, a young banker, drowned at his
party's barbecue for Richmond Negroes.[73]

The Conservatives hoped their conciliatory approach would attract many who might otherwise vote for Wells. In April, the *Whig*
had predicted that, if Withers would withdraw, the resulting coalition would elect Walker by a majority of sixty to a hundred thousand.[74] Such optimistic predictions reckoned without two compli-
cating factors. In the first place, many traditionalist Conservatives
were disaffected with the "new movement." When Colonel Lewis
E. Harvie announced that he would not vote for Walker or the
constitution, the Republican Richmond *State Journal* exultantly
predicted that fifty thousand traditionalists would boycott the
polls.[75] In the second place, Governor Wells, like his opponents,
increasingly approached the political "center" in search of marginal
votes. He claimed credit for persuading Grant to submit sections of

68. See Wise, *Lion's Skin*, pp. 243–45.

69. Richmond *Daily Whig*, June 8, 1869; Smith, "Virginia during Reconstruction,"
pp. 152–53; Eckenrode, *Political History*, p. 124.

70. W. W. Wing, quoted in Smith, "Virginia during Reconstruction," pp. 152–53.

71. Richmond *Daily Whig*, April 24, 1869.

72. *Ibid.*, March 23 and June 24, 1869.

73. *Ibid.*, July 6, 1869; Wise, *Lion's Skin*, pp. 244–45.

74. Richmond *Daily Whig*, April 13 and 15, 1869.

75. *Ibid.*, May 22, 1869.

the constitution for separate ratification and announced that he himself intended to vote against the test oath.[76] Wells's maneuvers testified to the effectiveness of the Conservatives' strategy.

Late in June, members of the Conservative Central Committee learned that the commanding general, E. R. S. Canby, intended to require all legislators-elect to sign the "iron clad oath" before taking their seats. Some Conservatives, in the spirit of the "new movement," began taking steps to withdraw their candidates in favor of men who had given no assistance to the Confederacy. This additional concession proved unnecessary. Stuart and John F. Lewis appealed privately to President Grant and, several days before the election, Grant instructed Canby not to require the oath.[77]

No turbulence marred the election on July 6. The Conservative-True Republican coalition won a decisive victory. Walker won 119,535 votes for governor, and Wells won 101,204. The voters rejected the test oath and disfranchisement clauses by majorities of about forty thousand each, and only 9,189 voted against the expurgated constitution. A hundred and thirty-eight Conservatives and forty-two Radicals won seats in the House of Delegates; thirty Conservatives and thirteen Radicals, in the state Senate. Six of the senators and twenty-one of the delegates were Negroes; three of the latter were Conservatives.[78]

On July 8, Gilbert C. Walker visited Richmond for a celebration of his triumph. The *Whig* observed that even its idol Henry Clay had never drawn as many enthusiastic Richmonders as Walker. Addressing his fellow citizens, the governor-elect reaffirmed his commitment to equal rights, to Grant's reconstruction policy as he understood it, and above all to economic development. He predicted that exploitation of resources, transportation lines, and immigration would make Virginia once again "the brightest in the galaxy of States."[79] Blaming Reconstruction social conditions for retarding economic recovery, Conservatives saw in the election a harbinger of coming prosperity. "Virginia," the *Whig* announced, "is now fairly open to capitalists and immigrants."[80] Horace Greeley's

76. Richmond *Daily Whig*, April 14 and 16, May 6, and June 4, 1869; Cahill, "Walker," p. 61.

77. Robertson, *Stuart*, pp. 457–61; A. W. Graves to James L. Kemper, June 18, 1869, Kemper Papers, University of Virginia.

78. *Annual Cyclopaedia, 1869*, p. 713; Smith, "Virginia during Reconstruction," pp. 156–57. The *Cyclopaedia* understates the number of Conservative delegates.

79. Richmond *Daily Whig*, July 9, 1869.

80. *Ibid.*, July 8, 1869.

New York *Tribune* led a chorus of Northern voices hailing the Virginia election as a model of responsible reconstruction denoting a sound field for Northern investment. The news from Virginia, the New York *Herald* averred, was "Better than a New Railroad to the Pacific."[81]

The *Whig* insisted that the victory belonged not to the Democratic party but to a union of men from many parties in favor of "President Grant's liberal Reconstruction policy."[82] "I started out," Walker told a Northern interviewer, "on a liberal Republican platform, and that is the name by which our party in Virginia should properly be designated. . . . There is a stronger tendency to Republicanism among the Virginians than perhaps among the natives of any other Southern state."[83] In the hour of "redemption," Conservatives saw President Grant in much the same way that their brethren farther south would see President Rutherford B. Hayes eight years later. The *Whig* depicted him as the inaugurator of a new "Era of Good Feeling," an Augustus saving the republic from chaos.[84] The crowd at the July 8 celebration cheered his name enthusiastically, and Chairman Daniel telegraphed him congratulations on "the triumph of your policy in Virginia."[85] The *Enquirer*, characteristically more traditionalist, remained skeptical about Grant.[86]

After the election, two and a half months followed without additional evidence from the White House of good intentions. Traditionalists repented of collaboration with the "new movement," and even General Mahone began to doubt the President's good faith.[87] Several prominent Virginians, including Mahone, traveled to New York and persuaded Greeley to ask Grant to have the military au-

81. *Ibid.*, July 9, 1869; Hesseltine, "Economic Factors," pp. 197–99.

82. Richmond *Daily Whig*, July 7, 1869.

83. *Ibid.*, July 16, 1869. The *Annual Cyclopaedia, 1869*, similarly, concluded that "the Radical and Conservative parties . . . consisted mainly of two discordant sections of the Republican organization." (p. 711).

84. Richmond *Daily Whig*, January 5 and 14, February 9 and 23, March 9, April 15, July 20, October 9, and December 14, 1869.

85. *Ibid.*, July 8 and 9, 1869. Wise, *Lion's Skin*, pp. 249, 275, and Pearson, *Readjuster Movement*, p. 21n, think Daniel meant his telegram ironically. In the context of the "new movement," his sincerity seems quite plausible.

86. Richmond *Enquirer-Examiner*, February 24, April 2, May 18, August 25, September 21, 1869.

87. Robert L. Montague to Robert M. T. Hunter, August 23, 1869, Hunter-Garnett Papers; William Mahone to Lewis D. Crenshaw (copy), August 14, 1869, Letter-Books, Mahone Papers.

thorities replace Wells with Walker.[88] Wells eventually resigned the governorship, probably because of official pressure, and on September 21, Walker assumed the office by General Canby's appointment.[89]

During 1869, moderate Republicans and innovative Conservatives had organized a movement for reconstruction under a constitution providing for "universal suffrage and universal amnesty," a businessman governor from the North, and an ethos valuing social peace and capitalist development. Businessmen and former nationalist Whigs had led both the Conservative and the True Republican columns of the "new movement." The Conservative members of the movement had won their party organization to it, by a combination of skillful manipulation and the collapse of the party's former program after the national election of 1868. With the Grant administration's hesitant co-operation, the Walker men took command of the Commonwealth.

The victory of the "new movement" in 1869 resulted from its leaders' ability and economic influence, its congruence with important social and political forces in the state and nation, and the failure of other groups to present viable alternatives. Its election victory did not reflect a numerical majority committed to its program.[90] The Radicals who had voted for Wells and the optional clauses were a large proportion of the electorate; the traditionalists who had failed to vote, or voted for Walker with strong misgivings, were another. For their numbers, the Conservatives committed to re-integration into the Northern-dominated Union and to capitalist development, rather than to Old Virginia policies and values, would exert great influence in their party and state during the ensuing years.

"Virginia is soon to be what Virginia never was," the Norfolk *Journal* boasted.[91] For other Virginians, the *Journal*'s cause for joy was the occasion for painful regret. "My very soul loathes the sight of the new order of things," the State-Rights Democrat J. Randolph Tucker wrote as the Conservatives assumed command. "Reconstruc-

88. Blake, *Mahone*, p. 109.

89. *Annual Cyclopaedia, 1869*, p. 713; Eckenrode, *Political History*, p. 126.

90. To the contrary, Pearson, *Readjuster Movement*, p. 21, infers from the events of 1869 "the preference of the white masses for moderation instead of for Radicalism or Bourbonism."

91. Reprinted in Richmond *Daily Whig*, July 9, 1869.

tion may make an Empire of *physical* Virginia—which may be great in its proportions and influential in the Counsels of the Union. But what can restore that social polity which constituted the Virginia of our pride?"[92] The question echoed down the endless corridor of years to come, unanswered.

92. J. Randolph Tucker to Robert M. T. Hunter, November 9, 1869, Hunter-Garnett Papers.

7.

The Walker Administration, 1869–1873

Gilbert C. Walker's administration occupied the first four years of Conservative supremacy in Virginia. Distinctive in some respects, it nevertheless set the tone for subsequent administrations in others. It witnessed the inception of most of the policy controversies that were to agitate the Commonwealth in the following years. Between 1869 and 1873, the new state government and the Conservative party crystallized into more definite forms. The resultant "Conservatism" was a moderate policy, entering upon the "new order of things" that traditionalism rejected but closing the door to the equalitarian thrust that Radicalism prefigured.

CHANGING OF THE GUARD

As soon as Walker assumed the governorship, he called the newly elected General Assembly to meet in special session on October 5 to complete the reconstruction process. To the disappointment of Virginia Radicals, federal Attorney General E. Rockwood Hoar ruled that the Reconstruction Acts did not require legislators to take the "iron clad oath" before performing the tasks precedent to readmission. State and federal officials agreed on a complex procedure for administering the oaths required of legislators. Each member must swear that he was not disqualified by participation in a duel. Each must also subscribe to one of two alternative oaths of allegiance. One oath merely affirmed loyalty to the federal and state constitutions for as long as the legislator might remain a citizen of Virginia, but the other included acceptance of "the civil and political equality of all men before the law." Only ten members, five of them Republicans, declined to sign the latter version. In addition, thirteen senators and forty-four delegates, almost all Republicans, took the "iron clad oath," administered as optional.[1]

Against poorly organized Radical opposition, the House elected Zephaniah Turner, Jr., as speaker, and John Bell Bigger as clerk, and the Senate chose Shelton C. Davis as its clerk. Proceeding to the business of reconstruction, the two houses ratified the Fourteenth and Fifteenth Amendments and submitted the newly adopted constitution to Congress. Only ten members, one a Negro Radical, opposed ratifying the Fourteenth Amendment, and only two opposed the Fifteenth. The legislature elected to the United States Senate Lieutenant Governor John F. Lewis and southwest Virginia judge John W. Johnston. The Radicals supported Dr. Alexander Sharpe (President Grant's brother-in-law) and L. H. Chandler for these offices.[2] State-Rights men tried without success to commit the Conservative caucus to elect Edmund Pendleton.[3] Mahone's railroads and the Old Dominion Steamship Company lobbied for Lewis.[4] Johnston, a prewar Democrat and Confederate major, complemented the Whig-Republican Lewis. He was, however, "reconstructed" in his opinions, and Congress had removed his political disabilities, at the suggestion of a Freedmen's Bureau officer, for his kind care of a suffering and abandoned Negro. Baldwin's clique had furthered the postwar political career of the new Senator, who soon after his election asked Mahone for political guidance.[5]

On January 26, Congress readmitted Virginia to representation,

1. *Daily Petersburg Index*, September 4, 1869; *Senate Journal* (1869–70), pp. 5–6, 22–24; Virginia *House Journal* (1869–70), pp. 17–21 (hereafter cited as *House Journal*); *Annual Cyclopaedia, 1869*, p. 713; Robert Maurice Ours, "Virginia's First Redeemer Legislature" (M.A. thesis, University of Virginia, 1966), p. 38 (hereafter cited as "Redeemer Legislature").

2. *Senate Journal* (1869–70), pp. 7–8, 27, 33–34; *House Journal* (1869–70), pp. 22–23, 36–37. Mahone's agent, Richard F. Walker, had for awhile considered supporting Sharpe and Chandler. Richard F. Walker to William Mahone, July 16, 1869; Walker to Mahone, July 21, 1869; and Walker to Mahone, September 26, 1869, William Mahone Papers, Duke University.

3. Richmond *Daily Whig*, October 25, 1869; John M. Pollard to J. Randolph Tucker, October 22, 1869, Tucker Family Papers, Southern Historical Collection, University of North Carolina at Chapel Hill.

4. Pearson, *Readjuster Movement*, p. 33n.

5. Richmond *Whig*, December 14, 1880, clipping in Frank Gildart Ruffin Scrapbook, Virginia State Library, I, 63–64; John W. Johnston, manuscript, "Reminiscences of Thirteen Years in the Senate," pp. 2–4 (hereafter cited as "Senate Reminiscences"), and Richmond *Evening State Journal*, undated clipping [1870], both in Johnston-McMullen Papers, Duke University; John B. Baldwin to Wyndham Robertson, March 14, 1869, Wyndham Robertson Papers, University of Chicago; John W. Johnston to William Mahone, October 21, 1869, William Mahone Papers.

on several conditions. All legislators must swear that they were eligible for office under the Fourteenth Amendment or that Congress had removed their disabilities. Virginia must never disfranchise citizens entitled to vote under the Underwood constitution, abridge citizens' rights to hold office, or deprive citizens of their rights in the new free-school system.[6] Congress promptly seated the members from Virginia. Lewis joined the Republican caucus in the Senate, and Johnston, after some hesitation, the Democratic.[7]

In February, the General Assembly, now officially recognized, reconvened and petitioned Congress to remove the disabilities of the few members ineligible under the Fourteenth Amendment. After some delay, congressional relief and broad interpretation qualified all members.[8] Governor Walker called on the legislators to "rebuild the edifice of state," combining the "broken and dismembered fragments" of the antebellum government with "the new materials which experience and the needs of the present demand." He reminded them that change was "the inexorable law of nature, more fundamental than paper constitutions," and warned them against gazing back at the glorious past to the exclusion of participating in a grander future.[9]

The House Committee on Courts of Justice reported an enabling bill to validate military appointees' official acts since readmission and to provide for filling offices that should fall vacant. Conservative delegates, seeking to gain additional patronage and depose Republican incumbents, amended the bill beyond recognition. One amendment permitted litigants to appeal decisions that the military-appointed Court of Appeals handed down during its January session to the new Supreme Court of Appeals. Another declared all judicial offices vacant; the legislature would appoint new judges for all courts, and the judges would appoint clerks, Commonwealth's

6. Text in Walter Lynwood Fleming, ed., *Documentary History of Reconstruction: Political, Military, Social, Religious, Educational & Industrial—1865 to the Present Time* (Cleveland: A. H. Clark Company, 1906–7), I, 488–90 (hereafter cited as *Documentary History*).

7. Smith, "Virginia during Reconstruction," pp. 160–61; sketch of Lewis in Samuel Bassett French Papers, Virginia State Library; John W. Johnston, "Senate Reminiscences," pp. 4–14. Johnston's account implies that he joined the Democratic caucus as soon as he took office—but see Richmond *Evening State Journal*, February 11, 1870, clipping in Richard F. Walker to William Mahone, February 12, 1870, and James W. Lewellen to Mahone, September 8, 1870, both in Mahone Papers.

8. Sylvia D. Vecellio, "John Warwick Daniel: Lame Lion of Lynchburg: Youth, Soldier, and Rising Politician, 1842–1885" (M.A. thesis, University of Virginia, 1956), pp. 63–64 (hereafter cited as "Daniel"); *Daily Petersburg Index*, February 25, 1870.

9. Governor's Message, February 8, 1870, *Senate Journal* (1869–70), pp. 40–41.

attorneys, and sheriffs to serve until the next election. Finally, Conservative Central Committee member Armstrong M. Keiley of Richmond added to the bill seven sections that authorized the governor, "for the more efficient government of the cities and towns," to appoint new municipal governing bodies, which would then appoint subordinate municipal officials. All these officials, supplanting existing city governments, would serve until the next regular election.[10] After these amendments, Radical Senator Franklin Wood appropriately moved to change the word "enable" in the bill's title to "disable."[11] The Conservatives, as General Mahone had already noticed, seemed even greedier for office than the carpetbaggers had been.[12]

Governor Walker used Keiley's amendment to the Enabling Act to appoint Conservatives to the "vacant" city council of Richmond. The council chose Henry K. Ellyson, publisher of the Richmond *Dispatch*, to the "vacant" office of mayor. Mayor George Chahoon and his Radical colleagues, not considering their offices vacant, refused to give place to Ellyson. A contest for control of city buildings followed. A mob of Conservatives, whom Ellyson deputized as policemen, surrounded the Chahoon group in a police station, isolating it from food and water. Chahoon appealed to Henry A. Wise for legal services, and the erratic patriarch, despising both parties but willing to defend the underdog, blustered his way through the besieging force to join his client. General Canby then intervened; both governments called off their police forces and shared access to the buildings, while the federal army kept order. Judge Underwood recognized Chahoon's administration, but Governor Walker insisted that Ellyson held the office.[13] The rival administrations agreed to bring the question before the new Supreme Court of Appeals in the form of habeas corpus proceedings in behalf of one another's prisoners. Their attorneys debated the complex problem in the language of constitutional law, but power politics, very likely, determined the outcome. The Supreme Court judges, all Conservatives, prepared a decision in favor of Ellyson.[14]

On the morning of April 27, Richmond's social leaders and Vir-

10. *House Journal* (1869–70), pp. 129–31, 136–38.
11. *Senate Journal* (1869–70), p. 116.
12. William Mahone to Thomas S. Flournoy (copy), August 15, 1869, Mahone Papers.
13. *Annual Cyclopaedia*, pp. 346–48; Wise, *Wise*, pp. 381–82; Wise, *Lion's Skin*, pp. 276–78.
14. *The Richmond Mayoralty Case*, 19 Grattan 676–719 (1870).

ginia's political leaders gathered in the Capitol to hear the decision on the mayoralty case, the first that the new court handed down. As the judges were taking their places on the bench, the gallery collapsed and caved in the floor of Jefferson's historic edifice. The disaster killed fifty-eight persons and injured almost all the survivors.[15] In consequence of the court's decision, Ellyson's Conservative administration was installed in power. In the municipal election a month later, the returns gave Chahoon a majority. The messenger carrying the return from the most heavily Republican ward was, however, attacked in broad daylight and robbed of the ballots. The Conservative commissioners of election, recognizing only the remaining returns, awarded the election to Ellyson. Conservative judges permitted that action to stand but called for a new election in November.[16]

In September, Richmond Conservatives sent Chahoon to prison for alleged fraud in office. As in April, tragedy struck: almost unprecedented floods of the James and the Shenandoah destroyed at least five million dollars' worth of property. In November, the Conservatives carried the Richmond municipal election by means that, their opponents charged, included importing "repeaters" from Baltimore and election judges' obstructing Negroes in voting. Once again, Nemesis turned triumph to sorrow. A major fire in December completed the series of events that fixed 1870 in Richmonders' memories as the Year of Disasters. The superstitious saw in these events a visitation of divine wrath. "It is remarkable," John S. Wise afterward reflected, ". . . how many terrible disasters attended the early demonstrations of the so-called Conservative party."[17]

THE GOVERNOR AND THE LEGISLATURE

"We must 'front face' and 'march,' " Governor Walker told his first legislature, "ever mindful to keep step to the music of the

15. Grattan's note to *ibid.*, 673; William Asbury Christian, *Richmond: Her Past and Present* (Richmond: L. H. Jenkins, 1912), p. 317 (hereafter cited as *Richmond*); Wise, *Lion's Skin*, pp. 278–83.

16. Christian, *Richmond*, p. 320; James H. Platt, Jr., in *Cong. Globe*, 42 Cong., 2 Sess., *Appendix*, 198.

17. Christian, *Richmond*, pp. 320–24; Platt in *Cong. Globe*, 42 Cong., 2 Sess., *Appendix*, 198–99; *Annual Cyclopaedia, 1870*, pp. 749–50; Lily Logan Morrill, *A Builder of the New South: Notes on the Career of Thomas M. Logan* (Boston: The Christopher Publishing House, 1940), p. 92 (hereafter cited as *Builder of the New South*); Robert Somers, *The Southern States since the War, 1870–1* (London and New York: Macmillan and Company, 1871), pp. 16, 25 (hereafter cited as *Southern States*); Wise, *Lion's Skin*, pp. 271–76, 283. Wise erroneously places this election before the original mayoralty controversy.

age in which it is our good fortune to live." To Walker, his was above all "an age of gigantic material development," characterized by the telegraph, the Atlantic cable, the transcontinental railroad, and the Suez Canal.[18] Intellectually, it was "the Utilitarian, the Practical, the Material Age. . . . The prevailing currents of human thought and human activity are the practical, the useful, the material."[19]

For all Walker's business experience and industrial orientation, in personal qualities he fitted the Gilded Age's ideal of a politician, not its ideal of a businessman. He proved effective as an administrator but defective as a maker of policy. As a humanitarian, he advocated free schools and enlightened treatment of prisoners and the insane. As an exponent of laissez-faire economics, he sought to substitute private for public ownership of railroads, to secure the public credit, and to limit public spending and social legislation. When the two principles clashed, and humanitarianism would cost the state money, Walker usually chose to stand by *laissez faire*. He vacillated in policy and followed the guidance of business interests. His principal programs—selling state railroad assets and funding the state debt in coupon bonds—became very unpopular.[20]

As a political leader, Walker was equally ineffective. He was often without opinions on important issues, kept his own counsel too much, and quarreled with his legislatures. He occasionally disgraced himself by public drunkenness.[21] During the 1870's, though, these shortcomings did not prevent other men from becoming powers in national politics if they had proper "connections." In 1871, Walker allied himself with the Pennsylvania Central Railroad, which purchased the Richmond *Enquirer* as the new partnership's organ.[22] In the summer of 1870 he coveted a seat in the United States Senate, but by October he raised his sights to the vice-presidency. Failing in 1872 to win the Liberal Republican nomination for vice-president, he joined traditionalist Virginia Democrats in demanding that the Democratic party run an independent national ticket—on which he doubtless hoped to find a place.[23]

18. Governor's Message, February 8, 1870, *Senate Journal* (1869–70), p. 41.

19. [Gilbert C. Walker], *Address of Gov. Gilbert C. Walker, Delivered at the Commencement of the Agricultural and Mechanical College, at Blacksburg, Montgomery County, Virginia, July 9th, 1873* (n.p., [1873]), p. 7 (hereafter cited as *Virginia A. & M. Address, 1873*).

20. Cahill, "Walker," pp. 105–7.

21. *Ibid.*, pp. 114–17; Wise, *Lion's Skin*, pp. 291–93.

22. Pearson, *Readjuster Movement*, p. 28.

23. Cahill, "Walker," pp. 117–26.

Walker's frustrated ambition found an outlet in ostentation. Critics accused him of maintaining a "corps of flunkies" at public expense.[24] They objected especially to the supposedly novel office of the governor's confidant Colonel W. F. Owens as uniformed aide-de-camp. In fact, the militia law of 1866 had created the office of aide-de-camp and set its salary, a little more than two thousand dollars a year. Owens' militia duties did not seem to merit such a salary, but he also performed unofficial secretarial work for Walker.[25] Owens' office was an example of favoritism if not of extravagance, for while the governor supported his friend with a position involving command of the militia, he treated Adjutant General William H. Richardson with contempt, leaving him unpaid for months.[26]

Walker's favoritism did not exceed that of his first General Assembly. Most of the new legislators were inexperienced. Their average age was about forty. Only seventeen had been legislators before, and only nine had served in any legislature before 1865. The election of 1869 presented the newcomers with no policy mandate. The elections to the legislature had attracted relatively little attention, and the parties had not taken official positions on the questions, principally economic, that would confront the General Assembly. These questions did not separate Conservative legislators from Radicals.[27]

Having declared all judgeships vacant in the Enabling Act, the legislators plunged upon the prizes like cormorants upon their victims. The House overwhelmingly resolved to elect only men eligible under the Fourteenth Amendment[28] but barred no other holds. "Intrigue and electioneering are ruling the day," wrote delegate John W. Daniel, who himself was trying to secure a judgeship for his brother-in-law.[29] A few members warned that to elect legislators to judgeships would violate the new constitution.[30] The majority showed no such scruples. The General Assembly chose eight members of the House of Delegates as judges.[31] "The House," a delegate

24. William H. Richardson to James L. Kemper, November 26, 1873, James Lawson Kemper Papers, University of Virginia.

25. *Senate Journal* (1871–72), pp. 214–15.

26. William H. Richardson to James L. Kemper, April 21, 1870, and Richardson to Kemper, April 26, 1870, Kemper Papers, University of Virginia.

27. Ours, "Redeemer Legislature," pp. 17, 19; McFarland, "Extension of Democracy," p. 78; William Smith, open letter on retrenchment, 1871, in Bell, *Smith*, pp. 276–77; Pearson, *Readjuster Movement*, p. 38.

28. Cahill, "Walker," p. 114.

29. Vecellio, "Daniel," pp. 61–62.

30. *Daily Petersburg Index*, February 25, 1870; *House Journal* (1869–70), p. 234.

31. *House Journal* (1869–70), pp. 255, 258, 262, 299, 340, 344, 365.

commented, "has been thined considerable by electing its members to Judges . . . I find it will not do to rely on any of our members when their own interest is concerned. The most of them are in the ring. And I find they are inconsistent what they would go for to day perhapes they would not to morrow."[32]

The first Conservative legislature set its members' compensation at six dollars a day, plus twenty cents a mile for travel from their homes to Richmond and back. The per diem struck a balance between the antebellum standard of four dollars and the Underwood convention's eight, but the mileage rate, at the prewar level, had become unrealistically high because of transportation improvements and railroads' gifts of passes to legislators. As before the War, no salary supplemented the per diem payment. Members collected their per diems when absent "on leave," often for private reasons. The procedure of "reconstructing" the state required three brief sessions between October, 1869, and March, 1870. During the third session, the members decided to treat the three as one continuous session, collecting per diems for each business day of the two recesses—without returning the mileage they had already collected for each recess! The legislators' extravagance in compensating themselves disturbed many Virginians.[33]

Even more disturbing were accusations of bribery in connection with the General Assembly's action on railroad charters and the state debt. The legislators elected by the "new movement," John Wise later remarked, fulfilled their pledge not to be constrained by traditional Virginia prejudices, "for until then Virginians had been prejudiced against legislative corruption." Popular anecdotes about Virginia's General Assembly, especially its black members, duplicated the tales Deep South conservatives told about corruption in their legislatures.[34] Little hard and fast evidence appeared to confirm the stories. The *Whig* called attention to rumors that Northern railroad companies had bribed legislators to oppose the charter Mahone wanted for his Atlantic, Mississippi and Ohio Railroad, but editor Alexander Moseley admitted to an investigating committee that he possessed no evidence of corruption.[35] Two black legislators

32. Thomas M. Shearman to James L. Kemper, April 14, 1870, Kemper Papers, University of Virginia.
33. William Smith, open letter on retrenchment, 1871, in Bell, *Smith*, pp. 279–81. Smith blamed the legislature's extravagance on three large elements in its membership: Radicals, young men susceptible to corruption by city life, and ruined planters who had run for office to improve their living conditions. *Ibid.*, pp. 282–83.
34. Wise, *Lion's Skin*, pp. 267–71.
35. *Senate Journal* (1869–70), Document X: *Report of the Senate Select Committee*

confessed to another committee that they had accepted money for votes on railroad charters, but one claimed that he had since returned the payment. Their colleagues took no action against them.[36] It appears that a disturbing number of legislators did take bribes but that suspicion far outran reality.[37] Whether or not bribery flourished, few doubted that, as John W. Daniel wrote, "Our Legislature is ruled by the influence of corporations."[38]

Men attached to Old Virginia standards detested the Gilded Age as it revealed its lineaments in the Walker administration and its General Assembly. The state government, L. Q. Washington found, had "a look of jobbery," and was "too much like the Northern Legislatures."[39] Former Congressman John Robertson had no confidence in "our Northern satrap—the war-democrat Walker."[40] "When I look," another traditionalist wrote, "at the statues of the good and great men surrounding the capitol building and then think of the purity and chivalry that always distinguished our Legislators in times past I am sickened and saddened at the corrupt scenes that have disgraced our legislature since the war."[41] Some considered Walker's administration no better than a Radical government and Virginia yet unredeemed.[42] Virginians better attuned to the postwar world, on the other hand, did not feel the traditionalists' revulsion. Such newspapers as the Richmond *Dispatch* spoke favorably of the General Assembly, and William Henry Ruffner, whom it placed in charge of the free-school system, considered it "an able body" that "contained a large proportion of men who represented the best type of Virginia mind and feeling."[43]

---

appointed to Investigate Charges Made by the Richmond Whig, pp. 4–6. Moseley challenged Senator Edmund W. Massey, who had initiated the investigation, to say who had drawn his attention to the editorial. Massey hesitated and equivocated for a long time before naming Major W. S. Wood. For a similar charge by the *Whig* in 1871, see Ours, "Redeemer Legislature," p. 120.

36. Vecellio, "Daniel," pp. 76–77; *House Journal* (1870–71), pp. 400–401.

37. See Ours, "Redeemer Legislature," pp. iii, 119–21, 140.

38. John W. Daniel to "Doctor" [?], December 16, 1870, John Warwick Daniel Papers, University of Virginia.

39. L. Q. Washington to Robert M. T. Hunter, July 25, 1871, Hunter-Garnett Papers, University of Virginia.

40. John Robertson to Wyndham Robertson, April 13, 1871, Robertson Papers. See T. Gibson to Robertson, March 14, 1871, *ibid.*

41. James S. Duckwall, quoted in Jones, "Conservative Virginian," p. 142.

42. See Frank G. Ruffin to Robert M. T. Hunter, March 5, 1872, Hunter-Garnett Papers; Robert L. Dabney to James L. Kemper, April 31 [!], 1872, and Joseph Mayo, Jr., to Kemper, March 25, 1871, both in Kemper Papers, University of Virginia.

43. Ours, "Redeemer Legislature," pp. 65, 122–23; [William Henry Ruffner], *The*

THE FUNDING ACT

Walker's first General Assembly left an especially profound imprint on Virginia's future because of the almost irreversible nature of its principal measures. After it had set up a free-school system, a future legislature would find difficulty in abolishing the program. After it had chartered railroads, future legislatures would find it difficult or impossible to amend the charters. After it had sold the state's railroad securities, the state could never recover them. Similarly, even later officials who disapproved of its settlement of the state debt considered the settlement an inviolable contract. From the course the Commonwealth took between 1869 and 1871, there was no drawing back except by measures too drastic for most Conservatives' tastes.

In regard to the state debt, even the legislature of 1869–71 was limited in its action by an earlier commitment by the Baldwin legislature. The War and its effects, reducing the state's assets and potential revenue by two-thirds, turned the manageable antebellum debt into an onerous burden. Conflict had devasted the transportation lines for whose construction Virginia had incurred the debt, and the bonds sold in 1865 at a third of their former market value. There was talk, at that time, of reducing the debt by repudiation or appeal to the bondholders, or at least of withholding wartime interest or delaying action until West Virginia might, as her constitution promised, assume part of the old Virginia debt.[44] The Baldwin legislature—dedicated to fiscal integrity, anxious to foster economic recovery by restoring public credit, and hoping for reunion with West Virginia—rejected these alternatives. In 1866, it assumed responsibility for the entire pre-1861 principal and provided for funding wartime interest in interest-bearing bonds. In the following year, the legislature found it necessary to decrease the interest payments from the stipulated 6 per cent to 4 per cent, until West Virginia should agree to divide the debt between the two states. However, since creditors holding coupon bonds could collect full interest by paying their coupons as taxes or dues to the state, the General Assembly out of fairness extended that privilege to holders of registered bonds as well.[45]

Public Free School System: Dr. Dabney Answered by Mr. Ruffner (n.p., [1876]), p. 13 (hereafter cited as *Public Free School System*).

44. Pearson, *Readjuster Movement*, pp. 7–10; Richmond *Whig and Public Advertiser*, January 16, 1866.

45. Pearson, *Readjuster Movement*, pp. 10–11.

At the beginning of Walker's administration, most Virginians felt no urgent need to arrange a new settlement of the debt. However the governor, a Northern businessman trying to attract Northern capital, saw "a dishonored state credit" as "the great evil that oppresses us."[46] In March, 1870, he proposed to the General Assembly that Virginia refund its debt in coupon bonds paying 6 per cent annual interest and accept the coupons when due for taxes and other payments. Coupon bonds, Walker thought, would enhance the state credit more than registered bonds and would command a higher market price. Since the state had no intention of defaulting, it could lose nothing by making the coupons tax receivable. The governor even expected that the coupons when mature would circulate as currency, relieving the money shortage. He thought that Virginia, until she could persuade or coerce West Virginia to pay a share, should pay 6 per cent on the entire debt of more than $45,000,000.[47] The fact that Virginians owned only a fourth of the bonds[48] only increased Walker's zeal, since his principal concern was to enhance Virginia's credit in Northern and foreign markets.[49] His plan delighted out-of-state capitalists. Many financiers expressed approval, and British bondholders for years honored Walker as "the father of the funding act."[50]

The most remarkable feature of the governor's proposal was his argument that Virginia could afford to pay full interest on all the bonds. Caught up in the current mood of business optimism, Walker expected that, in a few years, the James River and Kanawha Canal would equal the Suez Canal in commerical importance, and there would be a transcontinental railroad with its eastern terminus at Norfolk. He estimated that real estate had already recovered its valuation of 1860, that the value of personal property had quadrupled in the preceding four years, and that, consequently, the total

46. Governor's Message, December 7, 1870, *Senate Journal* (1870–71), p. 12.
47. *Ibid.*, pp. 13–15; Governor's Message, March 8, 1870, *Senate Journal* (1869–70), pp. 160–61.
48. Ours, "Redeemer Legislature," p. 113.
49. Governor's Message, December 7, 1870, *Senate Journal* (1870–71), pp. 13–15. Walker did suggest, in passing, that Virginia might tax bonds held by nonresidents. Governor's Message, March 8, 1870, *ibid.*, p. 159.
50. Governor's Message, December 7, 1870, *Senate Journal* (1870–71), p. 12; *Senate Journal* (1874–75), Document II: *Proceedings of a Conference with Virginia Creditors including an Exposition of the Debt, Finances, and Taxation of the State by the Governor, on the Tenth Day of November, 1874*, p. 6 (hereafter cited as *Conference with Creditors, 1874*).

value of property in Virginia was about $723,115,189.[51] Some months later, the governor blithely dismissed the auditor of public accounts' estimate of about half that amount, asserting that economic growth would rapidly correct any deficiency in ability to pay.[52] As a matter of fact, Virginia agriculture had entered on a period of stagnation, and statistical data accruing in the following years suggested that the actual value of property was about half as much as Governor Walker had claimed. Walker's estimate, in fact, was almost as high as the figure for 1860, including slave property and property in West Virginia.[53]

Since the General Assembly did not act at once on Walker's proposal, he reiterated it in December, 1870, claiming that if it had been in effect the preceding year the state would already have reduced the principal by more than ten million dollars and increased bond prices to 85 or 90 per cent of par.[54] The General Assembly overwhelmingly offered to settle the controversy with West Virginia by arbitration, but some members talked of more radical measures to reduce the debt.[55] The Joint Committee on Finance reported a bill that fitted Walker's specifications, except that it provided for issuing interest-bearing certificates instead of bonds for a third of the debt, which it expected West Virginia to pay. The bill also created a sinking fund, founded on proceeds from sale of state assets, to retire the debt.[56] Neither the legislature nor the press discussed thoroughly the Funding Bill's provisions, a less exciting subject than the simultaneous debates on railroad policy. Most newspapers expressed a vague approval of sound credit; some offered peripheral criticisms of the measure. The bill's critics, such as Speaker of the House "Zeph" Turner, wanted primarily to refuse to pay interest for the war years and explicitly to repudiate responsibility for the third of the debt assigned to West Virginia.[57]

51. Governor's Message, March 8, 1870, *Senate Journal* (1869–70), p. 158; see Governor's Message, February 8, 1870, *ibid.*, p. 42.

52. Governor's Message December 7, 1870, *Senate Journal* (1870–71), pp. 11–12; see Auditor's Office, manuscript report to Zephaniah Turner, Jr., February [n.d.], 1871, Gilbert Carlton Walker Executive Correspondence, Virginia State Library.

53. The Federal census of 1870 set the figure at $409,588,133; the state assessment of 1873, at $336,686,433.23. *Conference with Creditors, 1874*, pp. 15, 17–21; see also *House Journal* (1871–72), pp. 60–61.

54. Governor's Message, December 7, 1870, *Senate Journal* (1870–71), p. 12.

55. *Annual Cyclopaedia, 1871*, pp. 762–63.

56. Pearson, *Readjuster Movement*, pp. 29–30.

57. *Ibid.*, pp. 30, 32; Ours, "Redeemer Legislature," pp. 101–4, 109–10, 113.

Bondholders and speculators in bonds undertook to educate the legislators on the Funding Bill's merits. A syndicate of Northern bondholders retained John W. Jenkins, a Republican, and General Bradley T. Johnson, a Conservative, to lobby for the bill in return for a handsome compensation.[58] Governor Walker and his brother Jonas, personally interested in the bonds, cultivated the Radical delegates and allegedly bribed the Negroes among them. Other rumors had it that Walker's latest message had circulated on Wall Street before the General Assembly had received it and that a Conservative legislator had sold his vote for ten thousand dollars. The Pennsylvania Central Railroad, buying the *Enquirer*, turned it from opposition to support of the bill.[59]

The Senate readily passed the bill, majorities of both parties voting for it. Its supporters could not muster a majority of the delegates until the last evening of the session, when fourteen Conservatives and a Republican abruptly switched from opposition to support. The bill then passed by seventy-eight votes to forty-two, with the support of half the Conservative delegates and all the Radicals but one.[60] Richard F. Walker, Mahone's Richmond informant, heard that the Radicals had been "bought" the preceding evening and that Governor Walker and Jay Cooke were the speculators who stood to profit most from the measure.[61]

Only a few observers appreciated the potential political effects of the Funding Act. If the bill should pass through stock-jobbers' connivings, the *Whig* asked, "Will it not give a handle to demagogues to agitate for repudiation of the whole [debt]?"[62] While pending, the measure had occasioned little comment, but reports of the circumstances of its enactment touched off indignant protests in some western counties. The act was an important issue in a number of contests for the legislature that year, and the election in November

58. *House Journal* (1871–72), pp. 298–99. Jenkins, who had lobbied for Northern railroad interests during that session, refused before a House committee to identify his client or state the amount of the fee. Imprisoned for contempt, he defended himself in a thirty-minute revelation to the House, which promptly released him and dropped the investigation. *Ibid.*, pp. 299, 305–7, 320–24.

59. Cahill, "Walker," pp. 93–96; Pearson, *Readjuster Movement*, pp. 28–30, 32. Ours, a defender of this legislature's record, concludes that some corruption was involved, but less than critics charged, and that it is impossible now to identify the culprits for sure. Ours, "Redeemer Legislature," pp. 119–21.

60. Pearson, *Readjuster Movement*, p. 30; Ours, "Redeemer Legislature," pp. 114–19.

61. Cahill, "Walker," p. 94.

62. Quoted in Pearson, *Readjuster Movement*, p. 33; see also T. Gibson to Wyndham Robertson, March 14, 1871, Robertson Papers.

returned a majority hostile to the funding policy.[63] However, by the time the new legislature convened in December, 1871, bondholders had already funded two-thirds of the bonds under the new arrangement.[64] Future legislatures could change the status of that part of the debt only by acts of "repudiation."

WALKER AND THE CONSERVATIVE PARTY

As governmental policy and practice took on a definite form during the Walker period, so did the ruling party. In 1869, the "Whiggish" elements that led the "new movement" were a small if influential minority of the electorate,[65] and the Walker coalition seemed unlikely to cohere as a governing party. True Republicans sought to protect their position in the overwhelmingly Conservative coalition.[66] In the last months of 1869, many of the staunchest adherents of the "new movement" secretly tried to organize as an independent group, setting up an executive committee, similar to the Conservative party's, for the "Walker party." Democrat Abram Fulkerson, fiercely opposed, described the movement's leaders as Unionist Whigs and Republicans recently alienated from their party. Influential former Confederates, however, were also active in the plan. General Mahone and *Whig* editor Alexander Moseley were among its secret supporters. Most of the members of its Central Committee were Richmond businessmen.[67] Revenging himself on the Walker movement, Colonel Withers obtained the organizational plan of the "Walker party" and published it in his Lynchburg *News* with a savage editorial attack. The *Whig*, in reply, defended the move as necessary to purge the Conservative party of such "deadwood" as the *News*. Further controversy revealed widespread traditionalist hostility to the "Walker party." Many members of its Executive Committee repudiated it and denied their participation,

63. Pearson, *Readjuster Movement*, pp. 41–42; Cahill, "Walker," pp. 99–101; McFarland, "Extension of Democracy," pp. 82–84; Ours, "Redeemer Legislature," pp. 129–30.

64. *House Journal* (1871–72), pp. 60–61; Cahill, "Walker," p. 92.

65. See Abram Fulkerson to William Mahone, October 4, 1869, Mahone Papers.

66. Ours, "Redeemer Legislature," p. 25. Eckenrode, *Political History*, p. 125, holds that the fundamental cleavage was between True Republicans for Negro suffrage on principle and Conservatives for it only for expediency. In fact, this difference was neither as deep nor as apparent to contemporaries as Eckenrode thinks and never threatened to divide the movement.

67. Abram Fulkerson to William Mahone, December 2, 1869, and Alexander Moseley to Mahone, December 10, 1869, both in Mahone Papers; Richmond *Daily Whig*, December 3, 1869.

and the *Enquirer* agitated for the Conservatives to join the national Democratic party.[68] Although the "Walker party" died stillborn, many members of its Executive Committee remained powers among the Conservatives during the 1870's.[69]

Since the Walker party failed to organize, Governor Walker in his first message to the General Assembly declared himself independent of party. His political principles, he said, were dedication to the federal Union, maintenance of the public faith, honesty and economy in government, reduction of tariffs and taxes, universal free education, encouragement of labor, and universal amnesty and impartial suffrage. He would govern in accordance with those tenets, "it matters not what you may call them—whether republican, democratic or liberal."[70] In April, the Republican State Committee officially read Walker out of its party.[71] It called on the True Republicans to sever their connection with the Conservatives and return to the fold. Senator Lewis, Franklin Stearns, Lewis McKenzie, and a few others did so. Most True Republicans merged into the Conservative party. James W. Lewellen, who had been the secretary of the True Republicans' State Committee, thought that if the Republican party "had remained quiet, and permitted the *Enquirer* to *force* men into position, our Whig friends might have acted with the Republicans. Now our only course is, to stand by our own race, and beat the carpet baggers out of their boots."[72]

It remained to be seen whether the Conservative party would repudiate the "new movement" and embark on a traditionalist course. "Straight out" Democrats wanted to drop the name "Conservative," affiliate with the Democratic party, and adopt a Negrophobic program. In July, 1870, since the party had lapsed into disorganization, the Conservative members of Walker's first legislature, together with prominent Richmonders, reorganized it without calling a state convention. They appointed a new Executive Committee, consisting of a Central Committee of eleven Richmonders and two additional members from each congressional district. The new com-

68. Richmond *Daily Whig*, November 27, 1869; Cahill, "Walker," pp. 112–14; Richard F. Walker to Mahone, December 4, 1869, Mahone Papers.

69. These included Stuart, Marye, Flournoy, Waller R. Staples, Robert Whitehead, Charles S. Carrington, and Walter Herron Taylor. List in Richmond *Daily Whig*, December 3, 1869.

70. Governor's Message, February 8, 1870, *Senate Journal* (1869–70), p. 43.

71. Cahill, "Walker," p. 114.

72. James W. Lewellen to B. Johnson Barbour, April 26, 1870, B. Johnson Barbour Papers, University of Virginia.

mittee directed the party's congressional campaign. Consistently with the "new movement," it defined Conservative policy simply as home rule by the most competent.[73]

Internal dissension continued. During the election campaign, some thought the party was on the verge of disintegration.[74] The Conservatives won a statewide majority of only 2,239, and the Republicans elected eight of the eleven representatives. Traditionalists blamed the party's compromising policy. Party discipline weakened; Conservatives began to run for office as independents against the regular nominees. Admitting that the party was "in the throes of distraction," the Central Committee finally called the first state convention since 1869, the first indisputably regular one since 1868.[75]

The convention that met in Richmond on August 30, 1871, attracted many antebellum politicians previously inactive in New Virginia's politics. Former Lieutenant Governor Robert L. Montague presided over the gathering, and former Governor "Extra Billy" Smith chaired its Committee on Business. Some scholars, therefore, have seen in the personnel of this convention signs of a "Confederate reaction"[76] or traditionalist reaction in the Conservative party. In fact, the veneration of the Confederacy's trappings did not change the party's character. In the postbellum South, innovative groups often elevated Confederate officers and even antebellum statesmen to conspicuous positions, to invest innovation with the aegis of legitimacy.[77] The 1871 Convention did not end the Conservative party's rejection of antebellum Democratic statesmen, for it had never rejected them as individuals, and young Conservatives continued to resent "old fogies" until the last "old fogy" passed away. What ended in 1871 was many elder statesmen's deliberate aloofness from collaboration with the engineers of the "new movement." Their renewed participation probably did less to restrain adaptive tendencies in the party than to reconcile nostalgic traditionalists to those tendencies.

The convention's actions did not suggest traditionalist domina-

73. Pearson, *Readjuster Movement*, pp. 37–38; *Annual Cyclopaedia, 1870*, p. 745; *Virginia Conservative Address and Organization, 1870*, pp. 2–8 (hereafter cited as *Conservative Address, 1870*).

74. S. Bassett French to William Mahone, October 9, 1870, Mahone Papers.

75. Pearson, *Readjuster Movement*, pp. 38–39.

76. See *ibid.*, pp. 39, 40n.

77. See C. Vann Woodward, *Origins of the New South, 1877–1913* (Baton Rouge: Louisiana State University Press, 1951), pp. 14, 154–58 (hereafter cited as *Origins*).

tion. The delegates agreed to consider pre-1865 issues "dead." None expressed serious protest against universal suffrage or the Underwood constitution. The convention invited Governor Walker to join its sessions, thanking him for his services in 1869. General Jubal Early indignantly stormed out when the assemblage seated and applauded six Negro delegates from Richmond. The convention modified the party's local organization and had delegates from the congressional districts, rather than the president of the convention, select the "consulting members" of the Executive Committee. It adopted no platform. Its address to the voters, contrasting Virginia favorably with the Radical states of the Deep South, defined the issue for the forthcoming General Assembly election simply as "Conservative or Radical control?" The new Executive Committee warned Conservative voters not to vote for independent candidates and advised local units not to nominate candidates ineligible for office under the Fourteenth Amendment.[78]

In 1869, "Extra Billy" Smith had hoped that traditionalists would take control of the Conservative party and purge it of the leaders who had committed it to the "new movement." Unfolding events strikingly belied his prediction. By 1873, the "new movement" was more popular than ever. Its erstwhile opponent John Goode, Jr., admitted that he had erred; its latecomers tried to represent themselves as original adherents; and activity in the Walker campaign recommended an aspirant to office more highly than antebellum or wartime public service.[79] Throughout the period of Conservative ascendancy, advocates of innovation and compromise found the events of 1869 a convenient treasury of precedents.[80]

The Yankee governor himself found his political home in the party's leadership for the remainder of the Conservative decade. In August, 1870, four months after the Republican party had expelled him, Walker dropped his nonpartisan stance and announced himself a Conservative. After the traditionally Democratic *Enquirer* became his organ and he discovered personal advantage in a "straight out" Democratic ticket in 1872, he adopted the rhetoric of old-fashioned Virginia Democrats. Walker actively campaigned for the

78. Pearson, *Readjuster Movement*, pp. 39–40; Jones, "Conservative Virginian," p. 146.

79. John Goode, Jr., to William Mahone, August 30, 1872, Mahone Papers; *Daily Petersburg Index*, April 14, 1873; Petersburg *Index and Appeal*, December 12, 1873, and August 11, 1874.

80. See S. Bassett French to William Mahone, August 9, 1872, Mahone Papers; speech by Armstrong M. Keiley in Richmond *Dispatch*, May 25, 1876.

Conservative state ticket in 1873.[81] Although traditionalists scorned him, he was very popular in some Conservative circles. On his retirement, the Petersburg *Index* praised the "noble Governor" as "the eagle by day and the owl by night" to protect Virginia's interests from "birds of prey."[82] The Conservatives of the Richmond area twice elected the former governor to Congress, where he served from 1875 until 1879. At the Conservative State Convention of 1876, Walker and John W. Daniel received more calls for speeches than any of the party's other leaders.[83] "Extra Billy" Smith, who had hoped to proscribe the Walkerites, received no such recognition from his fellow Conservatives.[84]

In 1879, as the Readjuster movement against his Funding Act came to a head, Gilbert Walker returned northward to practice law in New York City, bringing to an end his remarkable role in Virginia's Conservative movement. A twentieth-century Virginian was to describe Walker as "the cleverest of all the carpetbaggers who ever came South," a "disastrous executive" who had nevertheless achieved political success by exploiting his Conservative affiliation.[85] It would be hard to find anything else that distinguished him from "carpetbag" governors whom conservatives in other Southern states were to remember with scorn.

81. Cahill, "Walker," pp. 114, 126–27.
82. Petersburg *Index and Appeal*, November 3, 1873. Perhaps the "birds of prey" were surprised to read that they had fared so meagerly under Walker.
83. Vecellio, "Daniel," p. 134.
84. A later student thought that when Walker left the governorship, "he was unquestionably the most popular man in Virginia, and the one term principle alone prevented his re-election." Tyler, ed., *Virginia Biography*, III, 4.
85. Eckenrode, "Virginia since 1865," p. 78.

8.
A "Kemper Redemption," 1873–1877?

If the Conservative party would only elect Gilbert Walker, John R. Edmunds promised the party conference of 1869, it would be able in 1873 to "nominate the gallant Withers or any other true hearted Virginian with assured success as the white man's candidate."[1] Many nostalgic Virginians thought Edmunds' prediction was being fulfilled when, in 1873, James Lawson Kemper, an antebellum Democratic legislator and Confederate general, succeeded Walker as governor. Traditionalists who had been cool to Walker convinced themselves that Kemper's election campaign, in which some Conservatives made racist appeals, was a true restoration of things past.[2]

Their hopes were shot through with illusion about the nature of the revolution since 1861. General Kemper, regardless of the role he had played in the time of slavery, no longer belonged to that era. To the limited extent that he did cherish old-fashioned ideas, he was unable to realize them in the postbellum world. Among native white Virginians, as well as outside that circle, there were influential groups with a stake in the new order, determined to resist backward steps.

THE ELECTION OF 1873

In considering whom to nominate for governor in 1873, Conservatives almost ignored the great powers of antebellum poli-

1. [John R. Edmunds], *Speech of John R. Edmunds of Halifax before the State Conservative Convention, April 28th, 1869* (n.p., [1869]), p. 8 (hereafter cited as *Edmunds Speech, 1869*).
2. Jubal A. Early to James L. Kemper, August 9, 1873, James Lawson Kemper Papers, University of Virginia; McFarland, "Extension of Democracy," p. 90; Charles E. Wynes, *Race Relations in Virginia, 1870–1902* (Charlottesville: University of Virginia Press, 1961), p. 6 (hereafter cited as *Race Relations*).

tics. J. Randolph Tucker, pre-eminent among the State-Rights lawyers, declined to run. He explained that he lacked funds, would be
unpopular for his traditionalist opinions, and wanted nothing to do
with politics under postbellum conditions.[3] Henry A. Wise, despising the Conservative party, played with the idea of running as an
independent.[4] "Extra Billy" Smith was disappointed in his hope
that the Conservative convention might "draft" him, and talk of
nominating John Letcher came to nothing.[5] A year before the nomination, the field already belonged not to the titans of the old State-
Rights Democracy but to two Confederate officers, Colonel Withers
and General Kemper.[6] Many of the traditionalists who had opposed
withdrawing Withers in 1869 now felt that the party owed him the
nomination.

Kemper, who had distinguished himself in the House of Delegates before 1861, had risen to the rank of brigadier general in the
Confederate army before a wound at the battle of Gettysburg had
brought about his retirement from active service. During the last
months of the War, he had directed the Confederate conscription
service in Virginia.[7] That part of his career gave him some claims on
traditionalists. Since 1865, though, Kemper had taken a new tack,
looking to capital and labor from the North to make Virginia "the
Eldorado of the South." He had supplemented his law practice with
a great variety of business projects. He had tried to attract a railroad
to his home county of Madison, to interest Northern investors in
farm and mineral land, and to attract immigrants. He had sought
the presidencies of two railroads and worked to further scientific
agriculture. He had become one of John Strode Barbour's associates in the Orange and Alexandria railroad interest. Although he
expressed regret that "the last of old Virginia" was "passing away,"
Kemper was preoccupied in the years before his governorship with
business considerations, not lost causes.[8]

3. (Nathaniel) Beverley Tucker to Robert M. T. Hunter, June 16, 1873, Hunter-
Garnett Papers, University of Virginia.

4. Richard F. Walker to William Mahone, May 26, 1873, and Walker to Mahone,
June 9, 1873, William Mahone Papers, Duke University; *Daily Petersburg Index*,
May 26 and June 3, 1873.

5. William Smith to James L. Kemper, August 19, 1873, and Joseph Mayo, Jr., to
Kemper, July 25, 1873, both in Kemper Papers, University of Virginia; John Letcher
to Wyndham Robertson, February 7, 1873, and James McDonald to Robertson, January 30, 1873, both in Wyndham Robertson Papers, University of Chicago.

6. S. Bassett French to William Mahone, July 6, 1872, Mahone Papers; Withers,
Autobiography, p. 313.

7. Jones, "Conservative Virginian," pp. ix–xi.

8. *Ibid.*, pp. 30–50, 71–73, 131, 136–38, 144–45, 153–54, 156n.

Kemper's candidacy originated from complex sources, without a unifying center. Some of his earliest supporters were traditionalists who wanted him to effect a second "redemption" against the Walker administration's innovations.[9] On the other hand, his varied experience, his residence in the center of the state, and his campaign efforts for the Greeley ticket in 1872 extended his appeal far beyond traditionalist circles. By the spring of 1873, Kemper had many adherents and appeared to be gaining on Withers in popularity.[10] He retarded his cause's growth, though, by clinging to the Virginia tradition against personally electioneering for office. His partisans were dispersed individuals, not a well-disciplined organization.[11]

Meanwhile General Mahone's Atlantic, Mississippi and Ohio railroad interest, a well-disciplined organization, was looking for a candidate to support. Unable to fulfill a charter obligation to build an extension from his line to Cumberland Gap by 1876, Mahone needed friends in Richmond to ward off demands for punitive measures.[12] Withers still opposed Mahone. Kemper was associated with the Orange and Alexandria Railroad, connected with Garrett's Baltimore and Ohio. By 1873, however, Mahone and Garrett had become allies against the incursions of the Pennsylvania Central Railroad. After Mahone failed to persuade Judge Waller R. Staples of the Supreme Court of Appeals to run, he sent Judge Samuel W. Thomas and Nathaniel B. Meade, the *Whig*'s editor, to sound Kemper on railroad policy. The visitors found him hostile to the "Bucktail" (Pennsylvania Central) interest, so Mahone put his forces to work for Kemper.[13]

The alliance with Mahone put a new life into Kemper's campaign, orienting it to railroad policies instead of memories of the past. Meade took charge of the campaign, and Mahone's men in every part of the state threw themselves into it.[14] The new adherents openly championed "Virginia railroads" against "Bucktails" and

9. *Ibid.*, pp. 140, 142–44; William H. Richardson to James L. Kemper, June 12, 1873, Kemper Papers, University of Virginia.

10. William Pope Dabney to James L. Kemper, January 14, 1873, Kemper Papers, University of Virginia; Jones, "Conservative Virginian," pp. 158–61.

11. Jones, "Conservative Virginian," pp. 166, 168.

12. See below, p. 158.

13. Jones, "Conservative Virginian," pp. 162–65, 167; see Pearson, *Readjuster Movement*, p. 28n.

14. *Ibid.*, p. 169; William Mahone to Nathaniel B. Meade, June 2, 1873; Meade to James L. Kemper, June 4, 1873; Samuel W. Thomas to Kemper, July 6, 1873; Thomas to Kemper, July 18, 1873; Meade to Kemper, November 10, 1873, all in Kemper Papers, University of Virginia.

hinted that some might bolt the ticket if Withers should win the nomination. Other railroad companies hostile to the Pennsylvania—the Orange and Alexandria, the Richmond, Fredericksburg, and Potomac, and the Seaboard and Roanoke—also supported Kemper.[15] The Mahone group's efforts were probably decisive in securing the nomination for him.[16]

The A. M. and O.'s intervention transformed the nature of the preconvention campaign. General Jubal Early, who was supporting Kemper for traditionalist reasons, warned him against Mahone, and the candidate continued to profess himself independent in policy matters. On July 15, he nevertheless met secretly in Baltimore with Mahone, Meade, and Thomas and satisfied Mahone that their railroad policies were mutually congruent.[17] The Pennsylvania Central put its resources behind Withers, but the course of the campaign showed the "Virginia railroad" cause so popular that even Withers would not uphold the "Bucktail" policy fully.[18]

When the Conservative Convention met in August, Mahone gave passes over his railroad only to delegates opposing Withers. In the convention's ballots, Kemper won support not only in the northern Piedmont and the Valley, where he had been popular from the first, but also in Richmond and Petersburg, in counties on the A. M. and O. route, and in the "Peninsula." The Kemper-Mahone forces won a large plurality on the first ballot and a majority on the second. After the delegates voted to declare the nomination unanimous, Mahone's friends seized their chief and carried him bodily to a tavern to celebrate. "Full well they knew," a reporter observed, "who had planned the battle and won the victory."[19]

15. Jones, "Conservative Virginian," pp. 172–74; see Jubal A. Early to Kemper, July 21, 1873, Kemper Papers, University of Virginia.

16. Robert R. Jones, who thinks that Charles C. Pearson and Nelson M. Blake exaggerate Mahone's influence in nominating Kemper, presents the matter as follows: Kemper was a strong candidate in his own right—but Withers, apparently stronger at the outset, campaigned actively and Kemper would not. The Mahone group provided Kemper with an active statewide campaign organization. Kemper would not have won the nomination if Mahone had opposed him but might have won if Mahone had exerted no influence. Jones, "Conservative Virginian," pp. 157, 166, 169, 177–78, 185–86.

17. *Ibid.,* pp. 157, 162–63, 175–76, 183–84; Jubal A. Early to James L. Kemper, July 21, 1873, Kemper Papers, University of Virginia.

18. Jones, "Conservative Virginian," pp. 177, 179; Nathaniel B. Meade to James L. Kemper, July 7, 1873, and Richard F. Walker to Kemper, July 6, 1873, Kemper Papers, University of Virginia.

19. Withers, *Autobiography,* p. 314; Jones, "Conservative Virginian," pp. 182–84, 395.

Withers left the convention floor, dispirited by his second exclusion from the governorship, but he soon heard from friends that the body had nominated him for lieutenant governor. He returned, intending to decline the nomination, but the delegates' ovation and the entreaties of his friends persuaded him to accept instead.[20] What Withers did not know was that he owed the "honor" to the rumor that he would not accept it if proffered. Hearing the rumor, General James A. Walker, the Mahone-Kemper candidate for lieutenant governor, had nominated Withers to enhance his own claims. Although Withers' traditionalist supporters saw the nomination as a vindication, many who had voted for him were outraged by his acceptance.[21] The convention went on to nominate party chairman Raleigh T. Daniel for attorney general, and Nathaniel B. Meade became the new chairman.

The convention adopted a platform that called for progress, not restoration. In fact, the document differed little from the Republicans' platform.[22] It endorsed the Walker administration, promised to administer equal justice to both races and to promote the prosperity of both, disclaimed captious hostility to the Grant administration, praised the free-school system, and asked the federal government to complete the James River and Kanawha Canal.[23] Kemper, in his letter of acceptance, combined pledges of honesty and economy with acceptance of the "new order." He committed himself to equal civil rights, sectional reconciliation, encouragement of education and economic development, and, in guarded language, to federal public works.[24] He presented himself as a thoroughly reconstructed Southerner.

Nor, except for some stridently racist pronouncements, did the Conservative campaign to elect him show a desire to undo the work of the preceding four years. Chairman Meade, a former Whig, noted with pleasure that the ticket balanced the former Democrat Kemper

20. Withers, *Autobiography*, pp. 313–16.
21. Richard F. Walker to James L. Kemper, August 8, 1873, and Nathaniel B. Meade to Kemper, "Fri." [August 8, 1873], both in Kemper Papers, University of Virginia.
22. As Jones, "Conservative Virginian," p. 189, points out.
23. Text in *Speech of Hon. R. M. T. Hunter, delivered at Richmond, Aug. 22, 1873; Biographical Sketches of Gen. James L. Kemper, Col. Robert E. Withers, and Hon. Raleigh T. Daniel, Conservative Nominees; Platform and Resolutions, Plan of Organization, State and Executive Committees* (n. p., [1873]), pp. 21–22 (hereafter cited as *Hunter Speech, 1873*).
24. Richmond *Daily Whig*, November 25, 1873, clipping in Kemper Papers, University of Virginia.

with two former Whigs, Withers and Daniel.[25] The State Committee inquired to make certain that Kemper had not been "an *early*
advocate" of secession.[26] Since Grant had carried Virginia in 1872,
Conservative leaders declared the canvass independent of national
politics. Their speakers attacked only the Virginia Republicans, not
the Grant administration or the national party.[27]

On one potential issue—the state debt question—the Conservative
press observed a studied silence during the campaign, for the sake
of party unity.[28] Meade, like Kemper, thought the Funding Act "the
greatest *fraud* ever imposed upon a people," but nonetheless an
inescapable contract.[29] Governor Walker, the perpetrator of the
"fraud," campaigned for Kemper, but campaign managers kept
Raleigh T. Daniel, an exceptionally fervent funder, from speaking
in antifunding areas.[30]

The election campaign took a mild course, revealing that the
differences between Republicans and Conservatives had decreased
greatly since 1868. Kemper's opponent, Robert W. Hughes, had
been a State-Rights Democrat before 1865 and a "co-operation" man
since then. After the election of 1869 Hughes, the editor of the Richmond *State Journal*, had won the ascendancy in the Republican
party and steered it in a moderate direction.[31] During the election
campaign. Hughes hedged on racial questions and appealed to the
poorer farmers by proposing relief to debtors, equitable taxes, and
increased school support. Although Mahone had helped to nominate Hughes as well as Kemper, the Republican candidate dropped
hints that the state might enforce on Mahone the charter requirement to build an extension to Cumberland Gap. The Pennsylvania
Central contributed to Hughes' campaign and Mahone, alarmed,
redoubled his efforts for the Conservative ticket.[32] In the election,

25. Nathaniel B. Meade to James L. Kemper, "Fri." [August 8, 1873], *ibid.*

26. Meade to Kemper, "Wed. night" [August 13, 1873?], *ibid.*

27. Meade to Kemper, June 24, 1873, *ibid.*; see below, p. 135; see also Charles
Martin to Wyndham Robertson, January 13, 1873, Robertson Papers.

28. See L. Q. Washington to Robert M. T. Hunter, September 25, 1873, Hunter-
Garnett Papers.

29. Nathaniel B. Meade to James L. Kemper, n.d. [1873?], Kemper Papers, University of Virginia.

30. Meade to Kemper, August 11, 1873, *ibid.*

31. Pearson, *Readjuster Movement*, pp. 36–37, 40; Richard F. Walker to Mahone,
December 4, 1869; Walker to Mahone, February 12, 1870; and Walker to Mahone,
February 16, 1870, all in Mahone Papers; *Annual Cyclopaedia, 1870*, pp. 745–46;
Annual Cyclopaedia, 1871, p. 766.

32. Pearson, *Readjuster Movement*, p. 48; *Annual Cyclopaedia, 1873*, pp. 766–67;
Jones, "Conservative Virginian," pp. 189, 195–96, 209–10; Alexandria *Virginia Sen-*

Kemper received 120,738 votes to Hughes' 93,439, and Conservatives elected two-thirds of the delegates and a larger proportion of state senators.[33] The outcome was a triumph not of traditionalist reaction, but of moderation and railroad influence.

KEMPER AND HIS ADMINISTRATION

As governor, Kemper disappointed many of his friends and supporters. John S. Wise, an ardent Kemperite in 1873, later depicted the governor as a physical wreck unable to discharge his duties, a vacillator who used eloquent language to conceal a lack of policy, and a hermit who alienated friends and resented advice.[34] His immediate associates often found him authoritarian, petty, and fickle. On the other hand, most Conservative politicians thought Kemper's policies commendable. His public appearances made favorable impressions on Virginia audiences, and his state papers were well received by out-of-state readers. His personality defects, perhaps the result of his Gettysburg wound, came out most severely in sustained personal contacts; he got along least well with those with whom he had to associate continually.[35] That problem did not, however, prevent him from exhibiting many qualities of a capable executive.

Acquaintances' most frequent charge against Kemper was that of ingratitude. "I went my full length for my old war commander J. L. Kemper," one of them wrote, "and have letters from him . . . which will speak for themselves, tho' he *droped* me like a hot potato after I had served his purpose!"[36] Kemper rationalized the acts of supposed ingratitude as avoiding the appearance of favoritism. Colonel Frank G. Ruffin attributed the governor's fickleness to unconscious motives—"jealousy, & constitutional weakness acting on ambition." He noticed that Kemper would often slight a friend said to have influence over him.[37] To Kemper, the habit was a reflex to protect the independence of his office; to the friend, it suggested jealousy, arrogance, or indecision.

---

tinel, September 10, 1873; E. E. Portlock to William Mahone, November 20, 1873, Mahone Papers.

33. *Annual Cyclopaedia, 1873,* p. 767.

34. Wise, *Lion's Skin,* p. 302.

35. See Jones, "Conservative Virginian," p. 163; Richard F. Walker to William Mahone, January 29, 1877, Mahone Papers.

36. C. B. Porter to Richard F. Walker, February 16, 1877, *ibid.*

37. James L. Kemper to Lewis E. Harvie (copy), April 8, 1876, James Lawson

Although Kemper's personality limited his effectiveness, his philosophy of government was more important in setting his course in office. Fluctuating in policy more than he cared to admit, he hewed to a norm of moderation and took pride in the relative political and social tranquility of his years in office.[38] To the chagrin of traditionalists, he set national reunification and capitalist development high among his goals. With those objectives he combined, perhaps inconsistently, a devotion to Jeffersonian tenets of cheap and simple government, and a moral absolutism that often sustained him in the conviction that his policies were the only just ones.[39]

Governor Kemper performed his administrative duties conscientiously, acting within a strictly defined frame of reference. He observed constitutional limitations to a fault, declaring it improper for him to testify before a legislative committee and responding with lectures on government to citizens who wrote to him about subjects in other officials' jurisdictions.[40] He practiced a parsimonious personal economy. His only important investment while in office, a southwest Virginia land speculation with General John D. Imboden and others, yielded little because of the partners' difficulty in expelling squatters. His salary of five thousand dollars did not pay the expenses of his office, and he left Richmond much poorer than he had come.[41] Kemper's ritual of simplicity contrasted with Walker's practice. On entering office, the new governor rejected his predecessor's suggestion of a public inaugural celebration as contrary to Virginia custom.[42] He left the controversial office of aide-de-camp

Kemper Papers, Virginia Historical Society; Frank G. Ruffin to Harvie, April 13, 1876, and Ruffin to Harvie, July 19, 1876, Lewis Evarts Harvie Papers, Virginia State Library.

38. See Jones, "Conservative Virginian," p. 361; Governor's Message, December 1, 1875, *Senate Journal* (1875–76), p. 14.

39. For these two characteristics, see Governor's Veto Message, March 12, 1874, *Senate Journal* (1874), p. 284; Meade C. Kemper (for James L. Kemper) to James A. Walker (copy), March 24, 1874 (and the thirty succeeding letters), James Lawson Kemper Executive Letter-Book (1874–75), Virginia State Library.

40. See James L. Kemper to Senate Committee on Public Institutions (copy), February 1, 1875, Kemper Executive Letter-Book (1875–77), Virginia Historical Society.

41. Jones, "Conservative Virginian," p. 356; F. M. Imboden and John D. Imboden agreement, July 17, 1874, and Dale Carter to John D. Imboden, August 9, 1875, both in John Daniel Imboden Papers, University of Virginia; A. D. Williams to Kemper, March 2, 1876, and Williams to Kemper, March 14, 1876, both in Kemper Papers, University of Virginia.

42. Gilbert C. Walker to James L. Kemper, November 25, 1873, Kemper Papers, University of Virginia; Kemper to Frederick W. M. Holliday, December 8, 1877, Frederick William Mackey Holliday Papers, Duke University.

vacant and asked the General Assembly to abolish it, obtaining authority to appoint voluntary, unpaid aides.[43] Such ritual acts appeased some of Walker's critics without reversing the adaptive policies on which the first Conservative administration had entered.

Kemper began his administration in close co-operation with General Mahone in policies and patronage. Relations between the two cooled later, largely because Kemper irritated Mahone's Richmond go-betweens and resented insinuations that Mahone controlled him. In 1875, the governor compensated for his greatest favor to Mahone[44] by denying Richard F. Walker a patronage request. Mahone urged Walker to keep his feelings to himself, since Kemper would remain in office for nearly three more years. Mahone's other Richmond agents later lost respect for Kemper, who consulted Mahone less and less frequently. He nevertheless continued to accept the railroad executive's advice and kept S. Bassett French, a Mahone ally, as one of his secretaries. The two did not "break"entirely until Kemper discountenanced Mahone's bid for the governorship in 1877.[45]

In his estrangement from Mahone, Kemper lost an important source of political leverage. Although he never became very unpopular, the governor lacked a permanent group of prominent men working with him to put his policies into effect. His own principles deterred him from trying to organize a political following; he simply stated his policies. Nor did he use the press to generate support; in fact, he shunned it.[46] "With only a dozen friends in the Legislature after one year's service," Richard F. Walker wondered in 1875, "what number can the Governor count on after four years have expired?"[47] It probably never occurred to Kemper to try to organize a bloc of legislators he could "count on." That neglect at times crippled his efforts to realize his desires.

Lackadaisical though his administration sometimes appeared, most Conservatives considered Kemper an acceptable governor. Leaders commended him for forward-looking policies, and his sym-

43. Governor's Message, January 1, 1874, *Senate Journal* (1874), pp. 25–26; Jones, "Conservative Virginian," pp. 219–20; George Wythe Munford to Kemper, February 24, 1874, Kemper Executive Correspondence, Virginia State Library.

44. See below, pp. 158–59.

45. Jones, "Conservative Virginian," pp. 290–91, 333–34, 351–52; see S. Bassett French to William Mahone, October 14, 1876, Mahone Papers.

46. See James L. Kemper to John J. Lafferty (copy), July 7, 1877, and Kemper to Otis F. Manson (copy), June 22, 1880, both in Kemper Papers, Virginia Historical Society.

47. Richard F. Walker to William Mahone, April 6, 1875, Mahone Papers.

bolic actions meanwhile appeased those who revered traditional standards of character and statecraft. If he lost popularity during his term, it was primarily because some of his followers of 1873 had fondly expected that he would somehow turn the clock back twenty years. In the very first months of the Kemper administration, those traditionalists were confounded to find their hero flirting with the Grant administration, insisting on equal rights for Negroes, and under attack from a traditionalist opposition led, amazingly, by followers of Gilbert C. Walker.[48] "Kemper . . . has been very flighty since he has been Governor—", the unreconstructed General William H. Payne complained, "Fancies that a 'new era' has dawned &c."[49]

In some respects, though, Kemper did desire a return to older customs. He did, for example, have a passion for the high antebellum standard of rectitude in Virginia's government, and he remained discontented with the Underwood constitution. In those respects, he took a conscientious stand for his convictions—but in both cases, he was frustrated by contrary forces within his own Conservative party.

THE BASEMENT OFFICE SCANDALS

In no way did Governor Kemper more legitimately personify the antebellum Virginia ideal than in his personal and official integrity. Postbellum conditions imposed a severe strain on his efforts to keep his administration untained by scandal. The aftermath of the War reduced many Conservatives from wealth to poverty, quickening their desires for income, and eroded some traditional inhibitions on means for acquiring it. Kemper knew that postwar periods often occasioned moral decay, and he feared that the intense struggle to make a livelihood would corrupt Virginians.[50] To his dismay, events within his own official family confirmed his fears.

The impecunious state government offered few temptations to the corruptible, but pre-eminent among the few was the complex of treasury offices in the basement of the capitol building. Until 1871, the Conservatives retained George Rye, the True Republican who had served as state treasurer under military authority, in office.

48. See below, pp. 135–37, 200–201.
49. William H. Payne to J. Randolph Tucker, December 31, 1874, Tucker Family Papers, Southern Historical Collection, University of North Carolina at Chapel Hill.
50. James L. Kemper, manuscript address at Virginia Agricultural and Mechanical College, August 8, 1876, Kemper Papers, Virginia Historical Society.

When Rye resigned in 1871, the General Assembly elected Joseph Mayo, Jr., to preside over the "basement offices." Mayo, then temporarily editing the *Enquirer*, was one of the first who called on James Lawson Kemper to run for governor to restore the Old Dominion to her ancient paths.[51]

The treasury officials had long operated on casual business and accounting procedures. The treasurer himself kept, "most wretchedly," the accounts of deposits from the state's banks of deposit. An independent investigator found the second auditor's system for keeping account of the state debt awkward, complicated, unnecessarily costly in labor, and inadequate in fundamental respects. The procedure by which committees of legislators annually inspected the accounts was, one committee complained, "a mere mockery and utterly destitute of any good results," allowing days for a task that would properly require months.[52]

The management of the sinking fund to retire the state debt fell short of even the basement offices' usual level of efficiency. The Funding Act made the treasurer and the two auditors commissioners of the fund, enabled them to co-opt a secretary, and gave them full authority, by majority vote, to use the fund to purchase state bonds. The act gave the commissioners no other instructions; it did not even require them to keep records or to report to the legislature. The commissioners took full advantage of their sweeping discretion. In August, 1871, the Board of Commissioners met, elected William F. Taylor—the auditor—as president, and William D. Coleman, a member of the Conservative Central Committee, as secretary. The board never met again. Coleman and Mayo decided on bond purchases in informal conference with one of the auditors. Coleman withdrew assets from the fund by presenting orders bearing his own signature to the second auditor, who then issued the necessary warrants to the treasurer. The board kept no record of its activities. Instead of canceling the retired bonds, it kept them and collected interest on them.[53]

51. Joseph Mayo, Jr., to James L. Kemper, March 25, 1871; Mayo to Kemper, July 29, 1871; Mayo to Kemper, August 19, 1871; and Mayo to Kemper, September 22, 1871, all in Kemper Papers, University of Virginia.

52. *Senate Journal* (1874–75), Document II: *Report of John O. Steger relative to the Condition and Management of the Capitol Basement Offices, to the Governor and Treasurer, together with Their Report to the General Assembly*, pp. 10, 27 (hereafter cited as *Steger Report, 1874*); *House Journal* (1874), p. 491.

53. *Steger Report, 1874*, pp. 8–9; *House Journal* (1874), Document II: *Report of the Joint Committee of Investigation into the Affairs of the Sinking Fund, submitted to the General Assembly, March 30, 1874*, p. 3 (hereafter cited as *Sinking Fund In-*

About the end of January, 1874, rumors circulated that Coleman was living on a standard far beyond his visible means and had been seen with official papers that should not be on his person. After conferring with Governor Kemper, the other three commissioners conducted an investigation. They concluded, from the imperfect records available, that six thousand dollars in bonds had disappeared from the fund and that Coleman had falsified treasury accounts to the amount of ten thousand dollars. Kemper suspended Coleman from office on suspicion, and his fellow commissioners preferred charges against him. Investigation revealed that the secretary had turned over to Richmond brokers large amounts of funded coupon bonds, in return for unfunded "peeler" bonds that commanded lower market prices after the legislature suspended funding in 1871. Coleman had pocketed the difference in price. In April, a Richmond court convicted him of forgery and sentenced him to four years in the penitentiary.[54]

By that time, an investigating committee of the General Assembly had confronted the treasurer with evidence of irregularity on his own part. Mayo first asked for time to examine his accounts. Then, immediately after testifying at Coleman's trial, he began to show signs of mental instability. On April 3, a panel of judges committed him to a state asylum. The investigating committee concluded that Mayo had participated in the exchange of "consol" bonds for "peelers," profiting more from the transactions than Coleman had. A more thorough investigation of the treasury revealed a deficiency of $16,599.89 in the sinking fund and uncovered evidence that Mayo had also removed $7,400 in bonds that banks of deposit had deposited in the treasury. A year and a half after the exposure, a Richmond jury decided that Mayo, discharged by then from the asylum, was currently insane and had been insane at the time of his illegal acts. He obtained release in his brother's custody. Not until three years after the defalcation did the General Assembly authorize the attorney general to proceed against Mayo's estate for the embezzled amount.[55]

---

vestigation); and Document VIII: *Report of the Committee for Courts of Justice, relative to the Responsibility of the Auditor, Second Auditor, and Late Treasurer for Default or Loss to the Sinking Fund*, p. 3 (hereafter cited as *Report on Responsibility, 1874*).

54. *Senate Journal* (1874), pp. 164–65; *Sinking Fund Investigation, 1874*, pp. 2–3; Jones, "Conservative Virginian," p. 241.

55. *Sinking Fund Investigation, 1874*, p. 3; *House Journal* (1874), pp. 358–59;

The Coleman-Mayo scandal cast embarrassing reflections on influential Conservatives. Both principals were members of the party's Central Committee and of the Kemper administration. A committee of the legislature suggested that the two auditors, as well as Coleman and Mayo, were financially responsible for the loss, because as commissioners they had tolerated the sinking fund's irregular procedures. Attorney General Daniel ruled that they were not liable.[56] Coleman, retaining the prominent Richmond attorney William L. Royall, applied to Governor Kemper for a pardon. Kemper, who had actively helped to expose the offenses, declined to grant the pardon, since a court had decided that Mayo had been temporarily sane on the day he had testified against Coleman. The governor was reticent in his social relations with Mayo, anticipating the possibility that he might be convicted and apply for pardon, but was hurt when the treasurer concluded that Kemper was his enemy.[57] Within a few years, Coleman and Mayo returned to social prominence and to influence in Conservative politics.[58]

Soon after the sinking fund scandal, the legislature, on Governor Kemper's recommendation, authorized a thorough investigation of the treasury. The investigating accountant, John O. Steger, discovered many irregularities, including a treasure-trove for pilferers: an open case of unissued coupon bonds, with two million dollars' worth of mature, tax-receivable coupons attached! In addition to destroying those bonds, Steger recommended a complete revision of the treasury's accounting system. Governor Kemper repeatedly urged the General Assembly to take action, but the legislators left the occupants of the basement offices to continue their careless practices.[59]

To Kemper's embarrassment, additional scandals came to light during his term. In 1876, disclosure of large arrearages due the

---

Senate Journal (1874), pp. 397–98; Jones, "Conservative Virginian," pp. 242–43; *Steger Report, 1874,* pp. 9–11.

56. *Sinking Fund Investigation, 1874,* p. 3; *Report on Responsibility, 1874,* pp. 2–5.

57. James L. Kemper to William L. Royall (copy), July 14, 1875, Kemper Executive Letter-Book (1874–75), Virginia State Library; Kemper to A. B. Guigon (copy), December 20, 1875, and Kemper to James Lyons (copy), January 6, 1877, both in Kemper Executive Letter-Books (1875–77), Virginia Historical Society; Kemper to William Wetmore Gordon (copy), March 25, 1878, Kemper Papers, Virginia Historical Society.

58. William D. Coleman to B. Johnson Barbour, July 10, 1878, B. Johnson Barbour Papers, University of Virginia; Jones, "Conservative Virginian," p. 326n.

59. *Steger Report, 1874,* pp. 13–14; Jones, "Conservative Virginian," p. 243; Petersburg *Index and Appeal,* May 9, 1877.

school fund cast doubt on the auditors' management and motives.[60] Early in 1877, a House of Delegates committee reported that Colonel C. T. Crittenden, the doorkeeper of the House, had falsified records to collect extra mileage for delegates, pay them their due, and pocket the difference.[61] Two more scandals broke during Kemper's last days in office. The new attorney general, James Gaven Field, found evidence that General Bradley T. Johnson, currently chairman of the state Senate's Committee on Finance, and other attorneys had cheated the Commonwealth out of about $243,000 in fees for settling claims during the Pierpont administration. Kemper promptly ordered prosecution of the suspects.[62] The very next day, the second auditor compounded the retiring governor's distress by disclosing evidence that parties unknown had removed retired bonds from the treasury and refunded them.[63] Kemper had often warned that the treasury's procedures were an open invitation to defalcation. But he was no more successful in reforming those procedures than in restraining in his subordinates the acquisitive drives characteristic of Gilded-Age America.

PERSISTENCE OF THE UNDERWOOD CONSTITUTION

Governor Kemper's inability to restore antebellum standards of governmental honesty was matched by his inability to implement his most traditionalist policy—to scrap the Radicals' Underwood constitution. In 1868, the Conservative party had vehemently opposed the Radical state constitution for its many revolutionary innovations. The expurgation of the proscriptive clauses removed only two of the document's drastic changes in government.[64] Many lukewarm supporters of the Walker movement hoped in 1869 that

60. See below, pp. 246–47; see also Asa G. Rogers to William A. Anderson, February 3, 1877, William A. Anderson Papers, University of Virginia.

61. Staunton *Vindicator*, March 30, 1877.

62. *House Journal* (1877–78), Document II: *Communication from the Governor of Virginia transmitting Report and Opinion of Messrs. James G. Field, M. B. Seawell and John M. Forbes, of the Johnson-Poe Settlement of the Chesapeake and Ohio Canal Matter*, pp. 3–41; James L. Kemper to James Gaven Field, John Murray Forbes, and M. B. Seawell (copy), December 4, 1877, Kemper Executive Letter-Book (1877), Virginia State Library; John Hammond Moore, "The Life of James Gaven Field, Virginia Populist (1826–1902)" (M.A. thesis, University of Virginia, 1953), pp. 49–51 (hereafter cited as "Field").

63. *Senate Journal* (1877–78), Document IV: *Communication from the Executive and the Treasurer and Second Auditor, in Relation to the Recently-Discovered Abstraction and Illegal Refunding of State Bonds*, pp. 2–7.

64. See the summary of the Constitution's innovations above, pp. 59–60.

the Conservatives, once in power, would discard the constitution or render it innocuous by amendment.

Governor Walker advised his first legislature to give the constitution a fair trial. He reminded the legislators that they had all endorsed it and that the voters had overwhelmingly ratified it. Although the handiwork of the "rude, inexperienced and incompetent" Radicals, the constitution was admirable in its main features and might well prove better than Virginia's traditional system of government. Walker urged the legislators to amend it only when convinced that change was necessary.[65]

The General Assembly followed the governor's advice. The first Conservative legislature approved only one amendment: to delete the usury clause. After approval by the subsequent legislature and ratification by a referendum, the amendment took effect in 1872. The second Conservative legislature voted to amend the clauses on local government to substitute "magisterial districts" for autonomous townships, make more offices appointive, and increase terms of office. Those amendments, which took effect in 1874, by no means restored the antebellum system of county government.[66] Although the Supreme Court of Appeals invalidated the homestead exemption provision, the Conservatives in power did not try to cast off the organic law they had pronounced intolerable in 1868.

Some Conservative leaders rapidly came to respect the hated Radicals' handiwork. Before the year 1869 ended, the *Enquirer* discovered that "the Bayne-Underwood Constitution, for a wonder, and no doubt by accident, improved on the late [judicial] system, and we are happy to find that much in it is free from censure."[67] Many traditionalists, in contrast, continued to detest "the shameful, self-abasing Constitution," canonized the nine thousand who had voted to reject it, and longed to redeem earlier Conservative pledges to revise it thoroughly.[68]

In a special message to his first General Assembly, Governor Kemper aligned himself with the advocates of revision. The constitution, he objected, made government complex and expensive, hampered the legislature's freedom to act, and retarded economic growth. It laid "sacreligious hands" on the venerable Bill of Rights by amending its text and placing it in the body of the document. It substi-

65. Governor's Message, February 8, 1870, *Senate Journal* (1869–70), pp. 40–41.
66. Thorpe, ed., *Constitutions*, VII, 3900–3901; see below, pp. 174–75.
67. Richmond *Enquirer-Examiner*, December 4, 1869.
68. O. Gray to J. Randolph Tucker, August 16, 1875, Tucker Family Papers; see also Jubal A. Early to James L. Kemper, August 9, 1873, Kemper Papers, University of Virginia.

tuted the ballot—"a source of fraud, dissimulation, and falsehood"—
for "our ancient, honest and manly mode of voting by the living
voice." Finding countless other features of the constitution (including its grammar and its references to the Confederacy) unacceptable,
Kemper concluded that an entirely new organic law would be necessary. However, he feared the expense and popular controversy that
would result if a legislature or convention should draft a new document. So he proposed a constitutional coup reminiscent of the Committee of Nine. He asked the General Assembly to appoint seven
statesmen to write a constitution and to initiate its adoption as an
amendment to the existing constitution—an "amendment" that
would strike the entire text and substitute another! The governor
implored the legislature to act hastily.[69]

The General Assembly gave the cold shoulder to the proposal for
a new organic law. One of its subcommittees, after adjournment,
did propose fourteen amendments, mostly reactionary in tendency,
that would have affected almost every branch of government.[70] In
the following session the legislature initiated a set of amendments
that stopped far short of the subcommittee's proposals, not to mention the governor's. Under the new amendments, persons convicted
of petty larceny would be disfranchised, as would those who had not
paid poll taxes for the year of the election. The membership of the
House would be reduced, after 1879, from 132 to between 60 and
100 and that of the Senate, from 43 to between 33 and 40. The General Assembly would meet only biennially, and legislators would receive salaries instead of per diems. State officials would be ineligible
to sit in the legislature. The General Assembly would possess broad
powers to reorganize courts and municipal governments and would
be able by a two-thirds majority in each house to remove duelists'
political disabilities. After approval by the next legislature and the
electorate, these amendments went into effect in 1876—the seventh
year of the Underwood constitution.[71]

By the end of his first year in office, Governor Kemper recognized
that he would have to settle for amendments to the constitution he
considered radically defective. At that time, he endorsed the amendments then pending in the legislature and suggested five others to
regulate corporations' practices. The constitution, he proposed,
should provide penalties for corrupt solicitation of officials and

69. Governor's Message, April 23, 1874, *House Journal* (1874), pp. 482–84.
70. *House Journal* (1874), pp. 484, 518; *Senate Journal* (1874), pp. 484, 530–31;
Petersburg *Index and Appeal*, August 31, 1874.
71. Thorpe, ed., *Constitutions*, VII, 3901–3.

should severely limit special legislation, exemption from taxes, and distribution of passes by railroads. On the other hand, it should exempt new manufacturing capital and immigrants' property from taxes for a specified number of years.[72] A year later, the governor recommended another series of constitutional changes, ostensibly designed for economy in government, which in fact would have canceled many of the Underwood constitution's reforms.[73]

Kemper's annual pleas for constitutional revision came to nothing. After 1876, the Conservatives made no more changes in the document they had once roundly condemned. The amendment that had made the poll tax a suffrage requirement was repealed in 1882. The Underwood constitution, unchanged thereafter, remained the organic law of Virginia until 1902.[74] Kemper had been afraid that his fellow Conservatives would come to accept the Radical constitution. "The longer we live under it," he had warned, "the greater the inclination to endure and to become reconciled to even such of its provisions as are vicious and demoralizing. Occasional and partial changes of some of its particulars only serve to increase the difficulty of ridding the State of the residue of the evil."[75] Within a few years after his warning, acquiescence had become general. In the 1880's, men who had been prominent opponents of the innovative document in 1868 declared that the Reconstruction constitution had, with a few important amendments, proven eminently satisfactory.[76] They thereby testified to their acceptance of what had originally been the Radical position on several controverted questions about state government.

Many traditionalists had looked to Governor Kemper to undo the work of the "new movement" and effect a sweeping political and social reaction. The governor did nothing of the kind. In part, the traditionalists mistook their man: Kemper was satisfied to accept and defend most of the changes that disturbed them. In part they mistook his party: in those respects in which Kemper did desire a retrograde movement, other Conservatives were ready to block his efforts. Even while it imposed a limit to the revolutionary potentialities of Reconstruction, Virginia Conservatism underscored William H. Seward's maxim that "revolutions never go backward."

72. Governor's Message, December 2, 1874, *Senate Journal* (1874–75), pp. 23–24.
73. See below, p. 222.
74. Thorpe, ed., *Constitutions*, VII, 3903–4.
75. Governor's Message, April 23, 1874, *House Journal* (1874), p. 482.
76. Waddell, *Augusta County*, p. 522; Cameron, *Interior Phases*.

9.

Virginia Conservatives and the New America

In 1861, Virginia political leaders found continuance in the Union intolerable, because of the Republican party's control of the federal government and the Northern majority's rejection of the Southern doctrine of State Rights. After Appomattox the former Confederates found themselves bereft of their old institutions and subjected to a Northern society and government more "Radical" than ever. Nevertheless, the Conservatives assimilated themselves rapidly to new roles in the reconstructed Union. During the 1870's they not only became American patriots but also reconciled themselves to federal centralization, and sometimes co-operated in national politics with the moderate elements of the Republican party.

THE NEW PATRIOTISM

By 1870 Conservative leaders were fairly well "reconstructed" to national loyalty. "No man who is not a fit subject for the lunatic asylum," Conservative Congressman George W. Booker, a wartime Unionist, said in that year, "has any other thought, expectation, or wish than that the Government of the United States and the Union under it should exist for all time to come." Conservative Senator John W. Johnston, a Confederate major, agreed.[1] In 1871, Richmonders held their first large Independence Day celebration in a decade. The journalist William D. Chesterman wrote that the sight of swarms of young Richmonders "making Independence speeches and drinking American cocktails on that glorious anniversary" would be the final evidence that "the past had been left be-

---

1. George W. Booker in *Cong. Globe*, 41 Cong., 3 Sess., *Appendix*, 11 (1870); John W. Johnston in *ibid.*, 41 Cong., 2 Sess., 3515 (1870).

hind, our reconstruction successfully completed, and the era of good feeling and reconciliation finally and fully restored."[2]

The Conservatives were proud to be citizens of the powerful and dynamic nation that had suppressed their own Confederacy. Edward A. Pollard, who in 1866 was still condemning the Union and its constitution, was dramatically converted in 1868. It was the appreciation of national strength that Southerners had learned by defeat, Pollard wrote, that had for the first time inspired in them a feeling of American loyalty.[3] Governor Kemper announced in 1875 that no others understood "the new conditions of union" as well, or would enforce them as jealously, as the defeated Confederate veterans.[4] Brigadier General Thomas M. Logan hoped in 1877 that the country was becoming "nationalized"—that the sectional issues were passing away, and that new differences, cutting across sectional lines, would result in equilibrium instead of civil war.[5] In 1878, Richmonders discarded their prejudice against observing Thanksgiving, a holiday supposedly of New England origin. The Reverend J. L. M. Curry, predicting a glorious future for the United States, asked worshippers to count among their blessings the nation's republican government, the abolition of slavery, and Northern assistance during the recent yellow fever epidemic.[6]

Some traditionalists, though, could never love the Union that had overthrown their cause. The romantic novelist John Esten Cooke dismissed the patriots as "a few optimists" who "with touching simplicity" refused to see that their "model republic" was fast becoming "a pure and unadulterated military despotism." The one thing, Jubal Early snarled, in which "this 'glorious union' " had made unparalleled progress in its first century had been "corruption and villainy among those in high places, and low too."[7] Those

2. *Daily Petersburg Index*, June 9, 1871.

3. Pollard, *Lost Cause Regained*, pp. 190–204; Edward A. Pollard, *The Key to the Ku-Klux* (Lynchburg: n.p., 1872), pp. 8–11; see Edward A. Pollard, *The Lost Cause: A New History of the War of the Confederates* (New York: E. B. Treat and Company, 1866), pp. 1–2, 37–39, 45, 51–52, 58.

4. Governor's Message, December 1, 1875, *Senate Journal* (1875–76), pp. 40–41.

5. Thomas M. Logan, "The Political Problem in the United States," manuscript speech in volume 3 (Thomas Muldrup Logan Papers, Southern Historical Collection, University of North Carolina at Chapel Hill), pp. 1–5, 10–12.

6. Edwin A. Alderman and Armistead C. Gordon, *J. L. M. Curry: A Biography* (New York: Macmillan Company, 1911), p. 247 (hereafter cited as *Curry*).

7. John Esten Cooke, manuscript "On the Road to Despotism," 1870, John Esten Cooke Papers, Duke University, pp. 1–2; Jubal A. Early to J. Randolph Tucker, March 23, 1876, Tucker Family Papers, Southern Historical Collection, University of North Carolina at Chapel Hill.

who kept up their "rebel" testimony against Yankee domination provided an index of the remarkable transfer of loyalties that the Conservative leaders had undergone.

Conservatives who rejected the unreconstructed attitude had somehow to reconcile their national patriotism with their memory of their lives as Confederates. They were not able, as a people, wholly to repent of a cause to which they had so fully committed themselves. However they might differ in their later opinions of secession and the Confederacy, they could not forget their ineffaceable solidarity with the Confederate dead.[8] "They are all unrepentant rebels," a British settler discovered.[9] Most felt loyalties both to some interpretation of the Confederacy's meaning and to the nation as it had become.

Most Conservatives, without rationalizing the relation between these loyalties, thought that their wartime actions deserved credit at least for sincerity. "Were we insincere, or wicked, or criminals?" Kemper asked a Northerner. "When I was shot to pieces in scaling your breastworks at Gettysburg . . . was I impelled by no higher motive than animates a penetentiary thief?"[10] Behind the perseverance that the Confederate soldier had showed, Mayor William E. Cameron of Petersburg said, "there must have been some grand faith, some moral conviction, before the purity of which the definitions of law and the verdict of power sink into insignificance."[11] Captain James Barron Hope, editor of the Norfolk *Landmark,* set the sentiment in verse:

> They thought that they were right and this
> Was hammered into those
> Who held that crest all drenched in blood
> Where the "Bloody Angle" rose.
> As for all else? It passes by
> As the idle wind that blows.[12]

8. *Daily Petersburg Index,* June 9, 1871.

9. [Allan-Olney], *New Virginians,* II, 204.

10. James L. Kemper to William A. Baker (copy), August 22, 1868, James Lawson Kemper Papers, Virginia Historical Society. See also Governor's Message, January 1, 1874, *Senate Journal* (1874), p. 18.

11. *Second Reunion of Mahone's Brigade, Held on the Anniversary of the Battle of the Crater, in the Opera House, Norfolk, July 31, 1876,* (Norfolk: Landmark Book and Job Company, 1876), p. 8.

12. James Barron Hope, *A Wreath of Virginia Bay-Leaves: Poems of James Barron Hope,* edited by Janey Hope Marr (Richmond: West, Johnston, and Company, 1895), pp. 152–53 (hereafter cited as *Bay-Leaves*).

That resolution could not satisfy everyone. A traditionalist, for whom Cameron's anonymous "grand faith" bore the specific name of Southern Rights, might insist that its rightness was more important than the soldiers' sincerity—not to mention "the idle wind that blows." The adaptive Conservative, on the other hand, was often quite ready to forget the issues of the conflict. The overpowering catastrophe of War had made the disputed questions of slavery and secession seem unreal to him.[13] For Hope, the Confederate soldiers' cause had been simply defense of their homes; he left the origins of the conflict to the future historian to unravel.[14] From that point of view, many Conservatives decided, Northerners and Southerners might disagree forever about past events but co-operate in mutual respect to advance their common nation.[15]

Losing sight of the contested issues, some found the War a common experience to unite participants on both sides. The veteran could feel that he "liked a man all the better after having had a fair fight with him."[16] Hope, in one of his poems, made the discovery of a Union and a Confederate corpse under the same blanket a symbol of the shared experience of combat. Building on that theme, he presented the War as a source of renewed American patriotism.[17] Others caught a vision of a new national consensus emerging from the conflict: the North would impress the objects for which it had fought on the country permanently, and Southerners must give up many cherished traditions—but the resulting consolidated nationality would incorporate both regions' contributions, and Southerners could influence the end product if they would put the past behind them and work to build the united nation.[18] Governor Frederick W. M. Holliday, Kemper's successor, hoped that under the "New Regime" Virginians would learn the value of labor and New Englanders, the value of "the gentler graces." Holliday used the figure of an arch rising from the graves of the dead on both sides to suggest "how individual rights and local government can live in sweet har-

13. *Daily Petersburg Index*, December 27, 1871.
14. Hope, *Bay-Leaves*, pp. 86–88.
15. James H. Skinner to William Cabell Rives, Jr., June 12, 1875, William Cabell Rives Papers, Library of Congress; Charles Triplett O'Ferrall, *Forty Years of Active Service* . . . (New York and Washington: Neale Publishing Company, 1904), p. 170 (hereafter cited as *Forty Years*).
16. Petersburg *Index and Appeal*, August 18, 1876.
17. Hope, *Bay-Leaves*, pp. 72, 147.
18. Daniel, ed., *Daniel Speeches*, pp. 111–18, 149–58; Wise, *Lion's Skin*, pp. 164–65.

mony with the central power and glory of the great Republic."[19] From the conflict of thesis and antithesis a higher synthesis would come into being.

It was Hope who, in his ode at the Yorktown centennial observance of 1881 gave the patriotic synthesis its classic formulation:

> Give us back the ties of Yorktown!
>   Perish all the modern hates!
> Let us stand together, brothers,
>   In defiance of the Fates;
> FOR THE SAFETY OF THE UNION
>   IS THE SAFETY OF THE STATES![20]

STATE RIGHTS AND FEDERAL AID

"The safety of the states," to Virginians of 1881, was a much more restricted concept than the State Rights doctrine of the 1850's. For some Conservatives, conquest had discredited the secessionists' abstractions. Others thought that the doctrine had once been correct, but that Northern victory had changed the Union's nature. Still others simply adjusted to the fact that contemporary national politics followed different axioms.

Some former State Rights men deserted their old positions altogether. "The strict construction that we thought right & proper 20 or 30 years ago," L. Q. Washington wrote, "is not accepted now by one person in ten in America, & is not going to be acted upon by any party or govt. in your day or mine. If this new theory of construction is to be the rule . . . are *we* to have & suffer all the mischiefs that can flow from its application, & at the same time reject any possible good that can come to us under this theory—appealing vainly to a discarded dogma of interpretation?"[21] John Tyler, Jr., who participated in conservative politics under the Pierpont government before he moved to Florida, went even farther. Conceiving of the nation as now a single consolidated unit, Tyler began about 1873 to advocate "Caesarism"—military despotism—as the South's new

19. Frederick W. M. Holliday, speech on June 6, 1879, and speech on May 24, 1881, to Boston and Providence Knights Templar, both clippings in Frederick W. M. Holliday Scrapbook (1850–99), Frederick William Mackey Holliday Papers, Duke University, Part II, pp. 26, 44.

20. Hope, *Bay-Leaves*, p. 131.

21. L. Q. Washington to Robert M. T. Hunter, June 8, 1873, Hunter-Garnett Papers, University of Virginia.

protection from the Northern majority.[22] The Richmond lawyer William Green, who had never believed in the constitutionality of secession, found more and more Virginians rejecting the "exploded dogma."[23]

Many who still valued strict construction believed fatalistically that it was doomed. "There need be no hope," the Richmond *Dispatch* wrote in 1872, "that State rights in any efficient and dignified form will ever be revived."[24] "Every day's history," Judge Waller Staples of the Supreme Court of Appeals thought, "but teaches the melancholy lesson that the Federal Courts, the Federal Legislature and Executive will, in the end, absorb every vestige of the rights of the States."[25] Governor Kemper similarly feared that centralization was inevitable. He hoped the trend might someday recede in part. "In the meantime," he told the Conservative State Convention in 1876, ". . . the resolutions of '98–9 are not among the living issues of this era. Let us quit looking backward."[26]

Those Conservatives who continued to talk about State Rights as a present reality revised the concept so drastically that its antebellum prophets would not have recognized it. Nullification, secession, and extraterritorial protection of states' "peculiar institutions"— pillars of the old State Rights credo—perished in 1865. Most Conservatives, in addition, greatly compromised the strict construction of federal powers. All that remained in the new "State Rights" was state control of purely intrastate concerns. Governor Kemper, wedded to the new standard, criticized the antebellum State Rights men for wasting their talents in "abstract, impractical and unprofitable controversy" about constitutional exegesis; they should have rested their case, he thought, on the general advantages of decentralized government.[27]

New Virginia inherited none of Old Virginia's reluctance to accept federal financial assistance. In 1870, the legislature requested federal aid to complete the James River and Kanawha Canal. In 1872, the Canal company and the General Assembly offered to give

22. John Tyler, Jr., to John D. Imboden, December 15, 1875, John Daniel Imboden Papers, University of Virginia.

23. William Green to J. Randolph Tucker, January 13, 1876, Tucker Family Papers.

24. Richmond *Dispatch*, December 18, 1872.

25. *Antoni v. Wright, Sheriff, &c. Wright, Sheriff, &c., v. Smith*, 22 Gratt. 864 (1872).

26. Jones, "Conservative Virginian," pp. 84, 324–25.

27. James L. Kemper manuscript address at Virginia Agricultural and Mechanical College, August 8, 1876, James Lawson Kemper Papers, Virginia Historical Society, pp. 7–8.

the federal government the Canal if it would complete construction. The Conservative State Convention of 1873 endorsed the proposition.[28] Many Conservatives wanted federal grants to states for public education, especially for freedmen. Superintendent of Public Instruction Ruffner argued that the federal government, by freeing the Negroes, had incurred an obligation to help educate them for citizenship and that eastern states were as much entitled to grants of public land for schools as western ones.[29] Virginia's public debt difficulties led Governor Walker to propose federal assumption of the states' debts.[30] Governor Kemper, in 1874, asked the federal government to complete the Canal, assume the Virginia debt, and provide funds for Negro education.[31] There were many proposals for federal aid for lesser projects. In 1876, the Richmond *Dispatch* expressed fear that Congress would end the era of federal largesse to transportation works before Virginia could receive her share.[32]

Eager to accept money from Washington, Conservatives nevertheless resisted federal encroachments on the Commonwealth's police power. Desiring federal aid for their free schools, they drew the line at measures that would have included federal direction.[33] The Virginia Conservatives in Congress opposed civil rights bills on the grounds that they would interfere with state police power.[34] The Walker administration battled Judge Underwood to keep cases involving civil rights issues in the state courts' jurisdiction.[35] Although the state in 1870 obtained federal troops to help sheriffs expel Negroes from former Freedmen's Bureau lands, Conservative leaders protested against the use of troops without state request to enforce civil rights.[36]

28. *Senate Journal* (1869–70), pp. 68, 126–27, 168–69; *House Journal* (1869–70), p. 192; Governor's Message, December 4, 1872, *Senate Journal* (1872–73), pp. 23–24; *Hunter Speech, 1873*, pp. 21–22.

29. *First Annual Report of the* [Virginia] *Superintendent of Public Instruction, for the Year Ending August 31, 1871* (Richmond: G. A. Schaffter, Superintendent of Public Printing, 1871), pp. 39–48, 99 (hereafter cited as *School Report, 1871*).

30. See below, p. 239.

31. Governor's Message, January 1, 1874, *Senate Journal* (1874), pp. 21–22, 24–25.

32. Richmond *Dispatch*, January 31, 1876. See also Richmond *Daily Whig*, January 1, 1869.

33. See *Cong. Globe*, 41 Cong., 3 Sess., pp. 1378–79 (1871).

34. *Ibid.*, 41 Cong., 2 Sess., 3514–18 (1870); 3 Sess., 1637–40 (1871); 42 Cong., 1 Sess., 484–85, and *Appendix*, 88–94, 210–16, 300–307 (1871).

35. *Senate Journal* (1871–72), Document X: *Communication from the Governor of Virginia transmitting Reports from the Attorney-General and Insurance Commissioner; and also a Memorial of the Virginia Historical Society*, pp. 1–2, 4–5, 10.

36. See Governor's Message, December 7, 1870, *Senate Journal* (1870–71), pp. 18–21; Governor's Message, December 6, 1871, *Senate Journal* (1871–72), pp. 33–37;

Congressman Richard T. W. Duke of Albemarle County exemplified the Conservatives' view of state-federal relations in its multiple aspects. "Do not suppose," Duke said when he entered Congress in 1870, "that I came here to revive the doctrine of State rights. That, sir, is dead." He referred to the antebellum State-Rights theories. When he argued for federal assumption of the James River and Kanawha Canal, Duke brushed the constitutional objection aside cavalierly. He nevertheless spoke against the Enforcement Acts as unwarranted intrusions on the minimal "State rights" of local self-government.[37] That "right," rarely challenged before 1861, had been of little importance to the champions of Southern Rights.

Old Virginia's foremost State-Rights spokesmen, R. M. T. Hunter and J. Randolph Tucker, manifested the concept's transformation remarkably. In 1873, when Hunter returned to political activity, his reconstructed protégé L. Q. Washington commended to him the popular desire that the federal government complete the James River and Kanawha Canal. In the ensuing exchange of ideas Hunter was slow to give up strict construction, but Washington insisted that the idea was meaningless since the War.[38]

On August 22, Hunter aired his conclusions in a campaign speech for the Conservative state ticket. State Rights, he announced, meant simply internal control of such internal concerns as education, alcoholic beverages, and marital and labor relations. State Rights had once, he remembered, had an additional meaning. "A respectable, but not the larger party" had tried to limit Congress' power to objects that the constitution explicitly enumerated or obviously implied. Although the position had been intellectually persuasive, State-Rights men had acquired a bad reputation by opposing beneficial public works that only the federal government could undertake. Since 1865 many had "put away" strict construction, and Hunter now proposed to soften it. Recalling Calhoun's Memphis

---

Senate Journal (1874–75), pp. 133–34, 138–39; *House Journal* (1874–75), pp. 121, 133–34, and Document V: *Correspondence between the Governor and the President of the United States in relation to the Employment of Military Force at Petersburg,* pp. 3–4.

37. Richard T. W. Duke in *Cong. Globe,* 41 Cong., 3 Sess., 207 (1870); 42 Cong., 1 Sess., *Appendix,* 88–94 (1871); 42 Cong., 3 Sess., *Appendix,* 68 (1873). For Senator John W. Johnston's distinction between the old and new versions of "State Rights," see *ibid.,* 41 Cong., 3 Sess., 749–50 (1871).

38. L. Q. Washington to Robert M. T. Hunter, May 15, 1873, Hunter-Garnett Papers.

speech of 1845, Hunter justified federal construction of interstate public works such as transcontinental railroads and the James River and Kanawha Canal. No political principle, Hunter pointed out, remained static. If Southerners would drop their opposition to federal public works, Northerners, wanting internal control of their capital-labor disputes, would recognize the home-rule variety of State Rights.[39] Hunter's speech attested a remarkable conversion. "Extra Billy" Smith declared that Hunter had renounced his lifelong principles to please the rulers of the day.[40]

J. Randolph Tucker, professor of law at Washington and Lee College and former attorney general of Virginia, encountered postbellum realities in 1874, when a curious turn in local rivalries resulted in his unexpected nomination as a candidate for Congress. Tucker found the voters of his district "mad" for federal completion of the Canal. Tucker wanted the Canal completed, but he worried about the "ancient Constitutional difficulty" and the danger of increasing federal power. Searching his soul, he began thinking about Hunter's speech of the preceding year.[41]

In his first speech in Congress—in January, 1876—Representative Tucker treated his colleagues to a dose of old-fashioned strict construction. In repartee with interrogators, he quibbled at length about the Constitution, making distinctions too elusive for most of his hearers to grasp.[42] Virginia Conservatives lauded Tucker for the ability his speech revealed but divided on the merits of his cause. The newspaperman J. Hampden Chamberlayne assured him that nine-tenths of all true Virginians approved the address.[43] L. Q. Washington, to the contrary, regretted that Tucker had taken "the old strict construction and States rights lines, which was superceded by the war and by the logic of events and [which] if carried out would defeat . . . the great works of internal improvement in which the South is interested."[44] The embittered Brigadier General Wil-

39. *Hunter Speech, 1873*, pp. 6–10; see also Robert M. T. Hunter to Lewis E. Harvie (copy), January 17, 1874, Lewis Evarts Harvie Papers, Virginia State Library.

40. William Smith to John A. Parker, August 28, 1873, in Bell, *Smith*, pp. 257–58. Bell replaces Hunter's name with a blank.

41. J. Randolph Tucker to Robert M. T. Hunter, September 4, 1874, Hunter-Garnett Papers.

42. *Congressional Record*, 44 Cong., 1 Sess., 509–14 (1876).

43. J. Hampden Chamberlayne to J. Randolph Tucker, January 28, 1876, Tucker Family Papers.

44. Typescript of L. Q. Washington, article in Richmond *Enquirer*, January 20, 1876, *ibid.*

liam H. Payne praised the speech as a swipe at the Yankees but admitted that he cared nothing for the Constitution.[45] The Richmond *Dispatch* ridiculed Tucker as a man who had unshakable faith in the stable lock even after the Yankees had stolen the horse.[46]

Before long, under influence from Virginians and others, Tucker began to shift his ground. Even before his initial speech, he had voted against a resolution condemning subsidies, appealing for justification to the statement's sweeping nature, its Northern authors' insincerity, and his constituents' views on the Canal.[47] A few months later, he took care to distinguish his assertion of state police power from the old ideas of nullification and secession.[48] After two years of additional compromises and clarifications, some constituents complained that Tucker was "not States Rights."[49] Historically, they were correct—for, in defending the police power of the states, the Conservatives were contending only for a single turret left standing among the ruins of the great symmetrical fortress that the Calhoun school had designed to defend the slaveholding South.

CONSERVATIVES, REPUBLICANS, AND DEMOCRATS

The Republican State Convention of 1870 criticized its opponents for "the contrivance, through means of a third party, termed 'Conservative,' to evade the issues between the great national parties—Republican and Democratic." Insofar as it was a movement opposed to Republicanism, the Republicans thought, the Conservative party must eventually be absorbed into the Democratic party in national concerns. It might also serve as "a convenient house of refuge for time-servers," opportunistically siding with whichever national party had the ascendancy at the moment.[50] The Republican criticism was in some respects a perceptive analysis of the Virginia Conservatives' strained attempt to preserve their independence of the two major national parties.

Conservatives differed about their relation to the national parties. Some former Democrats, such as Senator Johnston, simply regarded

45. William H. Payne to J. Randolph Tucker, February 8, 1876, *ibid.*
46. Richmond *Dispatch*, January 31, 1876.
47. J. Randolph Tucker to Henry St. George Tucker, January 9, 1876, Tucker Family Papers.
48. Richmond *Enquirer*, April 18 and 22, 1876, clippings in *ibid.*
49. J. Randolph Tucker to Edmund W. Hubard, July 30, 1876, Edmund Willcox Hubard Papers, Southern Historical Collection, University of North Carolina at Chapel Hill.
50. *Annual Cyclopaedia, 1870,* p. 746.

"Conservative" as the Democratic party's local name.[51] Others, especially former Whigs, felt more affinity to conservative Northern Republicans than to most Democrats. Some traditionalists were wary of all Northern parties. Most Conservatives, Governor Kemper thought, did not identify themselves with either national party. "The people of Virginia," the Richmond *Enquirer* stated in 1872, "are neither Democrats nor Republicans. They are Conservatives."[52]

Conservative leaders expected that the national parties of their day would soon disintegrate and that new ones would take form. They hoped that the Democratic-Republican polarization would give way to the domination of a national "center" party in which their Virginia group would play an important role. In the summer of 1865, a Loudoun County newspaper thought that there had never been "a more auspicious time for the organization of a great national Conservative party."[53] Early in 1869, the *Whig* expected President Grant to break with the congressional Radicals and initiate a moderate "Grant party."[54] In 1870, True Republican James W. Lewellen thought that the Democratic and Radical forces were almost defunct and that refugees fleeing "the two fires" might find a home in a national Conservative party that would unite southern conservatives and moderate Republicans.[55] Hope for realignment blazed high in the Liberal Republican movement of 1872 and survived its defeat. "The Conservative Party of Virginia—Can It Not Be Nationalized?" Thomas M. Logan asked in a newspaper editorial in 1874.[56] "The political elements," Governor Kemper wrote at that time, "are in process of transition. While many of them are ... drifting around us, the Conservative Party of Virginia stands on dry land. It stands on constitutional ground, broad enough and firm enough to receive and hold all true men of all parties. ... Sooner or later . . . accretions must crystallize in the perfect structure of a

51. John W. Johnston, "Senate Reminiscences," manuscript in Johnston-McMullen Papers, Duke University, pp. 12–13; Johnston in *Cong. Record*, 47 Cong., Special Session of Senate, pp. 56–57 (1881); William Smith in Richmond *Enquirer*, June 11, 1872.

52. Governor's Message, January 1, 1874, *Senate Journal* (1874), p. 20; Richmond *Enquirer*, May 25, 1872.

53. Quoted in Richmond *Whig and Public Advertiser*, August 8, 1865.

54. Richmond *Daily Whig*, March 11, 1869.

55. James W. Lewellen to William Mahone, September 8, 1870, William Mahone Papers, Duke University; see also Alexander Moseley to Mahone, November 18, 1870, *ibid*.

56. Morrill, *Builder of the New South*, p. 249.

great, national, constitutional party of Conservative ideas. . . ."[57] It was in such a party that the Conservatives hoped to find a congenial place in national politics.

Since the expected realignment did not occur, the Conservative party became increasingly identified with the Democratic party, adopting that name in 1883. From time to time, however, party leaders sought a rapprochement with moderate Northern Republicans, to whom they felt politically akin. Some argued that the Republicans might have controlled Southern politics if they had abjured forcible intervention and cultivated their "natural allies" of the governing class. "Make Republicanism respectable," the saying went, "and the Republican party will be as popular in the South as in the North."[58] The readiness of some Conservatives to work with the party that had brought about "the Last Capitalist Revolution" testified to their acceptance of the principal effects of the revolution, just as their opposition to the plebeian and Radical elements of that party testified to their determination to arrest the revolution short of its logical conclusion.

At the time of "redemption," Conservatives debated their policy in regard to the national parties. The *Enquirer* advocated joining the Democratic party and refusing any co-operation with Republicans.[59] The *Whig* took the opposite policy. "We are more indebted to President Grant alone," it declared, "than to all the Northern Democrats put together for our deliverance."[60] The organizers of the abortive Walker party intended to affiliate with the national Republican party on a platform that would include a moderately protective tariff, federally financed public works, a general amnesty, and approval of Grant's administration.[61] Their objective became a recurrent theme in the history of Virginia Conservatism.

The Liberal Republican movement of 1872—designed to reconcile the sections, uniting members of all previous parties and forget-

57. [James L. Kemper], *Letter from Governor Kemper: The Petersburg Charter; The Political Situation Considered; The Principles and Aims of the Conservative Party; Our Relations with the Federal Government* (n.p., [1874]), p. 3 (hereafter cited as *Kemper Letter, 1874*).

58. Petersburg *Index and Appeal*, August 26, 1876; undated editorial from Richmond *State* reprinted in Richmond *Whig*, October 9, 1880, clipping in Frank Gildart Ruffin Scrapbook, Virginia State Library, I, 53; see W. W. Forbes to Edmund W. Hubard, March 29, 1873, Hubard Papers.

59. Richmond *Enquirer-Examiner*, December 28, 1869.

60. Richmond *Daily Whig*, July 13, 1869; see also *ibid.*, March 23, April 15 and 21, 1869, and *Daily Petersburg Index*, February 25, 1870.

61. James W. Lewellen to William Mahone, October 25, 1869, Mahone Papers.

ting past controversies—naturally appealed to many Conservatives. At the end of 1871, L. Q. Washington found Virginia Conservatives more willing than Northern Democrats to support a conservative Republican for president.[62] Many Conservatives considered the Liberal movement an expanded version of their own "new movement."[63] The catchword "the New Departure," which they had used in 1869,[64] became the Liberal Republicans' national slogan. The *Whig* boasted, "The Virginia Conservatives . . . inaugurated Liberalism. . . . It spread from Virginia to Tennessee, from Tennessee to Missouri, and from Missouri, by means of the Cincinnati Convention, to the National arena."[65] A group of True Republicans of 1869 represented Virginia at the Liberal Republicans' national convention at Cincinnati in May, 1872. Governor Walker received seventy-five delegate votes for the vice-presidential nomination. Walker nevertheless went home to ally himself with those Virginians who, instead of endorsing the Cincinnati nominees, Horace Greeley and B. Gratz Brown, wanted a "straight-out" Democratic ticket.[66]

In June, the Conservative State Convention responded to the Democratic National Committee's invitation to "the Conservative citizens of Virginia" to send delegates to the Democratic National Convention. The majority of delegates—former Whigs in the lead—sought to pledge the delegation to support the Liberal Republican candidates at the Democratic convention. Others, including "Extra Billy" Smith, professed to support Greeley but opposed pledging the delegates, in order to leave the door ajar for a "straight-out" nomination. Former Congressman Thomas S. Bocock pointed out that the Conservative party "had avoided the name Democracy and the Cincinnati Convention had wisely avoided all connection with the Democratic party." The Convention, on General Kemper's motion, emphatically pledged its delegates to Greeley and Brown.[67]

62. L. Q. Washington to Robert M. T. Hunter, December 14, 1871, Hunter-Garnett Papers.

63. Richmond *Daily Whig*, May 13, 1872; W. A. Burke to Gilbert C. Walker, July 16, 1872, "Deaf Dumb & Blind Institute," Box 4, Gilbert Carlton Walker Executive Correspondence, Virginia State Library; Thomas F. Hill to James L. Kemper, August 11, 1872, James Lawson Kemper Papers, University of Virginia.

64. Richmond *Daily Whig*, February 11 and 15, 1869.

65. *Ibid.*, May 7, 1872.

66. Cahill, "Walker," pp. 123–26.

67. Richmond *Daily Whig*, May 11 and 31, June 28, 1872; L. Q. Washington to Robert M. T. Hunter, July 5, 1872, Hunter-Garnett Papers; Jones, "Conservative Virginian," pp. 151–52; Fahrner, "Smith," pp. 324–25. For Conservative expressions of

Even after the Democratic National Convention nominated Greeley, traditionalists found the antislavery crusader a bitter pill to swallow. Some supported him with reservations. Others opted for the "straight-out" Democratic ticket headed by Charles O'Conor. Colonel Harvie of the *Enquirer* refused to vote for Greeley.[68] Colonel John Singleton Mosby, after he despaired of a "straight-out" campaign, actually took the stump for Grant.[69] Henry A. Wise and his son John also decided that Grant was the lesser evil.[70] In 1872, Virginia politicians recognized, the marginal voters who would decide the election were not moderates but traditionalist Democrats. Greeley's opponents, to appeal to that group, circulated copies of the editor's antisouthern and racial-equality pronouncements.[71] Conservative managers pressed into service elder statesman R. M. T. Hunter to reconcile traditionalists to the Greeley ticket. In October, as the extent of disaffection became evident, Joseph Mayo stated that a speech by Hunter would "do more good . . . than all other influences combined."[72]

On election day, the adaptive Conservative leaders who championed Greeley proved unable to deliver the traditionalists' crucial votes. Republicans and "Grant Conservatives" voted their choice, the diehards did not vote, and Grant carried Virginia by about two thousand votes. The returns showed a decrease in the Conservative vote, not an increase in the Republican vote. "I thought . . . that we could carry the State," Colonel Withers wrote, "as I did not suppose 35 or 40,000 Conservatives would stay home."[73] The defeat did not, however, cause Conservative leaders to repent their collaboration with Liberal Republicanism. J. Randolph Tucker's support of Greeley restored his "availability" for office, and the Richmond *Dis-*

reluctance to endorse Greeley, see Richmond *Enquirer*, May 18 and 20, June 8, 11, 13, 15, 18, 1872.

68. Frank G. Ruffin to Robert M. T. Hunter, August 26, 1872, Hunter-Garnett Papers.

69. Virgil Carrington Jones, *Ranger Mosby* (Chapel Hill: University of North Carolina Press, 1944), pp. 286–90 (hereafter cited as *Ranger Mosby*); John Singleton Mosby to John S. Wise, July 1, 1872, John Sergeant Wise Papers, College of William and Mary.

70. Bear, ed., "Wise and 1873 Campaign," p. 332; Wise, *Lion's Skin*, pp. 294–95.

71. *Horace Greeley's Views on Virginia* (n.p., [1872]), pp. 1–8.

72. Robert M. T. Hunter to Augustus Schell (copy), August 19, 1872; Hunter to Schell (copy), n.d. [1872]; and Joseph Mayo, Jr., to Thomas Croxton, October 14, 1872, all in Hunter-Garnett Papers.

73. Richmond *Daily Whig*, November 12, 1872; Robert E. Withers to James L. Kemper, December 7, 1872, Kemper Papers, University of Virginia.

patch, in 1875, agreed with Georgia's General John B. Gordon that the Greeley movement had been "the wisest political movement in our political history."[74]

In the state election of 1873, the Conservative leadership resumed its flirtation with Grant Republicans. The State Convention, disavowing "captious hostility" to the president, promised to co-operate with him in beneficent programs as well as to oppose his errors.[75] The Conservatives declared that their campaign did not concern national issues, and such "Grant Conservatives" as Mosby, John S. Wise, and James Barbour campaigned for Kemper.[76] Conservative speakers distinguished between Northern and Southern Republicans. Colonel Withers said that "Republicanism in the North . . . comprised intelligence, virtue and worth, while Radicalism in the South was composed of men whose hearts are blacker than the negroes' skin." John W. Daniel made the same distinction.[77] One of the Conservatives' battery of speakers was O. T. Beard, a settler from Ohio, who explained that the principles of good government and social order that had made him a Republican in the North placed him among the Conservatives in Virginia.[78]

The Conservatives continued their conciliatory policy after the election. In his first message to the General Assembly, Governor Kemper stated that Virginia was committed to no party but would co-operate with members of any party to secure freedom from federal interference, fair settlement of her claims against the federal government, and national harmony with equal justice to every state and person.[79] The legislature reaffirmed the Conservative platform's position in regard to the Grant administration, promised to uphold the Fourteenth Amendment as the Supreme Court interpreted it, and opposed the pending federal civil rights bill intended to desegregate public accommodations.[80]

74. M. Harrison to J. Randolph Tucker, December 9, 1873, Tucker Family Papers; Richmond *Dispatch,* April 14, 1875.

75. *Hunter Speech, 1873,* p. 21.

76. Norfolk *Virginian,* November 8, 1873; Wise, *Lion's Skin,* p. 302; Bear, ed., "Wise and 1873 Campaign," pp. 322–24, 342; Jones, *Ranger Mosby,* pp. 292–93; John Singleton Mosby to James L. Kemper, August 13, 1873, Kemper Papers, University of Virginia.

77. Petersburg *Index and Appeal,* November 3, 1873; Richmond *Daily Whig,* October 9, 1873, clipping in John Warwick Daniel Papers, University of Virginia.

78. Petersburg *Index and Appeal,* October 17, 1873. Beard bore a grudge against United States District Attorney Henry H. Wells, Jr., who had prosecuted him for illegal distilling. *Ibid.,* April 14, 1873.

79. Governor's Message, January 1, 1874, *Senate Journal* (1874), p. 20.

80. *Senate Journal* (1874), pp. 33–34.

Kemper and his associates were playing for high stakes. The idea that President Grant would break with the Radical Republicans was again current.[81] Several of Kemper's advisors—Mosby, James Barbour, and Major John Scott of Warrenton—wanted, in that event, to spark a national party realignment by supporting the President for a third term. Kemper himself, during his election campaign, had written to Mosby that he and his party would go for Grant for a third or even a seventh term, if necessary, to keep Virginia out of the local Republicans' control. "This appears to be *our tide,*" Colonel James Gaven Field wrote to Kemper, "*Let us take it at its flood.*"[82]

In January, 1874, Governor Kemper had an interview with President Grant at the White House. Kemper tried to persuade Grant to use his influence against the civil rights bill. He apparently dropped the hint that under certain circumstances the Conservatives might support the president's re-election.[83] Kemper's primary concern was to preserve his party's freedom of action with respect to the national parties. The Conservative party, he recognized, included "extremists of two classes"—those who advocated general opposition to Grant's administration and those who advocated unconditional support—but he was confident that "the great body of the people repose silently between them, sympathizing with neither." In national politics, he said, the party would simply support those who supported its principles and oppose those who opposed them.[84]

Meanwhile, Gilbert Walker's Richmond *Enquirer* clique, now staunch Democrats, lay in wait for a chance to assail Kemper's dealings with administration Republicans. In June, when federal intervention in a Petersburg election made public opinion receptive, George C. Wedderburn of the *Enquirer* published the accusation that the Governor was trying to subvert the Conservative party to Republican interests. Wedderburn's claim, documented with quo-

81. James Gaven Field to James L. Kemper, January 16, 1874, Kemper Papers, University of Virginia; D. H. London to Robert M. T. Hunter, March 3, 1874, Hunter-Garnett Papers.

82. Jones, "Conservative Virginian," pp. 221–22, 240n; Field to Kemper, January 16, 1874, Kemper Papers, University of Virginia; James Barbour to Kemper, January 20, 1874, Kemper Papers, Virginia State Library.

83. Jones, "Conservative Virginian," p. 227; Kemper to John S. Mosby (copy), June 23, 1874, Kemper Executive Correspondence, Virginia State Library; Nathaniel B. Meade to Kemper, July 17, 1874, and Meade to Kemper, August 4, 1874, both in Kemper Papers, University of Virginia.

84. [Kemper], *Kemper Letter, 1874,* pp. 3–4.

tations from Kemper's 1873 letter to Mosby, touched off a traditionalist attack on Kemper and a rift between Kemper and Mosby. The discussion that ensued revealed that those who had talked of accord with the administration had differed in their interpretations of the accord they desired.[85] Nathaniel B. Meade continued to see Grant as "the winning card for the conservatives" and to envisage a Grant-Kemper ticket in 1876,[86] but the controversy had rendered an entente with the administration politically dangerous. Kemper remained willing to support Grant if he should take "our safe and constitutional ground," but he found in the president's record policies to censure as well as to commend.[87]

By 1876 there was no doubt that the Conservative party would again support the Democratic ticket—but in that course, too, it deferred to Northern leadership. Governor Kemper set the tone of Conservative participation in the nominating process. Observing that a conspicuous Southern following might prejudice Northern voters against a candidate, he hoped Southerners would not play conspicuous roles in the convention or campaign. They should, he wrote, let the past alone and "go for nothing but the practical and living measures which involve the future of the country and the equality of all its parts."[88] In practice, acquiescence in Northern leadership meant that the Conservatives, almost all inflationists, acquiesced in the leadership of hard-money Northeastern financial interests. The Richmond *Dispatch*, in January, wanted a western candidate who opposed immediate resumption of specie payments and rejected New York's governor, Samuel J. Tilden, as "the candidate of a club of New York swallow-tails." By May, however, the paper advocated nominating Tilden or someone else who would carry the decisive hard-money states of the Northeast.[89] S. B. Major of South Hill, who preferred the western inflationist Democrats,

85. Jones, "Conservative Virginian," pp. 237–40; Jones, *Ranger Mosby*, pp. 293–94; John S. Mosby, typescript of undated narrative, John Warwick Daniel Papers, Duke University; James L. Kemper to Mosby (copy), June 23, 1874, Kemper Executive Correspondence; L. Q. Washington to Kemper, June 19, 1874, and Nathaniel B. Meade to Kemper, July 17, 1874, both in Kemper Papers, University of Virginia.
86. Meade to Kemper, August 4, 1874, Kemper Papers, University of Virginia.
87. Kemper to John S. Mosby (copy), June 23, 1874, Kemper Executive Correspondence, Virginia State Library.
88. James L. Kemper to Montgomery Blair (copy), April 28, 1876, Kemper Executive Letter-Books (1875–77), Virginia Historical Society.
89. Richmond *Dispatch*, January 5, 6, and 7; February 1; May 17, 20, 24, 25, and 31, 1876.

similarly felt he must support Tilden as the only Democrat who could carry New York.[90] Virginia's delegates went to St. Louis uninstructed but there decided on Tilden as the Democrat most likely to win the election. On each ballot they gave "the candidate of a club of New York swallow-tails" seventeen of their twenty-two votes.[91] The Conservatives had restored the Virginia–New York axis—but with the order of precedence reversed.

During the campaign, the Conservative ranks held for Tilden with only trifling exceptions. Mosby and John Tyler, Jr., out of the Conservative camp by then, endorsed Hayes, whom Tyler commended as a gentleman of the finest Virginia ancestry.[92] General Imboden, then working in Pennsylvania, thought that Hayes might be as generous to the South as Tilden and better able to reconcile Northerners to his policy.[93] These deviants exerted no significant influence; Tilden carried Virginia.

When they learned that the election depended on twenty disputed electoral votes, Conservatives still hoped to inaugurate Tilden. Some expected that a new civil war would break out over the presidential succession.[94] Governor Kemper offered the Democratic National Chairman assistance in securing fair returns in Southern states, and State Chairman Meade organized a rally in Richmond for Tilden.[95] In January, Conservative leaders approved the compromise plan for an Electoral Commission to rule on the disputed returns. Most of them expected that the commission's findings would show Tilden the victor.[96]

After the commission ruled in Hayes' favor by a partisan majority, almost all Conservatives protested that they had been de-

90. S. B. Major to James L. Kemper, May 24, 1876, James Lawson Kemper Papers, University of Virginia.

91. [Democratic Party], *Official Proceedings of the National Democratic Convention Held in St. Louis, Mo., June 27th, 28th, and 29th, 1876* (St. Louis: Woodward, Tiernan and Hale, 1876), pp. 135–36, 144, 146.

92. *Letters of Col. Mosby and John Tyler, Jr.* (n.p., [1876]), pp. 1–8.

93. John D. Imboden to "Major" [John D. McCue?] (copy), October 3, 1876, Imboden Papers.

94. Petersburg *Index and Appeal*, November 28, 1876, and January 10, 1877; L. Q. Washington to Lewis E. Harvie, November 28, 1876, Harvie Papers.

95. James L. Kemper to Abram S. Hewitt (copy), November 11, 1876, Kemper Executive Letter-Book (1875–77), Virginia Historical Society; Petersburg *Index and Appeal*, January 10, 1877.

96. Richmond *Daily Whig*, January 29 and 31 and February 7, 1877; Staunton *Vindicator*, January 26, 1877; Petersburg *Index and Appeal*, January 24 and 31, 1877; John W. Daniel to J. Randolph Tucker, January 25, 1877, Tucker Family Papers; R. A. Banks to James L. Kemper, January 23, 1877, Kemper Executive Correspondence, Virginia State Library.

frauded. Gilbert C. Walker lapsed into several days of alcoholic despair.[97] Unwilling to admit that they had paved the way for Hayes's inauguration by agreeing to the Electoral Commission plan, Tilden's supporters looked about for scapegoats. Northern and Southern Democrats fell out, each group accusing the other of a fatal lack of firmness. Only a few Virginians assigned a share of the guilt to the Southern side.[98] Most blamed the Northern Democrats, or Tilden in particular.[99] J. Randolph Tucker was unusual in admitting that the Electoral Commission had been the only alternative to anarchy and military dictatorship and that the Democrats, after accepting the compromise plan, were bound to abide by the commission's decision.[100] The controversy again strained the tenuous bonds that united Virginia Conservatives and Northern Democrats.[101]

When President Hayes began to conciliate Southern conservatives, some Virginia Conservatives expressed a desire to co-operate with his administration.[102] The idea of party realignment was again in the air. Many Virginians, though, doubted Hayes' intentions or his ability to carry them out. Almost all opposed any immediate relaxation of party lines.[103] For eight years Conservatives had been disappointed in their hope of party realignment and alliance with a conservative Republican administration. By 1877 they appreciated the obstacles in the way of the change they sought. Hayes did win

97. Staunton *Vindicator*, February 23 and March 2, 1877; Petersburg *Index and Appeal*, February 14 and 19, 1877; James M. Fisher to Richard F. Walker, February 23, 1877, Mahone Papers.

98. Petersburg *Index and Appeal*, December 18, 1876, and February 27, 1877; Henry St. George Tucker to J. Randolph Tucker, December 14, 1876, Tucker Family Papers.

99. Petersburg *Index and Appeal*, February 14 and 21, 1877; Auburn L. Pridemore to [Richard F. Walker?], February 21, 1877, Mahone Papers; William E. Cameron to George W. Bagby, March 18, 1877, George William Bagby Papers, Virginia Historical Society.

100. J. Randolph Tucker to Henry St. George Tucker, February 25, 1877, Tucker Family Papers.

101. If the Northern Democrats should allow Hayes to take office, L. Q. Washington had written in November, Southern conservatives should dissolve their "alliance with a set of politicians who have not the courage to do more than bluster and protest." L. Q. Washington to Lewis E. Harvie, November 28, 1876, Harvie Papers.

102. Staunton *Vindicator*, March 9, 16, 23, 30, and April 27, 1877; Petersburg *Index and Appeal*, April 16, 1877; J. E. Stewart to Harrison H. Riddleberger, March 15, 1877, Harrison Holt Riddleberger Papers, College of William and Mary.

103. Petersburg *Index and Appeal*, May 5, June 20, July 7, September 13 and 21, and November 17, 1877; Staunton *Vindicator*, March 23 and April 20, 1877; Norfolk *Landmark*, March 25, 1877; Bagby, *Old Virginia Gentleman*, pp. 299, 302–5; William E. Cameron to George W. Bagby, March 18, 1877, Bagby Papers.

some Conservative friends in Virginia. Stuart corresponded with him, expressing a spirit of conciliation.[104] The Reverend J. L. M. Curry of Richmond, whom he had considered for a Cabinet position, worked to build his popularity in the Old Dominion. Virginians received Hayes warmly during his tour of Virginia in the autumn of 1877.[105] At the Conservative State Convention that year, former Congressman Daniel C. DeJarnette introduced a resolution commending President Hayes.[106]

That same summer General Thomas M. Logan, addressing a reunion in Waco, Texas, of Hood's Brigade, predicted that the Republican and Democratic parties would gradually dissolve into a new division between "progressive" and "conservative" parties. The conservative, propertied white men of the South would find their natural allies among the conservative, propertied white Republicans of the North, not among the Northern Democrats. Virginia's "new movement," Wade Hampton's conservative movement in South Carolina, and Hayes's policies were harbingers of the national conservative party of the future. Logan wanted the South to stay "solid" for awhile to prevent a resurgence of Radicalism, but he warned against politicians interested in perpetuating political sectionalism.[107] Logan's speech bore witness to the persistence of the strategy of alliance with moderate Republicans among the more advanced Virginia Conservatives.

One of the most remarkable features of that strategy was Ulysses S. Grant's continuing popularity in some Conservative circles. In 1874, Beverley Tucker and the Richmond *Dispatch*, as well as some of Kemper's advisors, regarded the president as a valuable ally in his racial and Southern policies.[108] In 1875, another Conservative, grateful for Grant's assistance in the crisis of 1869, warned others not to denounce hastily his intervention in Louisiana.[109] Logan, in 1877, described Grant and Hayes as representatives of "the best

104. Rutherford B. Hayes to Alexander H. H. Stuart, May 16, 1879, Alexander Hugh Holmes Stuart Papers, University of Virginia.

105. Alderman and Gordon, *Curry*, pp. 234–39, 242–43.

106. Petersburg *Index and Appeal*, August 10, 1877.

107. Morrill, *Builder of the New South*, pp. 123–25; Thomas M. Logan, "The Political Problem in the United States," Volume 3, Thomas Muldrup Logan Papers, pp. 5–12. Southern Historical Collection, University of North Carolina at Chapel Hill.

108. Petersburg *Index and Appeal*, August 11, 1874; (Nathaniel) Beverley Tucker to J. Randolph Tucker, n.d., [1874; only last four pages extant], Tucker Family Papers.

109. Alexandria *Virginia Sentinel*, January 10, 1875.

element of the liberal Republicans."[110] At the beginning of 1880, Dr. Richard A. Wise (a son of Henry A. Wise) announced at a session of the Conservative State Committee that he would prefer Grant to Tilden as president.[111] George W. Bagby attacked Wise for the statement—but Bagby himself was then trying to recover letters in which he had suggested re-electing Grant for a third term. E. S. Gregory, a Lynchburg newspaperman, thought that "some of the best people" in Virginia secretly shared that wish.[112] To a surprising degree, General Grant had conquered the hearts as well as the bodies of many former Confederates in Virginia.

During the fifteen years after 1865, Conservatives who had been Confederates adapted themselves to the United States as it had become and to contemporary Northern ideas of state-federal relations. The process required a painful readjustment of past to present loyalties, but most Conservatives managed to reduce their internal dissonance to a bearable level.

A telling index of adaptation was the Conservatives' role in national party politics. Even participating in the Democratic party required former Confederates to become "reconstructed" to a degree. The Virginia Conservatives, however, went farther. Hoping for the emergence of a moderate national party that would include moderate Republicans, they hesitated to identify themselves wholly with the Democratic party. Some of their foremost leaders, feeling a community of interest with Northern businessmen and professional men, repeatedly put out feelers to moderate Northern elements of the Republican party. Each attempt at rapprochement, nevertheless, foundered between the Scylla of the Radical Republicans and the Charybdis of the traditionalist Democrats.

Those Conservatives who sought party connections with conservative Northern Republicans were not entirely unrealistic. Some Northern Republicans, too, found it anomalous that their party consisted in the North of respectable, propertied moderates, and in the South of blacks and poor whites, corruptionists and wild-eyed Radicals. They, too, saw the logic of an alliance with Southern con-

110. Logan, "Political Problem in the United States," Volume 3, Logan Papers, p. 9.
111. [George W. Bagby], *John Brown and Wm. Mahone (1860–1880): An Historical Parallel, Foreshadowing Civil Trouble* (Richmond: C. F. Johnston, 1880), p. 15.
112. E. S. Gregory to George W. Bagby, January 14, 1880, Bagby Papers.

servatives who were adapting to industrial capitalism.[113] The projectors of the alliance did not err in discerning a long-term trend, but they did overestimate the rate at which the Northern-dominated nation was absorbing the South into its economic and political system. In the twentieth century, the appearance of a coalition between conservative Southern Democrats and Northern Republicans belatedly fulfilled the anticipations of many Virginia Conservative leaders of the 1870's.

113. Vincent P. De Santis, *Republicans Face the Southern Question: The New Departure Years, 1877–1897* ("Johns Hopkins University Studies in Historical and Political Science," LXXVII, No. 1 [Baltimore: The Johns Hopkins Press, 1959]), p. 88 (hereafter cited as *Republicans*); C. Vann Woodward, *Reunion and Reaction: The Compromise of 1877 and the End of Reconstruction* (New York: Little, Brown and Company, 1951), pp. 34–36 (hereafter cited as *Reunion and Reaction*).

10.

The Politics of Transportation

The influence of railroad companies pervaded the Virginia Conservatives' politics. "Redemption" ushered in a second "railroad era" for the Old Dominion.[1] Like the "railroad era" of the 1830's, the 1870's witnessed many promotional projects and much talk about railroading. Unlike the first era, it occasioned little new construction and a disappearance of state regulation. Another new characteristic was fierce conflict between established companies to control additional mileage, in which the contenders tried to use the state's power as a weapon in the fray. The promoters of the first railroad era had sought to help agriculturists market crops; the promoters of the second sought to organize channels for national trade and to open mineral resources to exploitation. The first era had created short, independent intrastate lines; the second combined old lines into interstate trunk lines, for whose control native Virginians engaged in unequal combat with Northern interlopers. Legislative chambers were often the arenas of the contest.

THE CONTEXT OF RAILROAD POLITICS

Despite an abundance of talk about new railroads, Governor Kemper in 1875 knew of no significant railroad construction in progress in Virginia.[2] During the 1870's, rail mileage increased only from 1,449 miles to 1,893.[3] The lack of construction was not sur-

1. See John D. Imboden, "Virginia," in *Report on the Internal Commerce of the United States, December 20, 1886, Appendix: The Commercial, Industrial, Transportation, and Other Interests of the Southern States*, House Document 7, Part II, 49 Cong., 2 Sess., 1886, p. 22 (hereafter cited as *Imboden Report, 1886*).

2. Meade C. Kemper (for James L. Kemper) to C. Maxwell Beach (copy), May 19, 1875, James Lawson Kemper Executive Letter-Book (1874–75), Virginia State Library.

3. Allen W. Moger, "Railroad Practices and Policies in Virginia after the Civil War," *Virginia Magazine of History and Biography*, LIX (October, 1951), 448n (hereafter cited as "Railroad Practices"). Mileage had increased by about a hundred miles between 1865 and 1870. Smith, "Virginia during Reconstruction," p. 258.

prising. The antebellum public works program had already provided service for most natural trade routes. Virginia railroads lacked financial resources. Even in the year that preceded the ruinous Panic of 1873, only two railroad companies in the state paid dividends.[4] The impoverished companies often had to repair war damage before they could extend their track. The Northern trunk lines, which could afford to expand, preferred to buy existing lines at depressed prices rather than build new ones.

Although new railroads were often imaginary, enthusiasm for them abounded. As the rail network matured, localities off the railroad routes recognized their disadvantage. Without a railroad, General Imboden predicted, Mecklenburg County would "become literally a wilderness in a few years more."[5] One of Imboden's friends "would like very much to live in So[uth] West Va. if there was a R. R. communication with the United States" but vowed that he would "never go out of the world but in one way."[6] Pleas and subsidies from desperate communities strangely deflected projected routes.[7] Small-town dreamers planned to run great national thoroughfares through their neighborhoods. Such a project was the "Washington, Cincinnati and St. Louis Railroad." The town of Harrisonburg subscribed its capital of fifty thousand dollars, and Senator Johnston and Representative John T. Harris introduced bills in its behalf in Congress. In 1873, during its only spurt of construction, the force at work numbered ten men. Construction ceased the following year, and the few miles of track around Harrisonburg lay untouched for a decade.[8] "We are . . . assured that the railway is really coming," a resident of another part of western Virginia wrote. "But that has been said so many times that I shall not believe it till I see the trains running."[9]

Not only towns and counties, but the capital city itself, became subservient to railroads' policies. In 1871, the Chesapeake and Ohio Railroad's directors declined the Richmond City Council's offer of $200,000 to build the Church Hill tunnel as too niggardly. The council at once met in special session, greatly increased the offer,

4. Petersburg *Index and Appeal*, October 27, 1873.

5. John D. Imboden to Annie Lockett, December 25, 1870, John Daniel Imboden Papers, University of Virginia.

6. B. Desha Harmon to Imboden, September 11, 1875, *ibid.*

7. Harmon to Imboden, August 27, 1872, *ibid.*

8. Wayland, *Rockingham County*, pp. 159, 230–31; *Cong. Globe*, 42 Cong., 3 Sess., 25, 897, 1308, 2082 (1873). Rockbridge County issued $400,000 in bonds for railroads that never materialized. Moger, "Railroad Practices," p. 450.

9. [Allan-Olney], *New Virginians*, II, 123.

and rescinded the conditions it had originally attached.[10] Despite a shocking accident rate in constructing the tunnel, the city coroner denied in 1873 that he had any authority to investigate charges of company negligence.[11] Cities customarily approved and underwrote companies' proposals without themselves taking initiative for planning.

Although the state no longer assisted railroads financially, it showed little more independence of the companies than city governments did. Many Virginians complained that their legislatures took up most of each session with transportation companies' applications for special favors and that they granted almost every application for a charter.[12] The Petersburg *Index* calculated that a fourth of the 1871–73 General Assembly's measures were charters, or amendments to charters, of private companies.[13] The antebellum tests—publicly expressed popular demand and provision of manifest public need—ceased to be applied.[14] Stuart, as chairman of the appropriate committee of the state Senate, introduced and withdrew railroad bills at the companies' behests.[15] The railroad lobby became, a critic charged, "as palpable, as undisguised a fact as the Capitol, and far more energetic than the Legislature on whose body it flourishes[,] a foul fungus."[16]

The railroad pass served as an instrument of corporate influence. General Mahone's Atlantic, Mississippi and Ohio Railroad gave legislators passes only as long as they voted in its interest. John M. Robinson—president of the Richmond, Fredericksburg and Potomac, and of the Seaboard and Roanoke Railroad—wrote off as "deadbeats" politicians who accepted passes without assisting his companies politically.[17] Even apart from such favoritism, critics of the

10. *Daily Petersburg Index*, November 30 and December 25, 1871.

11. *Ibid.*, January 16 and April 30, 1873.

12. *Ibid.*, January 1, 1872, and January 7, 1873; Governor's Message, March 8, 1870, *Senate Journal* (1869–70), p. 162; Governor's Message, December 2, 1874, *Senate Journal* (1874–75), pp. 19–21.

13. *Daily Petersburg Index*, April 8, 1873.

14. See [Robert Ould], *Speech of Judge Robt. Ould before the Senate Committee on Roads and Internal Navigation, on the Application of Mr. Reuben Ragland for an Amendment to the Charter of the Petersburg Railroad Company, Delivered February 15, 1873* (Richmond: Clemmitt and Jones, 1873), pp. 5–6 (hereafter cited as *Ould Speech, 1873*).

15. Richard F. Walker to William Mahone, February 7, 1874, William Mahone Papers, Duke University.

16. *Daily Petersburg Index*, January 7, 1873.

17. Richard F. Walker to William Mahone, October 6, 1874; Walker to Mahone, December 12, 1874; and John M. Robinson to Mahone, November 10, 1876, all in Mahone Papers.

system pointed out, passes subtly influenced the recipients—as well as defrauding the state of mileage compensation, encouraging absenteeism, and giving legislators special privileges.[18] Governor Kemper wanted to outlaw the practice, but he himself accepted passes.[19]

The Commonwealth's power to regulate railroads declined rapidly after 1865. The Board of Public Works customarily let companies select proxies to vote the state's stock in their boards, and the state undermined the board's regulatory influence by selling most of its railroad stock. The railroads increasingly ignored the board's remaining regulatory functions. By 1877, many had ceased even to file the required annual reports. William D. Chesterman concluded that "the State has no rights railroads are bound to respect" and that executives "look to the Board as their instructor, guide and friend, and don't want to be bothered by the State."[20] The board's atrophy gave the companies a free hand. Legislative suasion availed little: Judge John Lyon, attorney for the Petersburg Railroad, told a legislative committee that one could place no confidence in railroad officials' promises. The Chesapeake and Ohio disregarded the conditions that the state had attached to its formation.[21]

To restore a measure of regulation Governor Kemper proposed, at the end of 1874, the creation of a state commission to study and supervise railroads' practices. The law, he thought, should forbid higher freight rates for short hauls than for longer ones on the same lines and should regulate rates in noncompetitive areas. If ordinary means of enforcement should prove inadequate, the state should maintain a police on each line at the company's expense and should imprison violators.[22] Soon afterward Robert Ould, an attorney for John M. Robinson's railroads, introduced a railroad-commission bill in the House of Delegates. Almost all the companies united to oppose the measure. The House passed the commission bill, but the Senate committee reported adversely and the proposal died.[23] In

18. Richmond *Dispatch*, April 20, 1875.
19. Meade C. Kemper (for James L. Kemper) to John M. Robinson (copy), January 29, 1874, and M. C. Kemper (for J. L. Kemper) to Robinson (copy), February 2, 1875, both in Kemper Executive Letter-Book (1874–75), Virginia State Library.
20. Petersburg *Index and Appeal*, February 21, 1877.
21. *Ould Speech, 1873*, pp. 21, 29–30; *Senate Journal* (1876–77), Document XIII: *Communication from the Governor of Virginia in relation to the State's Interest in the Chesapeake and Ohio Railroad*, pp. 1–5, and Document XIV: *Contract Made between the State of Virginia and Huntington & Co. in regard to the Chesapeake and Ohio Railroad*, pp. 1–3.
22. Governor's Message, December 2, 1874, *Senate Journal* (1874), pp. 14–15.
23. Richard F. Walker to William Mahone, February 19, 1875; Walker to Mahone,

1877, the General Assembly did enact a law providing for one commissioner, to receive his compensation from the companies, with only nominal data-collecting functions.[24] The arrangement only caricatured the regulatory agency the governor had proposed.

Railroad companies paid only a pittance in taxes. In the year 1870–71, public-service corporations paid only $2,982 in all.[25] "Two years' taxes," Governor Walker informed the General Assembly, "are now due and uncollected from all of the most important railroads in the state. Some few of them shield themselves under some pretense of exemption from taxation by their charters, and others have no excuse at all." Pointing out that the state had chartered the corporations and burdened itself with debt to build their roads, Walker asked the legislature to repeal charter exemptions from taxation.[26] The General Assembly contented itself with levying a new tax of five mills per dollar on railroad bonds. However, the courts invalidated that tax insofar as it applied to nonresidents, and the legislature repealed it in 1874.[27]

The Commonwealth brought suit against the railroads that refused to pay taxes. The most conspicuous offender was the Chesapeake and Ohio, which General Williams C. Wickham had organized in 1868 by combining the Virginia Central and the Covington and Ohio Railroads. By 1870, the national railroad magnate Collis P. Huntington actually controlled the company.[28] Citing the Covington and Ohio's charter exemption and a state pledge not to tax the Virginia Central until its yearly earnings should exceed 10 per cent, the C. and O. held out until 1876, when the Supreme Court of the United States found it liable for taxes on the former Virginia Central line.[29] Newspapers estimated the company's back taxes for

---

February 20, 1875; Thomas N. Conrad to Mahone, February 22, 1875; Joseph R. Anderson to Mahone, February 27, 1875; Walker to Mahone, March 3, 1875; Walker to Mahone, March 5, 1875; C. B. Duffield to Mahone, March 11, 1875, all in Mahone Papers.

24. Vecellio, "Daniel," pp. 141–42.

25. Robert C. Burton, "The History of Taxation in Virginia, 1870–1901" (Ph.D. dissertation, University of Virginia, 1962), pp. 66–67 (hereafter cited as "Taxation").

26. Governor's Message, December 6, 1871, *Senate Journal* (1871–72), p. 29.

27. Burton, "Taxation," pp. 68, 70.

28. John F. Stover, *The Railroads of the South, 1865–1900: A Study in Finance and Control* (Chapel Hill: University of North Carolina Press, 1955), pp. 126–27 (hereafter cited as *Railroads of the South*).

29. *Senate Journal* (1871–72), Document XI: *Correspondence between the Auditor of Public Accounts and the President of the Chesapeake and Ohio Railroad Co. relative to the Taxation of the Company*, pp. 1–4; *Chesapeake and Ohio Railroad Company v. Virginia*, 94 U. S. 718–27 (1876).

eight years at $273,000, but it compromised with the state for $98,487.97.[30]

Officially, railroads were liable for the property tax (five mills per dollar), a tax of five mills per dollar on net earnings, and an additional five mills per dollar on net earnings exceeding a thousand dollars. From 1870 until 1880, nevertheless, public service corporations paid only $477,810—less than 2 per cent of all taxes the state collected. The most important factor contributing to the anomaly was not charter exemption but the law that permitted the companies to assess their own property for taxation.[31] The Conservative government did not seriously try to plug such loopholes.

Local governments were even less successful than the Commonwealth in taxing railroad property. Most did not even try. In 1872, the Supreme Court of Appeals ruled that a state grant of tax exemption included exemption from county taxes.[32] Six years later, the court decided in addition that the self-assessment system, by excluding railroad property from county assessments, precluded local governments from taxing it at all.[33] The General Assembly failed to act to restore county taxation of railroads.[34]

As they cast off public ownership, regulation, and taxation, the railroads also changed in their economic functions. Many promoters of the first Virginia "railroad era" had thought of the roads chiefly as facilities to market crops. By the early 1870's, the railroads were increasingly functioning to develop mining and manufacturing, rather than agriculture.[35] In contrast with the popularity of railroad development, Virginia shamefully neglected the public roads that growers needed for access to the railheads. A traveler, Edward A. Pollard pointed out, might step down "from swift, luxurious cars, [to find] naught of a road but the red galled strip . . . that served thirty or even fifty years ago the limited needs of the pioneer and the fieldhand."[36] Consequently, descendants of pioneers and fieldhands wondered what benefit the railroads conferred on them. The exchange of goods by rail, the Virginia Agricultural Society com-

30. Staunton *Vindicator*, May 11, 1877; Burton, "Taxation," p. 71n.

31. Burton, "Taxation," pp. 67–68, 70–71.

32. *City of Richmond* v. *Richmond and Danville Railroad Company*, 21 Gratt. 605–18 (1872).

33. *Virginia and Tennessee Railroad Company* v. *Washington County*, 30 Gratt. 471–86 (1878).

34. Vecellio, "Daniel," pp. 198–200.

35. See Governor's Message, December 4, 1872, *Senate Journal* (1872–73), p. 22.

36. Edward A. Pollard, "New Virginia," *Old and New*, V (March, 1872), 289 (hereafter cited as "New Virginia").

plained, might make Richmond a Cairo and Norfolk an Alexandria
—but "the country beyond, for any good railroads and canals can do
it, will be as barren as the sands of Egypt." Indeed, the railroads
harmed the Virginia farmer by introducing western competition.[37]

Another sweeping change was the enlarged scale of Reconstruction railroading. Antebellum entrepreneurs had constructed short,
independent lines; their postbellum successors consolidated those
lines, trying to put together interstate trunk lines. Collis P. Huntington worked to build a transcontinental rail empire by combining
the C. and O. with his western holdings. Thomas A. Scott of the
Pennsylvania Central and John W. Garrett of the Baltimore and
Ohio hoped to make their respective railroads the arteries for commerce between the industrial Northeast and the agricultural South.
Virginians William Mahone and John Moncure Robinson took
pride in their independence of out-of-state control. Nevertheless,
Mahone wanted to make his Atlantic, Mississippi and Ohio a trunk
line to tap the West, and Robinson dedicated his two lines to the
same role in the South Atlantic states.

The encroaching "foreign railroads" naturally came into conflict with Mahone's and Robinson's "Virginia railroads," which
posed as champions of Virginia interests resisting Northern invasion. General Mahone, the arch-foe of "foreign railroads," claimed
that his company recognized a responsibility to the Old Dominion
which no Northern concern could.[38] One of Mahone's correspondents marveled that "so many of our Virginia people could carry a
musket and fight through a fierce war for our integrity; and then . . .
shoulder northern Railways and fight for their commercial & financial enslavement. . . ."[39] Robert Ould described his client Robinson's railroads as "a breakwater against the sweeping flood of a
foreign invasion."[40] In 1877, a group of Augusta County farmers
protested that, because of "foreign" ownership,

The railroad system in Virginia has ceased to be a Virginia interest at
all. . . . Under this system the vast resources of Virginia are not going to
help to build her up, but as far as her true interests are concerned might

37. *Memorial of the Virginia State Agricultural Society on Immigration, Presented
to the General Assembly of Virginia, January 10th, 1872* (n.p., [1872]), p. 9 (hereafter
cited as *Agricultural Society Immigration Memorial, 1872*).
38. Blake, *Mahone*, p. 117; William Mahone to Harrison H. Riddleberger, June 6,
1875, Harrison Holt Riddleberger Papers, College of William and Mary.
39. C. R. Boyd to Mahone, May 31, 1875, Mahone Papers.
40. *Ould Speech, 1873*, p. 21.

as well be set down to the credit of other States. . . . These railroad owners in Virginia are as alien to her interests as if they lived in Holland. Have we nothing to fear from the influence of foreign gold and foreign bonds in shaping our state policy? To manipulate these roads in certain ways, must they not manipulate the State government?[41]

Not everyone saw it thus. Many Virginians did not believe their own interests were at stake in railroad rivalries and found "native" railroads no less alien to their needs than "foreign" ones. Besides, the Northerners commanded ample capital, and the "Virginia railroads" lacked funds to carry out their professed good intentions. Northern-controlled railroads, Thomas M. Logan thought, would afford Virginians the means to enrich themselves.[42]

The appearance of the question of "native" and "foreign" railroads depended, of course, on whose ox was being gored. The Pennsylvania Central adjusted its policy to the latitude, in Virginia preaching "free railroads" but in New Jersey invoking its charter privileges to keep out intruding competitors.[43] Mahone and Robinson, too, wanted to extend their power as "foreign capitalists" into adjoining states to benefit their Virginia interests. North Carolinians complained of oppression by Virginia-controlled railroads such as Robinson's.[44]

On fields of business and of government, rival executives did battle during the 1870's for control of trade routes. The contest was fierce, and for a time the advantage alternated between natives and Northerners. The latter group's victory marked an epoch in the region's transportation history.

SOUTHSIDE CONSOLIDATION AND FREE RAILROADS, 1870–1871

The effects of the War forced Virginia politicians to reconsider the antebellum public-works policy. In 1865, the Board of Public Works still held about half the capital stock of the principal railroads.[45] The state had no means to assist the companies in their task of rebuilding. For several years, Governor Letcher and others had suggested that the state sell its railroad assets.[46] Governor Pier-

---

41. Staunton *Vindicator*, May 25, 1877.
42. Morrill, *Builder of the New South*, pp. 94–95.
43. *Ould Speech, 1873*, p. 27.
44. C. P. Mebane to George W. Bagby, May 31, 1878, George William Bagby Papers, Virginia Historical Society.
45. Johnston, *Virginia Railroads*, p. 258.
46. Ours, "Redeemer Legislature," pp. 71–72; Boney, *Letcher*, p. 196.

pont proposed to consolidate the lines into a few privately owned systems. Hesitating to reverse the traditional policy, the Baldwin legislature gave several companies permission, under strict conditions, to buy the state stock in their lines and to consolidate. The Underwood convention terminated an era by forbidding in its constitution state financial assistance to transportation works.[47] In 1870, Virginia's future railroad policy was an open question.

The first inning was General Mahone's. In 1865, the general had returned to the presidency of the Norfolk and Petersburg and had become president also of the South Side Railroad from Petersburg to Lynchburg. Planning a trunk line to the West, he coveted the Virginia and Tennessee, from Lynchburg to Bristol, but most of its directors preferred to keep their informal relationship with the Orange and Alexandria. In 1867, Mahone received from the Baldwin legislature a charter that allowed his two lines, the Virginia and Tennessee, and the paper Virginia and Kentucky, to consolidate into the Atlantic, Mississippi and Ohio Railroad, whose name indicated the scale of the general's ambition. In November, 1867, Mahone finally won control of the Virginia and Tennessee, but he failed to complete the financial arrangements that the charter stipulated by May 1, 1868, and the act became inoperative. Undaunted, the general threw himself into Reconstruction politics. In the 1869 contest, he helped to elect a large number of sympathetic public officials.[48]

In the spring of 1870, Mahone's platoon of lobbyists went to work in the first Conservative legislature, using alcoholic and monetary arguments as well as verbal ones. The B. and O.'s agents retaliated, opposing the proposed consolidation. The House approved Mahone's charter by eighty-four votes to thirty-three, and the Senate, by twenty-six to sixteen, most members voting in accordance with their districts' railroad interests.[49] The new charter, more generous than the 1867 one, appointed commissioners to organize the A. M. and O. with a capital stock of $25,000,000 and to exchange shares on a voluntary basis with stockholders in the component lines. The merger would go into effect only when the commissioners should acquire a majority of the private stock in three of the companies.

47. Pearson, *Readjuster Movement,* pp. 13–14; Thorpe, ed., *Constitutions,* VII, 3894–95.
48. Blake, *Mahone,* pp. 72–87.
49. *Ibid.,* pp. 111–15; Moger, "Railroad Practices," p. 433; Ours, "Redeemer Legislature," pp. 49, 54, 56, 64–65.

Once the A. M. and O. should organize, the Board of Public Works would sell it the state's stock in the four companies. The A. M. and O. promised to complete the Virginia and Kentucky line, from Bristol to Cumberland Gap, in six years, and to pay the Commonwealth four million dollars in money or depreciated state bonds, securing the payment by a second mortage on its property. It might execute a first mortgage for as much as fifteen million dollars.[50]

The Baltimore interests made a last attempt to keep the Virginia and Tennessee link out of Mahone's control, by means of a stockholder suit. James E. Tyson of Baltimore, who had bought most of his unconverted V. and T. shares after the A. M. and O.'s formation, sued Mahone for consolidating the V. and T. with other roads without the stockholders' consent. Mahone had prepared for that eventuality by drafting his charter so as to organize the A. M. and O. by stockholders' voluntary action. Although the new company by November, 1871, owned two-thirds of the V. and T.'s shares and nearly all issued by the other companies, it kept separate accounts for each line, and a stockholder who declined to convert his shares could claim only a nebulous "injury." In view of these facts, federal judges Alexander Rives and Hugh L. Bond ruled that the A. M. and O. was operating quite legally.[51]

Enjoying legislative and judicial approval, General Mahone went to work to put his railroads in good running order. Initially, the roads were in poor condition and their stock, before consolidation, sold at a small fraction of face value.[52] The general repaired the roads and reinvigorated their operations. He improved their plant, safety record, rate of speed, and volume of traffic; he also reduced their operating expenses in proportion to revenue and made a good start toward paying their heavy debts.[53] He was unable, however, to accumulate the financial resources to put his project

50. Blake, *Mahone*, pp. 115–16.
51. *Tyson v. Virginia and Tennessee Railroad Company et al.*, 24 Federal Cases 493–97 (1871); *Daily Petersburg Index*, November 17, 1871.
52. *Senate Journal* (1872–73), Document XIX: *Report of Committee on Roads and Internal Navigation in response to Resolutions offered by the Senator from Scott and Russell concerning the Atlantic, Mississippi and Ohio Railroad Company*, p. 4 (hereafter cited as *Senate A. M. & O. Report, 1873*).
53. *The Case of the Foreign Bondholders and the Atlantic, Mississippi and Ohio R. R. Co.: The Answer of the Company and Accompanying Documents; Correspondence between General William Mahone, President, and John Collinson, Agent of the Company; also, General Mahone's Letter to Captain Tyler, Who Presided over the Meeting of Foreign Bondholders in London, &c., &c., &c.* (Richmond: n.p., 1876), pp. 7–11 (hereafter cited as *Case of Foreign Bondholders, 1876*).

on firm ground. This lack hampered his hope of westward extension and his battle against northern interests, and eventually it weakened even his grip on the A. M. and O.

While Mahone advanced in long strides, his Northern rivals outdistanced him with seven-league boots. The state government made their work easier by abandoning the mixed-enterprise tradition. For thirty years, Northern states had been transferring state-related banks, railroads, and canals to private owners. In 1865, *laissez faire* came to Virginia, too. Northern creditors, aided by Virginia bankers and lawyers, persuaded federal courts to entrust the state-related banks to receivers sympathetic to the Northern interests. The receiverships disbanded the banks, sending nearly all their remaining assets northward. Since the War's effects rendered worthless the deposits the state required from private banks, *laissez faire* reigned supreme in Virginia banking by 1870.[54] By that time, many Conservatives appreciated the case for private enterprise in transportation as well. In railroading as in banking, *laissez faire* and Northern economic penetration went hand in hand.

In March, 1870, Governor Walker commended to the legislature the laissez-faire ideas he had learned on Northern soil. Old Virginia's public-works policy, he stated, had been a costly error. State investment, he thought, was always unwise. It had artificially stimulated needless and unprofitable works, but private capitalists would have built the really necessary ones without state aid. The mixed-enterprise system combined the worst features of private and public ownership. Now, in 1870, Virginia had few assets to show for her folly. Government intervention in business, Walker thought, usually resulted in disaster. As a solution, he proposed the "free railroad" policy that Northeastern states had originated: to sell the state's railroad stock to private companies and to adopt a general-incorporation system that would give every company that complied with uniform procedures a charter to build a railroad, without special privileges. "Wherever," Walker said, "a railroad, or a canal, or a transportation company is needed, and people can be found who will invest the necessary capital, let the enterprise be organized and completed."[55]

54. *Senate Journal* (October session, 1870), Document IV: *Report of the Senate Committee on Banks relative to the Condition of the Virginia Banks at the Close of the Late War, and the Disposition of Their Assets: together with the Testimony Taken by the Committee, November, 1870,* pp. 3–15; *Steger Report, 1874,* p. 10.
55. Governor's Message, March 3, 1870, *Senate Journal* (1869–70), pp. 143–51, 162.

General Mahone stood to lose greatly from a "free railroad" policy, which would enable the Northern trunk lines to use their superior resources to full advantage. Ironically, Mahone in his 1870 effort had provided a precedent for those who would supplant him, both in his lobbying methods and in the provision of his charter which sold large amounts of state stock to the A. M. and O. on lenient terms. "Gen. Mahone . . . taught what could be done," the Staunton *Spectator* commented, "and 'what man has done, man can do.' "⁵⁶ The contest had begun in earnest.

Governor Walker, now siding with the Pennsylvania Central against Mahone, began the General Assembly session of 1870–71 with another plea for "free railroads."⁵⁷ Lobbyists for the Pennsylvania Central and the Baltimore and Ohio—including General Imboden and the governor's brother James Walker—promoted a bill for general sale of the state's railroad stock. The state's revenue needs and the lobbyists' lavish entertainment convinced the legislators. They passed the bill on March 28, and the governor signed it with some misgivings about its extremely generous terms.⁵⁸ The measure excited much public controversy. The *Whig*, expressing Mahone's views, thought it "ineffable infamy" to sell Virginia's "commercial independence and political autonomy, to a foreign corporation." The *Dispatch*, on the other hand, predicted a few months later that the "free railroad" policy would "in a few years put Virginia on the way to development and power which could never have been opened to her under the form of wasteful expenditure before the war."⁵⁹

Northern companies bought up the most desirable blocs of state stock at once. The Baltimore and Ohio purchased the state shares in the Orange and Alexandria Railroad, and the Southern Railway Security Company—a front for Tom Scott's Pennsylvania Central— acquired the Richmond and Danville and the Richmond and Petersburg shares. Mahone offered $200 a share for the R. and P. stock, but the Commonwealth sold to the Security Company at

56. Quoted in Jones, "Conservative Virginian," p. 141n.

57. Cahill, "Walker," pp. 80–84; Governor's Message, December 7, 1870, *Senate Journal* (1870–71), p. 25.

58. Moger, "Railroad Practices," pp. 438–39; Pearson, *Readjuster Movement*, pp. 28–29; John D. Imboden to Annie Lockett, February 21, 1871, Imboden Papers; *House Journal* (1871–72), p. 298; Cahill, "Walker," pp. 75–80; Ours, "Redeemer Legislature," pp. 84–90, 92–93, 95–96; Richard F. Walker to William Mahone, January 5, 1871, and Walker to Mahone, January 6, 1871, both in Mahone Papers.

59. Both quoted in Ours, "Redeemer Legislature," pp. 81–82, 99.

$150 after it learned that the general intended to pay out of the fund he had pledged for his debt to the state.[60] To console Mahone, the legislature authorized him to build a branch line to Richmond, but he lacked the money to do so.[61] Governor Walker had predicted that the stock sale would pay much of the state debt, but by 1874 the state had collected only $3,739,225.69 in state bonds from the sale. Virginia, General Imboden calculated in 1886, lost $10,982,773 on its antebellum investment in the sale of its railroad stock.[62]

The great beneficiary of the sales was the Pennsylvania Central's mushrooming rail empire in the South. By the end of 1871, the Southern Railway Security Company controlled eight Southern railroads, including the two Virginia acquistions, aggregating 1,191 miles. The company had paid only $3,478,850 to acquire control of the lines, which had cost about $32,000,000 to construct and which yielded net earnings of $1,461,208. A year later, at its peak of expansion, the company controlled thirteen Southern lines and 2,131 miles. The Richmond and Danville was a crucial link, since it was the northernmost segment connected with the bulk of the network and controlled the Atlanta and Richmond Air Line and the North Carolina Railroad.[63] After 1871, the Pennsylvania Central displaced the B. and O. as the principal Northern force in Virginia railroading, and Garrett joined Mahone in an uneasy entente against the Pennsylvania "Bucktails."[64]

"VIRGINIA RAILROADS" *vs.* "BUCKTAILS," 1872–1877

During the mid-1870's, railroad rivalries grew so fiercely competitive as to eliminate one contestant, General Mahone, entirely. No single interest won all that it desired, but an increase of Northern control was the general result. All players used political capitalism as a weapon, but the wealthier usually prevailed in the legislature as well as the countinghouse.

After 1871, Scott's Southern Railway Security Company controlled the direct rail routes from Richmond to Atlanta, Augusta,

60. Moger, "Railroad Practices," pp. 439–40; Vecellio, "Daniel," pp. 73–76.
61. *Senate Journal* (1870–71), pp. 43, 50, 54–57, 65.
62. *Steger Report, 1874*, p. 22; *Imboden Report, 1886*, pp. 75–77.
63. *Ould Speech, 1873*, pp. 26–27; Stover, *Railroads of the South*, pp. 106, 110–13, 118.
64. Stover, *Railroads of the South*, pp. 108–9; Blake, *Mahone*, p. 123; Jones, "Conservative Virginian," p. 288.

and Charleston, South Carolina. It then lacked only a route from Richmond to Washington to bind the principal Southeastern cities, by way of the Pennsylvania Central, to the principal Northeastern cities. "The keys are now in Virginia's girdle," Robert Ould declared. "Will she surrender them to the foreigner . . .?"[65] In 1871, the General Assembly approved a charter for a Richmond and Washington Railway Company, under Pennsylvania Central control, but attached to it amendments that rendered the road's construction uneconomical.[66] Colonel Sutherlin, a friend of the "Bucktails," perennially proposed a bill to complete the "free railroad" policy by adopting general incorporation. That measure, which would leave Scott's interests free to build a Richmond-Washington road, had little success.[67] The Security Company did acquire control of the Alexandria and Fredericksburg Railroad and completed its line from Alexandria to Quantico. At Quantico, however, its strained relations with the Richmond, Fredericksburg and Potomac Railroad limited through traffic to a single train each night.[68]

In trying to close their Quantico-Richmond gap, the Bucktails had to contend with John M. Robinson, whose Richmond, Fredericksburg and Potomac monopolized the Richmond-Washington rail route. Robinson operated the R. F. and P. mainly as a passenger road, developing his Seaboard and Roanoke line as part of a freight route that continued north from Norfolk by sea. The Pennsylvania interests tried through intermediaries to buy the R. F. and P., but Robinson discovered the principals' identity and determined to block their designs.[69]

In 1873, Reuben Ragland of Petersburg offered the Pennsylvania Central yet another chance to complete its network. Ragland and others bought the uneconomical Petersburg Railroad, which ran southward from that city into North Carolina, as a speculation to sell to some Northern company as a link for its route. When he found no takers, Ragland hit upon a plan to make his white elephant worth the Pennsylvania Central's trouble. The General Assembly would not authorize the Northern company to complete its

65. *Ould Speech, 1873*, pp. 26–27.

66. Moger, "Railroad Practices," p. 440.

67. Richmond *Daily Whig*, January 12, 1872; *Daily Petersburg Index*, January 7 and 10, 1873; Richard F. Walker to William Mahone, January 11, 1877, Mahone Papers.

68. Stover, *Railroads of the South*, p. 105; Petersburg *Index and Appeal*, November 21, 1873, and December 29, 1875.

69. *Ould Speech, 1873*, pp. 14–16, 18–23.

gap—but perhaps it would authorize the Petersburg Railroad to build a line to the Potomac. Claiming that the R. F. and P. would not transport cotton from his line northward at a reasonable rate, Ragland applied for a charter to extend his road. Robert Ould, the R. F. and P.'s attorney, pointed out that Robinson's rates were lower than Ragland's and that Ragland co-operated with the Bucktail lines to give Northern merchants rate advantages over Virginia ones. The legislature refused Ragland's request, and the Petersburg Railroad lost its meteoric prominence in the arena of political capitalism. Ragland "must be losing money on his road," Robinson wrote in 1874, "& he is worrying every one with whom he has business relations. He worries me less than might be expected."[70]

General Mahone might envy Robinson's secure position. Soon after he won his charter, the Southern Railway Security Company acquired the East Tennesssee, Virginia and Georgia Railroad, on which Mahone had counted for connections west of Bristol. The general also failed to secure the out-of-state connections he would need for his proposed Cumberland Gap extension. By thwarting Mahone's search for western connections, the Bucktails made the A. M. and O. a "Virginia Railroad" in a sense its founder had not intended.[71] They also menaced Mahone on his home ground, taking a hand in Flournoy's and Imboden's unsuccessful project for a Norfolk and Great Western line directly from Norfolk to Bristol.[72] Mahone stole a march on his foe by making it cheaper for Richmonders, in some cases, to ship goods down the river to Norfolk, then west by the A. M. and O., than to use the Richmond and Danville. The Bucktails gained ground, however, in 1872, when the Adams Express Company and its subsidiary Southern Express Company, losing their contract for the old V. and T. line, joined the coalition against Mahone. The express companies discontinued freight interchanges with the A. M. and O., and the Richmond and Petersburg and the Richmond and Danville made no arrangements for interchanges. The result was a virtual blockade on express service between Richmond and points on Mahone's route.[73]

70. *Ibid.*, pp. 6–9, 13–14, 24–30; *Daily Petersburg Index*, January 8, 10, and 15, 1873; John M. Robinson to William Mahone, October 17, 1874, Mahone Papers.

71. Stover, *Railroads of the South*, pp. 114–16; *Ould Speech, 1873*, p. 28; *Senate Journal* (1874), p. 210.

72. Stover, *Railroads of the South*, p. 109; Moger, "Railroad Practices," p. 449.

73. [William Mahone], *The Express Question: Correspondence between a Committee of Business Men of Richmond, and Wm. Mahone, President, Atlantic, Mississippi & Ohio R. R. Co., with an Appendix* (n.p.,[1874]), pp. 8–21.

Both the contending parties appreciated the value of political power to advance their interests. The "Executive and Legislative power," Mahone observed, were "the pass to the situation."[74] In the political game, however, the general's enemies held a trump card: the provision of the A. M. and O. charter that required the company to build an extension to Cumberland Gap by 1876. In 1873, the A. M. and O., lacking the Kentucky connections necessary to justify the extension, had not commenced it. Mahone's rivals, uniting with southwest Virginians who needed the extension, began pressing the legislature to enforce the charter requirement.[75]

By his strenuous political efforts in 1873, the general secured a sympathetic government in Richmond. A month after the election, he told stockholders that he would not begin the extension without assurance of Kentucky connections. In February, 1874, he defied a committee of the House of Delegates, declaring that the legislature was powerless to force him to build the extension. The General Assembly, in response to demands to prod Mahone, passed a joint resolution that in effect vindicated the general. Directing him only to begin work whenever he could obtain Kentucky connections, it allowed the A. M. and O., if it should fail to complete the extension by 1876, to divest itself painlessly of its Virginia and Kentucky component.[76]

In the session of 1874–75, General Mahone's influence in the legislature reached its apex.[77] Able to count on a large bloc of sympathetic members, the general brought about one of the most extraordinary coups of his career. During February, the Senate Committee on Roads, by adroit changes of wording, transformed a bill to extend the basic laws governing railroads and canals to other common carriers into a wholesale revision of the railroad laws. The Senate passed the bill on March 3, before a printed version existed. When the House Committee on Courts of Justice reported it on March 20 with a minor change, it seemed unlikely to reach the floor before the session's end. On March 29, nevertheless, General Mahone rallied his friends to a supreme effort. They managed to ram the bill through the House in the evening of March 30, the last of

74. Blake, *Mahone*, pp. 138–39.

75. *Senate A. M. & O. Report, 1873,* pp. 3, 6–7.

76. *Senate Journal* (1874), pp. 209–11, 523–24; *House Journal* (1874), pp. 160, 262, 498, 530–33; Blake, *Mahone,* p. 128.

77. Richard F. Walker to William Mahone, January 22, 1875; Walker to Mahone, February 15, 1875; Walker to Mahone, February 16, 1875; Walker to Mahone, February 26, 1875; Walker to Mahone, March 3, 1875, all in Mahone Papers.

the session, then promptly rushed the House version to the Senate, which promptly approved it as well. In the wee morning hours of March 31, railroad executives and lawyers rushed to the Capitol, trying to decipher the mysterious act's intent. Before anyone could move to reconsider, Richard F. Walker spirited the engrossed law to the nearby executive mansion, where Governor Kemper hastily signed it.[78]

Legal minds puzzled long over the Mahone group's "little dodger," so subtly drafted that few could guess its authors and purpose.[79] The ostensibly innocuous measure was in fact a master-stroke of political capitalism, stacking the cards in the game in Mahone's favor against the Bucktails. One change confined protection from rate discrimination to citizens of Virginia, excluding communities and nonresidents. Another made certain rate limitations inapplicable to *intrastate* commerce. A third altered the rule that the rate from an in-state to an out-of-state point might not exceed the rate in the opposite direction, to limit its protection to *cities*. A fourth made a company's *lowest* through-traffic rate per mile from an out-of-state point to a Virginia *city* its *maximum* rate from any Virginia city to any out-of-state point. A fifth change forbade railroads to issue through tickets and baggage checks for travel on out-of-state railroads that denied the same privileges to Virginia lines. A sixth, by one interpretation, banned interstate express companies from operating in Virginia.[80] The bill was expertly designed to harass the interstate trunk lines without interfering with the A. M. and O. For all its ingenuity, though, Mahone's coup did him little good because of the previous erosion of railroad regulation. The state proved as ineffective in applying the confusing provisions of the "little dodger" as it had in enforcing the common-carrier rules of the earlier law.

Mahone's political machinations could not compensate forever for his shortage of funds. After the Panic of 1873, even drastic econ-

78. Richmond *Dispatch*, April 21, 1875; William Mahone to Stith Bolling (copy), March 29, 1875, Letter-Books; Bolling to Mahone, March 29, 1875; Bolling to Mahone, March 30, 1875; R. F. Walker to Mahone, March 31, 1875; Walker to Mahone, April 3, 1875, all in Mahone Papers; *Senate Journal* (1874–75), pp. 147, 196, 208, 212, 234, 285, 457; *House Journal* (1874–75), pp. 297, 428, 446, 447.

79. R. F. Walker to Mahone, April 8, 1875, and Walker to Mahone, April 17, 1875, both in Mahone Papers.

80. Richmond *Dispatch*, April 14, 15, 17, 19, and 21, 1875. Mahone's confidants acknowledged that "Metropolis," the hostile author of this series, generally interpreted the bill correctly. C. B. Duffield to Mahone, April 16, 1875, and R. F. Walker to Mahone, April 21, 1875, both in Mahone Papers.

omies and layoffs did not enable the A. M. and O. to meet the interest payments on its debts. In 1875, Mahone visited London and negotiated a tacit agreement with his British bondholders and with his British agent, John Collinson. In March, 1876, however, Collinson resigned his position and the British bondholders' brokers brought suit against the A. M. and O. in federal court. Sending Collinson to America as their agent, they demanded receivership and a mortgage sale. For awhile, Mahone hoped to become receiver for his road, but in June, Judge Hugh L. Bond appointed Charles L. Perkins of New York and Major Henry Fink of Lynchburg as receivers.[81] Mahone, still president, accused the British interests of betrayal and struggled in vain to regain control of the company. The state made some effort to recover its interest in the A. M. and O. and belatedly questioned the constitutionality of some of the privileges it had given the company in 1870. In 1881, a group of New York and Philadelphia capitalists bought the company and reorganized it as the Norfolk and Western Railroad.[82] The "Virginia railroad" thus succumbed to Northern ownership.

With Mahone out of the way, Tom Scott enjoyed a free hand in Virginia. By 1876, Scott, having relinquished most of his Southern lines as unprofitable, was marshaling Southern political support for federal aid to his projected Texas and Pacific Railroad.[83] Mahone, Senator Johnston, and John W. Daniel refuted the T. and P.'s "Southern" pretensions, showing that Northerners controlled the company and that it would connect principally with Northern and Pennsylvania-owned lines.[84] Scott, nevertheless, commanded impressive support from prominent Virginians. General Imboden and Beverley Tucker, undeviating admirers of the Pennsylvanian, joined his payroll, and R. M. T. Hunter, L. Q. Washington, Franklin Stearns, and Colonel Edmund W. Hubard also drummed up enthusiasm for the transcontinental project.[85] In 1876, the General

81. Blake, *Mahone,* pp. 126–30; *Case of Foreign Bondholders,* pp. 5–7, 10–11.

82. Blake, *Mahone,* pp. 129–33; Vecellio, "Daniel," p. 197; Jones, "Conservative Virginian," pp. 348–49; Stover, *Railroads of the South,* p. 139.

83. Stover, *Railroads of the South,* pp. 118–20; Woodward, *Reunion and Reaction,* pp. 68–100. Woodward calls the southern support of the T. and P. "the apotheosis of carpetbaggery."

84. William Mahone to R. T. Wilson (copy), February 10, 1875, Letter-Books, Mahone Papers; Petersburg *Index and Appeal,* December 6, 1875; *Senate Journal* (1875–76), pp. 246–47; John W. Johnston in *Cong. Record,* 45 Cong., 1 Sess., 4124–29 (1878).

85. Governor James L. Kemper, Commission of Delegates to National Convention on the Texas & Pacific Railroad [1875], and John D. Imboden, manuscript speech on Texas & Pacific Railroad [1876–77?], both in Imboden Papers; (Nathaniel) Beverley

Assembly took up a great deal of time debating resolutions of support and opposition to the T. and P.'s request for federal aid.[86] In February, 1877, at the height of the T. and P.'s efforts in Congress, editor Meade put even Mahone's Richmond *Whig* on the record in favor of the appropriation.[87] In politics as well as in business, Scott's Bucktails had won most of the rounds against Mahone's natives in the contest to control Virginia's transportation facilities.

DEATH OF A DREAM

Of all the casualties of that struggle, none touched tradition-conscious Virginians more deeply than the fate of the James River and Kanawha Canal, the crowning glory of Old Virginia's public-works system. Intended to connect the Atlantic Coast and the Mississippi Valley, the Canal had won planters' and farmers' hearts as no railroad could have, and strict Democrats who had opposed all other public works had voted appropriations for it.[88] The Commonwealth's millions did not suffice for the purpose. In 1860, when railroad competition was becoming appreciable, the 198-mile waterway ending at Buchanan was only the beginning of a canal to the Kanawha.

Lee's surrender found the Canal in ruins, "a great gash across the heart of the Commonwealth." In that condition it did not justify the cost of construction, but to complete it would cost an additional forty million dollars. State assistance was now out of the question, and the decreased trade in agricultural products no longer sufficed

Tucker to J. Randolph Tucker (copy), September 4, 1877, Tucker Family Papers, Southern Historical Collection, University of North Carolina at Chapel Hill; (N.) B. Tucker to Edmund W. Hubard, April 18, 1878, Hubard Papers; L. Q. Washington to Robert M. T. Hunter, January 31, 1876, and George C. Brown to Hunter, February 12, 1876, Hunter-Garnett Papers, University of Virginia; Richard F. Walker to William Mahone, January 19, 1875; Stith Bolling to Mahone, January 20, 1875; and C. B. Duffield to Mahone, January 21, 1875, all in Mahone Papers.

86. Vecellio, "Daniel," pp. 131–132; *Senate Journal* (1875–76), pp. 245–47, 265, 277, 281, 284–85, 293–94; *House Journal* (1875–76), pp. 382, 396–97, 401, 409, 413–14. The Senate passed a resolution disapproving the project, but the House did not concur.

87. Richmond *Daily Whig*, February 5, 1877; Thomas S. Bocock to William Mahone, February 10, 1877, and John Goode, Jr., to Mahone, February 5, 1877, both in Mahone Papers.

88. Ambler, *Sectionalism*, pp. 105–7, 181–84; Bagby, *Old Virginia Gentleman*, pp. 67–69, 77; *Senate Journal* (1871–72), Document II: *Communication from the Governor of Virginia, transmitting Memorial of James River and Kanawha Company*, p. 5 (hereafter cited as *J. R. & K. Memorial, 1871*).

to pay the operating expenses.[89] Many Virginians, nevertheless, continued to believe that their Canal might become the great thoroughfare of trans-Appalachian trade. Governor Walker predicted in 1870 that the waterway, when complete, would "prove as valuable an adjunct to commerce as the far-famed Suez Canal." Others considered it at least a necessary supplement to the railroads.[90] "Our confidence in, and affection for, this measure," Robert W. Hughes wrote in 1871, "is traditional as well as actual. Our fathers cherished it, and our zeal for it descends to us by inheritance. . . ."[91]

Since neither the company nor the Commonwealth had the means to complete the Canal, its proponents looked for other sources of finance. Governor Walker, applying his laissez-faire policy, suggested that the state and other stockholders simply donate the Canal to a company of businessmen with stipulations about its completion, tolls, and management.[92] Most Canal advocates, unwilling to give away the fruit of decades of public effort, hoped that the federal government would assume the project.[93] Federal authorities were not willing to do so.

In 1874, the company embarked on a modest extension plan. It asked the legislature for permission to mortgage its property as security for a bond issue to improve the waterway and extend it twenty-eight miles to the Chesapeake and Ohio Railroad line at Clifton Forge.[94] Suspicion arose that President Charles S. Carrington and the company's managers, despite their professions, secretly intended a railroad, not a canal extension. Lewis E. Harvie and Frank Ruffin, watchdogs for farming interests among the stockholders, noticed that the legislature responded to Carrington's lobbying by chartering a railroad from Buchanan to Clifton Forge instead of consenting to the requested financial arrangement. In November, 1875, the stockholders instructed the company officers to seek a canal, not a

---

89. Pearson, *Readjuster Movement*, p. 7; Governor's Message, December 4, 1872, *Senate Journal* (1872–73), pp. 22–23; *Senate Journal* (1874–75), Document VI: *Memorial of the James River and Kanawha Company to the General Assembly*, pp. 5–6 (hereafter cited as *J. R. & K. Memorial, 1874*).

90. Governor's Message, February 8, 1870, *Senate Journal* (1869–70), p. 42; Richmond *Whig and Public Advertiser*, October 24, 1865; Richmond *Daily Whig*, January 16, 1868; Governor's Message, January 1, 1874, *Senate Journal* (1874), p. 24.

91. *J. R. & K. Memorial, 1871*, p. 5.

92. Governor's Message, December 4, 1872, *Senate Journal* (1872–73), pp. 22–24.

93. See I. D. Osborne to William Cabell Rives, Jr., January 18, 1872, William Cabell Rives Papers, Library of Congress, and above, pp. 126–27.

94. *J. R. and K. Memorial, 1874*, pp. 5–6; Governor's Message, December 2, 1874, *Senate Journal* (1874–75), p. 19.

railroad, extension. In the next session, however, the officers had the legislature postpone consideration of the bill to extend the Canal, and three company directors appeared among the incorporators of a railroad on the route. The urban businessmen who managed the company had apparently decided, against the stockholders' will, to supplant the venerable Canal with a railroad.[95] In 1876, the General Assembly chartered the Buchanan and Clifton Forge Railway Company, and the James River and Kanawha Company subscribed for four-sevenths of its stock. The company, however, seemed unable to surmount its financial obstacles,[96] and private interests were eager to try their hands. Time was working in favor of Gilbert Walker's private-enterprise plan.

In the spring of 1877, the General Assembly took a long stride toward private ownership. It granted the contracting firm of Mason, Gooch, and Hoge a charter for a Buchanan–Clifton Forge railroad and leased the James River and Kanawha Company, its property, and its assets to the firm for twenty years, on the condition that it build the railroad. Governor Kemper vetoed the sweeping measure on the obvious grounds that it conferred power unconstitutionally and tied the Commonwealth's hands in regard to one of its important interests for twenty years. Still hoping to save the "central water-line," Kemper begged the General Assembly at once to assist the J. R. and K. Company itself to build a railroad extension. The legislature passed a bill allowing the company to pre-empt all the convict laborers the state hired out in a final attempt to complete the connection. The effort devoured all the company's means, leaving the Canal unfinished.[97]

After the Mason-Gooch-Hoge episode, most Virginians gave up hope of "saving" the Canal. The attractiveness of the lease, William D. Chesterman thought, was that "the canal had become a bore and . . . Mason & Co. would relieve us of the trouble of thinking about

95. Norfolk *Virginian*, February 26, 1875; W. S. Morris to Lewis E. Harvie, February 21, 1876, and Frank G. Ruffin to Harvie, February 6, 1876, both in Lewis Evarts Harvie Papers, Virginia State Library; but see Petersburg *Index and Appeal*, January 17, 1877.

96. *Senate Journal* (1876–77), Document VI: *Communication from the President of the James River and Kanawha Co., in regard to the Stock of the Buchanan and Clifton Forge Railway Co., &c.*, pp. 1–2; Document XXII: *Communication from the President of the James River and Kanawha Co. and the Buchanan and Clifton Forge Railway Co. in response to Certain Interrogatories of the Senate Committee on Roads and Internal Navigation*, p. 353.

97. Vecellio, "Daniel," pp. 139–41; Staunton *Vindicator*, March 23, 1877; Jones, "Conservative Virginian," pp. 348–50; see below, p. 226.

it."[98] In a railroad age, the Canal seemed a pleasant anachronism that had "suited the old times."[99] In 1879, a group of promoters, mostly Northerners, secured from the General Assembly a charter for the Richmond and Alleghany Railroad and, in 1880, purchased the Canal property from the state, which, General Imboden figured, lost $10,436,869 on its investment. The Richmond and Alleghany then converted the entire Canal bed into a railroad from Richmond to Clifton Forge. That effort put it into receivership within two years. The Chesapeake and Ohio leased the railroad and finally acquired it in 1889.[100] Nostalgic Virginians such as George W. Bagby grieved inwardly when they understood at last that their ancestral "dream of the great canal to the Ohio . . . revolutionising the commerce of the United States . . . must be abandoned along with other dreams."[101]

The rivalries among Mahone, Robinson, Garrett, Scott, and Huntington—along with the passing of the James River and Kanawha Canal and the antebellum public-works system—profoundly transformed the control of transportation facilities. From the melee resulted a tendency from mixed enterprise to *laissez faire* and from local to Northern control. Most of the Conservative politicians gave active political assistance to one or another private interest. They furthered the laissez-faire tendency—some, with misgivings—but they divided in loyalties between "Virginia" and "foreign" railroads.

The Conservative ascendancy in Virginia became one of the most important stages of the process by which, during the late nineteenth century, Northern businessmen took control of almost the entire rail mileage of the South.[102] Once, the traditionalist clergyman Robert L. Dabney recalled in 1882, the Commonwealth had owned the great land and water highways, but giant corporations overshadowing the states had taken them over. "Each of these roads,"

98. Petersburg *Index and Appeal*, September 21, 1877.
99. Peyton H. Hoge and Howard R. Bayne, *The Travels of Ego and Alter: An Epistolary Narrative of a Tramp through the Old Dominion* (Richmond: West, Johnston, and Company, 1879), pp. 45–46 (hereafter cited as *Ego and Alter*).
100. Vecellio, "Daniel," pp. 200–201; *Imboden Report, 1886*, pp. 13, 16–17, 75; Moger, "Railroad Practices," pp. 430–31; Stover, *Railroads of the South*, p. 204.
101. Bagby, *Old Virginia Gentleman*, p. 78.
102. For a general view of the process, see Stover, *Railroads of the South*, pp. 280–84.

Dabney lamented, "points virtually to New York. To that city, yes, to one corner of Wall Street in that city, centre all their debts, their loans, their revenues, their chief management."[103] Against Yankee dictation in the economic realm, Conservative rule erected no barriers.

103. Quoted in Moger, "Railroad Practices," p. 457n.

II.

The Commonwealth
and the Countryside

The debacle of 1865 crippled the planter class as a social force. At the same time, it quickened the aspirations of the junior partners of the antebellum system: the small-scale farmers and the commercial capitalist class.

Henry A. Wise, speaking in 1867 at the dedication of Stonewall Cemetery at Winchester, expressed the farmers' hopes. "The plantation interest is gone," he announced. In its place he foresaw a utopia of intensive, diversified, small-unit farming by skilled freemen. Farms and towns, Wise expected, would appear in place of lonely unproductive plantations, and "a solid Caucasian yeomanry" would replace "ignorant lazy slaves of a degraded race!"[1]

Alexander H. H. Stuart, speaking at the University of Virginia in 1866, considered the plantation's downfall from the viewpoint of commerce and industry. In the future, he thought, refinement and culture would "be constrained, as in the North, to seek refuge in cities and towns." He, too, expected a division of estates, but he advised young men to seek careers primarily in manufacturing, mining, and transportation.[2]

The following fifteen years vindicated Stuart's capitalist prediction rather than Wise's agricultural vision. The remnants of the plantations, as both expected, stagnated. But the farmer, struggling to hold his own, saw the merchant, the banker, and the railroad executive advance to new peaks of wealth and power. In the transfer of resources and influence to those groups, the Conservative government in Richmond did not alleviate the farmers' hardship, far less redress the social imbalance.

1. Wise, *Wise*, pp. 398–99.
2. Robertson, *Stuart*, pp. 288–90.

DEBTS AND DEBTORS

The countryman who came home in 1865 to a devastated farm had to borrow heavily, often adding to old debts, to restore his buildings and replace his equipment and livestock. Although the maximum legal interest rate was 6 per cent, financiers took advantage of the dearth of capital to exact between 10 and 50 per cent on new loans. The agricultural prosperity that might make the debt burden bearable did not materialize. After the Panic of 1873, money became a scarce commodity in rural Virginia, and credit almost vanished. Farm families, deep in debt, were reduced to an abject standard of living.[3]

In the first postwar years, government gave the debtor some relief. In June, 1865, the Alexandria government's legislature enacted a law to stay collection of debts for several months. In the succeeding years first the Baldwin legislature, and then the commanding generals, extended the postponement. In 1870, however, the Underwood constitution went into effect, abrogating past stay laws and forbidding future ones.[4]

As the Conservatives assumed the reins of government, judicial sales threatened many Virginians. The stay law's expiration, the Richmond *Whig* reported, would place the southside and Tidewater people "in a condition of hopelessness and distress which has no parallel in the history of this country."[5] Some debtors demanded relief on the grounds that the War and emancipation had overthrown the whole system of economic relationships they had taken for granted in their prewar borrowing. Colonel Harvie of the *Enquirer* proposed a scaling down of all debts to distribute the effects of the War equitably.[6] Petitions and proposals for debt relief flooded the new General Assembly.[7]

3. Richmond *Whig and Public Advertiser*, January 9 and 12, 1866; *Conference with Creditors, 1874*, pp. 18–19; Pearson, *Readjuster Movement*, p. 14; Eckenrode, "Virginia since 1865," pp. 95–96; William L. Royall, *History of the Virginia Debt Controversy: The Negro's Vicious Influence in Politics* (Richmond: George M. West, 1897), pp. 9–12 (hereafter cited as *Debt Controversy*).

4. Jones, "Conservative Virginian," pp. 57, 59.

5. Quoted in Burton, "Taxation," p. 5.

6. "Many of the Oppressed" to Gilbert C. Walker, January 31, 1870; "A. G. R." to Walker, February 12, 1870; "Justice" to Walker, February 18, 1870; "Justice" to Walker, March 11, 1870; "Justice" to Walker, May [n.d.], 1870; "an umble [*sic*] Constituent" to Walker, March 22, 1872, all in "Letters on various subjects," Box 3, Gilbert Carlton Walker Executive Correspondence, Virginia State Library; Pearson, *Readjuster Movement*, p. 25; Jones, "Conservative Virginian," p. 149.

7. *Senate Journal* (1869–70), pp. 45–46, 62, 79; 119, 190, 219, 275, 413, 448, 455;

The Conservative officeholders responded to the pleas with half measures. Governor Walker rejected stay laws on principle and had doubts about other forms of debtor relief, but he admitted that the exceptional situation required some action. He estimated that the new homestead exemption, along with exemptions already in force, would protect three or four thousand dollars' worth of a debtor's property. Walker suggested that the legislature might also direct the courts to sell no property at less than its assessed value and give the creditor an option at that price if there were no higher bid.[8] In addition to enacting the homestead exemption, the General Assembly passed laws to regulate judicial sales and prevent the sacrifice of personal property.[9] Two years later the next assembly, more sympathetic to debtors, facilitated redemption of land held for delinquent taxes, reduced the maximum interest rate, and tried to avert judicial nullificaion of the homestead exemption.[10]

Until 1872, the homestead exemption was the debtor's best protection. The Baldwin legislature had exempted as much as 160 acres or $1,200 worth of property for each householder or head of family from execution for debt. The Underwood constitution required the General Assembly to enact a measure that might exempt as much as $2,000 in property. In 1870, the legislature passed a law allowing the debtor that amount, but the measure was not as benevolent as it appeared. The constitution excluded six kinds of transactions from the exemption's applicability, and the legislature narrowed its effect still more. The exceptions, critics claimed, crippled the law's protection to debtors.[11]

The homestead exemption survived for only two controversy-ridden years. Businessmen attacked it and lenders, in new loans, insisted on clauses to waive its protection.[12] Conservative Senator William M. Lackland of Botetourt County led a movement to

---

House Journal (1869–70), pp. 66, 76, 80, 106, 118, 159, 168, 176, 186, 201, 218, 229, 230, 266, 280, 308, 443, 640, 671; *Senate Journal* (December, 1870), p. 263.

8. Governor's Message, March 8, 1870, *Senate Journal* (1869–70), pp. 163–64.

9. *Senate Journal* (1869–70), pp. 75, 208, 378, 382, 548, 555–56, 568; 120, 190, 195, 359–60, 373, 374, 376, 450; *House Journal* (1869–70), pp. 410, 573, 574, 579; 404, 478–79.

10. Pearson, *Readjuster Movement*, p. 44.

11. Jones, "Conservative Virginian," p. 58; *Annual Cyclopaedia, 1871*, p. 766; William Smith, open letter on retrenchment, 1871, in Bell, *Smith*, pp. 284–85.

12. *Daily Petersburg Index*, February 25, 1870; V. Y. Conway to Gilbert C. Walker, April 18, 1870, Gilbert Carlton Walker Executive Correspondence; Jones, "Conservative Virginian," p. 59.

thwart that practice, liberalize the exemption, and make it easier for debtors to avail themselves of it. The legislature suspended forced sales affecting debtors who claimed the exemption until the courts should rule on its validity and asked Congress to amend the federal bankruptcy law to secure the measure's benefits to Virginia bankrupts.[13] In June, 1872, however, the Supreme Court of Appeals declared the exemption law and the state constitution's exemption provision void under the contracts clause of the federal Constitution, insofar as they applied to contracts antedating their enactment.[14] Since waiver clauses removed more recent loans from the exemption's application, it ceased to afford the debtor any protection.

In regard to interest on new loans, Conservative legislators offered him little more encouragement. The Underwood constitution established a maximum interest rate of 12 per cent. The first Conservative legislature permitted 12-per-cent loans, although it made 6 per cent "legal interest" for contracts that did not specify the rate.[15] The General Assembly of 1871–73 reduced the maximum to 8 per cent.[16] Many felt that in the prevailing depressed conditions usury laws would necessarily prove ineffective, except perhaps to make credit unavailable on any terms.[17] In 1872, the legislators and voters secured an amendment removing the usury clause of the constitution,[18] but later legislatures restored the 6 per cent maximum interest rate. There were accusations that lenders, including national banks, were actually charging illegally high rates.[19] All things considered, state protection to debtors deteriorated considerably during the Conservatives' first years in office.

13. *Senate Journal* (1871–72), pp. 71, 119, 229, 231, 235, 241, 270, 307, 323; *House Journal* (1871–72), pp. 49, 50, 58–59, 168, 177, 178, 184–85, 197, 219, 260, 266, 406, 419.

14. *The Homestead Cases*, 22 Gratt. 266, 279–301 (1872). Senator Lackland, in a final effort to save the exemption, introduced a resolution asking Congress to re-enact its provisions by an amendment to the bankruptcy law. *Senate Journal* (1872–73), pp. 122–23.

15. *Daily Petersburg Index*, February 25, 1870.

16. Pearson, *Readjuster Movement*, p. 44.

17. Richmond *Whig and Public Advertiser*, January 12 and February 9, 1866; *Journal of the Proceedings of a General Meeting of the Virginia State Agricultural Society and Convention of Virginia Farmers, held in Richmond on the 20th, 21st, and 22nd Nov., 1866*, pp. 17–19 (hereafter cited as *Agricultural Society Proceedings, 1866*).

18. Thorpe, ed., *Constitutions*, VII, 3900.

19. Richmond *Whig*, August 3, 1880, clipping in Frank Gildart Ruffin Scrapbook, Virginia State Library, I, 30.

THE TAX BURDEN

During the 1870's, the General Assembly rewrote the revenue laws with bewildering frequency, in response to fiscal difficulties and interest groups' efforts to shift the tax burden to one another's shoulders.[20] What remained constant was a tax structure that bore much more heavily on landowners, and much less heavily on businessmen, than the antebellum system had.

The halving of property values after the War, and state commitments to education and debt service, required a large tax increase at a time when farmers could ill afford additional expenses. In 1850, Virginians had paid 77.1 cents per capita in taxes; they paid $1.66 in 1870, and $1.88 in 1880.[21] The increase aroused sharp complaints, especially from rural landowners. Some argued that Virginia's taxes were among the nation's lowest, but almost all rural Virginians thought they were paying as much as they could tolerate. "Any material increase of taxation on lands, at this time," Governor Kemper admitted in 1874, "would be virtual confiscation of the lands."[22]

The first Conservative legislature enacted a tax law that relied very heavily on property taxes, heavily on capitation taxes, and relatively less on license taxes. It increased the property- and capitation-tax rates by two-thirds, setting the former at five mills per dollar and the latter at a dollar for each adult. Actual receipts from the property tax increased by 88 per cent from 1869 to 1870, while receipts from the capitation tax rose by 62 per cent. In 1870, the property tax provided 76.7 per cent of the revenue. Landed property alone accounted for 60.9 per cent, although in 1860 a wealthier landowning class had supplied only 48 per cent. The tax law hastened the planter's ruin and aggravated the farmer's trials. By 1880, because of new kinds of taxes, property taxes accounted for only 60.8 per cent of the revenue, but the landowner was still liable for five mills per dollar of property.[23]

Many businesses, unlike farms, escaped significant taxation under the 1870 law. In 1874, Stuart, the chairman of the Senate Commit-

20. Burton, "Taxation," pp. 82–83.

21. Ibid., p. iv.

22. Conference with Creditors, 1874, p. 23. For the argument that Virginia taxes were relatively low, see First Annual Report of the Commissioner of Agriculture, of the State of Virginia (Richmond: James E. Goode, 1877), p. 50 (hereafter cited as Agriculture Report, 1877).

23. Burton, "Taxation," pp. 38, 43–44, 76.

tee on Finance, found that half the merchants paid no business taxes and that many other businesses paid astonishingly little in proportion to their profits.[24] As a corrective, the legislature imposed a license tax on general merchants, from whose businesses property taxes could realize relatively little. The Richmond *Dispatch* recklessly accused rural legislators of bleeding commerce by taxes fifteen times higher than "landed gentlemen" paid. Merchants challenged the tax's validity in the courts, which upheld the levy. The tax, imposing inversely graduated rates on annual purchases, weighed more heavily on small businesses than on large ones.[25]

Businesses paid few taxes other than license taxes. During the 1870's, public-service corporations paid $47,781 in an average year; banks, $26,400; and insurance companies, $23,460. The tax on the oyster industry, Auditor William F. Taylor estimated, should yield $100,000 a year in net revenue, but under the collection system the state employed proceeds declined from $28,169.15 in fiscal year 1870–71 to $541.86 in 1878–79. Altogether, business taxes contributed 15.99 per cent of the tax receipts in 1870–71 and increased to a peak of 36.75 in 1877–78. For the decade, they provided about 27 per cent of the revenue. The most heavily taxed businessmen were general merchants and dealers in alcoholic beverages. The latter group regularly evaded the Moffett Law of 1877, which taxed liquor by the drink, and the relatively inelastic demand for their product enabled them to pass almost all their taxes on to the customers. Even general merchants could pay much of their tax bill by increasing the prices of a few items of inelastic demand.[26] Farmers, in a more competitive position, could not.

The countrymen were not wholly at a loss for remedies. The task of assessing property for taxation fell to elected county officials, unrestrained by procedures to equalize different counties' valuations. Since the assessor did not want his county to pay more than its share of state taxes, he was likely to assign low valuations. Successive assessments reduced the total of assessed property values in Virginia from $363,438 in 1870–71 to $303,993 in 1879–80.[27] Another form of rural tax strike was the breakdown in collection of the state income tax, which reduced its proceeds to about $35,000

24. Robertson, *Stuart*, p. 334.
25. Burton, "Taxation," pp. 52–56.
26. *Ibid.*, pp. 47–49, 55–57, 71–72, 74, 83–84.
27. *Ibid.*, pp. 75–77; Governor's Message, December 1, 1875, *Senate Journal* (1875–76), pp. 18–19; Richmond *Dispatch*, January 5, 1876; Petersburg *Index and Appeal*, January 16, 1878.

in an average year. Its administration failed most conspicuously in rural areas, where the few farmers who cleared enough to be liable for it took advantage of lax local enforcement and the difficulty of ascertaining farm income. Some counties did not pretend to assess incomes for taxation, and in many years all of rural Virginia paid less than ten dollars in income tax.[28]

In spite of tax evasion and the enactment of new business taxes, the insecure landowners apparently paid a higher proportion of their incomes to the Commonwealth in taxes than the more prosperous businessmen did.

THE TOBACCO CONTROVERSY

Governor Kemper attempted, in 1874, to strike a blow for agricultural interests in appointing the state tobacco inspectors. The system in force required growers to bring tobacco destined for out-of-state consumption to recognized "public" warehouses. At each warehouse, the governor and the warehouseowners each named an inspector—but it had become customary for the governor to appoint as state inspector whomever the owners might recommend. The owners' control of inspection, Kemper charged, enabled them to underpay the grower by biased grading, overtax him for the inspection cost, and give dealers drawbacks and rebates from the amount thus accrued. Determined to end the abuse, Kemper chose to introduce a countervailing force by appointing as state inspectors growers who would "stand by the planting interest against the rings of the town."[29]

The warehousemen resisted bipartisan inspection. Some large warehouses converted from "public" to "private" status to escape state inspection but continued to export tobacco from the state illegally. At the end of 1874, Governor Kemper asked the General Assembly to extend state inspection to *all* tobacco warehouses. Legislators sympathetic to the growers put up a hard fight for remedial legislation, but they were unsuccessful.[30] Kemper found himself

28. Burton, "Taxation," pp. 78–80.
29. Jones, "Conservative Virginian," pp. 245–46; James L. Kemper to Nathaniel B. Meade (copy), October 5, 1874, James Lawson Kemper Papers, University of Virginia.
30. Governor's Message, December 2, 1874, *Senate Journal* (1874–75), pp. 16–17; Stith Bolling to William Mahone, January 21, 1875, William Mahone Papers, Duke University; *Senate Journal* (1874–75), pp. 35–36, 43, 154, 167, 45, 54, 60, 65, 80, 91, 109, 139, 159, 167, 189, 220, 294–95, 299, 300–302, 304–5, 313–14, 316–17, 319–20,

fighting a losing battle. The two largest warehouses in Richmond went "private" to prevent Colonel Harvie's son Edwin J. Harvie from serving as state inspector.[31]

Going farther, the warehousemen launched a campaign to abolish state inspection altogether. In spite of mass meetings in the tobacco counties in favor of the system, the assembly excepted loose tobacco from inspection.[32] Unappeased, the warehouseowners continued to demand complete abolition. John W. Daniel and other politicians, regarding the inspection as only an inconvenience to wholesalers, endorsed their request. In 1877, the General Assembly abolished state inspection, extending the laissez-faire policy to the tobacco business. In the succeeding twelve years of wholly private inspection, the *Progressive Farmer* of North Carolina claimed, Virginia warehousemen tripled their inspection charges to growers.[33] The legislature had left the tobacco-growers at the mercy of the town merchants.

RURAL LOCAL GOVERNMENT

The Conservative government's policies affected power relationships among different rural groups as well as the relationship between country and town groups. The Underwood convention, hoping to democratize rural local government, introduced the township system. Each county, its constitution provided, would contain three or more townships. Each township would every year elect its own supervisor, clerk, assessor, collector, commissioner of roads, and overseer for the poor, and each would elect its three justices of the peace and three constables for staggered three-year terms. The supervisors of the townships would compose the county board of supervisors.[34] In 1868, Conservatives opposed the innovation. Traditionalist planters were appalled because it would overthrow their time-honored county court system,[35] but other Conservatives re-

---

164–65, 176, 185, 203, 251; *House Journal* (1874–75), pp. 30, 38, 167; 31; 64; 68; 179, 201; 184; 198; 208; 304–5; 328; 339; 377; 332, 413.

31. James L. Kemper to Lewis E. Harvie (copy), April 8, 1876, James Lawson Kemper Papers, Virginia Historical Society; Edwin J. Harvie to Lewis E. Harvie, April 26, 1876, Lewis Evarts Harvie Papers, Virginia State Library.

32. Benjamin W. Arnold, Jr., *History of the Tobacco Industry in Virginia from 1860 to 1894* ("Johns Hopkins University Studies in Historical and Political Science," XV, Nos. 1–2 [Baltimore: The Johns Hopkins Press, 1897]), pp. 44–45, 47.

33. *Ibid.*, p. 45; Vecellio, "Daniel," p. 133.

34. Thorpe, ed., *Constitutions*, VII, 3891.

35. See above, p. 12.

jected it mainly because it would give local black majorities control of many township governments in the southside.

Experience did not prove the township system unworkable in rural Virginia,[36] for the Conservatives did not give it a fair trial. The local commissioners who drew the township boundaries in 1870 took their task lightly. Many "butchered up" their counties arbitrarily, and some followed political criteria, putting almost all the Republican voters in a single township.[37] The supposition that Virginia's more dispersed rural population needed larger governmental units than New England's was not the verdict of experience. In some ways, dispersed populations needed even smaller governmental units and more officials than concentrated ones. Rural citizens sometimes complained that their townships were too large, and their people too scattered, for three justices of the peace to keep order.[38] For some purposes, Virginians found the township a convenient unit. In 1875, Conservative legislators even tried, unconstitutionally, to let each township or magisterial district in four specified counties elect its own commissioner of the revenue.[39]

Between 1872 and 1874, nevertheless, the Conservatives amended the constitution's sections on county and township government. They did not eliminate the township as a unit, nor did they restore antebellum institutions, but they did curtail the role of direct, local democracy.[40] The amendment added new county officials—elected commissioners of the revenue and an appointed surveyor—but deleted the provision that a large county might have more than one school superintendent. It made the office of overseer of the poor appointive and extended the county officials' terms of office. It changed

36. As Cappon, "County Government," p. 30, asserts.
37. J. E. Mallory to Gilbert C. Walker, April 22, [1870], "Letters on various subjects," Box 3, Gilbert Carlton Walker Executive Correspondence; *Second Annual Report of the Superintendent of Public Instruction, for the Year ending August 31, 1872. First Report of the Board of Visitors of the Agricultural and Mechanical College.* (Richmond: Robert F. Walker, Superintendent of Public Printing, 1872), pp. 12–13 (hereafter cited as *School Report, 1872*); Withers, *Autobiography*, p. 277; William W. Scott, *A History of Orange County, Virginia, from Its Formation in 1734 (O. S.) to the End of Reconstruction in 1870; Compiled Mainly from Original Records, with a Brief Sketch of the Beginnings of Virginia, a Summary of Local Events to 1907, and a Map* (Richmond: Everett Waddey Company, 1907), pp. 163–64.
38. E.g., John J. Tyler to Gilbert C. Walker, June 10, 1873, Gilbert Carlton Walker Executive Correspondence.
39. *School Report, 1872*, p. 12; Petersburg *Index and Appeal*, December 31, 1874; Governor's Veto Message, March 4, 1875, *Senate Journal* (1874–75), p. 296.
40. Some wished to go so far as to have the General Assembly appoint most county officials. Vecellio, "Daniel," pp. 29–30.

the time of county elections from November to May to escape federal intervention. Renaming the townships "magisterial districts," it abolished the offices of township clerk, assessor, collector, and road commissioner, and two of the three township constables. Township offices remained elective, but the amendment assigned to each a two-year term.[41]

Although the Conservatives modified the township system, they faithfully carried out the rest of the Underwood constitution's program to revolutionize local government. No preceding state constitution had dared to touch the ancient squirearchy of the county courts, but the new constitution uprooted it altogether. To appease the Eumenides of the Old Dominion, it provided for an institution called a "county court"—but that consisted of one salaried judge, whom the General Assembly appointed for a six-year term and who performed only judicial duties. Under the new order, the old court's administrative functions passed to the county board of supervisors—elected in magisterial districts—which became the county's principal governing body. In addition, the free-school system brought with it its own complex of local government institutions.[42] By implementing these sweeping innovations, Conservatives drastically modernized local government in rural Virginia.

Some continued to long for a restoration of the old county court, at least as a judicial institution. "Give us back our 'Old Squire,' " the Norfolk *Virginian* pleaded; "he was far better in the long run than his successor, the young county judge." Governor Kemper, in 1877, proposed changes looking toward such a restoration.[43] Most Conservative officials were not interested in such ideas. They were content to destroy the traditional oligarchic institutions and substitute more democratic ones—but they saw to it that the rule of the planters would not be succeeded by that of the freedmen.

DOGS AND FENCES

The Conservative administrations' local-government policies were not the only indication that, while deposing planters from the seats of power, they would also keep plebeian democrats from occupying them. The Conservatives taxed landowners heavily, but they also burdened the landless poor with the capitation tax. The

41. Thorpe, ed., *Constitutions*, VII, 3901.
42. Cappon, "County Government," pp. 29–30.
43. Norfolk *Virginian*, December 27, 1873; Governor's Message, December 5, 1877, *Senate Journal* (1877–78), p. 26.

abolition of state tobacco inspection harmed both the former slave-owner and the former slave. The poorest Virginians received little comfort from government on two of the Reconstruction issues that most vitally interested them: the "fence" and "dog" questions.

In the 1870's, herding was the "occupation" of the rural poor of both races—tenants, hired "hands," and squatters who eked out lives of misery on the margins of the agricultural economy. Many had to survive without meat and dairy products, since rent and bread consumed their incomes. Ordinarily, they lived outside the political process, cut off from information and required to vote, if at all, as their landlords or employers dictated. Some of the landless poor, however, had a few pigs or cattle that grazed on any accessible pasturage. This gave them a direct stake in the perennial "fence law" controversy—whether it was the landowner's responsibility to fence livestock out of his field or their owner's responsibility to fence them in.[44]

In the fence law of 1866, the legislature emphatically sided with the landowners, holding the owners of animals responsible for their depredations. About 1870, the rural residents engaged in fierce controversy over the law. Planters claimed that to fence in their fields would take so much land out of cultivation as to reduce their crops by a quarter.[45] Plebeians replied that they could survive only by keeping animals, that landowners would not even miss the grass and leaves that foraging animals would consume, and that "the heartless Godless Brother hateing money loveing minority" had gotten the law passed against the masses' desires.[46]

Despite modifications in 1872,[47] the fence law continued to discomfit the rural poor. "If the fence law remains," one of them complained, "numbers of us will be brought to starvation. We can not rent a pasture for one cow for less than $2 per month and there are thousands of acres of land lying waste only for the fence law we

44. [Anonymous] to Gilbert C. Walker, April 4, 1872, and "Your humble servants" to Walker, October 5, 1872, both in "Letters on various subjects," Box 3, Gilbert Carlton Walker Executive Correspondence, identical to handwriting, are a rare written expression of this class's plight. Some of its members found a way to use fenced-in pasturage, removing rails for their pigs to enter and eat. [Allan-Olney], *New Virginians*, I, 67–69.

45. J. D. Tisdale, J. B. Wilson, I. Thomas Tisdale, and R. W. Tisdale to Gilbert C. Walker, December 30, 1870, "Letters on various subjects," Box 3, Gilbert Carlton Walker Executive Correspondence.

46. Fifty-one "Citizens of Dinwiddie County" to Walker, n.d., *ibid.*

47. *House Journal* (1871–72), pp. 177, 384, 391, 433; 415, 519; *Senate Journal* (1871–72), pp. 374; 379; 383, 452.

could raise stock and live comfortable. . . . Many of us that owned cows had to sell them for less than half theair value or pay $2 per month for pasture."[48] ". . . The poor soulgers who served through the hole war," the same writer added, "is treated like dogs by our rich landholders."[49]

It was in regard to dogs that the more innovative landowners came simultaneously into conflict with the deposed aristocrats and the depressed poor. Heeding the gospel of diversification, the innovators began to pasture sheep on their uncultivated lands and thereby ran into trouble with their neighbors' dogs. The poor, especially Negroes, were intensely attached to their pets, and old-fashioned planters also kept foxhounds, whose unrestrained activities drove their neighbors to distraction. The sheep-raising entrepreneur was insensitive to the feelings of the Negro, the poor white, and the old Virginia gentleman—all unproductive classes in his eyes. They, in return, cared little for his economic interests when their beloved dogs were at stake. Sheep raisers asked the state for a dog tax to curb the canine menace, and their dog-loving neighbors resisted with spirit.[50]

Prominent Conservatives took the sheep raisers' side. Some spoke as though wolves were running loose. Superintendent of Public Instruction Ruffner published statistics to show that the keeping of dogs was an appalling drain on society's wealth, and Governor Kemper pronounced the "increasing prevalence of worthless and costly curs" a "grievous nuisance" depressing the economy. The General Assembly enacted dog taxes in certain counties for local revenue. In 1874, Kemper proposed a statewide dog tax to create in each county a fund to indemnify sheepowners for damage by dogs of unknown ownership.[51] The legislators were not willing to go that far. To advocate the "unpardonable sin" of taxing the "predatory, annoying, and vexatious animals," state Senator Charles T.

48. [Anonymous] to Gilbert C. Walker, April 4, 1872, "Letters on various subjects," Box 3, Gilbert Carlton Walker Executive Correspondence. Spelling as in original.

49. "Your humble servants" to Walker, October 5, 1872, *ibid*. Spelling as in original.

50. Coulter, *South during Reconstruction*, p. 227; [Allan-Olney], *New Virginians*, I, 235–36; Bradley, *Other Days*, pp. 285–88, 291–92, 296, 299–300.

51. *First Annual Report of the [Virginia] Superintendent of Public Instruction, for the Year ending August 31, 1871*. (Richmond: C. A. Schaffter, Superintendent of Public Printing, 1871), p. 53; Governor's Message, December 2, 1874, *Senate Journal* (1874–75), p. 18.

Smith of Nelson County complained, would end anyone's political career.[52]

There were sound reasons to question the dog-tax proposal. One did not have to be a dog-lover to see wisdom in the Norfolk *Virginian's* suggestion that sheepowners in Virginia employ shepherds, as those in the rest of the world did.[53] But Conservative leaders wanted to encourage sheep raisers and other capitalist entrepreneurs and valued their convenience above the rights of dogs and dogowners.

THE IMMIGRATION PANACEA

The principal object for which Virginia farmers sought positive state assistance was to encourage immigration.[54] The promoters of a new Virginia had little confidence in either the planters who owned much of the arable land or the Negroes and poor whites who constituted most of the labor force. Instead, they looked to immigration and investment from Europe and the North to regenerate their state. Immigration, the Norfolk *Virginian* proclaimed, "is a human Nile. Wherever its waves flow fertility is established . . . and abundant crops wave on spots which we have not the force or capital to cultivate."[55]

The demand for immigration was principally agricultural. Farmers' organizations were its most vocal exponents, and promoters sought primarily settlers engaged in agriculture and related pursuits.[56] "What immigration?" Henry A. Wise asked in 1867. He replied: "The first want is for *agriculture.*"[57] Wise advised farmers to *"advertise to select immigrants that you will gladly give to them one half of your superfluous lands and help them build and fence*

---

52. *Senate Journal* (1874), p. 176.
53. Norfolk *Virginian*, January 10, 1874.
54. See *Agricultural Society Immigration Memorial, 1872*, pp. 3–11.
55. Norfolk *Virginian*, July 7, 1871.
56. *Agricultural Society Immigration Memorial, 1872*, pp. 9–17; R. L. Ragland to Gilbert C. Walker, November 16, 1872, "Immigration," Box 4, Gilbert Carlton Walker Executive Correspondence; C. R. M. Pohle, "Rise for Virginia! a Call and Guide for German Immigrants to the State of Virginia, in the United States of America" (manuscript, 1866), enclosed in C. R. M. Pohle to State Board of Immigration, March 23, 1874, in James Lawson Kemper Executive Correspondence, Virginia State Library, pp. 7–8 (hereafter cited as "Rise for Virginia!").
57. Henry A. Wise to William T. Sutherlin, April 27, 1867, William Thomas Sutherlin Papers, Southern Historical Collection, University of North Carolina at Chapel Hill.

them. . . . Their settlement will make the other half far more valuable than was or is the whole."⁵⁸ Promoters, carried away with their own rhapsodies about opportunities for enrichment in Virginia, expected a large immigration. Gilbert Walker thought the state could attract between thirty and fifty thousand settlers a year and that each would add one or two thousand dollars to its wealth.⁵⁹

The Conservatives were not certain how to translate the panacea of immigration from a social myth into a public policy—not to mention a statistically significant reality. In 1866, the Baldwin legislature created a three-member Board of Immigration to advertise Virginia's attractions, but it required the board to finance its work from private contributions. Adjutant General Richardson, the commissioner of immigration, managed to raise only a donation of five hundred dollars and a loan of five hundred. On that budget, the board could do little. Worse still, when Richardson tried to arrange for a company of Scandinavian immigrants to buy land, landowners (moved by greed or prejudice) instantly raised their prices to an exorbitant level. During military Reconstruction, General Gaspar Tochman acted as the board's European agent, at his own expense. After "redemption," he joined with the private Virginia Immigration Society to request a ten-thousand-dollar appropriation and liens on land they might sell to immigrants. The legislature denied the request, and the European agency came to an end.⁶⁰

At the end of 1871, Governor Walker proposed a vigorous state program to attract immigrants. He asked the General Assembly to set up a State Bureau of Immigration, to maintain an office in Europe, distribute a pamphlet on Virginia's advantages, and sell land to settlers under power of attorney from landowners. Cooperating with localities and with adjoining states, the bureau would manage a depot at Norfolk to receive and trans-ship immigrants. Walker thought the agency would need an initial appropriation of twenty thousand dollars but would eventually become self-supporting.⁶¹

58. Quoted in Wise, *Wise*, p. 400.

59. Pollard, "New Virginia," pp. 279–83, 288; *Agricultural Society Immigration Memorial, 1872*, p. 16; Governor's Message, February 8, 1870, *Senate Journal* (1869–70), pp. 42–43.

60. Pollard, "New Virginia," pp. 284–85; Richmond *Whig and Public Advertiser,* January 8 and 25, 1867; *House Journal* (1869–70), p. 233; *Senate Journal* (1869–70), pp. 535–36, and Document III: *Report of the State Board of Immigration to the General Assembly*, pp. 2, 4 (hereafter cited as *Immigration Report, 1870*).

61. Governor's Message, December 6, 1871, *Senate Journal* (1871–72), pp. 16–18.

Walker's recommendation touched off a controversy on the propriety of state appropriations to encourage immigration. Colonel Edmund W. Hubard, speaking for the relatively successful immigration promoters of Mecklenburg County, objected that a system of state agents would be too expensive and would fall prey to special interests.[62] Colonel Frank Ruffin of the Virginia Agricultural Society and R. L. Ragland of the Halifax Agricultural Society advocated state aid. The laissez-faire policy, Ruffin warned, "dooms us to destruction through 'the laws of trade.' "[63] The governor, ordinarily a laissez-faire man, thought private enterprise inadequate in regard to immigration. The Commonwealth should act, he thought, to the extent of advertising Virginia and facilitating land sales to immigrants, perhaps even entering the real estate business on its own account.[64] The General Assembly shied away from Walker's plan, as from anything that would cost much money. The cause of state aid lay dormant for three more years.

In the session of 1874–75, Governor Kemper had more success with the legislature. On Kemper's recommendation, it established a new Board of Immigration, consisting of state officials acting ex officio, under the governor's chairmanship. The legislature appropriated ten thousand dollars for the board's work and authorized it to collect and publish information, employ agents at home and abroad, and contract with landowners to sell land to immigrants.[65] The project did not fulfill its initial promise. The appropriation obviously could finance only a few of the activities the bill authorized.[66] Very early, the board decided not to employ agents abroad or deal directly in real estate. It did plan a network of local agencies, which would finance their operations partly by commissions on land sales to immigrants, but these functioned sporadically if at all.[67]

62. Edmund W. Hubard to Gilbert C. Walker, November 2, 1872, and Hubard to Walker, November 27, 1872, both in "Immigration," Box 4, Gilbert Carlton Walker Executive Correspondence.

63. R. L. Ragland to Walker, November 16, 1872, *ibid.*; *Agricultural Society Immigration Memorial, 1872,* pp. 9–11, 16–17.

64. Walker to Edmund W. Hubard, November 20, 1872, Edmund Willcox Hubard Papers, Southern Historical Collection, University of North Carolina at Chapel Hill; Governor's Message, December 4, 1872, *Senate Journal* (1872–73), p. 14.

65. Governor's Message, December 2, 1874, *Senate Journal* (1874–75), p. 14; Jones, "Conservative Virginian," pp. 297–98.

66. See *Senate Journal* (1874–75), Document XVIII: *Memorial of the British Association of Virginia in relation to the Appointment of a Commissioner to Visit Europe in the Interest of Immigration,* pp. 1–2.

67. Meade C. Kemper (for James L. Kemper) to William Sherwood (copy), December 20, 1875, Kemper Executive Letter-Book (1875–77), Virginia Historical Society;

The board also belatedly published a revision of the "geographical and political summary of Virginia," which Major Jedidah Hotchkiss had compiled for that purpose in 1872. It neglected, however, the task Hotchkiss considered more important: *continuous* collection and dissemination of information on Virginia. The *Summary* sold slowly—because the board found that it had no power to establish channels to market or advertise the publication! "The immigration project and sale of Hotchkiss' pamphlet," William D. Chesterman wrote late in 1876, "have been a dead failure. The scheme has never had the breath of life put into it and fell still born."[68]

Many private organizations and companies worked to attract settlers. Some treated the immigrant laborer as a mere commodity of trade. Few lasted long or achieved significant results.[69] The principal exception, the Southside Virginia Board of Settlers, began when a promoter, selling land in a compact section of Mecklenburg County to immigrant colonies, generated the impetus among the settlers themselves to launch the board and its newspaper, the Chase City *Southside Virginian*. The group drew an impressive number of settlers to the area.[70]

In comparison with the "human Nile" that Conservative prophets foretold, actual foreign immigration to Virginia was a puny trickle. Of about 213,000 immigrants who entered the United States in 1868, only 713 came to Virginia. During the 1870's, only about 2,900 more foreign-born persons moved into Virginia than left the

---

M. C. Kemper (for J. L. Kemper) to John Bear Jones (copy), April 20, 1875, Kemper Executive Letter-Book (1874–75), Virginia State Library; Jones, "Conservative Virginian," p. 298.

68. *Senate Journal* (1874), Document V: *Communication from the Secretary of the Board of Immigration, in response to a Resolution of the Senate, Calling for Information as to What Steps Have Been Taken by That Board to Secure the Publication of a Geographical and Political Summary of Virginia,* pp. 2, 6–8; *Senate Journal* (1876–77), Document V: *Communication from the Governor of Virginia transmitting Report of the State Board of Immigration and the Secretary of the Board,* pp. 3–4; Petersburg *Index and Appeal,* November 21, 1876.

69. See W. W. Nevia to James L. Kemper, June 20, 1870; New York Southern Land Company broadside [July, 1870]; John Goode, Jr., to Kemper, January 10, 1873, all in Kemper Papers, University of Virginia; J. B. Compton to John D. Imboden, September 4, 1875, John Daniel Imboden Papers, University of Virginia; John W. Johnston to William T. Sutherlin, March 28, 1877, Sutherlin Papers.

70. Norfolk *Virginian,* January 24, 1875; J. Y. Ashehurst and Thomas Drew to Gilbert C. Walker, [n.d.], "Immigration," Box 4, Gilbert Carlton Walker Executive Correspondence; see map of Mecklenburg County, 1872, with settlers' lands marked, in Hubard Papers.

state. They did not begin to offset the net out-migration of about 54,000 native Americans.[71] In 1871, a Republican state senator caricatured Conservative proposals to encourage immigration by introducing a bill to *discourage emigration*.[72] Still believing in Virginia's basic attractiveness, promoters cast about for reasons as to why their expectations had miscarried. Their explanations—including the failure to provide state aid, the black population's presence, traditionalist newspapers and politicians, the Panic of 1873, and the suspension in 1872 of the Funding Act—were mere reflections of their authors' political preconceptions.[73]

In actuality, Conservatives were not prepared to welcome many typical European immigrants. Most advocates of immigration did not want working-class settlers. Only persons who could purchase farms or businesses on arrival, Commissioner Richardson and Governor Kemper believed, should come to Virginia. Edward A. Pollard warned that immigrant laborers could not prosper there, because they could not under-live black laborers, and that the effort to attract them only enabled labor agents to dump "the refuse of the human flesh-markets of Europe" in the state.[74] In 1870, the General Assembly showed more interest in excluding "pauper immigration" than in attracting immigrants. A rumor that five hundred Dutch settlers had become public charges in Amelia County inspired a legislative investigation, which showed that the colony in fact was prospering.[75]

Conservatives drew ethnic as well as class lines in defining desirable immigrants. The immigration law of 1866 authorized the Board of Immigration to encourage migration from England, Scotland, and perhaps "other British countries." The *Whig*, more lib-

71. Coulter, *South during Reconstruction*, p. 104; Bureau of Census, *Historical Statistics*, pp. 44–46.

72. *Daily Petersburg Index*, December 16, 1871.

73. W. B. McClure to James L. Kemper, July 24, 1876, Kemper Papers, University of Virginia; Bolling W. Haxall to B. Johnson Barbour, March 15, 1871, B. Johnson Barbour Papers, University of Virginia; Philip A. Bolling to Edmund W. Hubard, July 24, 1873, Hubard Papers; C. H. Peirce to Gilbert C. Walker, February 16, 1872, "Immigration," Box 4, Gilbert Carlton Walker Executive Correspondence; *Agriculture Report, 1877*, p. 49.

74. *Immigration Report, 1870*, p. 5; Governor's Message, December 2, 1874, *Senate Journal* (1874–75), p. 14; Meade C. Kemper (for James L. Kemper) to J. Smolinski (copy), July 29, 1874, and M. C. Kemper (for J. L. Kemper) to D. N. Davies (copy), March 27, 1875, both in Kemper Executive Letter-Book (1874–75), Virginia State Library; Pollard, "New Virginia," pp. 285–88.

75. *Senate Journal* (1869–70), pp. 187, 222, 237, 258, 265–66, 325, 366, 377, 440; *House Journal* (1869–70), p. 196.

eral, was willing to accept persons from Ireland, Scandinavia, and possibly even parts of Germany and France.[76] Commissioner Richardson and the Virginia Agricultural Society also preferred British settlers because they were the most readily assimilable.[77]

For all the popularity of immigration as a panacea, many rural Virginians did not like immigrants as neighbors. Some assaulted settlers and destroyed their property—and, in that case, Governor Kemper could only offer his sympathy and refer the victim to local law-enforcement officers.[78] Virginia farmers and immigrant laborers differed in their ideas about living conditions. One Virginia gentleman complacently showed a new crew of German workers to his cramped "Negro quarters" and found the next morning that his ungrateful "hands" had absconded "with such dismay that it is doubtful whether they stopped this side of the Atlantic."[79] Under such circumstances, the idea of attracting immigrants to regenerate the region was futility itself.

Under the Conservative ascendancy, middle-class farmers fared better than the former planter aristocrats and much better than their hired farm workers, the most poorly compensated in the United States.[80] Even so, they only held their own. Their quest for immigration reflected the general problems of their position. They dreamed of the ripe apples of prosperity, but the persistent reality turned the dream to ashes in their mouths. The state government, attentive to commercial and industrial interests, neglected those of farmers. But the landowners' own narrowness of vision contributed greatly to their disappointment. In conceiving of immigration as a necessity for development, they closed their eyes to the existence of the "bottom rails" of the rural population, whom their control of the land condemned to lives of degradation.

76. Richmond *Whig and Public Advertiser*, May 8 and August 7, 1866.

77. *Immigration Report, 1870*, pp. 7–8; *Agricultural Society Immigration Memorial, 1872*, pp. 15–16.

78. James L. Kemper to T. B. Nielson (copy), January 17, 1877, and Kemper to Nielson (copy), March 24, 1877, both in Kemper Executive Letter-Book (1875–77), Virginia Historical Society.

79. Pollard, "New Virginia," p. 288.

80. On farmhands' compensation, see *Agriculture Report, 1877*, p. 49.

12.

White Supremacy
in Theory and Practice

"White supremacy" was an article of faith for Southern conservatives of the Reconstruction era. Later writers have distorted the phrase's meaning by describing as "white supremacists" only persons who voice an arrant Negrophobia and support such crass forms of race control as segregation laws, disfranchisement, and lynching. The usage is misleading. The conservatives first formulated the slogan in resistance to the black bid for power during Reconstruction. In that context, it meant simply what its words said: that the reins of government and society should remain in the hands of members of the white race. Within that broad policy, there was room for many ideas about race and techniques of race control, including a sophisticated elitism under equalitarian legal forms.

Although the white supremacists of the 1870's included advocates of gross means of repression, most of them saw no need for such means as long as everyday social arrangements kept Negroes from acquiring social power. In Virginia, after 1870, black militance abated. In 1878, when a strike by black farmhands briefly interrupted the tranquility, William D. Chesterman took comfort in the fact that urban Negroes appeared less susceptible to "the contagion of communism" than white workers.[1] In so stable a social environment, the Virginia Conservatives were able to uphold the forms of equality before the law and treat Negroes respectfully, without compromising the fundamental condition of white supremacy.

IMAGES OF THE "INVISIBLE MAN"

In 1877, a Northern visitor found Virginians willing, as they had not been in slavery days, to discuss race relations freely

1. Petersburg *Index and Appeal*, June 22, 1878.

with outsiders. They seemed no more concerned about the freed-
man "than about any poor man" and were content "to let you have
your own views about him just as you have them about sheep or
oxen." The visitor heard "a great variety of opinions about him,
mostly depreciatory, it is true, but still varying in degree as well as
in kind."[2]

After the specter of plebeian insurgence passed, Conservatives
evaluated the freedmen almost exclusively by a single criterion:
their efficiency as laborers. Most Conservatives, putting away proslavery ideas, recognized the new labor system as economically superior to the old. Colonel Sutherlin said that emancipation, injur-
ing only a parasitic minority, had given "the vigorous young men
of the time" unprecedented opportunities to make fortunes.[3] Henry
A. Wise stated that slavery had been a curse to character and economic progress and that emancipation had freed whites as well as
blacks from the incubus.[4] The "blight" of slavery, the Staunton
Vindicator declared, had so retarded Virginia's growth that only a
generation growing up in its absence could introduce there the
energy, thrift, and prosperity of the North.[5] A speaker on agriculture estimated that supervised field labor was twice as productive
in Virginia in 1879 as in the slave era.[6]

Agreeing that slavery had retarded the South's development,
Conservatives differed about Negroes' abilities as free laborers.
Some answered emphatically in the negative. In 1866, a German-
Virginian recklessly asserted that the freedmen, economically use-
less, had scattered in idleness and indigence throughout the United
States.[7] Hugh Blair Grigsby claimed that "no contract made in January with a stalwart unmarried negro is worth a cent after the 1st
of June."[8] General Imboden believed that his two English servants
"will do the work of at least 4 negroes, and are more respectful in
their deportment."[9] "I have always observed," General Lee re-

2. [Anonymous], "Some Recent Observations in Virginia," *The Nation*, XXV (September 13, 1877), 164.

3. *Agricultural Society Proceedings, 1866*, pp. 26–27.

4. Wise, *Wise*, pp. 378, 385, 398–99, 412–13.

5. Staunton *Vindicator*, January 12, 1877.

6. William Henry Ruffner, "General Notes" notebook (c. 1879), William Henry
Ruffner Papers, Historical Foundation of the Presbyterian and Reformed Churches.

7. Pohle, "Rise for Virginia!" Preface and p. 3.

8. Hugh Blair Grigsby to Alexander H. H. Stuart, November 24, 1873, Alexander
Hugh Holmes Stuart Papers, University of Virginia.

9. John D. Imboden to Mrs. John D. Imboden, June 13, 1873, John Daniel Imboden Papers, University of Virginia.

marked in 1865, "that wherever you find the Negro, everything is going down around him, and wherever you find the white man, you see everything about him improving."[10]

Other Conservatives were just as certain that black workers were quite competent. If employers would treat them fairly, the *Whig* argued in 1867, Negroes would probably be the best possible "hands" for Virginia agriculture.[11] The Britisher Robert Somers found that almost every "effective employer" held that opinion and that skilled black workers received wages approaching those of their white counterparts.[12] In 1866, Colonel Sutherlin amazed experienced planters by describing his success in farming with black labor, applying the managerial techniques he used in his factories.[13] Thomas Pollard, Virginia's first commissioner of agriculture, calculated in 1877 that black farmhands in Virginia did more daily work than white ones in Massachusetts, although they were paid barely two-fifths as much.[14] Edward A. Pollard, finding black workers industrious, urged employers to grant them better terms and hoped they would become independent craftsmen and farmers.[15]

Some Conservatives imagined that the black population, once freed, was sure to decrease in proportion to the white. In 1866, a Halifax County clergyman wrote that Negroes increased slowly in freedom and that white immigration would render them such a small minority that whites could "keep the few negroes who will be among us . . . as a rarity."[16] In 1869, John R. Edmunds made the strange prediction that, under a Conservative administration, whites would increase by 10 per cent a year and blacks would decrease at the same rate.[17] Even Sutherlin expected that Negroes would eventually disappear.[18] In 1873, Stuart suggested colonizing them abroad to make sure.[19]

10. Freeman, *Lee*, IV, 199.

11. Richmond *Whig and Public Advertiser*, January 18 and 22, 1867.

12. Somers, *Southern States*, pp. 17–18.

13. *Agricultural Society Proceedings, 1866*, pp. 24–26.

14. *Agriculture Report, 1877*, pp. 48–49.

15. Pollard, "New Virginia," pp. 286–87.

16. Richmond *Whig and Public Advertiser,* January 18 and 22, 1866. He argued that conservatives could therefore afford to grant qualified Negro suffrage.

17. *Edmunds Speech, 1869,* p. 7. Misprint "increase" for "decrease." In the first months of Conservative rule, a large number of Negroes did leave the state. See John W. Johnston in *Cong. Globe*, 40 Cong., 2 Sess., 4999 (1870); Edward A. Pollard, "The Negro in the South," *Lippincott's Magazine*, V (April, 1870), 385–86.

18. *Agricultural Society Proceedings, 1866,* p. 26.

19. Robert C. Winthrop to Alexander H. H. Stuart, November 13, 1873; A. D.

On the other hand, the white-supremacy idea afforded room for the expectation that freedmen not only would survive but might improve racially, approaching equality with white men. General Logan attributed Negroes' defects during slavery to "limited race education and advantages."[20] The Staunton *Vindicator* thought that slavery had degraded the race. After two generations of education and self-help, it predicted, "the virus of slavery will be out of the black man and he will be a different and better citizen."[21] Superintendent Ruffner, the only Conservative who attempted a scholarly study of race, concluded that the Negroes were descended from the founders of the first human civilization, that of ancient Ethiopia. The race, he thought, had degenerated in the debilitating environment of tropical Africa but was again evolving upward in America. Since emancipation, Negroes had progressed so rapidly that they might someday become one of the world's most advanced peoples. Race prejudice, Ruffner lightly assumed, would die out as they advanced.[22] Even Ruffner, though, did not question the need for white supremacy in his own day. He defended school segregation, advised Negroes that their progress must be gradual, and refrained from publishing his most novel racial ideas.

Conservatives defined Negroes' "progress" as assimilation to white society's standards, by white men's assistance. A typical philanthropic effort was the one Colonel James H. Skinner launched in the Young Men's Christian Association at Staunton. Skinner deplored the effects of Negro suffrage and hoped to remedy them by benevolent assistance—a work "of temporal benefit to ourselves" as well as one "to the praise and glory of God." The Staunton *Vindicator* agreed that blacks needed the kind of Christianity that produced "citizens more profitable to the state." After a month of YMCA discussion, several white "missionaries" finally visited a Negro church, unexpectedly, and offered their ministrations. The

---

Dickinson to Stuart, November 20, 1873; and Hugh Blair Grigsby to Stuart, November 24, 1873; all in Stuart Papers; E. C. Burks to Wyndham Robertson, October 4, 1873, Wyndham Robertson Papers, University of Chicago.

20. Quoted in Morrill, *Builder of the New South*, p. 132.

21. Staunton *Vindicator*, January 12, 1877.

22. Ruffner, "General Notes" notebook (c. 1879), Ruffner Papers; "Proceedings of the Department of Superintendence of the National Education Association at Its Meeting at Washington, D. C., February 18–20, 1880," *Circulars of Information of the [United States] Bureau of Education, 1880*, II, 80 (hereafter cited as "Department of Superintendence, 1880"); William Henry Ruffner, "The Co-education of the White and Colored Races," *Scribner's Monthly*, VIII (May, 1874), pp. 89–90 (hereafter cited as "Co-education of Races").

"heathen" politely rebuffed those who sought to improve them, and the philanthropists' enthusiasm waned.[23]

Lacking sophisticated theories of racial superiority, Conservatives operated on a variety of working assumptions within the scope of white supremacy. They took for granted that black persons were inferior to whites in intellectual ability, that they should enjoy ordinary legal rights but occupy a subordinate social status, and that they should possess the franchise but not exert political power in proportion to their numbers.

CIVIL RIGHTS

White supremacists took up a version of the laissez-faire philosophy that had inspired the attack on slavery. Edward A. Pollard's policy in 1868 was to give the Negro basic legal rights and "leave him to gravitate to the condition which nature and experience shall assign to him."[24] In 1872, the House of Delegates resolved that since all Virginians were constitutionally guaranteed equal civil rights, there was no need for civil rights legislation.[25] Equality, as the Conservatives recognized it, was almost entirely a matter of formal legal status.

The Conservatives followed a moderate policy in regard to civil rights. Governor Kemper promised that his administration would uphold the Reconstruction amendments to the federal Constitution but would insist on state control of race relations within the limits the amendments set. They defined a national consensus in which, Kemper said, "the political equality of the races is settled, and the social equality of the races is a settled impossibility." It would be "political insanity" for "the weaker and relatively diminishing race" to try to take control of the state government. On the other hand, the whites—with the advantages of numbers, wealth, education, and power—could afford to conciliate the blacks. Racial conflict weakened the state and slowed economic growth; it might invite federal intervention or provoke blacks to militance. The Conservatives' cardinal principle in civil-rights policy, Kemper declared, was to enact no law that explicitly discriminated against either race.[26] Generally speaking, the party carried out that policy.

23. Staunton *Vindicator*, January 12 and 26, and February 16, 1877.
24. Pollard, *Lost Cause Regained*, p. 185.
25. *House Journal* (1871–72), p. 241.
26. Governor's Message, January 1, 1874, *Senate Journal* (1874), pp. 17–18; Governor's Veto Message, March 12, 1874, *ibid.*, p. 186.

Conservatives did not consider laws against interracial marriage discriminations against either race. In 1873, the General Assembly enacted a law subjecting a white person who married a Negro to a maximum punishment of a year in prison and a fine of a hundred dollars. In 1878, it declared such marriages "offenses against morality and decency" and provided prison sentences of between two and five years for couples who left the state to marry and returned at once. But it was not until 1879 that the legislature declared marriages beween white persons and those of as much as one-fourth Negro ancestry legally void.[27]

The Commonwealth operated its own institutions on a segregated basis. Governor Walker set up the Central Lunatic Asylum exclusively for Negroes, and each public school and college was for students of a single race. Conservatives even threatened to scuttle the free-school system if Congress should pass laws against school segregation.[28] Some of them subscribed to the "separate but equal" doctrine of dividing school funds between the races in proportion to their numbers. Superintendent Ruffner advocated it but failed to realize it in his school system, and Congressman R. T. W. Duke wrote it into a bill for federal aid to Virginia schools.[29] In 1872, twenty Conservatives voted in the House of Delegates to give black institutions five-twelfths—the population ratio—of Virginia's Morrill Act fund for technical colleges. The majority gave black colleges only a third of the fund.[30]

Outside its own institutions, the Commonwealth did not require segregation in public accommodations. In private conduct, there was no strict, generally accepted code of racial mores. The white social leadership was gradually developing a racial etiquette, complicated by variants and exceptions, that required Negroes to occupy subordinate roles when the races came into contact. "We give

27. Wynes, *Race Relations*, pp. 92–93. The 1873 law was vulnerable to the objection that, by the Conservatives' standards, it discriminated against white persons.

28. Governor's Message, February 9, 1870, *Senate Journal* (1869–70), p. 53; Governor's Message, December 6, 1871, *Senate Journal* (1871–72), pp. 19–20; Jones, "Conservative Virginian," p. 233n; Norfolk *Journal*, January 10, 1874; *Fourth Annual Report of the Superintendent of Public Instruction, for the Year ending August 31, 1874; with Reports of the Virginia Agricultural and Mechanical College, and Hampton Normal and Agricultural Institute* (Richmond: Richard F. Walker, Superintendent of Public Printing, 1874), pp. 42–52 (hereafter cited as *School Report, 1874*); Ruffner, "Co-education of Races," p. 89; Wynes, *Race Relations*, p. 124.

29. Ruffner, "Co-education of Races," p. 89; Wynes, *Race Relations*, p. 128; *Cong. Globe*, 41 Cong., 3 Sess., pp. 491, 676.

30. *House Journal* (1871–72), pp. 237, 466–67.

the colored race equal political and legal rights," Congressman John T. Harris of Harrisonburg said, "but social equality, never! never! never!" Since Negroes resented overt subordination, interracial contact progressively declined.[31] White businessmen often practiced segregation, but not in the rigid, uniform system that was later to appear. Hotels and restaurants ordinarily operated on a segregated basis. Lecture-halls provided separate seating for Negroes but did not always enforce separation.[32] Railroad companies expected white passengers to ride first-class and Negroes second-class, and some even provided "Jim Crow" cars. However individuals of each race departed with impunity from the custom. After 1875 railroad officials stopped trying to enforce segregation, and both races rode in the same cars until the turn of the century.[33]

Perhaps the integration of railroads in Virginia was the only lasting effect of the public-accommodations sections of the Civil Rights Act of 1875. After Congress passed the law, a few Virginia Negroes challenged segregation, and some previously segregated businesses served them. By monolithic unity, though, whites usually kept their mores intact. On a packet-boat on the James River and Kanawha Canal, for instance, the white passengers refused to enter the dining hall until the sole black passenger finished his dinner. At night the captain, exercising his customary prerogative, assigned the Negro the steward's berth, apart from the white passengers.[34] In 1883, the Supreme Court of the United States invalidated the Civil Rights Act insofar as it applied to private practices. The court's civil-rights policy accorded with the Conservatives'—that racial discrimination should not appear on the face of a law.

In administering justice, Conservatives showed conventional racial biases, with local variations. The state judges in Richmond, reported a black correspondent, accorded more respect to black attorneys than did District of Columbia judges. In rural justice-of-the peace courts, on the other hand, white litigants, justices, and lawyers regularly intimidated Negroes.[35] With occasional excep-

31. John T. Harris in *Cong. Globe*, 42 Cong., 2 Sess., 853–56 (1872); Wynes, *Race Relations*, pp. 68, 82–83, 90–91; Philip Alexander Bruce, *The Plantation Negro as a Freeman: Observations on His Character, Condition, and Prospects in Virginia* (New York and London: G. P. Putnam's Sons, 1889), pp. 44–57, 242–43 (hereafter cited as *Plantation Negro*).
32. Wynes, *Race Relations*, pp. 76–80; [Allan-Olney], *New Virginians*, I, 238.
33. Wynes, *Race Relations*, pp. 68–75.
34. *Ibid.*, pp. 77–78, 116–17; [Allan-Olney], *New Virginians*, I, 237–38; II, 100–105.
35. Alexandria *People's Advocate*, May 13, 1876; [Allan-Olney], *New Virginians*, II, 80–84.

tions, Conservative court officers summoned only white men for jury service. Legislators claimed that, since neither constitution nor laws excluded Negroes from serving, there was no need for legislation to secure them the right to serve.[36]

In 1878, Conservative jury practices came under the scrutiny of federal courts, in which Negroes did serve on juries. The federal grand jury for the Western District of Virginia indicted county judge J. D. Coles of Pittsylvania County for excluding Negroes on racial grounds. Judge Alexander Rives of the Western District also removed to his court the murder trial of two black youths in Patrick County, where no Negro had ever been a juryman, on the grounds that they could not receive a fair trial in the local court. The state government called on the United States Supreme Court to free Judge Coles and remand the Patrick County defendants to state custody. In 1879, the Supreme Court's majority upheld Coles's arrest and arraignment under the Civil Rights Act, but the same justices, taking at face value the state constitution's statement that all qualified citizens were eligible for jury duty, required the Patrick County youths to seek redress in state courts.[37] As in the later Civil Rights Cases, the court's ideas partly resembled those of the Conservatives.

As moderate white supremacists, the Conservatives kept race relations more stable and less violent in Virginia than in other southern states. Negroes and Northern white men bore witness to the difference.[38] Such organizations as the Ku Klux Klan did not take hold, and some Conservatives condemned the Klan's violence in other states.[39] The tranquility was only relative; acts of political and racial violence did occur in Virginia.[40] Nor did the relative placidity prove that racial and partisan oppression were absent—only that they were well institutionalized. Since Conservatives were in power in Virginia, Republican Congressman Charles H. Porter of Rich-

36. Wynes, *Race Relations*, pp. 138–41. Federal courts, Conservatives claimed, exercised similar prerogatives to exclude Conservatives from federal juries. Richard T. W. Duke in *Cong. Globe*, 42 Cong., 1 Sess., 2243 (1871).

37. *Virginia v. Rives*, 100 U. S. 313–24 (1879); *Ex parte Virginia*, 100 U. S. 339–49 (1879).

38. Wynes, *Race Relations*, pp. 95–96.

39. Richard T. W. Duke in *Cong. Globe*, 42 Cong., 1 Sess., *Appendix*, 90 (1871).

40. Petersburg *Index and Appeal*, August 11, 1877; [Allan-Olney], *New Virginians*, II, 164; Mrs. Adeline Dobbs to Gilbert C. Walker, November 8, 1870; J. R. Bailey to Walker, November 25, 1870; Bailey to Walker, May 8, 1871; and Bailey to Walker, n.d. [1871], all in "Letters on various subjects," Box 3, Gilbert Carlton Walker Executive Correspondence, Virginia State Library.

mond said, they needed no Ku Klux Klan: "The outrages committed upon loyal men there are under the forms of law."[41] The Conservatives managed to "keep the lid on" their society, rarely enraging either Negroes or Negrophobes.

They never banished the possibility of civil disturbance from their minds, however. On the eve of the presidential election of 1876, premonitions of a black uprising spread among whites in all parts of the state. Local officials and militia officers applied to Richmond for additional arms. Governor Kemper discredited the hysteria and refused the arms. Frantic arming by white militia, he pointed out, might itself inspire Negro violence or federal intervention. The federal government did send soldiers to Petersburg but no disorder occurred. The prophets of danger could point only to a "Negro disturbance" in the streets of Richmond—actually an informal election celebration, dispersed by a few policemen.[42]

In view of the social structure's instability, Conservatives considered the state militia important to preserve order. In 1870, Adjutant General Richardson, anxious to organize the militia, warned that "the negroes have arms almost or quite to a man."[43] Governor Walker wanted a militia to repress outbreaks against the Conservative government.[44] Governor Kemper thought that "the new and abnormal society of a Southern State" made it necessary to equip the militia for camp and combat.[45] He insisted on a volunteer militia, instead of one consisting of all adult males, to insure that white officers would control it. He rejected the idea of two segregated inclusive militia organizations, since combat situations might put black officers in command of white units.[46] Kemper was willing to use black militia in disturbances, but only under white command.

The Virginia militia consisted of segregated volunteer companies, white units greatly predominating. Adjutant General Richardson and his associates sometimes tried, by partisan application of rules, to obstruct the formation and continuance of black companies. Kemper, who presided in 1874 over a review of black mili-

41. Charles H. Porter in *Cong. Globe*, 42 Cong., 1 Sess., *Appendix*, 277 (1871).

42. Jones, "Conservative Virginian," pp. 326–28; Frank G. Ruffin to Lewis E. Harvie, November 10, 1876, Lewis Evarts Harvie Papers, Virginia State Library.

43. William H. Richardson to James L. Kemper, May 20, 1870, James Lawson Kemper Papers, University of Virginia.

44. Governor's Message, December 7, 1870, *Senate Journal* (1870–71), pp. 17, 21.

45. James L. Kemper to George H. Williams (copy), October 6, 1874, James Lawson Kemper Executive Letter-Book (1874–75), Virginia State Library.

46. Kemper to Dabney H. Maury (copy), May 2, 1876, Kemper Executive Letter-Book (1875–77), Virginia Historical Society.

tia, defended the units.[47] The companies performed an ornamental function in ceremonies. The black militia of Richmond participated in the funeral of Confederate General George Pickett on October 24, 1876, and were scheduled to take part in the unveiling, two days later, of the Foley statue of General "Stonewall" Jackson on Monument Avenue. General Jubal Early objected to the interracial aspect of the ceremony, predicting that the black companies would carry banners honoring Lincoln and the Fifteenth Amendment. Governor Kemper—finding that Richmond Negroes, Mrs. Jackson, and the available Confederate leaders all wanted the black troops present—left the program unaltered. Early, incensed at the governor, denounced the program as *"an insult to all Confederates who have any respect for themselves left,"* and Kemper urged the Negrophobic general to stay away from the ceremony, fearing that his very presence would touch off a race riot. The black companies, for unexplained reasons, did not take part in the unveiling, but Negroes who had been attendants in the Stonewall Brigade marched with its veterans.[48] The incident illustrated the difficulties of Conservative leaders who tried by brokerage to adjust the irreconcilable demands of Negroes and of Negrophobes.

The Conservatives' policy in civil rights was to uphold equality of rights in the forms of law but (by the everyday use of their economic and governmental power) to continue the black race's social subordination. The second objective required them sometimes to stretch, but hardly ever to violate, the first. Official impartiality—as Conservatives interpreted it—usually afforded ample means to uphold white supremacy. A case in point occurred when a group of Negroes asked to use the state Capitol to celebrate the anniversary of their emancipation. Governor Kemper managed to refuse the request while still adhering to the rule of official impartiality by discontinuing the customary use of the Capitol for "political or quasi-political" meetings.[49] "Equality before the law" did not disturb the distribution of social power.

47. *Daily Petersburg Index*, November 17, 1871; Robert L. Hobson to Kemper, February 17, 1874, Kemper Executive Correspondence, Virginia State Library; Meade C. Kemper (for J. L. Kemper) to Hobson (copy), February 19, 1874, Kemper Executive Letter-Book (1874–75), Virginia State Library; Petersburg *Index and Appeal*, February 24, 1874; Kemper to William H. Richardson, June 15, 1876, Kemper Executive Letter-Book (1875–77), Virginia Historical Society.

48. Jones, "Conservative Virginian," pp. 276, 300–303.

49. James L. Kemper to R. E. Blankenship (copy), September 19, 1877, Kemper Executive Letter-Book (1875–77), Virginia Historical Society.

POLITICAL RIGHTS

The Conservative leaders recognized the active political rights of Negroes to the same extent that they recognized passive civil rights. Some may have hoped to disfranchise Negroes at some future time,[50] but most neither wanted to nor expected an opportunity to do so. They were content with Negro suffrage as long as it did not give the black five-twelfths of the population much political power. President Grant's reconstruction policy, the Conservative leadership approvingly said in 1870, had "recognized the political enfranchisement of the negro" but given the whites "the opportunity to secure for themselves the control of the State forever."[51] As long as the white majority observed the "color line" in voting, the Conservatives would control the state government, whose centralized structure would limit the power of local black majorities. In addition, Conservatives hoped in 1869 that the white population would outstrip the black in growth and that many Negroes would come to vote the Conservative ticket. The Negroes' votes, therefore, would not give them real power.

Paternalistic white supremacists believed that the Negro's best interest consisted "more in being governed well, than in directing Government."[52] His "true interest," Conservatives decided, was for racial harmony and solidarity with his employer. For several years after "redemption," therefore, they hoped that many Negroes would vote their ticket.[53] When freedmen continued to vote overwhelmingly Republican, they postponed their hopes to the future. In 1873, R. M. T. Hunter disappointedly announced that the Negroes were not true Virginians because they supported an alien party against the state's rulers. He still predicted, though, that they would someday join the Conservative fold.[54] The Conservatives' purpose, Governor Kemper asserted in 1874, was not to subject the Negro to the white man; it was only to break down the carpetbaggers' "oathbound" Republican organization, so Negroes would "come under

50. "If I had the power," J. S. Duckwall, a traditionalist living in West Virginia, wrote in 1874, ". . . I would not allow the negroes to vote at all. The Time has not come for this species of legislation. . . ." J. S. Duckwall to Kemper, March 31, 1874, Kemper Papers, University of Virginia. See also John Robertson to Wyndham Robertson, November 19, 1869, Robertson Papers.

51. *Conservative Address, 1870,* p. 4.

52. Robert M. T. Hunter, manuscript Conservative Address to Congress, 1868, Hunter-Garnett Papers, University of Virginia.

53. Pearson, *Readjuster Movement,* p. 35; see Bruce, *Plantation Negro,* pp. 67–69.

54. *Hunter Speech, 1873,* pp. 3–4.

the same influences which governed other men in forming party affiliations."[55] Believing their own rule was in the best interest of all, white Conservative leaders saw no need for a countervailing political force.

Conservatives alternated their invitations to Negroes with racist appeals to white solidarity. In the gubernatorial election of 1873, in particular, they made much of the "color line." Party Chairman Meade led "a red hot campaign on the issue of races." Kemper described the parties as "the white man's party and the negro party" and called Hughes a "Judas" for running on the latter's ticket. Withers declared that "wherever the issue is made by which the white man is on one side and the negro on the other he would always be found on the side with his race."[56]

The 1873 campaign did not, in fact, reflect a sharp change in Conservative race policy.[57] Before and after 1873, the Conservative party was a paternalistic white supremacist party that presented itself to white voters as embodying the "expressed will" of their race[58] and welcomed black voters on the basis of their "true interest." From a paternalist viewpoint, the two appeals were consistent, although Conservatives differed in their emphases. In the 1873 campaign, Kemper, as candidate of "the white man's party," promised to uphold Negroes' equal rights under the law. Other Conservatives solicited Negroes' votes and criticized Meade's racist strategy.[59] Meade himself was using the racist emphasis, in part, to divert attention from economic issues that would divide his party.[60] Conservatives directed the "color line" especially to white laborers and craftsmen, whom Hughes was trying to win by his economic policies.[61]

The Conservatives never ceased to seek the support of Negroes. In 1874, they persuaded a considerable number of Negroes to vote their ticket in Petersburg and Norfolk city elections.[62] In the Richmond mayoralty election of 1876, Conservative candidate Charles S. Carrington so openly and successfully courted the black vote that

55. *Kemper Letter, 1874*, p. 2.
56. Jones, "Conservative Virginian," pp. 199–200; Petersburg *Index and Appeal*, November 3, 1873.
57. Pearson, *Readjuster Movement*, p. 49, and Wynes, *Race Relations*, pp. 10–12, argue that it did.
58. *Conservative Address, 1870*, p. 4.
59. Jones, "Conservative Virginian," pp. 200, 202–3; Fahrner, "Smith," p. 326.
60. See quotation in Jones, "Conservative Virginian," p. 200.
61. See Petersburg *Index and Appeal*, November 3, 1873.
62. Jones, "Conservative Virginian," p. 234.

the Republican J. Ambler Smith, running as an independent, attacked Carrington as a Negrophile.[63] A few months later, Conservatives lionized the Reverend J. W. Dungee of Richmond, a former conductor on the "underground railroad," who broke with other black leaders to support Tilden.[64] It did not pay, Conservatives learned, to scorn the black vote. Stith Bolling, defeated in 1873 as a candidate for the House of Delegates, blamed Conservatives who had decided they did not want Negroes' votes.[65]

Some Conservatives used foul means instead of fair, to win or neutralize the black vote. Gerrymandering, intimidation, bribery, election violence, and fraud figured from time to time in their campaign methods.[66] Conservative officials, using separate ballot boxes for the races, sometimes limited the number of Negroes who could vote in the allotted time by delaying them with technicalities.[67] In the congressional election of 1874, ballots bearing the label "Regular Republican Ticket" and the name of Conservative candidate Gilbert C. Walker circulated in Richmond.[68] In 1875, election judges in one Richmond ward, drinking heavily while on duty, assigned only thirteen votes to the Republican candidate for state senator. Fifty-six literate and fifty illiterate voters later claimed to have voted Republican, and the ballot box contained seventy Conservative ballots that looked as though they had been deposited at the same time.[69] Some campaigners specialized in rounding up black voters. "I have voted about 20 American citizens of African

63. Richmond *Dispatch*, May 25, 1876.
64. Petersburg *Index and Appeal*, August 5 and 28, September 13, and October 31, 1876; Alexandria *People's Advocate*, July 15, 1876.
65. Stith Bolling to William Mahone, November 11, 1873, William Mahone Papers, Duke University.
66. James H. Platt, Jr., in *Cong. Globe*, 42 Cong., 2 Sess., 1439, and *Appendix*, 196, 199–200 (1872); Petersburg *Index and Appeal*, November 13 and December 12, 1873; Richard F. Walker to William Mahone, November 20, 1868, and Abram Fulkerson to Mahone, November 5, 1873, both in Mahone Papers; J. R. Watkins to Gilbert C. Walker, September 22, 1873; T. L. R. Baker to Walker, October 27, 1873; John W. Lawson to Walker, November 1, 1873, all in Gilbert Carlton Walker Executive Correspondence; Henry P. Drain to James L. Kemper, n.d., Kemper Executive Correspondence, Virginia State Library; George T. Peers to J. Randolph Tucker, November 6, 1878, Tucker Family Papers, Southern Historical Collection, University of North Carolina at Chapel Hill; Avary, *Dixie after the War*, p. 288.
67. James H. Platt, Jr., in *Cong. Globe*, 42 Cong., 2 Sess., 1439, and *Appendix*, 196, 198, 200 (1872).
68. Ballots enclosed in Richard F. Walker to William Mahone, November 4, 1874, Mahone Papers.
69. *Senate Journal* (1875–76), Document XIII: *Reports of the Senate Committee of Privileges and Elections in the Case of Knight vs. Johnson in the Senate of Virginia*, pp. 37–38 (hereafter cited as *Knight-Johnson Contest, 1876*).

'scent' for you . . .," General William Skeen wrote to J. Randolph Tucker in 1874. "Remember the darkie as I have, kindly; for it is his misfortune & not his fault that he is cursed with freedom."[70]

The few black voters who joined the Conservatives acted on a variety of motives. The sophisticated—such as the leaders of the State Association of Colored Conservatives, which functioned in 1876—had become disillusioned with the Republican party's corruption and subservience to wealth and hoped that dividing the black vote would increase the race's leverage in both parties.[71] Others, though, were Conservative out of ignorance, authoritarian moralism, desire for white men's approval, snobbery, displaced self-hatred, or simple opportunism.[72] They were a small group; the great majority of Negroes remained Republicans.

Negroes' political behavior, incomprehensible to Conservatives, drove them almost to distraction. To whites, the blacks appeared completely apathetic until election day when they flocked to the polls and voted as a bloc. Conservatives usually attributed the phenomenon to the black community's coercive discipline. Some concluded that the Negro's politics consisted of a perverse opposition to whomever and whatever the whites supported.[73] The Negroes' incurable Republicanism eventually revived Conservatives' latent doubts about Negro suffrage. "It creates a mournful realization of the unhappy state of our country," John W. Daniel wrote in 1876, "to reflect that political power should be at all reposed in beings so utterly disqualified for its responsible and intelligent use" as illiterate Negroes.[74]

The idea of making payment of poll taxes a suffrage qualification originated in Conservative leaders' search for revenue. In 1871, Governor Walker proposed to double the capitation tax, financing the schools entirely from that source. Incidentally, he suggested

70. William Skeen to J. Randolph Tucker, November 3, 1874, Tucker Family Papers.

71. Petersburg *Index and Appeal*, October 31, 1876.

72. See—a remarkable psychological document—[Anonymous] to James L. Kemper, April 8, 1875, "Letters on various subjects," Box 3, Gilbert Carlton Walker Executive Correspondence; see also William Henry Ruffner, 1894 reminiscence based on Ruffner Diary (Ruffner Papers), for February 13, 1848.

73. Richard T. W. Duke in *Cong. Globe*, 42 Cong., 1 Sess., *Appendix*, 90–91; [Allan-Olney], *New Virginians*, II, 148–50; Petersburg *Index and Appeal*, August 5, 1876; Bruce, *Plantation Negro*, pp. 62–65, 74–75; Royall, *Reminiscences*, p. 103. Superintendent Ruffner showed somewhat greater understanding. "Department of Superintendence, 1880," p. 80.

74. *Knight-Johnson Contest, 1876*, p. 23.

making payment of the tax a suffrage condition, as a means to enforce its collection. It would then be, he claimed, "the most thoroughly collected tax imposed."[75] A year later, though, Walker added a second justification: "to preserve . . . the purity of elections" and "throw an additional safeguard around the ballot box."[76] The two objects were inconsistent: insofar as the requirement would accomplish one, it would fail to accomplish the other.[77] Most Conservatives probably thought it would be a good thing in either case.

In 1876, by amending the state constitution, the Conservatives made payment of the poll tax a prerequisite for voting, made conviction for petty larceny a suffrage disqualification, and allowed the legislature by two-thirds vote to re-enfranchise men disqualified for dueling. Without mentioning race, the amendments tended to disfranchise the poor, and the bulk of Negroes were poor. It was difficult to measure the political effect of these restrictions.[78] For about three years before the amendments, Negroes, finding that their votes had negligible effect on public policy, had been voting in smaller numbers. Nevertheless, the Richmond *State* and Petersburg *Index* thought the amendments effected "almost . . . a political revolution" in deterring Negroes from voting in 1877.[79] By subtracting enough black voters to decide elections in some of the darker counties, they rendered voting futile for a much larger number not directly disfranchised.

The right to hold office, like the right to vote, did not of itself transfer social power to black hands. For a generation after the "new movement," Negroes sat in the General Assembly and held local offices. The number of black legislators declined from thirty in 1869–70 to five in 1878–79. Only in the assembly of 1869–71 were any of them Conservatives. The black members sponsored bills for civil rights and penal reform but exerted little influence on legisla-

75. Governor's Message, December 6, 1871, *Senate Journal* (1871–72), p. 22.

76. Governor's Message, December 4, 1872, *Senate Journal* (1872–73), p. 13.

77. Superintendent Ruffner showed a similar ambivalence. *Third Annual Report of the Superintendent of Public Instruction, for the Year ending August 31, 1873; with Reports of the Virginia Agricultural and Mechanical College, and Hampton Normal and Agricultural Institute* (Richmond: Richard F. Walker, Superintendent of Public Printing, 1873), pp. 177–79 (hereafter cited as *School Report, 1873*).

78. See the differing views of Pearson, *Readjuster Movement*, pp. 49–50; Wynes, *Race Relations*, pp. 12–14, 135–36; Jones, "Conservative Virginian," pp. 292–96. In 1875, about an eighth of the liable whites and a fourth of the liable blacks failed to pay the capitation tax. *Senate Journal* (1876–77), Document XVII: *Communication from the Auditor of Public Accounts in response to Senate Resolution Calling for a Statement concerning Capitation Tax for the Year 1875*, p. 4.

79. Petersburg *Index and Appeal*, November 8, 1877.

tion.[80] Traditionalist George Wythe Munford, who had been clerk of the antebellum House of Delegates, could not bear to watch the "Big Black Buck negroes" legislating in the seats of the Fathers. The Conservative members, on the contrary, associated amicably with their black colleagues and accorded them the usual signs of respect.[81]

Only extremists among the Conservatives were opposed on principle to Negroes holding any offices. Conservatives sometimes supported black candidates against white Republicans, and the Staunton *Spectator* pronounced Louisa County's black superintendent of the poor superior to his white predecessors. Principal Samuel Chapman Armstrong of Hampton Institute observed that, although white Virginians would not tolerate being governed by Negroes, they did not begrudge them minority representation in the legislature.[82] In 1870, Governor Walker appointed Thomas Campbell, a Staunton Negro, to the Board of Governors of the Central Lunatic Asylum, and the state Senate elected Abraham Hall, a black Conservative, its doorkeeper.[83] Subsequently, Conservatives rarely if ever appointed Negroes to even minor positions. Conservative leaders in Norfolk were unable to persuade Governor Walker to appoint even a black notary there.[84]

Conceding to Negroes only token representation in government, Conservative officials recognized them as members of their constituencies and consulted with their "leaders" to adjust relations between the state and the black community. Kemper boasted that he had "influence with them [Negroes] through their preachers and leaders."[85] The relationship allowed room for consultation and benevolence, but the white Conservatives made the decisions.

80. Luther Porter Jackson, *Negro Office-Holders in Virginia, 1865–1895* (Norfolk: Guide Quality Press, 1945), pp. 72–79 (hereafter cited as *Negro Office-Holders*).

81. George Wythe Munford to Wyndham Robertson, February 13, 1874, Robertson Papers; Somers, *Southern States*, p. 17; Pearson, *Readjuster Movement*, p. 35n; *Senate Journal* (1869–70), pp. 365–66, 498; [Anonymous], "Personnel of the General Assembly," *The Old Dominion*, IV (May 15, 1870), 299–300; James Shepherd Pike Diary, Calais Free Library (typescript copy in possession of Professor Robert F. Durden, Duke University), January 21, 1873.

82. Wynes, *Race Relations*, pp. 85–88.

83. Staunton *Vindicator*, March 23, 1877.

84. Richard Lewellen to Gilbert C. Walker, January 11, 1872; James E. Fuller to Walker, January 11, 1872; T. R. Borland to Walker, January 18, 1872; Borland to Walker, December 30, 1873; Fuller to James L. Kemper, March 21, 1874; Borland to Kemper, March 23, 1874; and Fuller to Kemper, November 11, 1874, all in Gilbert Carlton Walker Executive Correspondence.

85. *Cong. Globe*, 40 Cong., 2 Sess., 2385 (1870); Jones, "Conservative Virginian," p. 300n.

THE PETERSBURG STORY

Negro suffrage, even under a Conservative state government, deprived the planters in predominantly black counties of the political power they had once enjoyed, since Republicans represented their districts at Richmond and Washington. Conservatives in southern and eastern Virginia chafed under that situation,[86] which Conservative rule in the state did not alter. In 1876 Governor Kemper refused, in the absence of a nonpartisan pretext, to reschedule an election in a black district to reduce Negroes' participation. In the same year, the State Board of Canvassers "counted in" a black state senator and a white Republican congressman in southeastern Virginia.[87] Conservatives in that area, unable to win local elections, wanted appointive offices or representation on the state ticket as a consolation. Conservatives in the rest of the state paid little attention to them. The Conservative party never nominated a resident of the rural southeast for one of the three principal state offices.[88] Conservatives of "the Black Country" raged that they had "to contend alike with Africa and the [federal] administration, apparently without moving the sympathy and certainly without receiving the active aid, of other more favored and more secure sections of the state."[89]

For years after 1869, Republicans controlled the governments of several heavily black cities—notably Petersburg, where, between 1872 and 1874, forty-one Negroes held city offices ranging from city councilman to policeman.[90] Petersburg Conservatives could show little in the way of "oppression." Many residents found life there downright dull.[91] They were determined, nevertheless, to realize white supremacy in their city. In 1874, they put their trust in a proposal for a new municipal charter that would transfer many municipal powers from the Republican city council to a board of commissioners to be appointed by the Conservative city judge.[92] The legislature approved the coup readily. "The bill is on the home-

86. Charles Bowen to William Cabell Rives, Jr., November 9, 1877, William Cabell Rives Papers, Library of Congress; A. D. Dickinson to Alexander H. H. Stuart, November 20, 1875, Stuart Papers.

87. James L. Kemper to William Mahone, July 25, 1876, Mahone Papers; Petersburg *Index and Appeal*, November 28, 1876.

88. Norfolk *Virginian*, November 22, 1873; Philip W. McKinney to James L. Kemper, July 8, 1873, Kemper Papers, University of Virginia.

89. Petersburg *Index and Appeal*, November 28, 1876.

90. Jackson, *Negro Office-Holders*, p. 86.

91. *Daily Petersburg Index*, November 17, 1871; Petersburg *Progress*, quoted in Richmond *Enquirer*, May 24, 1872.

92. Jones, "Conservative Virginian," p. 228.

stretch," the Petersburg *Index* reported shortly before final passage, "and any body who runs across the tracks deserves to be run over."[93]

To the Petersburgers' chagrin, their governor "ran across the tracks" by interposing his veto. Kemper objected that the instrument subverted republican government by reducing the regular, elected government to impotence. He pointed out that it was not for the legislature to judge the Petersburg voters' competence and that federal authorities would recognize the coup as an act of racial discrimination. The way to remedy municipal mismanagement in Petersburg, Kemper suggested, would be to pass a general law putting limits on all cities' tax rates, debts, and spending. The state senate chose not to override the charter veto.[94]

The racists of Petersburg knew no bounds in their hatred of Kemper. Some wrote to the governor, calling him a "deep dyed damn rascal," wishing that he had been killed at Gettysburg, and suggesting that he "tender his resignation & join the negro party who he is truly serving." An outburst of racist violence further discredited the "law and order" party in Petersburg.[95] However, two-thirds of the Conservative newspapers in Virginia approved the governor's decision, and prominent conservatives from all over the South commended him. Their statements, coinciding with those of Northern newspapers, showed that a compromising national consensus on race relations was crystallizing in both sections.[96]

Deprived of the *coup d'état* they desired, Petersburg Conservatives went to work to win control of their city by the electoral process. In a city election on May 29, they turned out in force to vote. Many Negroes did not vote, and some voted for Conservatives. The presence of federal troops, requested by the Republicans, did not affect the result. The Conservatives won a victory that surprised their own leaders. Intimidation of Negroes may have played a part in the result but so did the reassurance Kemper's veto gave to moderates discontented with the incumbent administration.[97]

93. Petersburg *Index and Appeal*, February 24, 1874.

94. Governor's Veto Message, March 12, 1874, *Senate Journal* (1874), pp. 283–87.

95. "Gettysburg veterans, who now curse you" to James L. Kemper, March 12, 1874; "Many 100 Voters" to Kemper, March 12, 1874; "Gettysburg Veteron [sic]" to Kemper, n.d., and other letters in Kemper Executive Correspondence Virginia State Library; James P. Riely to Kemper, March 16, 1874, Kemper Papers, University of Virginia.

96. Jones, "Conservative Virginian," pp. 231–34; Alexander H. Stephens to Kemper, March 15, 1874; Preston H. Leslie to Kemper, March 17, 1874; John Letcher to Kemper, March 17, 1874, and other letters in Kemper Papers, University of Virginia.

97. Petersburg *Index and Appeal*, May 30, 1874; Jones, "Conservative Virginian,"

Petersburg's troubles did not end after the election. In July, the new Conservative city council, usurping power, declared the school board memberships vacant and appointed a new board, which the State Board of Education recognized after four months of inquiry.[98] After seven months in office, the Conservative administration found itself the target of the same charges of extravagance and corruption that its members had directed against their predecessors. To escape political peril, it initiated a new charter revision in the legislature, to postpone the next election from May, 1875, to May, 1876, and to alter the structure of government in favor of the propertyowners. The General Assembly passed the charter and, since it did not overthrow political democracy but merely slanted the rules in the Conservatives' favor, Governor Kemper approved it.[99]

Reflecting on city government problems, Kemper devised a plan to make municipal government "a just republican system" instead of "the rule of an unrestrained numerical majority." He proposed to give every city and town a bicameral legislature. In choosing one house, all adult males would vote; in choosing the other, only those who met a property or tax-paying qualification. Kemper thought his idea would help to contain urban social unrest in all parts of the nation.[100] His suggestion, like the Petersburg charters of 1874 and 1875, was designed to strengthen the hands of white propertyowners in conflicts with propertyless blacks. The bicameral plan and the 1875 charter, which Kemper approved, differed from the 1874 charter in that they did not arbitrarily circumvent political processes and did not explicitly discriminate against Negroes as Negroes. The difference was one of means, not of ends. The Petersburg story bore out the Conservative leaders' policy of combining official overt impartiality in racial matters with subtle covert assistance to the propertied class to which the leaders belonged.

Many twentieth-century writers have tried to fit all the Southern white supremacists of Reconstruction days into the image of a later

---

pp. 236–37; *House Journal* (1874–75), Document V: *Correspondence between the Governor and the President of the United States in relation to the Employment of Military Force at Petersburg,* pp. 3–4.

98. *Senate Journal* (1874–75), Document XIX: *Communication from the Board of Education in reference to the Resolutions Adopted by the Board of Public Schools in the City of Petersburg, Relating to Certain Charges Made by the Superintendent of Public Instruction in His Last Annual Report,* pp. 5–6.

99. Norfolk *Virginian,* February 26, 1875; John C. Armistead to William Mahone, January 20, 1875, Mahone Papers; Jones, "Conservative Virginian," p. 186n.

100. Governor's Message, December 2, 1874, *Senate Journal* (1874–75), pp. 22–23.

South of mob violence, Negrophobia, segregation, and disfranchise-ment laws. To Virginia Conservatives, in fact, "white supremacy" meant simply seeing that Negroes did not win social and political power. Able during the 1870's to secure that condition without wholesale violence or blatant legislative discrimination, the Con-servatives did not use those instruments. In the relative absence of black militance, they could afford to treat Negroes with paternal-istic benevolence.

By distorting the meaning of "white supremacy," later liberal writers concealed the foundations of their own racial edifice. The Conservative policy of the 1870's was broad enough to contain al-most all the white liberal policies of the early twentieth century as well as the "extremist" ones. Racial liberals stood for racial har-mony and benevolence, law and order, and formal equality under law—as had the more enlightened Conservatives. They did not im-peril, any more than the Conservatives had, the fundamental con-dition of the white race's supremacy in social power. They were, therefore, exceptionally enlightened white supremacists, in the phrase's historical meaning. In the end, as in the beginning, White Supremacy was nothing but the negation of Black Power.

13.
The Educational Revolution

In no way did Conservatives more completely abandon their antebellum heritage for the "new order" than in their educational policies. The antebellum South had not been receptive to universal free public education, even after the cause had captured almost all the free states. The South had excelled, rather, in higher education of its elite in classical colleges and universities. On the bayonets of Yankee soldiers came an educational revolution, part and parcel of the new order of nineteenth-century liberal capitalism. Its principal innovations were the public common school and a "practical" or technical curriculum. Opposed by traditionalists, it found an eager welcome not only from freedmen and poor whites but also from middle-class groups of entrepreneurial bent. Radicals first took the initiative in the revolution, but the more advanced Conservatives carried it to an impressive, if limited, completion.

INCEPTION OF THE FREE-SCHOOL SYSTEM

There was little in Virginia's antebellum traditions to encourage advocates of universal public free education. The Old Dominion had never set up even the beginnings of a general free-school system. The county oligarchies had refused to implement the school law of 1796, and the dedication in 1810 of part of the state Literary Fund to "pauper schools" had not been, in the eyes of later reformers, "even a tolerable substitute for a general system of education." During the 1840's there had been a movement for a state public-school system, but the permissive free-school law of 1846 had given rise to only a few schools, most of them short-lived.[1] The state government, before the War, exercised no supervision over local "pauper schools" and contributed to their support only part of the Literary Fund and, after 1851, the capitation-tax pro-

1. *School Report, 1871,* pp. 86–91.

ceeds.[2] Illiteracy had been common among even white Virginians before 1865.[3]

Between 1865 and 1867, conservative Virginians showed few signs of departing from the traditional educational policy. The Baldwin legislature took no action. Even the *Whig*, one of the most enlightened conservative newspapers, continued to dismiss universal education as a Yankee error.[4] The Educational Association of Virginia, at its annual convention in 1866, discussed free schools and Negro education only as abstract possibilities and assigned them low priorities in its agenda.[5] A few conservatives approved of teaching freedmen the "three R's," but almost all the people actually doing that work were Northern teachers working for the Freedmen's Bureau and Northern philanthropic agencies.[6]

In the Underwood convention, the Republican majority wrote free schools into the state constitution. The Conservative members did not oppose the system in essence, but they introduced amendments to limit its cost and segregate the schools by race.[7] The Peabody Education Fund, then beginning its task of providing Northern assistance to Southern schools, influenced the convention behind the scenes. The fund's general agent Dr. Barnas Sears, who had recently been president of Brown University, addressed the convention and lobbied for a moderate free-school provision that enlightened Conservatives might accept. Rumor credited him with authorship of the constitution's educational sections.[8] The constitution provided that the Commonwealth should set up a complete free-school system by 1876. The General Assembly should elect a superintendent of public instruction to administer the system, and the

2. Edgar W. Knight, "Reconstruction and Education in Virginia," *South Atlantic Quarterly*, XV (January, 1916), 26, 39–40 (hereafter cited as "Reconstruction and Education").

3. *School Report, 1871*, pp. 24–25.

4. Richmond *Whig and Public Advertiser*, August 14 and 31, 1866.

5. [Educational Association of Virginia], *Minutes of the Educational Association of Virginia Assembled in University Hall, Charlottesville, Virginia, Tuesday, July 17th, 1866* (Richmond: C. H. Wynne, 1866), pp. 7–8.

6. Fleming, ed., *Documentary History*, II, 183–84; unidentified clipping from a Clasksville newspaper, *Cong. Globe*, 41 Cong., 3 Sess., 1379 (1871); Taylor, *Negro in Reconstruction*, pp. 138–45.

7. Knight, "Reconstruction and Education," pp. 27–34.

8. Jabez L. M. Curry, *A Brief Sketch of George Peabody and a History of the Peabody Education Fund through Thirty Years* (Cambridge, Mass.: University Press: John Wilson and Son, 1898), p. 42 (hereafter cited as *Peabody Fund*); Charles C. Pearson, "William Henry Ruffner: Reconstruction Statesman of Virginia," *South Atlantic Quarterly*, XX (January, 1921), 31 (hereafter cited as "Ruffner").

superintendent, governor, and attorney general would constitute the State Board of Education. The state would contribute to the school system at least the interest on the Literary Fund and the proceeds of the capitation tax. Counties might levy property taxes of as much as five mills per dollar for school support. The convention left the question of school segregation open.[9]

After the Conservatives became the executors of the Underwood constitution, many traditionalists hoped that they would not take its mandate for free schools seriously. The legislature, indeed, provided a discouragingly low salary for the superintendent of public instruction.[10] Nevertheless, about a dozen candidates sought the office. The Conservative caucus selected as its candidate the Reverend William Henry Ruffner of Lexington, who had the endorsements of John B. Baldwin, of General Lee and his Washington College colleagues, and very likely of Barnas Sears. The Republican legislators accepted Ruffner, and on March 2, 1870, the General Assembly elected him on joint ballot, with only one dissenting vote.[11]

The Conservative who would administer the free-school system for its first twelve years lacked strong ties to the dominant interests and traditions of antebellum Virginia. His ancestors had been German pioneers and entrepreneurs around Charleston, West Virginia. His uncle, Lewis Ruffner, had been a founder of the Unionist state of West Virginia. His father, the Reverend Henry Ruffner, had been driven from the presidency of Washington College in 1848 by the proslavery condemnation of his pamphlet advocating emancipation.[12] William Henry Ruffner had himself been a maverick from the Old Virginia norm. As a student at Washington College, he had imbibed a lasting passion for science and technology. Opposed to slavery on economic grounds, he had acted in Virginia as an agent

9. Thorpe, ed., *Constitutions*, VII, 3892–93.

10. Charles S. Venable to B. Johnson Barbour, February 14, 1870, Barbour-Ellis Papers, University of Virginia.

11. Pearson, "Ruffner," p. 30; William Henry Ruffner Diary (1870–87), March 2 and 5, 1870, William Henry Ruffner Papers, Historical Foundation of the Presbyterian and Reformed Churches; Celestia S. Parrish, "Problems and Progress of Universal Education at the South" (article in unidentified volume of Association of Collegiate Alumnae *Proceedings*; copy in Ruffner Papers), p. 53 (hereafter cited as "Problems and Progress").

12. William Henry Ruffner, "The History of Washington College, Now Washington and Lee University, during the First Half of the Nineteenth Century: A Continuation of the 'Early History of Washington College, by Rev. Henry Ruffner, D.D., LL. D.,'" *Washington College Historical Papers*, IV (1893), 52–54, 97–99; V (1895), 3–20; VI (1904), 3–57, 103–8.

of the American Colonization Society. As a Presbyterian minister in Philadelphia, he had opposed parochial education, rebuked fellow churchmen for ignoring social problems, and become a disciple of the "nationalist" economist Stephen Colwell. In 1853, Ruffner had returned for his health to Rockbridge County to engage in scientific farming and geological exploration. A conditional Unionist, he had exhibited the ordinary signs of Confederate loyalty during the War. Since then, he had renewed his study of social questions, opposing Radicalism but advocating the eventual establishment of public free schools for both races.[13] Ruffner was eminently qualified for innovative, nontraditional leadership, and the Conservative legislators showed by selecting him the course they intended to pursue in education.

During March, Ruffner worked with members of the University of Virginia faculty and with Barnas Sears of the Peabody Fund to prepare his plan for a school system. The document, based on the constitutional provisions and on Northern and foreign models, left many questions for future decision. For the succeeding year, it proposed to set up the system's administrative machinery and to start in each county between one and three district schools, whose popularity would facilitate completion of the system by 1876. The program called for racial segregation with equitable division of funds between white and black schools. Consulting with Sears and with Professor John B. Minor of the University of Virginia, Ruffner wrote his plan's principles into a free-school bill to present to the General Assembly.[14]

The first Conservative legislature went even farther than Ruffner had hoped in supporting the adventurous proposal. Amending the bill, it devoted a fifth of the property-tax revenue, as well as the Literary Fund income and capitation-tax proceeds, to the school fund. The additional funds brought about a change of strategy: instead of beginning with a few model schools and expanding gradually, the Board of Education worked to set up the system rapidly on a statewide basis.[15] Ruffner and his associates and local officials

---

13. *Ibid.*, VI, 22–27, 91, 96, 102–3; Pearson, "Ruffner," pp. 25–29; Richmond *Enquirer*, April 6, 1876; Henry F. May, *The Protestant Churches and Industrial America* (New York: Harper, 1949), pp. 18–19; Ruffner, 1894 reminiscences based on antebellum diaries; Ruffner diaries (1860–61), Ruffner Papers.

14. Ruffner Diary (1870–87), March 2–April 26, 1870, Ruffner Papers; *Senate Journal* (1869–70), Document XIII: *Report of the Superintendent of Public Instruction*, pp. 1–11 (hereafter cited as *School Plan, 1870*).

15. [Ruffner], *Public Free School System*, p. 13.

spent most of the remainder of 1870 in administrative preparation for opening the first schools. During the winter of 1870–71, about 3,000 teachers taught 130,000 pupils in 2,900 schools for an average term of 4.5 months.[16] The Conservatives had made a promising start in establishing one of the most progressive Reconstruction reforms in their state.

THE POLITICAL ECONOMY OF PUBLIC EDUCATION

Old Virginia's educational arrangements had functioned as an integral feature of its social system. The free-school system's architects designed it to operate as an integral feature of a New Virginia social system. Superintendent Ruffner, a student of economic theory, envisioned the free schools as a force for economic modernization. He believed that labor, the source of value, was much more susceptible of improvement than land or capital. Labor consisted of the combined effort of body and mind. Since the mind was capable of almost limitless improvement, so was labor power. Properly speaking, there was no "unskilled labor."[17] Only by developing competent labor power could Virginia generate the economic growth she would need to compete with developed regions.[18] "In this day," Ruffner wrote, "no civilization can hold its own without a union of working and reading."[19] The proposition conspicuously negated the proslavery philosophy of the preceding era.

Rebuking traditionalists who believed in a fixed class stratification, Ruffner preached the free-enterprise gospel of social mobility. A competent and honest laborer, he felt sure, could work hard, save, invest, and thereby become a prosperous farmer or businessman by middle age.[20] Schooling not only would develop the faculties the worker used in his job, but it would motivate him to work harder

16. *Senate Journal* (October, 1870), Document II: *Report of the Board of Education, October 1, 1870,* p. 1; Cornelius J. Heatwole, *A History of Education in Virginia* (New York: Macmillan Company, 1916), p. 220 (hereafter cited as *Education in Virginia*).

17. *Eighth Annual Report of the Superintendent of Public Instruction, for the Year ending July 31, 1878* (Richmond: R E. Frazier, Superintendent of Public Printing, 1878), p. 50 (hereafter cited as *School Report, 1878*); *School Report, 1871,* pp. 62–65; [Ruffner], *Public Free School System,* p. 3.

18. *School Report, 1878,* pp. 64H–64J; [Ruffner], *Public Free School System,* p. 4; *School Report, 1871,* p. 76.

19. [Ruffner], *Public Free School System,* pp. 5–6.

20. [William Henry Ruffner], *The Proper Educational Policy for the Colored People: Extract from an Address Delivered by W. H. Ruffner at the Hampton Institute, June 11,* [1873] (n.p., n.d.), p. 4 (hereafter cited as *Educational Policy for Colored People*).

by increasing his material wants. Ambition would thus replace compulsion and physical necessity as the motive for labor.[21] Every person, Ruffner thought, had a "certain intrinsic value to the State," equal to "his productive power, minus his running expenses." The "public value" of an unschooled laborer was about eight hundred dollars. Elementary education increased his productive power, and thereby his "public value," by 25 per cent. Colleges were "the most profitable factories known in society," because they could increase the cash value of a human life to ten thousand dollars![22]

Universal education, the superintendent believed, would also further social stability. Because of the laborers' ignorance, emancipation and universal suffrage had opened the door to crime, social disorganization, misgovernment, and radical agitation. Once "educated in the right views and habits," however, the workers would become "the unconquerable defenders of order and property."[23] Educated laborers and the economic growth they would bring about would enhance the value of property, and educated voters and officeholders would increase its security. Free schools would also reduce crime.[24]

Ruffner's case for public schools followed logically from his economic argument for universal elementary education. Only the state could command the resources to educate all children, especially in an impoverished state. A relaxation of the laissez-faire principle was therefore in order.[25] Since the state educated to improve its citizens and increase its wealth, free schools were a collective enterprise, not a luxury or a charity. In the long run the schools would pay for themselves many times over.[26]

Superintendent Ruffner's arguments reflected his Conservative associates' less polished ideas of the social function of public education. A British traveler echoed the current expectation that Virginia's free schools would "be a source of much profit in the end, and . . . make her labor more profitable, and her wide domains more

21. *School Report, 1878*, pp. 51–59.
22. *School Report, 1871*, pp. 106–7; *School Report, 1872*, Part II, 107.
23. "Department of Superintendence, 1880," p. 81.
24. *School Report, 1878*, pp. 64C–64E.
25. *School Report, 1871*, pp. 128–29; *Sixth Annual Report of the Superintendent of Public Instruction, for the Year ending July 31, 1876* (Richmond: Richard F. Walker, Superintendent of Public Printing, 1876), pp. 12–13 (hereafter cited as *School Report, 1876*); *School Report, 1872*, II, 101.
26. [Ruffner], *Public Free School System*, p. 9; *School Report, 1871*, pp. 38, 49–50; *School Report, 1872*, II, 1; *School Report, 1878*, p. 42.

attractive and more pleasant to settlers of every class."[27] "Progressive countries," Thomas M. Logan wrote, "are forced to adopt some system of public instruction, or be distanced in the industrial race of the nations."[28] Governor Walker saw free schools as a concomitant of *laissez faire*: the maxim "That country is best governed which is least governed" could be realized only "through the education and consequent mental and moral elevation of the people."[29]

Conservatives valued public schools also as a force to stabilize society. "The stubborn, disorderly, and vicious negroes . . . ," a Clarksville editor wrote, "are not those who have been educated, but the ignorant who scarcely know the difference between right and wrong." Only a drastic program to educate Negroes, therefore, would bring about "a peaceful, quiet, and prosperous state of things."[30] "I am in favor of educating your people," a former governor allegedly told a Negro, "for *it is the only way I can keep you out of my corn crib*."[31] Logan wrote that the lower classes, in acquiring political power, needed education to direct their demands into realistic, reformist channels.[32] Stuart advocated universal education in order to reconcile the masses to the social order and cure them of belief in "the assumed antagonism between capital and labor." Stuart especially hoped that schooling would teach lower-class Southern voters to honor their states' public debts.[33] The free-school system, these Conservatives recognized, was part of the essential machinery of the postbellum social structure.

THE CONFLICT OVER FREE SCHOOLS

Conversely, traditionalists alienated from the postbellum order opposed the school system. Ruffner was kept constantly aware of the special Southern "unbelief" in popular education, born of the traditions of slavery days.[34] "The new common-school system," Washington County's school superintendent recalled in 1885, ". . . was . . . in many features, contrary to all our cherished notions and hereditary traditions. . . . The opposition and distrust were decid-

27. Somers, *Southern States*, p. 20.

28. Quoted in Morrill, *Builder of the New South*, pp. 130–31.

29. Governor's Message, December 4, 1872, *Senate Journal* (1872–73), p. 12.

30. Unidentified editorial from a Clarksville newspaper, in *Cong. Globe*, 41 Cong., 3 Sess., 1379 (1871).

31. [Virginia Department of Public Instruction], Circular No. 89: *Public School Difficulties Removed*, p. 3.

32. Morrill, *Builder of the New South*, pp. 127–28.

33. Robertson, *Stuart*, pp. 471–72.

34. *School Plan, 1870*, p. 1; "Department of Superintendence, 1880," 74–75.

edly outspoken in this county for several years."[35] Twelve superintendents, in their annual reports for 1876, reported significant opposition in their counties.[36] At the Conservative State Convention of 1877, a delegate introduced a resolution to abolish the free schools.[37] The system, a minister protested in 1878, was "essentially communistic, 'supported by the votes of those who do not pay for it & the money of those who do not vote for it.' "[38]

The system's traditionalist opponents, disgusted with the Conservative officeholders' enthusiasm for it, attacked openly in 1875. Under the pseudonym "Civis," Professor Bennett L. Puryear of Richmond College wrote for the *Religious Herald* a much-discussed series of articles opposing mass education on principle.[39] A year later, Professor Robert L. Dabney of Union Theological Seminary near Farmville presented, in the *Planter and Farmer*, the most thorough critique of public education from an unyielding traditionalist viewpoint. Dabney claimed that the system gave demagogic politicians control of education and that public schools, constitutionally barred from imparting religious instruction, were by nature anti-Christian. He believed firmly in a fixed distinction between leisure and laboring classes, in which each child's status was determined from birth by "Providence, social laws, and parental virtues and efforts." Only evil, he thought, could come of "leveling" attempts to educate the masses. At best, the laborers would relapse into illiteracy. At worst, schooling would lead them into the vices of Northern and European workers: idleness, crime, drunkenness, radicalism, and vulgar mass culture. Negroes, Dabney thought, were racially immune from education—but if whites should accept them as educated, the result would be racial amalgamation, and the consequent destruction of civilization. For whites, Dabney wanted a return to the days of the private school and the "pauper school," but for blacks he foresaw only re-enslavement or extermination.[40]

Ruffner, engaging in a newspaper debate with Dabney, played up

35. Quoted in Mayo, "Education," p. 904.
36. *School Report, 1876*, pp. 28–37.
37. Petersburg *Index and Appeal*, August 10, 1877.
38. Kinloch Nelson to Frederick W. M. Holliday, December 19, 1878, Frederick William Mackey Holliday Papers, Duke University.
39. [Richmond] *Religious Herald*, April 1 and 8, May 20 and 27, June 3 and 10, 1875.
40. Robert Lewis Dabney, *Discussions by Robert L. Dabney, D.D., LL.D., Recently Professor of Moral Philosophy in the University of Texas, and for Many Years Professor of Theology in Union Theological Seminary in Virginia*, edited by Clement Read Vaughn (Mexico, Mo.: Crescent Book House, 1897), IV, 176–90, 193–94, 200–14 (hereafter cited as *Discussions*).

his opponent's repudiation of nineteenth-century liberal values. He classed Dabney with French ultramontanists and others who wanted to push society back from industrial capitalism to the feudalism of the Dark Ages. The superintendent particularly attacked Dabney's reliance on the proslavery "mud-sills" view of society. The white masses' services to the Confederacy, he thought, should have refuted that concept. The middle classes, he believed, were superior to the upper, and in any case the reshuffling of classes during Reconstruction had disrupted the antebellum stratification.[41]

Confronted with traditionalist opposition, school officials made propaganda for public education one of their principal tasks. In writings, speeches, and travels, Ruffner seized every opportunity to argue the case for free schools. The 1870 school law explicitly made the role of propagandist an important part of the county superintendent's job.[42] The contest to convert public opinion was a desperate one.

The Conservative proponents of public education did not hesitate to use Northern assistance. Superintendent Ruffner acknowledged his system's indebtedness to Northern schools as models and to the Freedmen's Bureau and Republicans for educational work in Virginia in the late 1860's.[43] Virginia schoolmen asked Congress for federal aid. In its absence, the main Northern financial assistance came from the fund that the Yankee merchant George Peabody had dedicated to education in the South. Peabody and Sears, moved by missionary zeal to export the educational system of their native New England, intended the fund to assist public common schools, not colleges or private academies.[44] Settling in Staunton, Sears greatly influenced the public schools of his adopted state. He and Ruffner often conferred, and almost always agreed, about educational policy. At one time, Sears served as school superintendent for Augusta County. He regularly praised Virginia's school system in his reports, and between 1870 and 1882, the Peabody Fund gave $233,000—a fifth of all its donations—to Virginia free schools.[45] The Northern money was a great asset to the free-school cause.

41. [Ruffner], *Public Free School System*, pp. 14, 39, 41.
42. *School Report, 1872*, II, 78.
43. [Ruffner], *Public Free School System*, p. 5; *Educational Journal of Virginia*, II (May, 1871), 174–78, and (June, 1871), 315–20; *School Report, 1871*, pp. 17–21, 115–17, 203–4.
44. Curry, *Peabody Fund*, pp. 3, 24–26; *Proceedings of the Trustees of the Peabody Education Fund, 1874–1881* (Boston: University Press: John Wilson and Son, 1898), p. 422 (hereafter cited as *Peabody Trustees Proceedings, 1874–1881*).
45. *Peabody Trustees Proceedings, 1874–1881*, pp. 12, 65, 99–101, 151–52, 212–14,

In the battle for public education, the innovators at first met indifference, and occasional hostility, from the Educational Association of Virginia, which consisted mainly of private-school teachers. Professor Minor was unable in 1869 to persuade the association to endorse public education, and at its convention in 1870, the oceanographer Matthew Fontaine Maury spoke bitterly of "this system of common schools which has been thrust upon us."[46] But the public-school forces possessed one resource to win the association's co-operation: money. The association needed funds to publish its *Educational Journal of Virginia*. In return for state and Peabody Fund money, the editors agreed to carry in each issue a section by Ruffner addressed to free-school personnel and to send the *Journal* without charge to county school officials.[47] By that arrangement, the association gradually came around to a co-operative attitude to the free schools.

As the free schools demonstrated their benefits, public opinion became increasingly favorable to them. In its platform of 1873, the Conservative party held up the school system as its greatest accomplishment. In 1875 and 1876, there were indignation meetings in several counties against the views of Puryear and Dabney.[48] After that, there seemed to be little doubt about majority feeling. In 1877, the Staunton *Vindicator* asserted that any candidate for office who would announce himself opposed to free schools would insure his defeat in any county in Virginia. A farmer, the story went, told his legislator: "Kill the public schools, will you? Do it if you dare and this will be your last winter in Richmond."[49]

In 1875, when it reached maturity, the free-school system employed 4,262 teachers and boasted an enrollment of 184,486 pupils and an average daily attendance of 103,927. Although it lacked prestige in comparison with private schools, it provided almost

261, 380; *Senate Journal* (October, 1870), p. 68; Heatwole, *Education in Virginia*, pp. 239–40.

46. [Educational Association of Virginia], *Minutes of the Educational Association of Virginia. Fourth Annual Session, held in Lexington, Virginia, July 13–16, 1869* (Lynchburg: Schaffter and Bryant, 1870), p. 10; *Minutes of the Educational Association of Virginia. Fifth Annual Session, held in Warrenton, Virginia, July 12–15, 1870* (Richmond: Educational Journal Printer, 1870), pp. 7, 11, 12, 24; Ruffner Diary (1870–87), July 12–15, 1870, and Charles Martin to William Henry Ruffner, April 30, 1870, both in Ruffner Papers.

47. *School Report, 1874*, pp. 130–31.

48. *Hunter Speech, 1873*, p. 21; McFarland, "Extension of Democracy," p. 96; see Charles Martin to William Henry Ruffner, February 1, 1876, Ruffner Papers.

49. Staunton *Vindicator*, January 12, 1877; Parrish, "Problems and Progress," p. 54.

all the formal elementary education available in Virginia. Its limitations were obvious. The one-room, single-teacher school was standard in most rural districts, and even that was absent in some sparsely populated areas. The minimum school term was officially five months, and the state average, only a little longer.[50] Each teacher received a minimum of twenty dollars a month during the term; the average stipend in 1871 was only thirty dollars.[51] Quality of instruction left something to be desired. The few secondary schools in the system were supported entirely by county funds and did not adequately prepare students for study at the state's university.[52] The free schools, nevertheless, made training in the "three R's" available to many thousands of children on a scale that no previous generaton of Virginians had dreamed of. It was in cities and other densely populated areas that the Conservative architects of the system were able to set up effective graded schools as models for later development elsewhere.[53] Their blueprint for a free-school system—like their blueprint for a New South that would include it—was far-sighted, but circumstances delayed their ambitious schedule for construction.

"PRACTICALITY" IN HIGHER EDUCATION

Concurrently with the introduction of free schools came a curriculum revision in institutions of higher learning. After 1865, adaptive Southerners criticized the classical education that Southern gentlemen had boasted before the War and looked with new respect at "technical" curricula born of the industrial revolution. New and old colleges alike turned to "practical" and "technical" education.

Conservative leaders welcomed federal land-grant assistance for agricultural and technical colleges under the Morrill Act of 1862. Washington College, the Virginia Military Institute, and even the serene aristocratic University at Charlottesville projected new agri-

50. Heatwole, *Education in Virginia*, p. 244.

51. *School Report, 1871*, p. 14; *Senate Journal* (1872–73), Document X: *Communication from the Superintendent of Public Instruction in response to a Resolution of the Senate Requesting to be Furnished with a Statement of the Number of Additional Teachers and Schools for Each County Necessary to Carry into Successful Operation the Free School System in the State*, p. 1.

52. *School Report, 1873*, pp. 9–10; *School Report, 1872*, II, 10; Philip Alexander Bruce, *History of the University of Virginia, 1819–1919: The Lengthened Shadow of One Man* (New York: Macmillan Company, 1920–22), IV, 236.

53. Heatwole, *Education in Virginia*, pp. 262–79; James L. Kemper, manuscript address to State Educational Convention, 1876, James Lawson Kemper Papers, Virginia Historical Society.

cultural and technical programs to qualify for aid under the program.[54] Rejecting their claims, the General Assembly, in 1872, allotted two-thirds of Virginia's land-grant fund to creating the Virginia Agricultural and Mechanical College at Blacksburg for white students and one-third to advancing the Hampton Normal and Agricultural Institute at Hampton for black ones.[55] These, unlike the other applicants, were new schools, specifically dedicated to "practical" concerns.

The declared purpose of the Virginia A. and M. College was to train Virginians for leadership roles in the powerful and growing realms of business and industry. The institution's planners, careful to accentuate its technical emphasis, made it a manual-labor college and dropped the ancient languages from its curriculum. During the 1870's, however, its mechanical instruction was—for want of proper equipment—mostly theoretical. Its faction-ridden faculty was badly divided about how to carry out its technical-education mission.[56]

Hampton Institute was the project of Samuel C. Armstrong, who had been a Union colonel and a Freedmen's Bureau official. Armstrong made Hampton a manual-labor school to train black students to become farmers and craftsmen, by instilling industrious and moral habits, as well as formal education, in them.[57] Many white Virginians wary of academic higher education for Negroes approved of Hampton's "practical" training.[58] Negroes, however, were indignant that the school, controlled by white paternalists, conditioned students to subordination and taught them to despise the great majority of their race.[59] During the 1870's, the institute was an "industrial" college mainly in that it enabled students to work their way

54. Manuscript plan for joint Washington College–Virginia Military Institute application for federal land donation, 1869, Ruffner Papers; *Report of the Rector of the University of Virginia in reference to the "Congressional Grant of Lands for Agricultural and Technical Schools"* (n.p., [1870]), pp. 1–8.

55. *House Journal* (1871–72), pp. 237, 466–67.

56. [Walker], *Virginia A. & M. Address, 1873,* pp. 1–8; James L. Kemper, manuscript address at Virginia Agricultural and Mechanical College, August 8, 1876, pp. 1–2, Kemper Papers, Virginia Historical Society; *School Report, 1872,* II, 11–14; *First Report of the Board of Visitors of the Agricultural and Mechanical College* (section of *School Report, 1872*), pp 1–36; *School Report, 1874,* p. 142; F. H. Imboden to John D. Imboden, September 16, 1875, John Daniel Imboden Papers, University of Virginia; Scott Ship to William Henry Ruffner, November 29, 1879, Ruffner Papers; *Senate Journal* (1876–77), *Communication from the Faculty of the Virginia Mechanical and Agricultural College to the General Assembly,* pp. 1–3.

57. Talbot, *Armstrong,* p. 144n.

58. [Ruffner], *Educational Policy for Colored People,* pp. 3–5; Bruce, *Plantation Negro,* pp. 173–74.

59. "Moses" in Alexandria *People's Advocate,* June 10, 1876, and "Aquila" in *ibid.,* July 1, 1876.

through school and taught them the rudiments of efficient farming. Few learned skilled trades there.[60]

The technical emphasis extended beyond the land-grant colleges. Lexington's two institutions, pioneers in technical instruction before the War, increased the emphasis afterward. During General Lee's presidency, Washington College reorganized its curriculum to emphasize practical and technical studies.[61] The Virginia Military Institute, now that Virginians were unlikely to enter military careers, presented itself as an engineering school and an agency in industrialization.[62]

The University of Virginia, once a stronghold of Southern Rights, underwent changes in the late 1860's. For the first time, students of Whig and conditional Unionist backgrounds attended in large numbers, altering the climate of student opinion. Faculty changes took the same direction.[63] B. Johnson Barbour, the university's Unionist rector, initiated an attempt "to make the Institution more in accord with the practical spirit of the age." Schools of applied mathematics, civil engineering, and applied chemistry appeared, and authorities projected a school of agriculture. Barbour recognized the training of public-school teachers as one of the university's chief functions. Many of the long-established faculty resisted the trend.[64] After Barbour resigned in 1870, Governor Walker used his appointive power to restore control of the institution to the humanist old guard. That group departed less from traditional policies, but its counterrevolution could not restore the university's ancient grandeur.[65]

Still more traditional, and more sterile, was the College of William and Mary. The end of the War found its buildings destroyed

60. Horace Mann Bond, *Negro Education in Alabama: A Study in Cotton and Steel* (Washington: Associated Publishers, 1939), pp. 196, 219.

61. Freeman, *Lee*, IV, 320–32.

62. *Senate Journal* (1874), Document IV: *Semi-annual Report of the Board of Visitors of the Virginia Military Institute, with Accompanying Papers*, p. 6; James L. Kemper, manuscript speech welcoming Virginia Military Institute cadets to Richmond, 1876, Kemper Papers, Virginia Historical Society.

63. Wise, *Lion's Skin*, pp. 82, 84–85.

64. Smith, "Virginia during Reconstruction," p. 314; B. Johnson Barbour to William Cabell Rives, Jr., February 19, 1869, William Cabell Rives Papers, Library of Congress; John W. Mallet to Barbour, January 14, 1870; Mallet to Barbour, February 11, 1870; manuscript of Rector's Report to Governor for University of Virginia, March 25, 1870; Charles S. Venable to Barbour, May 17, 1870, all in Barbour-Ellis Papers.

65. Robert W. Hughes to Barbour, May 12, 1872, Barbour-Ellis Papers; Maximilian Schele de Vere to William Cabell Rives, Jr., April 29, 1872, Rives Papers.

or damaged and its endowment funds unproductive. Its president, General Benjamin S. Ewell, pleading the weight of tradition and the supposed advantages of rural isolation, resisted efforts to change the school's location. The college remained under traditionalist influence. The classics continued to dominate its curriculum, and in 1870, Henry A. Wise and Robert L. Montague were the speakers at its first postwar commencement exercises. In its obstinate resistance to change, the institution did not prosper. In 1881, it again had to suspend its operations.[66]

Lack of money—the Virginia Conservatives' constant nemesis—tormented the new education as well as the old. The free-school system lived on precarious revenues, and the cost of apparatus, Colonel Armstrong found, put the quietus on almost every attempt to found a real technical college.[67] Virginia colleges found it harder than ever to compete with well-financed Northern ones. President Charles S. Venable feared that the state university was fighting a losing battle "against the splendid and costly equipments of Harvard and Yale."[68] The only solution seemed to be to tap the Northern industrial economy on which the rivals drew. During the years that followed the surrender at Appomattox, officers of Virginia colleges periodically re-enacted that event in desperate supplications to Northern men of wealth.[69]

Free schools and technical colleges were institutions of the industrial capitalism maturing in the North. In Virginia, they were new institutions in the Reconstruction era. By embracing them, the Conservatives embraced much more, for they saw the transformation of education as a means to the transformation of their entire society. Although they did not have the means to bring about the larger industrial revolution quickly, they tried to hasten it by transplanting to Virginia the educational institutions of liberal capitalism.

66. Smith, "Virginia during Reconstruction," pp. 330–33; Petersburg *Index and Appeal*, February 25, 1870; Tyler, ed., *Virginia Biography*, III, 197.
67. Samuel C. Armstrong to William Henry Ruffner, February 16, 1874, Ruffner Papers.
68. Charles S. Venable to James L. Kemper, December 12, 1873, Kemper Papers, University of Virginia.
69. Freeman, *Lee*, IV, 348–51; Ruffner Diary (1870–87), July 30–August 8, 1870, Ruffner Papers; William Cabell Rives, Jr., to B. Johnson Barbour, February 20, 1869, and Benjamin S. Ewell to Rives, May 5, 1869, both in Rives Papers; *Annual Cyclopaedia, 1876*, p. 802.

14.
Making Ends Meet

Financial stringency haunted the Conservatives through their years in power. The War and its effects greatly reduced Virginia's resources. Although the Commonwealth's potential revenue declined, its financial commitments increased. Unwilling to try drastic remedies to break the chains that limited the government's freedom of action, the Conservatives made them tighter by observing strict fiscal orthodoxy. For years, to reduce government spending was almost the sum of their financial policy, and the policy acted as a brake on many of their adaptive intentions.

THE ORDEAL OF STATE FINANCE

Arguing for his funding plan in 1870, Governor Walker presented an optimistic view of the Commonwealth's finances. He estimated that the state government would spend, apart from free schools, about $3,303,000 a year: $550,000 for the ordinary government expenses and $2,753,000 to service the state debt. Estimating the amount of taxable property at $723,115,000, he calculated that the nonschool taxes would provide $3,364,000 a year. By simple arithmetic, Walker concluded, the state could carry out his funding plan and still realize a surplus of $61,000 each year.[1] Since the General Assembly, in the Funding Act, committed itself to pay interest on only two-thirds of the antebellum debt Walker wanted to assume, a credulous Virginian might have expected large budgetary surpluses on the basis of Walker's figures.

Actual experience refuted Governor Walker's confident predictions. The value of property in Virginia—and, consequently, the property-tax income—turned out to be about half the amount he had calculated. Ordinary government expenses ran to two or three times his expectation. The sale of state railroad stock brought in

1. Governor's Message, March 8, 1870, *Senate Journal* (1869–70), pp. 141, 157–59.

not the $12,661,044 he had foreseen, but a mere $3,900,843.[2] To meet the state's obligations therefore became not an easy matter but a very difficult one.

The Funding Act's operation played havoc with the Commonwealth's finances. State officials never received enough revenue to pay the stipulated 6 per cent interest. Nevertheless, owners of funded coupon bonds collected almost their full interest by using coupons to pay taxes and dues to the state or by selling them to others to use for that purpose. The practice reduced the cash revenue the state needed to carry on other activities and pay interest on the noncoupon bonds. In the ten years the Funding Act was in force, consequently, the state accepted $8,707,615.50 in coupons as dues but paid only $2,415,973.56 in cash interest. By both modes together, it paid less than two-thirds of the stipulated interest on the debt.[3] Owners of funded coupon bonds ("consols") collected most of their interest, but owners of unfunded "peeler" bonds received only a small fraction. The state, receiving two-fifths of its revenue in coupons,[4] lacked money for its activities. Governor Kemper objected in 1874 that the coupons, "thrust upon the treasury, in large amounts, at the most inopportune periods of each fiscal year . . . periodically threaten to suspend the operations of the government."[5]

In the fiscal year 1870–71, before the Funding Act, the Commonwealth enjoyed a budgetary surplus of $81,703.16. During 1870–71, the funding process suspended most interest payment for a year, yielding a surplus of $877,245.99. Thereafter, as the state accepted coupons for dues, each year's accounts showed a deficit, as high as $570,636.37 for 1873–74.[6] No one seemed able to alter the trend. Governor Kemper boasted in 1875 that conditions had so far improved that the state had paid 5 per cent on the debt that year. Critics noticed, however, that to accomplish the feat the state had borrowed $230,000 from financiers in short-term loans. In the very month of his boast, Kemper himself had to lend the state about $200,000 in anticipation of expected revenue.[7] In 1875–76, the an-

2. Burton, "Taxation," p. 125.

3. *Ibid.*, p. 140.

4. *Ibid.*, p. 137.

5. Governor's Message, December 2, 1874, *Senate Journal* (1874–75), p. 7.

6. *Conference with Creditors, 1874,* p. 24; see Burton "Taxation," p. 42.

7. Governor's Message, December 1, 1875, *Senate Journal* (1875–76), pp. 14–16; Petersburg *Index and Appeal,* December 6, 1875; James L. Kemper to Robert M. T. Hunter and Asa G. Rogers, January 18, 1879; Kemper to William F. Taylor, January

nual deficit was $610,691; two years later, it was $854,953.[8] "At present," William D. Chesterman reported in September, 1877, "there is not a dollar in the State Treasury—not unless it has been borrowed from the banks to-day."[9] The situation posed a serious challenge to Conservative statesmen.

Conservative leaders who looked to increased revenue to solve the problem were most unconvincing. Blithe assurances that economic progress would soon enable the state to meet all its commitments went unfulfilled year after year. The staunchest "debt-payers," such as Stuart, proposed to increase taxation[10]—but neither the numerous farmers nor the powerful businessmen would tolerate higher taxes.

Unable to increase revenue, Conservatives turned to the idea of reducing state spending. Some wondered why Virginia's government should cost much more in the 1870's than it had in the 1850's. The phenomenon, in actuality, was not mysterious. Emancipation had transferred to government the police and welfare expenses for the freedmen, previously the responsibility of individual slaveowners. The Underwood constitution had instituted the free-school system and increased the number of public officials.[11] There was some official extravagance during the Walker administration, but those who expected economy alone to solve the financial problem greatly exaggerated its role. Nevertheless, "retrenchment"—reduction of public spending—became the Conservatives' favorite remedy. By presenting the problem as one of economy in government, they obscured the contradiction between the different elements of their program. For the time being, all Conservatives could agree to test the benefits of "retrenchment," or at least to talk about testing them.

RETRENCHMENT

Although "debt-payers" or "funders" ordinarily outnumbered the "readjusters" who wanted to scale down the debt or give debt service low priority in the state budget, the state never paid

28, 1879; manuscript "Reply of James L. Kemper to a Communication from the Auditor of Public Accounts to the Senate in relation to the payment of certain interest in 1875," February 8, 1879; and Kemper to Taylor, February 5, 1879, all in James Lawson Kemper Papers, Virginia Historical Society.

8. Burton, "Taxation," p. 158.

9. Petersburg *Index and Appeal*, September 13, 1877.

10. Robertson, *Stuart*, pp. 338–39, 341–42; Staunton *Vindicator*, June 29, 1877.

11. See Governor's Message, January 1, 1874, *Senate Journal* (1874), p. 22.

full interest on the bonds to which the Funding Act pledged its revenue. The apparent paradox raised the question of whether the price of carrying out the act were not higher, in taxes or reduction of government services, than the funders—or, at least, their constituents—were willing to pay. Refusing to admit an affirmative answer, funders tried conscientiously to balance the state budget. To the readjusters' question, "Is it to be readjustment, or repudiation?" the Petersburg *Index* replied, "It is neither. The issue is retrenchment in public expenses, or increase of taxation."[12] Retrenchment became the experiment that would determine the feasibility of the funding policy. If it succeeded, most critics of the policy would be satisfied. If it failed, more and more Virginians would see truth in the popular gibe that a debt-payer "would rather owe you all his life than cheat you out of a cent."[13]

The retrenchment impulse first took form in the reaction against the reputation for extravagance of Governor Walker and his first legislature. Critics objected to many expenditures, and "Extra Billy" Smith claimed that a few obvious reforms would reduce the General Assembly's annual cost from $220,000 to $75,000.[14] Governor Walker himself, though, soon seized the initiative from his critics. In December, 1871, hoping to divert the new legislature from an attack on his funding policy, he recommended severe reductions in legislative and judicial—not executive—expenses. Walker estimated that the General Assembly could reduce its cost by three-fifths by limiting its session to the statutory sixty days, paying members' actual traveling expenses instead of twenty cents a mile, and cutting clerical, paper, and printing expenses to the bone. He proposed also to reduce the number of courts, make them support themselves entirely by fees, give justices of the peace original jurisdiction over all misdemeanors, and have each county pay for criminal prosecution within its bounds. Eventually, Walker hoped, the state could also abolish the office of second auditor and devolve tax collection to city and county officials. Characteristically, he expressed confidence that economy measures would enable the state to pay full interest on the debt.[15]

Governor Walker's economy recommendations did not deter the legislators from obstructing debt service; in fact they had no effect

12. Petersburg *Index and Appeal*, October 9, 1877.
13. Quoted in Wise, *Lion's Skin*, p. 303.
14. William Smith, open letter on retrenchment, 1871, in Bell, *Smith*, pp. 277–83.
15. Governor's Message, December 6, 1871, *Senate Journal* (1871–72), pp. 26–29.

at all on them. The press recognized that the proposals to delegate state functions to localities would reduce Virginia to "an aggregate of petty communes."[16] The legislators did discuss proposals to reduce their compensation—often with tongue in cheek. On one occasion the members of the House, carried away in a mood of hilarity, passed a bill to cut their pay from six dollars a day to two—only to consider on the morrow how to undo their joke on themselves.[17]

Governor Kemper, after he despaired of negotiating a new debt settlement, also turned to drastic retrenchment as the solution. In December, 1875, he pointed out that state expenditures (apart from schools and debt service) were 84 per cent greater than before the War. Blaming the Underwood constitution for the difference, he proposed to return to the antebellum level of per capita state spending. The "economy" program Kemper recommended was a reactionary proposal to have local governments assume all criminal expenses not relating to felonies and to revive viva-voce voting and the antebellum system of county government. Even that drastic program, he thought, would solve the financial problem only if the state would also impose new taxes on alcoholic beverages and church property, enforce the oyster tax, and adopt a stricter assessment system.[18]

Wishing neither to increase taxes nor to restore antebellum institutions, the legislature could not follow Kemper's proposals. It did approve the constitutional amendments, ratified in 1876, to reduce the General Assembly's membership, hold sessions biennially instead of annually, and pay legislators salaries instead of per diems. The amendments, however, did not actually go into effect until 1879.[19]

In the 1876–77 session, the governor presented a more realistic economy program, but a drastic one nevertheless. For the treasury, he recommended a long-due modernization of office practices, doubling the officials' working hours, concentrating the clerks under their superiors' eyes, and eliminating "interruption, and needless waste of time." Kemper proposed also to abolish the offices of adjutant general, superintendent of public printing, register of the land

16. Norfolk *Virginian*, February 28, 1874; Richmond *Dispatch*, reprinted in *Daily Petersburg Index*, January 16, 1873.

17. Richmond *Daily Whig*, March 2, 1872.

18. Governor's Message, December 1, 1875, *Senate Journal* (1875–76), pp. 17–19, 25–29.

19. Thorpe, ed., *Constitutions*, VII, 3901–3.

office, and second auditor, and to assign their duties to other officials.[20] The recommendations realistically stated the extreme economies that would be necessary to do justice to both debt service and education, but very few political leaders could support them all, and if enacted they would have crippled the administration of government. S. Bassett French, Kemper's secretary, was sorry that the governor had been "so wild" as to "fritter down to the little end of nothing."[21]

Kemper did bring about important reductions. By 1876, the offices of aide-de-camp and superintendent of public buildings had disappeared, and the number and salaries of treasury clerks had declined. The General Assembly reduced the adjutant general's salary from two thousand dollars to one hundred, after which the secretary of the Commonwealth usually served as adjutant general as well.[22]

The most extreme funders, persisting in the delusion that excessive spending accounted for the whole financial problem, accused even Kemper's administration of extravagance. In 1877, newspapers claimed that state expenditures were still 50 per cent too high.[23] The legislature investigated charges that the governor had spent too much for Foley's statue of Stonewall Jackson.[24] An irate retrencher took Kemper to task for requesting appropriations for such "humbugs" as fisheries, immigration, and observance of the centennial of American independence. "If this appropriation system is to continue," he concluded, "we had better repudiate at once, (it will bring us to it) & worry the people no longer."[25]

After 1877, funders found it harder than ever to argue that Virginia, under economical government, could pay full interest on the debt. Kemper's strenuous efforts—reducing ordinary government expenses from about $1,057,000 to about $967,000 after four years—did not even approach the goal. Each year, Conservatives tried more desperately to save money. In 1878, the General Assembly reduced the amount of state salaries and the number of treasury clerks. In 1879, it instituted a new penal code intended to save money by

20. Governor's Message, December 6, 1876, *Senate Journal* (1876–77), pp. 14–15; Jones, "Conservative Virginian," pp. 341–43.
21. Quoted in Jones, "Conservative Virginian," p. 343.
22. *Ibid.*, pp. 343–45.
23. Petersburg *Index and Appeal*, July 23, 1877.
24. *Ibid.*, January 17, 1877; *House Journal* (1876–77), Document IV: *Special Message of the Governor of Virginia in response to the Resolution of the House of Delegates concerning the Inauguration of the Jackson Statue*, pp. 1–6.
25. J. W. Ware to James L. Kemper, March 23, 1876, James Lawson Kemper Papers, University of Virginia.

using summary procedures and substituting direct punishments for imprisonment.[26] In these last years of their united rule, the Conservatives made their most impressive reductions in spending, but state finance remained in desperate condition. The failure of repeated "retrenchment" efforts necessarily called into question either the Conservative officeholders' sincerity or Virginia's ability to pay even the interest on her debt. Since the largest reductions in spending—in General Assembly cost and officials' compensation—were those which fell chiefly on the officeholders themselves,[27] the defect more and more appeared to be one of ability rather than sincerity.

BREAD (STATE INSTITUTIONS) . . .

The impulse to "retrenchment" played havoc with the modest social services that the Commonwealth provided. The free schools were the most important victims, but not the only ones. In the conduct of the state prison and institutions for the insane, the dearth of money and the drive to reduce public spending exacted a high cost in human suffering.

One of Governor Walker's ambitions was to make the State Penitentiary in Richmond pay its own expenses. He succeeded in reducing its cost to the state from almost $67,000 in 1870–71 to about $40,000 in 1871–72.[28] Skeptical of Walker's prediction that he would yet eliminate the cost entirely, the legislature considered leasing the institution to a private contractor.[29] The state was already in the practice of leasing the position of general agent and storekeeper for the prison to a private businessman. In 1874, Governor Kemper found it necessary to remove the general agent and one of the penitentiary's three directors from their offices for conspiring to defraud the state in institutional purchases.[30] Later, as an economy measure, Kemper even suggested that the General Assembly abolish the penitentiary board, leaving control of the institution entirely to the supervisory officials.[31]

The Commonwealth's financial stringency cost the prisoners

26. Jones, "Conservative Virginian," pp. 345–46.
27. Burton, "Taxation," pp. 152, 154.
28. Governor's Message, December 4, 1872, *Senate Journal* (1872–73), p. 18.
29. *Daily Petersburg Index*, January 10, 1873.
30. John A. Sloan to James L. Kemper, July 16, 1874, James Lawson Kemper Executive Correspondence, Virginia State Library; Kemper to Otis F. Manson (copy), June 16, 1880, and Kemper to Manson (copy), June 22, 1880, both in Kemper Papers, Virginia Historical Society.
31. Governor's Message, December 2, 1874, *Senate Journal* (1874–75), pp. 13–14.

heavily. They suffered from congestion in the dilapidated structure. Often, the penitentiary directors reported in 1875, four or five were "confined in a small room, barely ventilated and imperfectly warmed—a state of things which must engender disease, as well as endanger the security of the inmates." In 1876, the 729 male inmates occupied only 171 cells.[32] The state operated the prison parsimoniously, spending about thirty-five cents a day for each convict's maintenance, clothing, policing, and medical care, and an additional nine to fourteen cents for his food.[33]

It was the penitentiary's inadequacy that first inspired the hiring-out of convicts' labor power to private contractors. During 1869, the number of inmates increased from 357 to 601 and the prison expenses increased by about one-fifth. The state, administrators decided, did not have the means either to employ all its prisoners or to construct adequate facilities for them. In 1870, consequently, the General Assembly, on Governor Walker's recommendation, introduced the "convict-leasing" system.[34] At first Walker expected that the state would contract with private companies to employ convicts in manufacturing on the penitentiary property.[35] Since the legislature would not appropriate enough money to the prison to make that possible, however, the state hired the convicts out for work outside the walls.

Once the practice began, the same budgetary considerations perpetuated it. The state lacked the means, Governor Kemper admitted, to house the hired-out convicts or employ them on its public works.[36] Many came to regard the system as a positive good. The Richmond *Dispatch* deplored the "Wasted Labor" of the prisoners who remained at the penitentiary.[37] It was the black convicts whom penitentiary officials chose to hire out; for years, hardly a single white was among the hundreds working outside the prison.[38] The

32. Wynes, *Race Relations*, p. 138; *Annual Cyclopaedia, 1876*, p. 799.

33. Meade C. Kemper (for James L. Kemper) to Samuel P. Waddill (copy), July 30, 1877, Kemper Executive Letter-Book (1875–77), Virginia Historical Society.

34. Governor's Message, February 9, 1870, *Senate Journal* (1869–70), pp. 48–49; *Senate Journal* (1869–70), pp. 63, 69, 70, 273–74, 294; *House Journal* (1869–70), pp. 68, 71, 76, 78, 81, 260, 287, 291–92, 301, 314, 319.

35. Governor's Message, December 7, 1870, *Senate Journal* (1870–71), pp. 23–24.

36. *Senate Journal* (1874–75), Document IX: *Communication from the Governor of Virginia transmitting communication from the Superintendent of the Penitentiary, in reference to Convicts Hired on the Valley Railroad*, p. 2; Meade C. Kemper (for James L. Kemper) to D. F. Bailey (copy), April 20, 1877, Kemper Executive Letter-Book (1875–77), Virginia Historical Society.

37. Richmond *Dispatch*, February 1, 1876.

38. Wynes, *Race Relations*, p. 137; manuscript monthly reports of George F. Stro-

practice grew, however, to include the great majority of the prisoners. In October, 1877, officials reported that there were no convicts fit for outdoor work left at the penitentiary.[39]

Only a few companies, designated by law, leased prisoners. Until 1876, the only contractors were the Old Dominion Granite Quarry and Mason, Gooch, and Hoge, who used convict labor to build the Chesapeake and Ohio tunnel in Richmond.[40] Later, transportation companies entered the field, some of them prevailing on the General Assembly to give them prior claims on the pool of unfree manpower.[41] In 1877, the James River and Kanawha Company, in its final desperate attempt to complete the railroad extension to Clifton Forge, secured an act that enabled it to pre-empt all able-bodied prisoners to work on its line. Barely able to pay even the low rates for convict labor, it employed all the hired-out convicts. Its prisoners died at the appalling rate of 8 per cent in 1878 and 5 per cent in 1879, in contrast with 2.5 per cent for the less healthy convicts in the penitentiary.[42] The Canal company, in its death-throes, took a host of humbler Virginians with it to destruction.

Contractors for hired labor secured a phenomenal bargain. Under the first contracts, the contractor paid the state twenty-five cents a day for each prisoner and assumed responsibility for the men's care and custody. In 1872, Governor Walker increased the rate to forty cents and restored to the penitentiary surgeon the medical care and superintendence of the laborers.[43] Mason, Gooch, and Hoge continued to pay the low rate of their contract, which was

ther, Superintendent of Virginia Penitentiary, to Gilbert C. Walker for October, 1872, and January–November, 1873, "Rept. Supt. Pen.," Box 3, Gilbert Carlton Walker Executive Correspondence, Virginia State Library.

39. Charles Rutledge Whipple (for James L. Kemper) to [illegible] (for Henrico County Board of Supervisors) (copy), October 16, 1877, Kemper Executive Letter-Book (1877), Virginia State Library.

40. Manuscript monthly reports of Superintendent George F. Strother to Gilbert C. Walker for October, 1872, and January –November, 1873, "Rept. Supt. Pen.," Box 3, Gilbert Carlton Walker Executive Correspondence.

41. James L. Kemper to Christopher Y. Thomas (copy), April 13, 1876, and Kemper to Mason, Gooch and Hoge (copy), October 23, 1876, both in Kemper Executive Letter-Book (1875–77), Virginia Historical Society.

42. Kemper to William T. Sutherlin (copy), January 4, 1877, and Meade C. Kemper (for J. L. Kemper) to Thomas Dunlap (copy), April 11, 1877, both in *ibid.*; Charles Rutledge Whipple (for J. L. Kemper) to T. Trimble (copy), December 13, 1877, Kemper Executive Letter-Book (1877), Virginia State Library; Governor's Message, December 4, 1878, *Senate Journal* (1878–79), p. 27; Wynes, *Race Relations*, p. 157.

43. Governor's Message, December 4, 1872, *Senate Journal* (1872–73), p. 18.

legally irrevocable. Governor Kemper tried, but failed, to increase the hiring rate to seventy-five cents. Even the forty-cent rate suffered encroachments. In 1876 and 1877, the Old Dominion Granite Company, letting its contract lapse, was allowed to hire 171 convicts for months at twenty-five cents a day for each. Some companies, knowing that the Commonwealth could not afford to maintain the convicts itself, offered to lease them without paying it *anything*.[44] The prisoners, of course, had no stake in either the state's or the contractors' claim to the profits of their labor.

There was some disapproval of convict-hiring. Residents of areas where black convicts worked objected to their presence.[45] Richmond stonecutters charged that the Old Dominion Granite Company was training prisoners in stonecutting, creating servile competition for free craftsmen.[46] General Mahone, running for governor in 1877, argued that the state should employ convicts on public works instead of leasing them.[47] In 1878, Governor Holliday expressed grave doubts about the policy but saw no ready alternative.[48]

Almost no one objected to convict-hiring on the grounds of hardship to the prisoners. Mary Allan-Olney, a British lady living near the Canal route, did not think the convicts ill-treated. Living in congested quarters, she thought, came as naturally to Negroes as to barnyard animals. She condoned overwork, flogging, and shooting down escapees as just punishment for crime; she was "sure that a negro—or a white man either—who really gets himself into prison must have done something very bad indeed."[49] Governor Walker even worried that the hiring system, providing moderate outdoor

44. Governor's Message, December 2, 1874, *Senate Journal* (1874–75), p. 13; James L. Kemper to Mason, Gooch and Hoge (copy), June 3, 1874; Kemper to Christopher Y. Thomas (copy), April 13, 1876; Kemper to Mason, Gooch and Hoge (copy), October 30, 1876; Kemper to Mason, Gooch and Hoge (copy), November 2, 1876, all in Kemper Executive Letter-Book (1875–77), Virginia Historical Society; *Senate Journal* (1876–77), Document XI: *Communication from the Governor of Virginia relative to Applications Made to Him for Employment of Convict Labor*, pp. 1–2.

45. Governor's Message, December 7, 1870, *Senate Journal* (1870–71), pp. 23–24; [Allan-Olney], *New Virginians*, II, 114–17.

46. James C. Taylor to Gilbert C. Walker, December 20, 1872, and enclosed documents, "Letters on various subjects," Box 3, Gilbert Carlton Walker Executive Correspondence.

47. [William Mahone], *General Mahone against Convict Labor in Competition with Honest Labour and Private Enterprise* (n.p., [1877]), pp. 3–4.

48. Governor's Message, December 4, 1878, *Senate Journal* (1878–79), p. 27.

49. [Allan-Olney], *New Virginians*, II, 117–19.

work, would pamper the convicts and provide an inducement to crime.[50]

Virginia's penal arrangements were unenlightened in other respects as well. The state did not abolish corporal punishment as a penalty until the 1880's.[51] It maintained no reformatory, so juveniles when convicted went to the penitentiary.[52] Raleigh T. Daniel, as attorney general from 1874 to 1877, insisted on the principle that a convict possessed no legal rights at all. Even a prisoner entitled by law to good-behavior time, Daniel ruled, could not receive it unless the governor chose to grant it as an act of clemency.[53]

The state's institutions for the insane were as inadequate as its prison. In 1869, Governor Walker found that both the Eastern State Lunatic Asylum in Williamsburg and the Western State Lunatic Asylum in Staunton were "filled to overflowing" and that many additional insane persons were lodged in county jails. Walker temporarily alleviated the problem by creating the Central Lunatic Asylum in Richmond for black inmates.[54] The white asylums remained unequal to their task. "For every vacancy," the governor's office reported in 1877, "there are scores of applications."[55] For lack of asylum accommodations, the penitentiary, in 1873, had to retain an obviously insane prisoner, and many Virginians had to send relatives to out-of-state institutions at twice the Virginia asylums' rates.[56]

In the face of the retrenchment campaigns, the asylums could make little headway. For financial reasons, the state neither bought the Richmond land that the Central Asylum occupied nor found it

50. Governor's Message, December 7, 1870, *Senate Journal* (1870–71), p. 24.
51. Pearson, *Readjuster Movement*, p. 147; see Richmond *Enquirer*, June 21, 1872.
52. *Senate Journal* (1874–75), Document XII: *Message of the Governor of Virginia to the General Assembly, stating All Pardons Granted and Punishments Commuted during the Year 1874, with the Reasons Therefor*, p. 9.
53. George F. Strother to James L. Kemper, January 20, 1874, and Raleigh T. Daniel to P. F. Howard, January 22, 1874, both in Kemper Executive Correspondence, Virginia State Library.
54. Governor's Message, February 9, 1870, *Senate Journal* (1869–70), p. 53.
55. Meade C. Kemper (for James L. Kemper) to Thomas W. Valentine (copy), June 7, 1877, Kemper Executive Letter-Book (1875–77), Virginia Historical Society.
56. D. R. Brown to George F. Strother, February 8, 1873; Francis T. Stribling to Strother, February 8, 1873; Strother to Gilbert C. Walker, February 12, 1873, all in "Rept. Supt. Pen.," Box 3, Gilbert Carlton Walker Executive Correspondence; *Senate Journal* (1874), Document XV: *Report of Auditor [of] Public Accounts, in response to Resolution Calling for Information as to Number of Lunatics in the Several State Asylums Whose Estates Are Sufficient to Meet Their Expenses*, p. 3 (hereafter cited as *Auditor's Report on Asylums, 1874*).

a permanent home elsewhere.[57] Not until the late 1870's did the government enlarge the asylums even slightly. Advocates of retrenchment denied that the facilities were inadequate[58] and argued that debt service should take precedence over social services. Superintendent Francis T. Stribling of the Western Asylum voiced a humanitarian dissent. "In all civilized communities," he asked, "is it not a fact that, however impoverished—whatever the indebtedness of the parents—if there be an afflicted child under the roof, the fond father and the loving mother will ignore all other claims and devote their means and energies to its proper care? . . . Why should not our good old mother, Virginia, treat with a similar affection her afflicted children?"[59]

The constant pressure to reduce public spending precluded significant progress for Virginia's penitentiary and asylums during the Conservative period. Not until the Readjuster party scaled down the state debt in 1882 did appropriations for social services increase greatly.[60]

. . . AND CIRCUSES (THE PHILADELPHIA CENTENNIAL)

Financial pressure sometimes impeded even symbolic expressions of the Conservative elite's adaptation to the national consensus. In 1871, Philadelphia interests persuaded Congress to sponsor an industrial exposition in that city in 1876 to commemorate the centennial of American independence. The General Assembly of Virginia endorsed the celebration.[61] Many Conservatives enthusiastically promoted the exposition for both its political aspect, to express the renewal of national unity, and its economic one, to exhibit industrial accomplishments and potentialities. They hoped to attract Northern capital by advertising Virginia's channels for investment.[62] The enthusiasts—such as Colonel Frederick W. M.

57. *Senate Journal* (1874), pp. 162–63.
58. Norfolk *Virginian*, February 26, 1875.
59. *Auditor's Report on Asylums, 1874*, p. 5.
60. Pearson, *Readjuster Movement*, pp. 145–46.
61. *Senate Journal* (1872–73), pp. 256–57; *House Journal* (1872–73), p. 285.
62. *Senate Journal* (1872–73), pp. 256–57; Frederick W. M. Holliday to John D. Imboden, December 27, 1875; T. J. Moorman to Imboden, December 23, 1875; E. J. M. Pace to Imboden, January 10, 1876; and William G. Neilson to Imboden, February 21, 1876, all in John Daniel Imboden Papers, University of Virginia; Jubal A. Early to J. Randolph Tucker, March 23, 1876, Tucker Family Papers, Southern Historical Collection, University of North Carolina at Chapel Hill.

Holliday of Winchester, chairman of Virginia's committee for the exposition—wanted the state to sponsor a large exhibit of the Old Dominion's business attractions.[63]

On the other hand, many Virginians of traditionalist bent saw no good in the centennial. Its political aspect, in their eyes, amounted to the North's celebrating, in the name of American liberty, its triumph over the South. "The very men," the Petersburg *Index* complained, "who have exerted their utmost energy to destroy all that was of value in our constitution . . . are to be the ring leaders in the celebration of the centennial anniversary of the achievement of these liberties."[64] Other traditionalists took offense at the observance's economic aspect. Some saw in "That Peddlers' Centennial" a swindle by which Philadelphia merchants had tricked federal and state governments into financing a scheme to enrich them.[65] Jubal Early summed up the traditionalist objections: "As a speculation, the Yankees will have infinitely the advantage of us, and as a matter of sentiment they will pervert it to the establishment of their own views."[66]

Nationalist and entrepreneurial Conservatives advocated participation in the centennial and traditionalists opposed it, but retrenchment cast the deciding vote. The General Assembly endorsed the exposition in 1873, but it appropriated not a cent for the Virginia commissioners' expenses.[67] Holliday and General Imboden proceeded, anticipating forthcoming appropriations, to organize exhibits and reserve space in Philadelphia.[68] In December, 1875, Governor Kemper asked the General Assembly to appropriate ten thousand dollars to pay for Virginia's role in the observance. Radical Republicanism, he assured the legislators, was a passing phenomenon, and Virginians could hasten sectional reconciliation by demonstrating their adaptation to "the new conditions of union."[69]

63. See *Shall Virginia Be Represented at the Philadelphia Industrial Exhibition? And, If So, How?* (n.p., n.d.; copy in Frederick William Mackey Holliday Papers, Duke University), pp. 1–4.

64. Petersburg *Index and Appeal*, November 13, 1873.

65. J. Randolph Tucker in *Cong. Record*, 44 Cong., 1 Sess., p. 509 (1874); Norfolk *Virginian*, January 31, 1874; Charles M. Fauntleroy to James L. Kemper, October 10, 1876, and J. W. Ware to Kemper, March 23, 1876, both in Kemper Papers, University of Virginia.

66. Jubal A. Early to Frederick W. M. Holliday, October 10, 1875, Holliday Papers.

67. *Senate Journal* (1872–73), p. 382.

68. James L. Kemper to Frederick W. M. Holliday (copy), September 7, 1875, Kemper Executive Letter-Book (1875–77), Virginia Historical Society; Jones, "Conservative Virginian," pp. 311–12.

69. Governor's Message, December 1, 1875, *Senate Journal* (1875–76), pp. 36–41.

After a long debate the House of Delegates—more in a spirit of economy than of traditionalist protest—voted down all appropriation bills for participation in the exposition. As long as Virginia could not pay the interest on its debt, many thought, it would be wrong to appropriate money for the centennial.[70] However, many Northerners interpreted the legislature's action as an expression of Southern disaffection.

The General Assembly's refusal of funds decided the state's official action. Governor Kemper began to waver in his support of the exposition.[71] On October 7, he informed the centennial officials that he would not attend the festival on "Virginia Day," October 17, lest he might thereby appear disrespectful to his assembly. He could not advise Virginians to spend money in Philadelphia, he wrote, when Virginia needed it badly. He nevertheless assured the officials that the "true centennial spirit" pervaded the Old Dominion.[72] The Virginia Military Institute cadets did go to Philadelphia. Superintendent Francis H. Smith justified the journey as indispensable to their "scientific and practical studies," but he financed it from non-public funds.[73]

The state's inaction made way for a curious form of private enterprise. Edward G. Booth, a Philadelphia contractor of Virginia origin, undertook to fill the breach by building on the exposition grounds a "Virginia pavilion"—a two-room square box with a wide veranda and glass roof. After the legislature failed to provide state funds, Holliday's committee had no choice but to accept Booth's offer. Booth assigned the state one room for exhibits and retained the other as a resting-place where he ostentatiously exhibited his own Virginia hospitality. Centennial officials considered his "pavilion" an eyesore that violated in spirit the rule against a private individual's erecting a building on the grounds. Judge Alexander Rives found the center a pleasant place to relax—until Booth appeared to distribute refreshments, bask complacently in compli-

---

70. *Senate Journal* (1875–76), pp. 78–80, 85–86, 102; *House Journal* (1875–76), pp. 119, 121–22, 133–34, 137, 139, 142–43; Walter Herron Taylor to James L. Kemper, November 16, 1875, enclosed in Kemper to John D. Imboden, November 19, 1875, Imboden Papers.

71. Kemper to James M. Smith (copy), October 2, 1876, all in Kemper Executive Letter-Book (1875–77), Virginia Historical Society.

72. Kemper to J. E. Peyton, October 7, 1876, in *Senate Journal* (1876–77), Document I: *Documents accompanying the Governor's Message to the General Assembly, December 6, 1876*, pp. 11–13.

73. *House Journal* (1876–77), Document VII: *Semi-Annual Report of the Superintendent of the Virginia Military Institute to the Board of Visitors*, p. 5.

ments to his generosity, and lecture Rives *ad nauseam* about the celebrities he had invited to visit the "pavilion."[74]

Just as the Conservatives' financial policies hamstrung their states' symbolic participation in the Philadelphia centennial, they also hamstrung its substantive social services. On both levels, Conservative leaders ordinarily accepted the relatively progressive standards of the United States in their day. Their progress in meeting those standards, however, was retarded, not only by their antebellum inheritance and their lack of means, but also by the internal contradictions of their own program, evident in their debt and financial policies. When adaptation required positive state action, "retrenchment" and the priority of debt service repeatedly proved a stumbling-block to adaptive Conservatives. The contradiction within the Conservative program was a source of continual strain on the party and the state government. In the last years of Conservative rule, it became a wedge, splitting the party into antagonistic factions.

74. Edward G. Booth to John D. Imboden, October 15, 1875, and A. T. Goshorn to Imboden, November 15, 1875, Imboden Papers; Joseph R. Hawley to Frederick W. M. Holliday, March 4, 1876, and Alexander R. Boteler to Holliday, March 18, 1876, both in Holliday Papers; Booth to Lewis E. Harvie, May 3, 1876, Lewis Evarts Harvie Papers, Virginia State Library; Withers, *Autobiography*, p. 346; Alexander Rives to B. Johnson Barbour, July 2, 1876, Barbour-Ellis Papers, University of Virginia.

15.

Emergence of the
State Debt Issue, 1871–1877

In March, 1871, one would hardly have expected that the passage of the Funding Act would give rise to a controversy that, eight years later, would tear the Conservative party apart. At the time, there was little public discussion of the measure and less articulate opposition. Most critics of the bill were concerned with peripheral problems: West Virginia's share, wartime interest, and the timeliness of the action. Only a handful of legislators, mostly from southwest Virginia, questioned the validity of the debt.[1]

In the succeeding years, the debt question grew by degrees until it overshadowed all other issues in state politics. An articulate group of spokesmen for agricultural interests became a nucleus of "antifunder" or "readjuster" sentiment. The nucleus' growth, however, depended less on the actions of its initial members than on those of the "debt-payers" who directed the state government. It was they who, by their repeated efforts to carry out the Funding Act's provisions at a tolerable social cost, demonstrated the state's apparent inability to do so. It was they, consequently, who repeatedly found it necessary to bring questions about the debt to the attention of the voters, who eventually turned to answers too radical for the men who had posed the questions.

ANTIFUNDING: AGRARIAN ORIGINS

The two prominent Virginians who, in 1871, proposed policies tending to repudiation or scaling-down of the state debt were Lewis E. Harvie and Henry A. Wise. Neither wielded power in the Conservative regime. They spoke in defense of agricultural inter-

---

1. Pearson, *Readjuster Movement*, pp. 26–27, 32–33.

ests and rationalized those interests in the vocabulary of Southern tradition.

Colonel Harvie, the publisher of the Richmond *Enquirer*, sought to alleviate the distress of rural debtors. War and emancipation, he pointed out, had overthrown the usual state guarantee of property rights and catastrophically stripped private debtors and the state itself of many of their resources. Harvie thought that the legislature, in the interest of equity, should divide the loss between creditors and debtors by scaling down all debts, public and private, by half.[2] While the Funding Bill was pending, funders allied to Governor Walker acquired control of the *Enquirer* and committed it to the funding policy, but Harvie continued to express his opinions privately.[3]

While the legislature was considering the bill, Wise attacked it on a number of grounds in newspaper articles. His most original argument—a reflecton of his alienation from postbellum Virginia—was the assertion, "The thing now called Virginia is no more the legal entity which contracted that debt than is Massachusetts or Dakota." The federal government, Wise claimed, had destroyed the government of Virginia and set up in its former territory, by right of conquest, two entirely new states. By conquest, therefore, the United States had assumed liability for the antebellum Virginia debt. Virginia, Wise thought, should pay nothing until bondholders might bring suit, and then it should argue his legal case before the Supreme Court of the United States.[4]

Wise may have intended his argument as a tactical dodge. Federal judges would be most unlikely to accept his theory—but even if they did not, he pointed out, the state would gain time to assess its resources and might obtain better terms from courts or creditors than it would assume in the Funding Act.[5] Whatever Wise had in mind, his constitutional theory gave some Virginia taxpayers a rationale to argue that Virginia was not irrevocably bound to pay the debt. After the act passed, Wise continued to state his position, insisting that the state should not pay a cent.[6]

In March, 1871, Harvie's and Wise's pronouncements fell on deaf

2. *Ibid.*, p. 25; Jones, "Conservative Virginian," p. 149.

3. Pearson, *Readjuster Movement*, pp. 28–29; Richmond *Daily Whig*, January 17 and 23, 1872.

4. Wise, *Lion's Skin*, pp. 287–90; Pike Diary, January 23, 1873, Calais Free Library.

5. Wise, *Lion's Skin*, pp. 288, 290.

6. Blake, *Mahone*, p. 165n.

ears; but a few months later, the election of a new legislature revealed a more widespread reaction against the Funding Act. The act became a campaign issue, especially in the Valley, and most of the successful candidates considered it either an error or a fraud.[7] When the new legislature convened in December, the members passed a joint resolution to suspend funding of the debt—ostensibly a temporary measure pending study of the problem. Walker vetoed the resolution, defending his policy and pointing out the inequity of discriminating against bondholders who had not yet been able to fund their bonds. Although the Senate failed to override the veto by two-thirds, the legislature carried the point that Walker's action was invalid on technical grounds. The treasury stopped funding bonds.[8]

The General Assembly followed up the suspension with more attempts to undo the Funding Act. It passed, over Walker's veto, a bill forbidding the treasury to accept coupons in payment for taxes. It ordered payment of 4 per cent interest instead of the stipulated 6, imposed a tax on the bonds, investigated the circumstances of the Funding Act's passage, and provided for full interest payment on bonds owned by Virginia colleges.[9] Some legislators toyed with more radical proposals, hinting at outright repudiation.[10] Most of the legislators were not repudiators. They were—as their measures of tax and debt relief testified—a group especially responsive to agricultural interests.[11] In regard to the state debt, they wanted to gain time, to reassert control over the revenue, and to prevent an increase in landowners' taxes. A tax increase adequate to carry out the Funding Act's terms, Delegate J. A. Early of Albemarle predicted, would crush agriculture, "the chief and only great interest of the state." "Let this legislature increase taxation," Early warned, "and the next legislature will assuredly be composed of repudiationists."[12]

The Supreme Court of Appeals thwarted the legislature's attempt

7. Pearson, *Readjuster Movement*, pp. 41–43.
8. *Ibid.*, p. 42; Governor's Message, December 6, 1871, *Senate Journal* (1871–72), pp. 23–31; *Daily Petersburg Index*, December 16, 1871; Governor's Veto Message, December 28, 1871, *House Journal* (1871–72), pp. 106–9; *House Journal* (1871–72), pp. 147–50, 168–69; *Senate Journal* (1871–72), p. 144.
9. Pearson, *Readjuster Movement*, pp. 42–43.
10. *Senate Journal* (1871–72), pp. 93–94; *House Journal* (1871–72), pp. 279, 290.
11. Pearson, *Readjuster Movement*, pp. 44–45. William D. Chesterman wrote, "The tendency of nearly all legislation at this session, so far projected or effected, is oppressive to the cities and towns of Virginia." *Daily Petersburg Index*, January 22, 1873.
12. *Daily Petersburg Index*, January 5, 1872.

to stop the acceptance of coupons in payment of taxes. In November, 1872, three of the four judges ruled that the Funding Act was an irrepealable contract and that the legislature could not, therefore, prevent the reception of coupons for taxes. The judges nevertheless recognized the suspension of funding as valid.[13] The holders of the "consol" bonds funded before the suspension—about two-thirds of the state debt—therefore possessed—in their tax-receivable coupons—a privilege not available to holders of unfunded "peelers." The discrimination was an arbitrary one. In 1874, nonresidents of Virginia owned between three-fourths and four-fifths of the "consol" bonds.[14]

Supreme Court Judge Waller R. Staples contributed to the antifunding cause by dissenting from the majority decision in the coupon cases. Staples did not press his doubt of the Funding Act's constitutionality but argued that the act against receiving coupons for taxes was valid because a legislature could not constitutionally grant a lien on future revenues.[15] Most "antifunders," for the time being, took Staples' dissenting opinion as their ground rather than Harvie's and Wise's more extreme teachings and contented themselves with trying to give Virginia's needs a higher claim on the revenue than debt service. Some held more radical proposals in reserve for the future.

The General Assembly, meanwhile, took such additional antifunding action as the judicial decision left open to it. It subjected all persons buying or selling coupons to the license tax for brokers and forbade tax-collectors to convert their collections into coupons for the treasury and pocket the difference. The laws did not stem the trade in coupons. The General Assembly continued to authorize payment of only 4 per cent interest, but "consol" holders continued to collect more by using their coupons. In 1873, a committee of the legislature conferred with representatives of the bondholders, but the discussion only deepened the mutual antagonism.[16] The debt question had reached a stalemate.

Powerless for the present, Conservative "readjusters" nevertheless formulated a program and rationale for scaling down the state

13. *Antoni* v. *Wright,* 22 Gratt. 833–87 (1872).
14. Pearson, *Readjuster Movement,* p. 43; *Conference with Creditors, 1874,* p. 34; see above, p. 219.
15. *Antoni* v. *Wright,* 22 Gratt. 859–76 (1872).
16. Burton, "Taxation," pp. 80–82, 136–38. In 1880, the federal Supreme Court declared the tax on coupons invalid in its application to nonresidents. The General Assembly then repealed it.

debt. In 1875, "Parson" John E. Massey of Albemarle County—a Baptist minister who had become a country gentleman and a member of the legislature—set down in his pamphlet *Debts and Taxes* the most thorough statement of the readjuster position, drawing on the ideas of Harvie, Wise, and Staples. Massey began with an exposition of the theory that Virginia was not liable for the antebellum debt, citing both Wise's ideas and Jefferson's dictum that "the earth belongs always to the living generation"—but he soon dropped that argument, which led logically to total repudiation. Conceding for the sake of argument that the debt followed the soil, he animadverted on the circumstances of the Funding Act's passage, claimed that its authors had meant it to burden Virginia with even West Virginia's third of the old debt, and presented evidence that Virginia lacked the resources to pay the debt.[17]

Massey rested his case primarily on the effects of the War. In 1860, the debt had amounted to one-twenty-second of the value of property in Virginia; in 1875, including West Virginia's share, it was one-seventh of that value. The bondholders, Northern and local, shared in responsibility for the War, which had wrought the change, so they should share the loss with Virginia taxpayers. Was it equitable, Massey asked, that a war for which all were equally responsible should have wiped out the value of the planter's slaves and halved that of his land but left the bondholder's wealth intact? Massey presented a plan to distribute the War's effects evenly. Virginia should explicitly repudiate all responsibility for West Virginia's third of the debt. She should concede no interest for the War years. She should scale down the interest on American-owned bonds in proportion to the reduction of Virginia property values resulting from the War. European bondholders, not responsible for the War, should receive the full value of their bonds—but from the federal government, not the state.[18]

In 1875, Massey did not speak for an organized movement—but agriculturists, who found his opinions congenial, were beginning to organize for common concerns. At the beginning of 1876, the Patrons of Husbandry, or "Grangers," claimed 18,783 members in Virginia. The order, in which Colonel Harvie was active, professed a purpose to protect the weak, restrain the strong, distribute bur-

17. John E. Massey, "Debts and Taxes," in Elizabeth H. Hancock, ed., *The Autobiography of John E. Massey* (New York and Washington: Neale Publishing Company, 1909), pp. 60–88 (hereafter cited as *Massey Autobiography*).

18. *Ibid.*, pp. 81, 88–96.

dens and power equitably, and seek the greatest good for the greatest number.[19] Some Conservative politicians feared that it would become an independent political force and that a Republican-Granger coalition would dethrone the Conservative party.[20] By 1877, the Grangers were manifesting insurgent attitudes toward the political establishment and the state debt, and there was talk of an independent Granger candidacy for governor.[21] More and more Virginia farmers were ready to take up "Parson" Massey's ideas.

WALKER, 1873

In the early 1870's, a powerful farm-based movement to readjust the state debt was only a potentiality. Readjuster writers were only isolated individuals, and hard-pressed farmers had not yet found a reform program to articulate their discontent. Ironically, the succession of controversies that reinforced, united, and drew recruits to these "outsiders" originated inside the funder leadership that they eventually deposed.

The "funders," many of whom thought the Funding Act had been an unwise policy, considered it an irrevocable contract from which the state could never escape without the bondholders' consent. Therefore, some funders realized, simply to treat the debt as a debatable issue—even by agitating for full payment—was a dangerous concession, opening the door to repudiation. "Bringing . . . the debt-question before the people in any form," former Governor Kemper wrote in 1880, "falsely implies that the debtor-party may do as it pleases with the contract; it virtually submits to the body of the debtors the question whether they, without consulting the creditor, will or will not pay the debt they owe; and such a question, thus brought into a spurious forum, of itself teaches the people the lesson of repudiation, for it addresses their selfish passions and interests, tells them they have the power to keep the creditors' money

19. Pearson, *Readjuster Movement*, p. 59; Alexandria *Virginia Sentinel,* January 16, 1875; John Ott to Lewis E. Harvie, May 16, 1878, Lewis Evarts Harvie Papers, Virginia State Library; J. M. Blanton to Edmund W. Hubard, May 23, 1877, Edmund Willcox Hubard Papers, Southern Historical Collection, University of North Carolina at Chapel Hill.

20. George R. Calvert to Harrison H. Riddleberger, February 10, 1874, Harrison Holt Riddleberger Papers, College of William and Mary.

21. Petersburg *Index and Appeal,* February 14 and September 21, 1877; S. Bassett French to William Mahone, November 21, 1876, William Mahone Papers, Duke University.

as their own, and invites them to keep it."[22] It would seem, then, that to avert readjustment Conservative leaders would have concerted their efforts to preclude controversy about the debt or questioning of the Funding Act. In fact, the unworkable system of state finance under the act made consistency in that strategy impossible. Financial difficulties impelled the Conservative leaders themselves, again and again, to make the debt a subject of controversy, inviting measures more drastic than they were prepared to sanction.

Gilbert C. Walker, "the father of the funding act," was the first to reopen the dangerous controversy. Walker realized by 1872 that his measure was unpopular and that it complicated state finance. He urgently needed to increase his popularity. Disturbed by the inconsistencies of the financial legislation in force, he asked the legislature to formulate some coherent, workable system of finance[23]— but the illogical *status quo* mirrored the legislators' attitudes better than any coherent policy could.

In February, 1873, making one of the sharpest turns of his zigzag career, Governor Walker proposed that the federal government assume all the states' public debts, forbidding them by constitutional amendment to incur debt in the future. The measure, Walker said, would help to secure national credit, restore intersectional harmony, and absorb the federal budgetary surplus. Without admitting that the Funding Act had been a blunder, he pointed out his plan's obvious applicability to Virginia's financial problems. Playing with fire, he even referred favorably to the effort by Wise's followers to have Congress assume the Virginia debt.[24] The General Assembly petitioned Congress to assume the states' debts and, strange to say, some Virginians believed that Congress really was about to unburden them of their state debt.[25]

Keen observers recognized in Walker's plan for federal assumption the dangerous implication that Virginians might not, after all, have to carry out the Funding Act's requirements. A Canadian critic

22. James L. Kemper to H. Sheppard (copy), March 18, 1880, James Lawson Kemper Papers, Virginia Historical Society.

23. Governor's Message, December 4, 1872, *Senate Journal* (1872–73), pp. 13–14.

24. *Senate Journal* (1872–73), Document XV: *Special Message of Governor Walker to the General Assembly of Virginia, on the Debt of the States, February 18, 1873*, pp. 1–8.

25. *Senate Journal* (1872–73), pp. 242–43, 255–56, 270–71; *House Journal* (1872–73), pp. 285–87, 301, 461; *Senate Journal* (1874), pp. 275–76, 417; Alexandria *Virginia Sentinel*, September 10, 1873.

warned the governor that his proposal would distract Southerners from their duty to settle their public debts honorably.[26] Nathaniel B. Meade prevented the Conservative State Convention of 1873 from endorsing federal assumption, since the proposal would alienate bondholders and brokers. "They know," Meade wrote, "the *Federal Government* will never pay the debt. Whilst even such a resolution would turn the eyes of the people from *themselves,* who are *primarily* bound for it, to another, and thus *encourage* the idea of repudiation . . . [since] if this *Government* is bound, *we are not.* It is a dangerous question and must be nicely handled."[27] Walker, perhaps seeing the peril in his proposal, ceased to press it. Governor Kemper, after advocating it for a time, also came to appreciate its dangerous tendency. To pause in effort to pay the debt and ask for outside aid, he said in 1876, was "to divert the public mind from the line of duty, to awaken false hopes, and to discourage the only practicable fulfillment of our undertakings. Such a policy, however patriotically conceived, marches on the line of repudiation."[28] The fact that funders like Walker and Kemper sometimes "marched on the line of repudiation" showed the inherent difficulty of the funder position.

KEMPER, 1874

The debt and financial problems plagued Governor Kemper from his first days in office. Finding the Commonwealth's financial condition much worse than he had expected, the new governor concluded that the Funding Act had been a "disastrous mistake" and that only the antifunding legislation of 1871 and 1872 had saved Virginia from financial ruin.[29] He observed with concern, however, that that legislation had shaken the business world's confidence in Virginia. The Council of Foreign Bondholders, the principal organization of British owners of American bonds, had condemned the measures as a form of repudiation. Virginia's bonds were selling at 52 per cent of face value—lower than those of Egypt, Turkey, and Peru. Believing state credit essential to the health of

26. "A friendly Canadian" to Gilbert C. Walker, n.d., "Letters on various subjects," Box 3, Gilbert Carlton Walker Executive Correspondence, Virginia State Library.

27. Nathaniel B. Meade to James L. Kemper, n.d. [1873], James Lawson Kemper Papers, University of Virginia.

28. Governor's Message, December 6, 1876, *Senate Journal* (1876–77), p. 10.

29. Governor's Message, March 27, 1874, *House Journal* (1874), pp. 343–44; *Conference with Creditors, 1874,* pp. 25–27, 30.

society, Kemper found the situation intolerable.[30] In his first message to the legislature, he endorsed federal assumption and dropped a hint of Wise's idea that the federal government had destroyed antebellum Virginia. He nevertheless warned that a violation of public honor would be the worst of disasters and proposed a program of economy and taxation to convince the bondholders and the federal government that Virginians were doing their best to pay the debt.[31]

During the next three months, Kemper saw the situation deteriorate. The Panic of 1873 was depressing the revenue, almost half of which was coming in in the form of coupons. State credit did not improve; the Council of Foreign Bondholders issued another blast against the state's policies. Instead of increasing the property tax, the General Assembly considered a joint resolution for "further readjustment" of the debt. A rumor circulated that the governor was going to propose scaling the debt down to its market value. Meade begged Kemper not to reopen the dangerous question. The state's financial peril, however, left the governor no choice.[32]

On March 27, in a special message to the General Assembly, Kemper denounced the Funding Act in terms as fierce as any readjuster's and pronounced its fulfillment impossible. Considering it a binding contract, however, he warned against any hint of repudiaton or forcible readjustment. He proposed to use all surplus revenue to pay interest, abandoning efforts to retire the principal. The only way Kemper could see to revive state credit and obtain relief was to restore understanding with the creditors. Perhaps both parties could agree on a new settlement that the state could realistically afford to carry out.[33]

Kemper's realistic pronouncement, a marked contrast to Walker's soothing syrup, pleased many Virginians and satisfied some American bondholders that Virginia was paying as much as she could. The General Assembly authorized the governor to call a

30. *Annual Cyclopaedia, 1872*, p. 795; *Conference with Creditors, 1874*, p. 32; Burton, "Taxation," p. 135n; Governor's Message, March 27, 1874, *House Journal* (1874), pp. 347–48.

31. Governor's Message, January 1, 1874, *Senate Journal* (1874), pp. 21–23.

32. *Senate Journal* (1874), Document III: *Communications from the Auditor of Public Accounts, in response to a Resolution of the Senate, Calling for Information as to What Amount of Taxes of the Present Fiscal Year Has Been Paid in Coupons, and What Amount in Currency, January 19, 1874*, pp. 1–2; Document XVII: *Communication from the Governor, March 27, 1874*, pp. 9–10; *Daily Petersburg Index*, January 24, 1874; Jones, "Conservative Virginian," pp. 249–50, 260.

33. Governor's Message, March 27, 1874, *House Journal* (1874), pp. 348–50.

conference of bondholders and appointed him and R. M. T. Hunter, recently chosen as state treasurer, to represent the Commonwealth. To reassure the bondholders, it authorized cash payment of two-thirds of the interest on the funded debt and if possible on the unfunded, provided certificates representing unpaid interest, and levied a number of new taxes.[34] All was not smooth sailing for Kemper's effort to restore public credit, however. On May 10, the Council of Foreign Bondholders, convinced that Kemper's government was bent on "spoliation," voted to discountenance Virginian's attempts to raise capital in Europe. The governor, angered by personal insult and by sabotage to his state's credit, broke off communications with the council.[35]

At the bondholders' conference at Richmond on November 10, Governor Kemper presented the bleak facts of Virginia's finances in a carefully prepared address. Easily refuting Walker's calculations of 1870, he concluded that the state was not able to pay the full interest the Funding Act stipulated. Unless it could gain a respite from the Act's obligations, it must either repudiate them or impose taxes that would crush its economy, leaving the creditors still unsatisfied.[36] The presentation dispelled most suspicious that the state was not trying to pay its debt.

Kemper went yet further, trying to frighten the bondholders into conceding terms less favorable to themselves. He presented an alarming tableau of the anarchy that would have resulted if the state had funded West Virginia's third of the antebellum debt as well. He intimated that the citizens would rise in resistance if the bondholders should carry their exactions too far. He spoke respectfully of other Virginians' opinions that the Funding Act and the new taxes were unconstitutional.[37] In his effort to bring the bondholders to accept a readjustment, Kemper set the prospect of repudiation before them—and, incidentally, before Virginia taxpayers as well.

Suggesting a new settlement, the governor said the state could

---

34. Jones, "Conservative Virginian," pp. 257–58, 260–61.
35. *Conference with Creditors, 1874,* pp. 5–10; James L. Kemper to Andrew J. Rogers (copy), May 18, 1874, and Kemper to Scott Brothers (copy), June 5, 1874, both in James Lawson Kemper Executive Letter-Book (1874–75), Virginia State Library.
36. *Conference with Creditors, 1874,* pp. 3–4, 15–23.
37. *Ibid.,* pp. 24–27, 29–31. Kemper had inquired into possible legal grounds for repudiating the Funding Act. James L. Kemper to Jeremiah S. Black (copy), September 11, 1874, Kemper Executive Letter-Book (1874–75), Virginia State Library.

not currently pay more than 4 per cent interest and that a new plan would have to treat all creditors equally, ending the distinction between "consols" and "peelers." He would accept an absolute state guarantee of semiannual payment at convenient places. Within those limits, Kemper invited the bondholders to propose a refunding settlement. He objected, however, that all previous proposals by creditors would impose intolerable financial burdens on the state. No plan, he warned, could succeed unless holders of consol bonds would stop presenting their coupons to pay taxes so that the treasury would have money to pay partial interest on the "peelers."[38]

The conference's committee to consider Kemper's address presented a conciliatory report, expressing hope that most out-of-state owners of consol bonds would surrender their coupons in return for a permanent arrangement that would guarantee prompt payment of at least 4 per cent annually at convenient places. The committee referred favorably to an offer by the American Bond-Funding and Banking Association of London, to refund the debt in bonds that would pay 4 per cent for ten years and 5 per cent for the following twenty. In the general session, the conference resolved that the state should permanently dedicate a specific source of revenue to pay 4 per cent interest yearly and should issue certificates for unpaid interest, to be funded into 4 per cent bonds after ten years. It should begin to pay full interest as soon as its means might permit. The representative of the Council of Foreign Bondholders—former Secretary of the Treasury Hugh McCulloch—did not participate in the conference's deliberations but merely informed the council of their result.[39]

A month after the conference, Governor Kemper told the General Assembly that the meeting had proved a great success, in that it had helped convince the bondholders of the state's good faith and had enhanced the market value of Virginia bonds. Aware that his recent pronouncements had fed the flames of antifunder agitation, he asked the legislature to act hastily to refund the debt. "If we further postpone a financial settlement," he warned, "we engender such internal difficulties and agitations as may . . . tear the vitals of our state."[40]

38. *Conference with Creditors, 1874*, pp. 26–28.
39. *Ibid.*, pp. 31–34.
40. Governor's Message, December 4, 1874, *Senate Journal* (1874–75), pp. 6–8.

No recapitalization came about, however. The General Assembly did not act. The administration concluded that the American Bond-Funding Association was unreliable and that its terms were unacceptable.[41] The consol holders were not disposed to give up their privileged position. Kemper had said that, to allow any plan to succeed, they must withhold almost all their coupons—but the revenue paid in coupons diminished only slightly and temporarily.[42] Kemper again did lip-service to refunding in his 1875 message to the legislature, but after that, he ceased to press the subject.[43] All parties seemed content, for the time being, to forget about recapitalizing the debt.[44]

Even though no recapitalization resulted from the bondholders' conference of 1874, it served its initiator's chief purpose—to restore the state's credit. "If no adjustment be agreed on here," Kemper had said at the conference, "yet if this meeting cause creditors to understand the real condition of Virignia, and restore confidence and good will between them and the state, then the labors of all connected with this effort will have been amply compensated."[45] After the prospect of refunding began to fade, Kemper still boasted that the conference had done more than any other event since the War "towards . . . recovering to the State the confidence of creditors and capitalists."[46] Any refunding proposal, to Kemper, was secondary to that objective—and since the conference had enhanced Virginia's credit, he was well satisfied with its outcome.

The governor found, however, that his initiative concerning the

41. *Senate Journal* (1874–75), Document IV: *Correspondence of the Governor with the Agent of the American Bond-Funding and Banking Association (Limited), in respect to the Recapitalization of the Debt of Va.*, pp. 3–11; Hugh McCulloch to James L. Kemper, November 20, 1874, Kemper Papers, University of Virginia; Jones, "Conservative Virginian," pp. 267–71.

42. Jones, "Conservative Virginian," p. 272n, considers the decline important. Kemper, on the contrary, complained at that time that bondholders were continually paying in or selling coupons to collect the full 6 per cent interest. James L. Kemper to C. E. Nicol (copy), September 13, 1875, Kemper Papers, Virginia Historical Society.

43. Jones, "Conservative Virginian," pp. 271–72; James L. Kemper to John S. Willett (copy), October 18, 1877, Kemper Executive Letter-Book (1877), Virginia State Library.

44. Pearson, *Readjuster Movement*, p. 53, blames the holders of consol bonds for the failure to recapitalize. Jones, "Conservative Virginian," pp. 273–74, blames the General Assembly and public opinion. The question matters little if, as the following paragraph suggests, Kemper himself did not take the proposal as seriously as these writers believe.

45. *Conference with Creditors, 1874*, p. 29.

46. James L. Kemper to Thomas Branch and Company (copy), June 24, 1875, Kemper Executive Correspondence, Virginia State Library.

debt had also had an unintended result: encouraging antifunder sentiment in Virginia. Readjusters were quoting Kemper's menacing statements with delight, and funders were blaming him for repudiationist agitation.[47] Afraid of the fire he had rekindled, Kemper began trying to extinguish it. In the spring of 1875, he threatened to veto the tax bill if it should include readjuster amendments. "This, coming from an avowed anti-Funder, astonished everybody," Richard F. Walker noticed.[48] When the banking house of Thomas Branch and Company announced to the financial world that the governor had broken with the "repudiation party," Kemper indignantly denied that he had ever been a repudiator. The bank's statement, he felt, impugned his honor and the state's credit as badly as would a notice that he had given up stealing.[49]

Kemper had not changed his policy, but—disturbed by the growing readjuster feeling—he had altered his emphasis, tone, and strategy. Instead of frightening creditors with the specter of repudiation, he now assured them that there was no repudiation movement in Virginia.[50] There was no alternative, he now acknowledged, to paying the entire debt. Seizing on a temporary relaxation of economic stringency, he took up Walker's prediction that economic growth would rapidly enable the state to meet its obligations.[51] "What we want," he taught, "is to put an end to agitation—to have less talk and more action."[52] He remained critical, still, of out-of-state capitalists who criticized the state for not adopting extreme measures to pay full interest. They were defeating their purpose, Kemper warned them, because their propaganda was discouraging the investment that would enable Virginia to pay and was provoking an antifunding reaction within the state.[53]

47. *Ibid.*; Hancock, ed., *Massey Autobiography*, pp. 62, 82–85.
48. Richard F. Walker to William Mahone, April 8, 1875, Mahone Papers.
49. James L. Kemper to Thomas Branch and Company (copy), June 24, 1875, Kemper Executive Correspondence, Virginia State Library.
50. *Ibid.*; Kemper to John S. Willett (copy), October 18, 1877, Kemper Executive Letter-Book (1877), Virginia State Library.
51. Kemper to P. Hairston (copy), May 24, 1875, *ibid.* (1874–75); Governor's Message, December 1, 1875, *Senate Journal* (1875–76), pp. 14, 24; Governor's Message, December 5, 1877, *Senate Journal* (1877–78), pp. 16, 20.
52. Kemper to C. E. Nicol (copy), September 13, 1875, Kemper Papers, Virginia Historical Society.
53. Kemper to Thomas Branch and Company (copy), June 24, 1875, and Kemper to Hugh McCulloch (copy), December 8, 1875, both in Kemper Executive Correspondence; Kemper to Baring Brothers and Company (copy), May 18, 1876, Kemper Executive Letter-Book (1875–77), Virginia Historical Society.

RUFFNER, 1876

The inadequacy and uncertainty of the school revenue was a continual torment to Superintendent Ruffner. The school fund received the proceeds from the capitation tax and a fifth of those from the property tax, as well as city and county funds. Local support was often meager, and tax payment in coupons rendered state support irregular. In 1870, the school taxes yielded $435,182, but in 1872, the first full year of the Funding Act's operation, they brought in only $184,672. To make the problem worse, the General Assembly, in 1872, passed a measure that so severely restricted local appropriations for schools as to subtract $200,000 more from the schools' income. During the school year 1872–73, therefore, the free schools enjoyed only half the income they had received the preceding year. Ruffner was afraid at first to publish the alarming news that the adventurous school system might wither as suddenly as it had sprung up. In March, 1873, the crisis left him no choice but to spring the facts of school finance on the General Assembly. The legislature was cool to his plea for emergency assistance, but, carrying out his suggestions for long-term reform, it allowed localities freer rein in levying local school taxes and provided that the school fund should receive its share of the revenue in cash, not coupons.[54]

After the Panic of 1873, school finance became even more precarious, and Ruffner searched ceaselessly for dependable sources of revenue. In 1876, his allies had the House of Delegates pass a resolution requiring Auditor Taylor to provide him with a statement of the proceeds from the taxes dedicated to school purposes. The auditor revealed, with embarrassment, that he did not himself know exactly how much the taxes yielded, since he received the revenue in bulk and learned its sources only after paying Ruffner the estimated school revenue. From available records, Ruffner calculated that by 1874 the free schools had received $382,732 less than the amount to which they were entitled and that by 1876 the arrearages probably amounted to about $550,000.[55]

54. *Senate Journal* (1872–73), pp. 453, 510, and Document XVII: *Communication from the Superintendent of Public Instruction, in response to a Resolution of the Senate Calling for Information as to the Financial Condition of the Public Free School System, March 14, 1873*, pp. 1–2; *House Journal* (1872–73), pp. 149, 266, 384, 401, 415–16, 432, 487–88.

55. *House Journal* (1875–76), Document VII: *Communication from the Superintendent of Public Instruction transmitting a Table Showing the Amount of State Tax Paid and Received for School Purposes in Each County and City in the State for the Year 1873*, p. 1; *Seventh Annual Report of the Superintendent of Public Instruction,*

By publicizing the discrepancy, Ruffner brought the debt issue again to the fore, since the tax-receivable coupons were at the heart of the revenue problem. The readjusters, seizing on his revelations, demanded to know why the state had, the preceding year, paid some of the overdue interest on the peeler bonds, "diverting" money due to the schools. State officials replied that no one had known of the discrepancy at that time.[56] Taylor explained the difficulty of ascertaining the amount of school revenue. Even if he had known of the "diversion," he nevertheless continued, he would not have paid the school fund the entire amount due. The treasury did not receive enough to meet all the state's commitments, and Taylor thought that schools, debt service, and government operations were equal in their claims on the revenue. He had paid the school fund its share of ascertained revenue balances and more than its share of incoming cash. The treasury, he insisted, could not afford to do more.[57]

Other state officials sided with Taylor against Ruffner in regard to the relative claims of schools and debt on the revenue. Governor Kemper suggested administrative reforms to prevent a future diversion of school income, and even intimated that paying school taxes in coupons might be unconstitutional. He nevertheless defended past practices, pointing out that the school fund enjoyed the privilege of receiving all its income in cash.[58] The General Assembly instructed the auditor, if practicable, to pay the undisputed $382,732.26 of arrearages to the school fund in quarterly payments of $15,000 each, but Taylor decided each quarter that the state of the treasury made payment impossible.[59] Governor Kemper, on leaving office, warned that to pay the schools their allotted revenue promptly in cash would imperil the government's existence. "Does the bond of the constitution," he asked, "so . . . exalt any one of the departments, over all others, that it may, whenever the letter of the bond is forfeit, cut its pound of flesh from the body of the state, nearest its heart, even at the sacrifice of the life of the state?"[60]

---

for the Year ending July 31, 1877 (Richmond: R. E. Frazier, Superintendent of Public Printing, 1877), pp. 12–13 (hereafter cited as *School Report, 1877*).

56. Jones, "Conservative Virginian," p. 316; James L. Kemper to Robert M. T. Hunter and Asa G. Rogers (copy), January 18, 1879, Kemper Papers, Virginia Historical Society; *School Report, 1876*, p. 10.

57. Reprinted in *School Report, 1877*, pp. 13–14.

58. Governor's Message, December 6, 1876, *Senate Journal* (1876–77), pp. 15–18.

59. Burton, "Taxation," pp. 150–51.

60. Governor's Message, December 5, 1877, *Senate Journal* (1877–78), p. 28.

In fact it was the bondholders, not the school system, who appeared to possess that privilege.

Ruffner, no more an antifunder than Kemper had been in 1874, carried his fight for school support to lengths that embarrassed the funders and encouraged the readjusters. He pressed the "diversion" issue for two years. He disrupted the unity of the state administration by protracted disputes with Taylor.[61] He encouraged the readjusters' campaign to guarantee that the schools would receive their funds promptly, in cash, regardless of the consequences to the bondholders. He blamed the "diversion" on the Funding Act's coupon provision. He argued that the schools' claims were legally and morally prior to the bondholders' and that free schools were necessary for the economic growth without which Virginia could never pay the debt. In 1878, as schools closed for lack of funds, Ruffner warned the funders, as Kemper had warned the bondholders, that too strict an adherence to the Funding Act would give rise to plebeian insurgence.[62]

Like Kemper before him, though, Ruffner provided only a temporary inspiration for readjuster strategy. He, too, was unwilling to press the controversy he had aroused to its logical conclusion. Personally, he considered the debt a sacred obligation and thought repudiation would be "moral death" and "eternal damnation." He advocated an increase in taxes as the solution to the revenue problem.[63] As the "diversion" controversy continued and the readjuster movement gained strength, Ruffner took caution and retreated, as Walker and Kemper had earlier done. In 1879, the General Assembly passed legislation enabling the superintendent to claim any balance of money in the treasury until the arrearages should be repaid. To the readjusters' chagrin, Ruffner declined their invitation to increase school income and, incidentally, paralyze debt service.[64]

MAHONE, 1877

The gubernatorial election of 1877 attracted as candidates a number of Confederate officers who, at first, did not divide over policies. Their bases of support were mainly geographical. Colonel

61. *School Report, 1877*, p. 13n; *School Report, 1878*, pp. 11–24; William F. Taylor to James L. Kemper, October 24, 1878, Kemper Papers, University of Virginia.

62. *School Report, 1878*, pp. 6, 24–25, 37–42.

63. *Ibid.*, pp. 35–36; *School Report, 1871*, pp. 49–55.

64. W. N. Newman to Lewis E. Harvie, June 18, 1879, Harvie Papers.

Frederick W. M. Holliday was the Valley's "favorite son"; Brigadier General William Terry, the Southwest's; and Major General William B. Taliaferro, the Tidewater's. Major John W. Daniel was strongest in the Piedmont, Brigadier General William Mahone retained his popularity in the southside, and Major General Fitzhugh Lee stood by as a possible compromise candidate.[65] Neither the debt nor any other divisive issue seemed likely, initially, to figure in the contest for the Conservative nomination.

William Mahone had reached the turning point of his career. During the preceding decade, Mahone's political activity had centered on his business interest. In the 1869 election, his first concern had been to secure the A. M. and O. charter; in 1873, it had been to escape from the charter's requirement about the Cumberland Gap extension. He had rarely tried to commit his associates on nonrailroad issues, much less to organize a multi-issue movement. Often a kingmaker, he had never before aspired to a crown of his own. In 1875, he had rejected the idea of going to the United States Senate, preferring to stick to his business.[66] Mahone's departure from his orbit to run for governor in 1877 resulted from his business reverses. He hoped to use the office to recover control of the A. M. and O., or at least to keep it out of his Northern adversaries' hands.[67]

The Mahone coterie aroused itself again, but it soon encountered unaccustomed obstacles. Although the general's varied activities had given him valuable experience and prestige as a defender of Virginia against Northern encroachment, he suffered from many handicaps as a candidate. He had made many enemies, and his power and arrogance inspired distrust. His business failure had diminished his resources, his personal connections, and his public image. His dealings with the state had savored of the same questionable practices as those of his "Bucktail" opponents.[68] The other candidates' adherents combined to attack Mahone. "Four pluck one is the game," Richard F. Walker commented. Newspapers assaulted him mercilessly, and the state Conservative organization made rulings prejudicial to his candidacy.[69] Beset by the hostility of estab-

65. Pearson, *Readjuster Movement*, p. 68.

66. William Mahone to D. C. Dunn (copy), May 17, 1875, Letter-Books, Mahone Papers.

67. William Mahone to Harrison H. Riddleberger (copy), August 19, 1877, Riddleberger Papers; Pearson, *Readjuster Movement*, p. 71.

68. Pearson, *Readjuster Movement*, pp. 70–71.

69. Blake, *Mahone*, pp. 148–49; Staunton *Vindicator*, April 20, 1877.

lished politicians, Mahone found it advantageous to substitute issue politics for personality politics.[70]

The time was ripe to reappraise the state's debt policy. Unpaid interest had increased the total debt from $31,145,711 in 1874 to $33,538,967 in 1877.[71] To pay off the debt obviously would require a great increase of exertion. The Richmond *Dispatch*, a funder paper, expressed impatience with "the lingering, loitering, Micawberlike policy" of waiting for economic recovery. "It is time," the *Dispatch* wrote, "that the State had determined either to pay the interest upon her debt, or to let her creditors know that she does not intend to pay it."[72]

Until 1877, Mahone's policy on the debt question had been quite conventional. He had not personally opposed the Funding Act in 1871, and he had approved Kemper's policy in 1874.[73] His political associates included both funders and readjusters. In 1875, the general had exerted himself to persuade the latter group to support a funder for lieutenant governor. As late as March, 1877, he intended, if nominated, to include Attorney General Raleigh T. Daniel, an extreme funder, on his ticket.[74] Many agrarian and working-class readjusters had no love for Mahone. In May, 1877, readjuster farmers in Augusta County resolved to oppose the election of any railroad executive as governor.[75] Mahone's practices as an employer did not entitle him to labor support. Many of his own employees opposed his candidacy and would prefer an independent "repudiation" candidate.[76]

On the other hand, there were significant bases for alliance between Mahone and the readjusters. The general had experienced the same financial stringency that had brought farmers to question the debt, and he, too, had suffered at the hands of foreign bond-

70. See William C. Pendleton, *Political History of Appalachian Virginia, 1776–1927* (Dayton, Va.: Shenandoah Press, 1927), p. 318 (hereafter cited as *Appalachian Virginia*).

71. Burton, "Taxation," p. 141.

72. Quoted in *ibid.*, p. 142.

73. Cahill, "Walker," pp. 96–98; Blake, *Mahone*, p. 165n; Ours, "Redeemer Legislature," p. 102; Jones, "Conservative Virginian," pp. 250, 266–67; John W. Johnston in *Cong. Record*, 47 Cong., Special Senate Sess., p. 56 (1881).

74. Richard F. Walker to William Mahone, February 8, 1875; Walker to Mahone, February 9, 1875; Walker to Mahone, February 15, 1875; Walker to Mahone, March 27, 1877; and Mahone to Walker (copy), February 11, 1875, Letter-Books, all in Mahone Papers.

75. Staunton *Vindicator*, May 25 and June 15, 1877.

76. Richard F. Walker to William Mahone, February 26, 1870, and L. F. Johnson to Mahone, June 19, 1877, both in Mahone Papers.

holders. His appeal to cheap-transportation sentiment and his opposition to absentee-owned railroads had endeared him to some
farming elements. His political friends included readjusters Abram
Fulkerson, Harrison H. Riddleberger, and (as suspicious allies)
Lewis E. Harvie and Frank G. Ruffin.

On June 29, Mahone broached the financial question in an open
letter. He would sooner "let the very wheels of government stand
still," he declared, than tolerate "the perversion or conversion of
the public-school fund to any other purpose than that for which it
was created." On July 4, in a second letter, the general condemned
the Funding Act as a "grievous mistake" that had led to "practical,
though unwilling, repudiation" since the state could not pay full
interest. "We should," he proposed, "seek and insist upon, urge,
and, if necessary, demand a compromise and readjustment of the
debt of the Commonwealth and of the annual liabilities thereunder
which shall be within the certain and reasonable capacity of the
people to regularly meet."[77] Mahone's letters added nothing to
earlier readjuster pronouncements, but they gave the movement a
powerful recruit, and Mahone a new source of political support.

Contrary to most readers' impressions, Mahone had not irrevocably committed himself to forcible readjustment in the July 4
letter. The Petersburg *Index* and Norfolk *Landmark*, funder papers
close to the general, interpreted it as calling for no more than
"voluntary readjustment"—a bilateral agreement with the bondholders.[78] Mahone himself later explained to acquaintances that he
had hoped only, by hinting at forcible readjustment, to frighten the
bondholders into accepting a compromise that would reduce the
interest rate and put peeler and consol bonds on the same basis. The
strategy succeeded, temporarily, in that it drove the price of consol
bonds down from 74 to 63 per cent of par.[79]

Mahone's letters disturbed political circles as deeply as financial
ones. In consternation, funders exclaimed that Mahone and his advisors were "conspirators against the life of the Conservative party"
and that his "villainous letter" had precipitated "a wretched division of sentiment" on the debt. The *Enquirer*, finding in the letters
a revolutionary menace to property, intimated that if Mahone

77. Both quoted in Blake, *Mahone*, pp. 149–50.
78. Petersburg *Index and Appeal*, July 7, 1877; Pearson, *Readjuster Movement*, p.
74n.
79. William Mahone to Harrison H. Riddleberger, August 19, 1877, Riddleberger
Papers; Mahone to R. L. Brockett, September 17, 1877, in Staunton *Vindicator*, September 28, 1877.

should win the nomination the funders would unite with the Republicans to defeat him.[80] Most of the other candidates for governor temporized on the financial question. Colonel Holliday evasively stated that the question was for the legislature to decide and that, as governor, he would not interfere with its decision. Some thought Holliday was favorable to readjustment, but he made it clear to his associates that he would not countenance a forcible readjustment. John W. Daniel, who openly took that position, privately sought an entente with Holliday on debt policy.[81]

On August 8, when the Conservative State Convention met at Richmond, the debt issue became a source of open conflict in the party. Colonel William E. Lamb made his welcoming speech an extreme statement of the funder position, but was shouted down by readjuster delegates. The funders won the next round, electing Marshall Hanger of Augusta County, the speaker of the House of Delegates, as president of the convention, and Delegate James H. Dooley of Richmond, as chairman of the Committee on Resolutions. Because of Granger and Valley objections to Mahone's railroad record, the readjusters could not agree on a gubernatorial candidate. They tried to have the convention adopt a platform before nominating candidates, but Hanger prevented the maneuver.[82]

The balloting showed that Mahone, although the choice of the largest bloc of delegates, could not win a majority. In the first six ballots, Mahone and Daniel proved the most popular contenders, Mahone leading in all but the fourth. It was evident that the other candidates were determined not to release their delegates to support Mahone. On the seventh ballot, John S. Wise, Mahone's floor leader, released the Mahone men to vote for Holliday, who then received a majority of 852 votes against 568 for Daniel and one holdout for Mahone.[83] The long-standing hostility between Ma-

80. W. F. Drinkard to James L. Kemper, July 9, 1877, Kemper Papers, University of Virginia; James H. Skinner to Frederick W. M. Holliday, July 31, 1877, Frederick William Mackey Holliday Papers, Duke University; Pearson, *Readjuster Movement*, p. 73.

81. Pearson, *Readjuster Movement*, p. 73; Blake, *Mahone*, p. 153; Vecellio, "Daniel," pp. 146–48; Frederick W. M. Holliday to Norman Bell (copy), July 20, 1877, and John W. Daniel to Holliday, July 11, 1877, both in Holliday Papers.

82. Petersburg *Index and Appeal*, August 9, 1877; McFarland, "Extension of Democracy," pp. 101–3.

83. Vecellio, "Daniel," pp. 157–61. Daniel's and Holliday's floor managers denied charges of collusion between their blocs. Petersburg *Index and Appeal*, August 11, 1877. For whatever reason, the Daniel men were certain, before the first ballot, that

hone and Daniel accounted adequately for Mahone's supporting Holliday, but Daniel's funder pronouncements and the readjuster sympathies of some of Holliday's Valley supporters may have confirmed the decision.[84] The convention completed the ticket with two funders: General James A. Walker for lieutenant governor and the incumbent Raleigh T. Daniel for attorney general.

The convention's platform rejected any repudiation of just obligations but promised to try by all honorable means to effect an adjustment that would permit prompt interest payment without increasing taxes. It also advocated economy in government and called on Conservatives to settle their differences inside the party.[85] Readjusters interpreted the platform as committing the party to readjustment by whatever means might prove necessary. The funders who had drafted the ambiguous document understood it as a statement of their own policy.[86] A readjuster delegate parodied the funders' lip-service to voluntary readjustment by introducing a resolution for "a voluntary adjustment of all matters between the sheep and the dogs of this State," pledging the party "to support any scheme for the protection of the innocent lambs which will not contravene the natural and legal rights of the hungry dog."[87] The funders had gotten their way at the convention, but the readjusters could claim some symbolic concessions.

So far, General Mahone's course on readjustment paralleled the previous courses of Walker, Kemper, and Ruffner. Not personally committed to forcible readjustment, he had been impelled by public and personal considerations to bring the debt question to public attention. To frighten bondholders into compromise, he had used menacing language hinting at forcible measures. After August, 1877, though, Mahone's course diverged sharply from the example his predecessors had set. Entrenched in the political establishment, they had given ground when their actions appeared to be encouraging forcible readjustment. Mahone, in contrast, was losing his railroad power and had now become a pariah to most of the Conserva-

---

Mahone could not win a majority. John E. Penn to John W. Daniel, telegram, August 9, 1877, John Warwick Daniel Papers, University of Virginia.

84. McFarland, "Extension of Democracy," p. 103, thinks that many believed Holliday sympathetic to readjustment.

85. Text in Petersburg *Index and Appeal*, August 11, 1877.

86. Pearson, *Readjuster Movement*, p. 76n; see A. Dudley Mann to James L. Kemper, October 3, 1877, Kemper Papers, University of Virginia.

87. Petersburg *Index and Appeal*, August 11, 1877.

tive leadership. Having almost no stake left in the *status quo* to lose, he could afford to build a new career as a readjuster leader.

Mahone at once took the lead in an effort to make the election campaign a forum in which to express the readjuster position. Readjusters, he insisted, must press their interpretation of the platform, elect legislators of their persuasion, and form an independent readjuster caucus in the next legislature. Still hoping that menacing gestures by a readjuster government would convert the bondholders to voluntary readjustment, the general directed a readjuster campaign within the Conservative campaign.[88]

In many districts, readjusters battled funders in Conservative conventions and even in general elections. Each faction made a candidate's debt policy the supreme test of his worthiness for office. Conservative rallies became debates between the two factions, sometimes by readjusters forcing funders to divide the time.[89] When Attorney General Daniel died a week after the convention, the Conservative State Committee, as a sop to the readjusters, replaced him on the ticket with Colonel James Gaven Field, an Albemarle County farmer and lawyer who had been Daniel's opponent for the convention nomination. Field, whom Governor Kemper appointed to complete Daniel's term in office, warmly advocated a readjustment without committing himself about "forcible" means.[90] While Field campaigned on that basis, General Walker took an unyielding funder position in his campaign speeches. Readjusters demanded that Walker be removed from the ticket for deviating from the platform, but most party leaders found his policy at least as consistent with their interpretations of the platform as Field's.[91] Members of each faction launched independent legislature candidacies against regular Conservative nominees of the other. Twenty-two independents, nearly all readjusters, won seats in the House of Dele-

88. William Mahone to Harrison H. Riddleberger, August 19, 1877, and Mahone to Riddleberger, August 31, 1877, both in Riddleberger Papers.

89. See Staunton *Vindicator*, July 6 and September 14, 1877; J. Randolph Tucker to Henry St. George Tucker, October 22, 1877, Tucker Family Papers, Southern Historical Collection, University of North Carolina at Chapel Hill.

90. Moore, "Field," pp. iii, 54–55; Staunton *Vindicator*, September 28, 1877, and September 11, 1879. In 1892, Field ran for Vice-president of the United States on the Populist ticket.

91. James A. Walker, manuscript 1877 campaign speeches, James Alexander Walker Papers, Southern Historical Collection, University of North Carolina at Chapel Hill; William Mahone to Harrison H. Riddleberger, September 20, 1877; Mahone to Riddleberger, September 28, 1877; and Mahone to Riddleberger, October 8, 1877, all in Riddleberger Papers; Staunton *Vindicator*, September 28, 1877; Petersburg *Index and Appeal*, October 9, 1877.

gates.[92] General Mahone, aware that the Conservative party was crumbling, was working to reorganize parties on the lines of the debt issue.[93]

"The public debt and credit of Virginia," Governor Kemper regretfully observed, "are being bedraggled in the arena of party politics and are among the issues in the canvass . . . which now agitates the State."[94] That situation marked an era in the history of the Conservative leadership as well as in that of the debt issue. Again and again in the preceding six years, the recurrent crises of state finance had led Conservative leaders who were not themselves forcible readjusters to bring explosive questions about the state debt before the citizens. Each time, some Conservatives who thought about the questions found satisfaction in the readjusters' answers. By degrees, the debt question had grown to become the principal issue dividing political factions. Now, in the latter part of 1877, funders and readjusters confronted one another across a battle line that no belated desire to suppress the controversy would be able to erase.

92. Petersburg *Index and Appeal*, October 9, 1877; Pearson, *Readjuster Movement*, p. 77.

93. William Mahone to Harrison H. Riddleberger, August 31, 1877, Riddleberger Papers.

94. James L. Kemper to R. E. Blankenship (copy), September 20, 1877, Kemper Executive Letter-Book (1875–77), Virginia Historical Society.

16.

Disintegration of the Conservative Party, 1877–1879

Frederick W. M. Holliday's unopposed election to the governorship on the Conservative ticket was the apex of his party's dominance and the beginning of its disintegration. In the two succeeding years, the controversy over readjustment split the party into sharply differentiated funder and readjuster factions, which in 1879 became separate organizations antagonistic to each other. The funders controlled the Conservative party organization, but each party claimed to be the true representative of the politics of Virginia Conservatism. The Readjuster party elected a majority of members of the legislature in November, 1879, bringing the decade of Conservative dominance to an end.

CONFRONTATION

The chasm that separated funders and readjusters was social as well as political. Businessmen, city-dwellers, planters, and white men in largely black counties were usually funders. The opponents of the debt were mostly hard-pressed farm people: yeomen in the Valley, "hillbillies" in the Southwest, and Negroes and some poor whites in planting regions.[1] Farmers' meetings adopted readjuster resolutions.[2] In 1877, the funder-dominated Senate Finance Committee attributed the readjuster agitation to the transfer of wealth, by "a law as certain as the law of gravitation," from the rural chivalry to the urban business class.[3] It was yeomen, however, not

1. Pearson, *Readjuster Movement*, pp. 103–17, 127–29. John S. Wise, a prominent readjuster, pointed out that former Democratic regions tended to elect readjusters, and former Whig ones, funders. Wise, *Lion's Skin*, pp. 309, 323–26.
2. Staunton *Vindicator*, May 25, 1877. The *Vindicator* denied that the meeting represented the opinions of most farmers. *Ibid.*, June 1, 8, 15, and 29, 1877.
3. McFarland, "Extension of Democracy," pp. 107–9.

[256]

planters, who gave the movement its thrust, and it was popular also among the propertyless. Funders often expressed contempt for readjusters as the poorer, less educated "tag rag and bobtail" of society.[4] The funders portrayed their opponents, further, as enemies of property—but two Richmonders who hiked through many readjuster counties in 1879 discovered no trace of socialist sentiment.[5] The movement drew its leadership not from the real "bottom rails" of society but from small-scale farmers, plus Mahone's railroad clique and country gentlemen such as Massey, Harvie, and Ruffin.

The impulse for readjustment sprang largely from farmers' economic distress, especially their lack of currency. The national banking system provided the Southern states with a disproportionately small amount of its notes. Virginia, Governor Kemper estimated, had only a third the share of the national currency to which her population entitled her and less than a third the banking capital and currency that the area of postwar Virginia had possessed in 1861, before emancipation increased the need for circulating medium. In isolated areas, men conducted business on a barter basis. To suggest that Virginia accumulate adequate circulating medium through the provisions of the National Banking Act of 1864 was, the Governor asserted, "as ineffectual as the advice to a starving and destitute man to buy bread for cash."[6] Rural residents, the most disadvantaged, took the lead in inflationist and readjuster movements, and city dwellers, enjoying more credit facilities, tried to restrain the movements.

Virginians could find no direct remedy for their currency problem. In regard to federal policy, even the most orthodox fiscal thinkers in Virginia were inflationists by Northeastern standards.[7] Congressman Eppa Hunton, typifying their ambivalence, declared

4. Richmond *Whig*, August 3, 1880, clipping in Frank Gildart Ruffin Scrapbook, I, 30, Virginia State Library; Robert E. Withers to James Barron Hope, October 4, 1879, James Barron Hope Papers, College of William and Mary; Willie Walker Caldwell, "Life of General James A. Walker," p. 243, typescript in James Alexander Walker Papers, Southern Historical Collection, University of North Carolina at Chapel Hill (hereafter cited as Caldwell, "Walker"); Hoge and Bayne, *Ego and Alter*, p. 11; George W. Booker to James L. Kemper, January 10, 1878, James Lawson Kemper Papers, University of Virginia.

5. Hoge and Bayne, *Ego and Alter*, p. 48.

6. Governor's Message, January 1, 1874, *Senate Journal* (1874), pp. 22–23; Governor's Message, December 2, 1874, *Senate Journal* (1874–75), p. 10.

7. See Richmond *Enquirer*, August 17, 1875; Richmond *Dispatch*, January 5 and 6 and July 11, 1876; J. Randolph Tucker to Edmund W. Hubard, July 30, 1878, Edmund Willcox Hubard Papers, Southern Historical Collection, University of North Carolina at Chapel Hill.

"that he was a hard money man, but thought the interests of his people required more currency and was for inflation."[8] In federal politics, however, Virginians could do little to solve their problem. Since each national party was divided internally on the currency, neither would undertake a serious reform program.[9] Stymied at the federal level, some Conservatives devised projects for inflation by state action. Almost all the plans advocated a state-bank currency, and presupposed the repeal of the prohibitory federal tax on notes of state-chartered banks.[10] Few legislators took seriously even State Treasurer R. M. T. Hunter's carefully prepared proposal for a land bank, which Governor Kemper endorsed.[11]

Unable to surmount their difficulties by monetary policy, Virginia farmers resented the reduction of their inadequate incomes by taxes that went to out-of-state bondholders. Studying the readjusters' criticisms of the wisdom, feasibility, and validity of the Funding Act, many resolved to end that drain on their fortunes.

To funders, the crux of the question was the illegitimacy of unilateral repudiation of contractual obligations. Some funders criticized the legislature's actions on the debt in 1866 and 1871 as severely as did readjusters, but they considered them binding contracts from which the state could not withdraw without the bondholders' consent.[12] The "debt-payers" deeply reverenced honor and public morality. "Temporary relief from pecuniary pressure is too dearly bought," Judge Wood Bouldin of the Supreme Court of Appeals wrote in 1872, "at the price of the violated faith of Virginia."[13] "The honor of a State is above price," Governor Holliday asserted. "It cannot be measured by money."[14] The Reverend

8. Alexandria *Virginia Sentinel*, August 27, 1874.

9. Robert E. Withers to Lewis E. Harvie, February 29, 1876, Lewis Evarts Harvie Papers, Virginia State Library.

10. See John W. Daniel, "The Financial Crisis and How to Deal with It," manuscript speech in Senate of Virginia, March 11, 1878, John Warwick Daniel Papers, University of Virginia (hereafter cited as "Financial Crisis").

11. *Senate Journal* (1874–75), Document III: *Plan Providing for a Constitutional Currency, proposed by Hon. R. M. T. Hunter, State Treasurer,* pp. 3–8; Governor's Message, December 2, 1874, *Senate Journal* (1874–75), p. 10; Nathaniel B. Meade to Richard F. Walker, December 26, 1874, William Mahone Papers, Duke University.

12. Richmond *Dispatch*, November 18, 1874, quoted in Burton, "Taxation," p. 140; Governor's Message, December 5, 1877, *Senate Journal* (1877–78), pp. 13–14, 17–21.

13. *Antoni* v. *Wright*, 22 Gratt. 859 (1872).

14. [Frederick William Mackey Holliday], *Inaugural Address of Gov. Fred. W. M. Holliday, delivered in Richmond, Va., Jan. 1, 1878* (n.p., [1878]), p. 6 (hereafter cited as *Inaugural Address*).

J. L. M. Curry stated the moral case against readjustment in an address on "Law and Morals."[15]

Frank S. Blair, a Wytheville lawyer, replied to the funder talk of "honor" with the Falstaffian rejoinder: "Honor won't buy a breakfast."[16] To many an impoverished farmer, that argument was compelling. Few readjuster leaders, however, dismissed the problem of "honor" so lightly. Judge Waller Staples argued that Virginia's sufferings since 1861 had amply redeemed her honor and that to compromise her sovereignty by alienating future revenues was less honorable than to reclaim control over the revenue.[17] Mahone and Riddleberger charged that the funders, not the readjusters, were "repudiators," since they paid no interest on the peelers, levied taxes inadequate to pay interest on the debt, and repudiated obligations to the school system by diverting funds.[18] Mahone thought of the readjuster program as the alternative to repudiation.[19]

Legalism as well as moralism characterized the funder position.[20] Forcible readjustment, funders insisted, was not only immoral but impossible, since the courts would have to invalidate it. Some claimed that the readjusters were not sincere in their political program—since their professed object was unattainable—but were merely using demagogy about the debt to worm their way into office.[21] Funders naturally took a high view of the judiciary's prerogatives. Holliday believed that the "strength and purity" of judges were "the firmest bulwarks of freedom and peace," and Lieutenant Governor Walker warned that barbarism and oppression of the weak would result from any attack on judicial independence.[22] By 1878, readjusters, on the other hand, carped at the Supreme Court of Appeals and looked for opportunities to reconstruct the courts.[23]

15. Alderman and Gordon, *Curry*, p. 246.
16. Quoted in Caldwell, "Walker," p. 246.
17. *Antoni* v. *Wright*, 22 Gratt. 865–67, 870–71 (1872).
18. William Mahone to Harrison H. Riddleberger, August 31, 1877, Harrison Holt Riddleberger Papers, College of William and Mary; Harrison H. Riddleberger, "Bourbonism in Virginia," *The North American Review*, CXXXIV (April, 1882), 418–25 (hereafter cited as "Bourbonism in Virginia"); Staunton *Vindicator*, June 1, 1877.
19. Mahone to Lewis E. Harvie, January 5, 1879, Harvie Papers.
20. See anecdote on Raleigh T. Daniel in O'Ferrall, *Forty Years*, p. 426.
21. Richmond *Dispatch*, April 22, 1875; Staunton *Vindicator*, June 15, 1877; Petersburg *Index and Appeal*, October 9, 1877.
22. Governor's Veto Message, February 27, 1878, *House Journal* (1877–78), p. 426; James A. Walker, manuscript speech in Richmond, September, 1878 (James Alexander Walker Papers, Southern Historical Collection, University of North Carolina at Chapel Hill), pp. 20–21. See also Governor's Message, December 4, 1878, *Senate Journal* (1878–79), p. 13.
23. Edward C. Burks to J. Randolph Tucker, June 12, 1878, Tucker Family Papers;

Funders were almost as anxious about Virginia's currency and credit shortage and her slow economic growth as were readjusters. They saw the problem, however, through businessmen's eyes. Believing that only an influx of Northern capital could bring prosperity, they thought that forcible readjustment would greatly retard development instead of stimulating it. "To repudiate," Kemper warned, "is to stain her [Virginia's] honor, to shut out immigration and capital which would otherwise come here and to inflict upon the state damages and losses . . . many times greater . . . than the thirty millions of debt."[24] "Let the dark shadow of repudiation rest upon our State," Colonel William E. Lamb told the Conservative State Convention of 1877, "and who would trust us? Our own capitalists would send their surplus means abroad, and all hope of foreign aid would be a delusion and a snare."[25] Jedidah Hotchkiss and A. Dudley Mann testified that readjuster agitation was hurting their efforts to attract foreign investment to Virginia.[26] Conversely, Holliday believed, "so soon as we indicate a willingness and ability to pay the interest promptly, our Bonds will at once go to par and Capital and population [will] flow into our borders;—and never till then."[27] Funders therefore thought, "It will cost more not to pay, than it will to pay" and defended their policy as "the most *selfish* thing the state could do."[28]

Funder Conservatives looked to Northern assistance in their conflict with the readjusters. Some of the most active funders, such as Bradley T. Johnson and William L. Royall, represented out-of-state bondholders as attorneys and lobbyists. Others, such as the principal Richmond bankers, acted as brokers for them in coupon transactions. The only conspicuous business interest on the readjuster side, significantly, was General Mahone's, which had long

---

John Echols to Charles T. O'Ferrall, December 14, 1878, Charles Triplett O'Ferrall Papers, College of William and Mary; Richmond *Whig*, November 20 and 29, 1880, clippings in Ruffin Scrapbook, I, 54–56.

24. Quoted in Jones, "Conservative Virginian," p. 315.

25. Petersburg *Index and Appeal*, August 9, 1877.

26. Richmond *Dispatch*, April 9, 1875; A. Dudley Mann to James L. Kemper, April 17, 1878, Kemper Papers, University of Virginia.

27. Frederick W. M. Holliday to Michael G. Harman, April 12, 1877, in unidentified clipping, Holliday Scrapbook (1850–99), Part II, p. 5, Frederick William Mackey Holliday Papers, Duke University. See also Governor's Message, December 4, 1878, *Senate Journal* (1878–79), p. 11.

28. George W. Booker to James L. Kemper, February 11, 1878, Kemper Papers, University of Virginia; (Nathaniel) Beverley Tucker to Edmund W. Hubard, April 18, 1878, Hubard Papers.

exemplified native capital in its rivalry with Northern capitalists. Funders counted on the federal judiciary and perhaps the executive as well, to intervene if necessary to prevent forcible readjustment.[29] Governor Kemper remarked that repudiation would be equivalent to secession and added pointedly that "no lesson from the past is needed to inform us that the power of Virginia is not equal to the power of the United States." In 1880, Kemper welcomed what he considered usurpations of power by the Supreme Court of the United States, because he believed that the Court would use the new powers to thwart attempts at readjusment.[30] Readjusters, in reply, cultivated memories of the antebellum State-Rights ideas. When the majority of the Supreme Court of Appeals cited federal Supreme Court decisions as authority for the funder position, the dissenter Judge Staples called to mind the doctrines of Spencer Roane.[31] Extreme funders felt betrayed in 1883, when the Supreme Court at Washington briefly countenanced the readjuster position.[32]

By the end of 1877, the controversy over the state's debt and finances had given rise to two distinctive brands of Conservative thought. The differences between funder and readjuster extended beyond the initial issue and, indeed, defined divergent roads to the Conservatives' utopia of economic modernization and prosperity. The case for separate party organizations was already apparent to some; after two more years, it would be apparent to all.

THE BARBOUR BILL

The financial problem was the great issue that faced the members of the General Assembly when they came together in December, 1877. The outgoing governor congratulated the legislature on the absence of an "organized party of repudiation" and expressed confidence that the existing revenue system, with minor changes, would soon suffice to pay full interest on the debt.[33] The incoming governor, against Kemper's advice, yielded to young Conservatives' desire for a spirited inaugural celebration, unprecedented in Vir-

29. See Staunton *Vindicator*, July 20, 1877; Bradley T. Johnson, "Can States Be Compelled to Pay Their Debts?" *The American Law Review*, XII (July, 1878), 625–59.
30. Governor's Message, December 5, 1877, *Senate Journal* (1877–78), pp. 19–20; James L. Kemper to Frederick W. M. Holliday, March 15, 1880, Holliday Papers.
31. *Antoni* v. *Wright*, 22 Gratt. 841–47, 863–64 (1872).
32. Royall, *Debt Controversy*, pp. 74–75.
33. Governor's Message, December 5, 1877, *Senate Journal* (1877–78), pp. 16, 18, 20.

ginia practice.[34] In his inaugural address Holliday, too, warned against radical agitation and class strife and urged full payment of the debt.[35]

Meanwhile, the readjuster legislators, under General Mahone's prompting, organized a separate caucus, open to all antifunders regardless of party or race, for concerted action. Initially, Mahone hoped that the readjusters might elect the speaker of the House and perhaps impeach some treasury officials, to impress the bondholders with the expendience of accepting a compromise settlement.[36] John W. Daniel, appreciating the disruptive significance of the readjusters' proceedings, proposed that the Conservative caucus discontinue its former practice of admitting Conservatives who had been elected as independents. The caucus voted to exclude the twenty-two independent delegates, whereupon the regularly elected Conservative readjusters also withdrew. An informal committee of prominent Conservative legislators defended the caucus action, on the grounds that past lassitude had now brought about a crisis in party unity and that most of the independents had run with Republican support and joined the bipartisan readjuster caucus. When the regularly elected Conservative legislators refused to return alone, nevertheless, the caucus eventually relented and admitted the independents.[37]

At the beginning of the session, many thought that the "Simon Pure Readjusters" had a clear majority of the legislature.[38] The maneuvers of the first two weeks revealed, however, that many men elected as favorable to "readjustment" were not willing to take drastic steps toward that goal. Some tried to organize a separate "Honest Readjuster" bloc, and others would not act consistently with the readjuster caucus. The caucus members could not agree on candidates for offices.[39] Unable at the time to mount a formidable

34. James L. Kemper to Frederick W. M. Holliday, December 8, 1877, and Kemper to Holliday, December 17, 1877, both in Holliday Papers; Henry St. George Tucker to J. Randolph Tucker, December 30, 1877, Tucker Family Papers, Southern Historical Collection, University of North Carolina at Chapel Hill.

35. [Holliday], *Inaugural Address*, pp. 2–8.

36. William Mahone to Harrison H. Riddleberger, December 10, 1877, Riddleberger Papers; Petersburg *Index and Appeal*, December 10, 1877.

37. Vecellio, "Daniel," pp. 166–67; Petersburg *Index and Appeal*, January 16, 1878; Pearson, *Readjuster Movement*, p. 80.

38. F. H. Armistead to William Mahone, December 11, 1877, Mahone Papers.

39. Abram Fulkerson to Mahone, December 13, 1877; Richard F. Walker to Mahone, December 14, 1877; I. C. Fowler to Mahone, December 18, 1877; Walker to Mahone (two letters), December 19, 1877; and Fulkerson to Mahone, December 19, 1877, all in *ibid*.

direct attack on the debt, the hard-line readjusters worked in a broader coalition to give the state's needs first claim on the revenue. They supported the "Barbour bill," which declared that in allocating its revenue the state should look first to preserving the government, secondly to supporting free schools, and only thirdly to paying the interest on the debt. The bill provided that half of the incoming funds should go to government operations, a fifth to schools, and three-tenths to debt service, and that the government and schools should receive their shares in cash. John W. Daniel and other funder leaders opposed the bill as a precursor of repudiation. The House passed it by a margin of thirty-one votes and the Senate by five, the members from the cities opposing it overwhelmingly.[40]

Governor Holliday vetoed the Barbour bill, aligning himself clearly with the funders in his veto message. The bill, he asserted, was an unconstitutional violation of contract. The debt was by nature a higher obligation than support of the free schools, which earlier and more virtuous generations of Virginians had not found necessary. Holliday seemed to agree with John W. Daniel's recent remark that it would be better to burn the free schools than to repudiate the debt.[41] The governor also vetoed, on the same grounds, "Parson" Massey's bill to collect the school revenue separately, in cash, and maintain it as a distinct, inviolable fund.[42]

At that critical juncture a number of funders decided, in view of the majority coalition's programmatic vagueness, to contain its agitation by supporting a proposal for voluntary readjustment. Thomas S. Bocock, a moderate funder, and I. C. Fowler, a moderate readjuster, sponsored a bill that authorized the governor to receive outstanding bonds in exchange for registered bonds that would pay 3 per cent interest for eighteen years and 4 per cent for the remaining twenty-two years of their lives. The bill also invited bondholders to propose plans for readjustment. The General Assembly passed the Bocock-Fowler Bill and Governor Holliday signed it, but no significant group of bondholders—least of all, holders of consol bonds—showed interest in it.[43]

40. Pearson, *Readjuster Movement*, pp. 78–79; McFarland, "Extension of Democracy," pp. 107, 109–10; Vecellio, "Daniel," p. 179.
41. Governor's Veto Message, February 27, 1878, *House Journal* (1877–78), pp. 425–30; Vecellio, "Daniel," pp. 179–80; Frederick W. M. Holliday to James L. Kemper, March 7, 1878, Kemper Papers, University of Virginia.
42. Hancock, ed., *Massey Autobiography*, pp. 135–41.
43. Burton, "Taxation," pp. 140–41; McFarland, "Extension of Democracy," p. 111, Pearson, *Readjuster Movement*, p. 79.

Such diversions as the Bocock-Fowler Bill could not greatly retard the readjuster movement's progress as long as the system of state finance proved inadequate. In 1878, coupons made up about 47 per cent of incoming revenue. The most promising new tax in years—the "Moffett Punch Law" of 1877 to tax alcoholic beverages by the drink—had proven unpopular but, because of evasion, had yielded little of the revenue its advocates had predicted. Governor Holliday found that the existing sources of state income, which Kemper in December had pronounced adequate, would probably continue to provide about $800,000 a year less than the Commonwealth needed. To meet all obligations, he estimated, would require increasing the property tax from five mills on the dollar to eight or nine—or raising an equivalent amount from other taxes— in a time of economic stagnation. The auditor calculated that the state could pay 4 per cent interest on the debt for 1878 only if assessments should remain constant. He expected, however, that they would decline by 20 or 25 per cent.[44] The free schools suffered intensely from the financial emergency. School revenue declined from $460,024 in 1875 to $243,244 in 1878. Almost half the schools in Virginia failed to operate during the session of 1878–79.[45] The curtailment of the Commonwealth's principal social service made the readjuster program appealing to a large number of previously indifferent Virginians.

ORGANIZATION AND AGITATION, 1878

On the night that the session of 1877–78 ended, a group of readjuster legislators met at the *Whig* office and appointed a seven-member committee to plan organization and tactics. On April 25, a secret conference of readjusters, called by the committee, met in Richmond and adopted an appeal to be published over the signatures of the readjuster members of the legislature. The document condemned the veto of the Barbour bill and a recent Supreme Court of Appeals decision that invited the state to increase taxes to carry out the Funding Act, as contrary to the Conservative platform of 1877. It insisted on honesty and economy in government and on Virginians' sovereignty in determining their own fiscal and educa-

44. Burton, "Taxation," pp. 56, 58–61, 145–47, 151; Petersburg *Index and Appeal*, September 13 and 21, 1877, and January 8, 1878; Pearson, *Readjuster Movement*, pp. 57, 76.
45. Burton, "Taxation," pp. 149–52; McFarland, "Extension of Democracy," pp. 96–98.

tional policies. It advocated a constitutional convention to settle the debt problem and to consider other reforms and summoned readjusters to organize to elect men of their persuasion to Congress that autumn.[46] The Richmond *Dispatch* published the circular prematurely, to expose the readjusters' activities, and many wavering Conservatives found it necessary at once to take sides with or against the movement.[47] Readjusters began to organize independently but proceeded slowly and secretly in the hostile Tidewater and southside.[48]

The principal question in the congressional election—whether to redeem the national debt in gold or "greenbacks"—involved many of the same principles as the readjustment issue. Mahone and his followers planned to draw funder-readjuster lines in choosing congressmen and to extend their appeal by taking the "greenbacker" position. Where readjusters could not carry Conservative conventions, they were to nominate their candidates independently and contest the general elections. In the other camp, the Richmond *State* advised its readers to support funder candidates against readjusters, outside as well as inside the Conservative party.[49]

Initially, some funders intended to oppose both readjustment and greenbackism in the congressional elections. So popular was the inflationist cause, however, that their orthodox strategy would have imperilled their electoral prospects. John W. Daniel, preferring to oppose readjustment by diversionary tactics and interested in J. Randolph Tucker's seat in Congress, broke ranks with the champions of monetary orthodoxy.[50] For some time, Daniel had called attention to Virginia's currency shortage and proposed creating note-issuing banks and monetizing silver.[51] In August, 1878, he began preaching inflation with a vengeance. He attributed Virginia's financial plight not to her debt but to the national bank system,

46. William Mahone to James Neeson (copy), March 18, 1878, Letter-Books, Mahone Papers; Pearson, *Readjuster Movement*, p. 80; Blake, *Mahone*, pp. 170–71.
47. Mahone to Harrison H. Riddleberger, July 15, 1878, Riddleberger Papers.
48. Mahone to Lewis E. Harvie, January 5, 1879, Harvie Papers; Pendleton, *Appalachian Virginia*, p. 335.
49. Pearson, *Readjuster Movement*, p. 81; Mahone to Harrison H. Riddleberger, July 15, 1877, and Mahone to Riddleberger, July 20, 1878, both in Riddleberger Papers.
50. In the legislative session of 1877–78, Daniel proposed to retire the state debt by floating a new bond issue on the same terms as the Funding Act. He hoped that economic conditions would improve and agitation abate before interest on the new bonds would fall due. Vecellio, "Daniel," p. 168.
51. *Ibid.*, pp. 170–72; Daniel, "Financial Crisis."

which had relegated the South and West to colonial status, "aggrandized the few at the expense of the many," and "created a plutocracy to live on the industries of the country . . . at war with popular interests." Daniel's remedy was to abolish the national banks, allow state banks to issue notes, accept greenbacks for all payments to the federal government, and redeem the national debt in greenbacks instead of gold. That program, he thought, would stimulate business, restore the state's control over its finances, and bring the antidebt movement to an end.[52]

Daniel drafted a series of inflationist resolutions to present to the Conservative nominating convention for the Seventh District and threatened to bolt the ticket if Congressman Tucker should win renomination but refuse to accept the resolutions as his platform.[53] Tucker, orthodox in financial matters, found Daniel's resolutions embarrassing but published as inflationist a statement of policy as he conscientiously could. The District Convention, satisfied, renominated Tucker and adopted Daniel's resolutions in an amended form acceptable to Tucker.[54] Insistent on containing inflationist demands within the Conservative party, Daniel campaigned for Tucker against an independent greenbacker. After the election, he continued his effort to divert readjuster agitation from the state debt to the federal currency policy.[55] He warned Northern businessmen that unless currency reform occurred, repudiation would "roll like a whirlwind" and the people would "reassert their right of self government in such a way as to make the money tyrants tremble and weep for their gains."[56]

In other districts as well, funders adopted Daniel's election strategy. All regular Conservative nominees except Tucker and General Joseph E. Johnston of Richmond endorsed the greenback cause, taking the wind out of the readjusters' sails. Although readjusters contested both nominations and elections, only two—and those,

52. Vecellio, "Daniel," pp. 184–86.

53. *Ibid.*, pp. 186–90.

54. *Ibid.*, pp. 184, 191–92; Robert M. T. Hunter to J. Randolph Tucker (copy), August 29, 1878, Hunter-Garnett Papers, University of Virginia; John Dunscombe Horseley to J. R. Tucker, June 17, 1878; J. R. Tucker to Henry St. George Tucker, August 23, 1878; Thomas S. Bocock to J. R. Tucker, August 28, 1878; Bocock to J. R. Tucker, August 29, 1878; Edward S. Hutter to J. R. Tucker, August 29, 1878; Eppa Hunton to J. R. Tucker, September 5, 1878; and J. R. Tucker to H. St. G. Tucker, September 6, 1878, all in Tucker Family Papers.

55. Vecellio, "Daniel," pp. 193, 204–5.

56. Daniel, "Financial Crisis."

moderates—won seats in Congress.[57] Greenbackism, General Mahone found, was serving as a ruse to divert public attention from the debt.[58]

The diversion did not outlast the election campaign, and the debt quickly returned to the center of the stage. The division of opinion about debt policy now overrode formal party lines in the eyes of both factions' leaders. George W. Booker had written, months before, that the Conservative party was disintegrating in the absence of Republican competition.[59] After the congressional election, some funders tried to form a tightly disciplined factional organization.

William L. Royall, the attorney for a group of bondholders, organized thirty-nine prominent citizens, largely businessmen and clergymen, into a "Society to Preserve the Credit of the State." The group included three prominent Republicans: federal judges Alexander Rives and Robert W. Hughes, and General Williams C. Wickham of the C. and O. The society called for the formation of local organizations of funders, regardless of party or race, to support "debt-paying" candidates for the legislature in 1879. It not only opposed readjustment but advocated increasing the property tax from five mills on the dollar to seven.[60] Royall hoped to collect a large campaign fund by soliciting donations from bondholders and from every chamber of commerce in the nation. The society would work through the Conservative party in some counties, but not in others. "Parties may go to the dogs," Royall wrote, "as far as their platforms enjoin dishonesty upon me."[61] The society proved unpopular except in Richmond. Its tactics made it hard for other funders to accuse readjusters of disrupting the Conservative party. It alienated many by proposing a tax increase, contrary to the Conservative platform of 1877, and by introducing bondholders, federal judges, and ministers as controversialists in the discussion of the debt. Meeting little support and much opposition, the society soon ceased to function.[62]

57. Pearson, *Readjuster Movement*, pp. 81–83; McFarland, "Extension of Democracy," pp. 112–13.
58. William Mahone to Harrison H. Riddleberger, October 7, 1878, Riddleberger Papers.
59. George W. Booker to James L. Kemper, February 11, 1878, Kemper Papers, University of Virginia.
60. Pearson, *Readjuster Movement*, pp. 83, 84n.
61. William L. Royall to James L. Kemper, September 5, 1878, Kemper Papers, University of Virginia.
62. Pearson, *Readjuster Movement*, pp. 83–84.

Even more ambitious than Royall's project was one that Alexander H. H. Stuart pondered but apparently never proposed publicly. The debt problem, Stuart decided, was beyond the legislature's competence. "It is a business question," he wrote, "& businessmen are the proper parties to settle it." Stuart thought that the principal businessmen of Richmond should confer with the bondholders' attorneys to determine what the creditors could reasonably expect from the state and what guarantees would be necessary to assure the fulfillment of those terms. A convention of half a dozen members from each county—hand-picked for "integrity, intelligence, & business capacity"—should ratify the plan and organize a movement to carry the next legislative election for it. Stuart cited his own Committee of Nine as a precedent for this extraconstitutional initiation of policy.[63] Having inaugurated the Conservatives' rule by a *coup d'état*, "Senex" hoped to preserve it by a second.

THE MC CULLOCH ACT

Although Stuart's project never materialized, an influential group of businessmen took the initiative in another way. During 1878 some bondholders and brokers, aware of the danger of readjustment, became willing to offer concessions to appease the discontented. The Council of Foreign Bondholders in London and the Funding Association of the United States of America in New York offered Governor Holliday their assistance in persuading bondholders to accept a settlement that would place all bonds on the same basis and require no more than 4 per cent interest initially. Combining their efforts, the London and New York groups drafted a bill that former Secretary of the Treasury Hugh McCulloch presented to a committee of the General Assembly during the 1878–79 session, in response to the Bocock-Fowler Bill's invitation. Since the authors of the "McCulloch Bill" were brokers who contracted to persuade bondholders to accept its terms, advocates of forcible readjustment called the plan "the Brokers' Bill" and questioned the brokers' ability to elicit the bondholders' consent.[64]

Under the McCulloch bill, bondholders would surrender their

63. "Senex" [Alexander H. H. Stuart], "Some suggestions about the Public debt question, A new mode of effecting establishment," manuscript, n.d. [1880], Alexander Hugh Holmes Stuart Papers, University of Virginia. See Staunton *Vindicator*, September 7, 1877.

64. Pearson, *Readjuster Movement*, pp. 85–86, 89; Hancock, ed., *Massey Autobiography*, p. 142; Riddleberger, "Bourbonism in Virginia," pp. 422–23.

bonds to the contracting agencies, in lots no more than a third of which could consist of peeler bonds plus half the convertible interest on them since 1871. In exchange, the creditors would receive new coupon bonds paying 3 per cent for ten years, 4 per cent for the following twenty, and 10 per cent for the remaining three years of their term. The state would accept coupons for taxes and dues, and the bonds and coupons would be exempt from taxation. Bondholders would also receive certificates for West Virginia's third of the antebellum debt, and by accepting these they would release Virginia from any liability for that part. After 1885, the state would levy a special property tax of a fifth of a mill on the dollar for a sinking fund to retire the bonds. The Funding Association and the Council of Foreign Bondholders would be the sole agents in the funding process, provided that they should file acceptance of the terms by May 1, 1879, fund at least eight million dollars in bonds by January 1, 1880, and fund the remainder at the rate of five million dollars in bonds each six months.[65]

Funders supported the McCulloch proposal. Governor Holliday, in his annual message, described it as a generous offer. The plan, John W. Daniel said, had many advantages: it would reduce taxpaying by coupons, require no tax increase, restore public credit, reduce the interest rate, give all bondholders equal treatment, and constitute a reasonable compromise.[66] Readjusters objected on a number of grounds. The hard core among them complained that the bill capitalized unpaid interest into principal, authorized fiduciaries to refund bonds held in trust without court permission, limited the state's freedom of action, and put both state and bondholders in the hands of the brokers' syndicate. The requirement that one present consols and peelers together would, they asserted, enable the syndicate, after cornering the consol market, to force holders of peeler bonds to sacrifice them at great losses. The provisions for tax exemption and tax-receivable coupons would largely cancel out the reduction of interest.[67]

Many members of the coalition that had passed the Barbour Bill were much more moderate, objecting to the McCulloch measure mainly because it contained no provision to protect the school fund.

65. Pearson, *Readjuster Movement*, pp. 86–87; Vecellio, "Daniel," pp. 211–13.
66. Governor's Message, December 4, 1878, *Senate Journal* (1878–79), pp. 24–27; Vecellio, "Daniel," pp. 207–9.
67. Hancock, ed., *Massey Autobiography*, p. 143; Riddleberger, "Bourbonism in Virginia," p. 423.

Noticing that the funder-dominated Senate Committee on Finance was reporting bills to slash school support to a nominal level, they feared a serious funder attack on the school system.[68] The McCulloch bill's managers negotiated a compromise agreement with these moderate readjusters. The funders agreed to assure the passage of D. W. Henkel's readjuster bill to authorize tax collectors to deliver three-fourths of their city's or county's estimated amount of state school aid in cash, as collected, to a special local school fund. The bill would therefore guarantee the schools that amount in case the treasury should lack cash to pay the entire amount due. In return for funder support of the Henkel bill, moderate readjusters supported not only the McCulloch bill but also the "Allen amendment" to that bill, which authorized the auditor to insure prompt interest payment by obtaining short-term loans and, if necessary, by selling noninterest-bearing tax-receivable certificates at as little as three-fourths their face value. The amendment, hard-line readjusters objected, required the state to redeem the certificates at a value a third higher than that for which it sold them. Enough moderates, nevertheless, broke ranks to add the "Allen amendment" to the bill and to pass it by substantial majorities in both houses. Funders hailed the law as the final resolution of uncertainty and controversy about the debt.[69]

The New York–London syndicate succeeded in funding eight million dollars' worth of bonds before the deadline of January 1, 1880. Readjusters charged that the syndicate had been allowed to use the state's sinking fund to conduct the refunding, that by cornering the consol bonds it had bought depreciated peeler bonds and exchanged them for new consols, and that it had thereby realized a million-dollar profit in refunding bonds worth eight million. By the time it had completed this initial task, the controversy resulting from the McCulloch Act had given militant readjusters a majority in the General Assembly. The syndicate then dropped its contract with the state, and the act ceased to have any practical effect.[70]

The McCulloch Act opened the curtain on a new scene in the debt controversy, in which the players defined their roles more clearly than ever before. Since the act seemed the bondholders' max-

68. McFarland, "Extension of Democracy," pp. 114–15; Pendleton, *Appalachian Virginia*, pp. 330–31.

69. Pearson, *Readjuster Movement*, pp. 86–88; Vecellio, "Daniel," pp. 211–13; Riddleberger, "Bourbonism in Virginia," p. 423; Burton, "Taxation," p. 148.

70. Riddleberger, "Bourbonism in Virginia," pp. 423–24; Hancock, ed., *Massey Autobiography*, pp. 144–45.

imum concession, those who rejected it were "forcible readjusters" almost by definition. Its proponents, although previously divided, became a new coalition of "funders" in the broadest sense. The state election of 1879 became a referendum on the debt question as the McCulloch Act defined it, and new parties formed in accordance with the division of opinion on that question.

THE ELECTION OF 1879

During the General Assembly session of 1878–79, a fourth of the members of the legislature issued a call for supporters of the Barbour bill to select delegates to a readjuster state convention. Mahone's associates worked hard to stimulate enthusiasm for the conclave, but most of the press attacked it and the Conservative party's officials tacitly opposed it. Many men chosen as delegates refused to attend. In some counties, the delegates represented impressive movements; in others, unimportant cliques.[71]

About 175 delegates, from fifty-nine counties and three cities, participated in the convention that met at Mozart Hall in Richmond on February 25 and 26. Members of the Conservative party predominated, but Republicans, Greenbackers, and independents also attended. Negroes took part as delegates from Halifax and New Kent counties. The few delegates known beyond their own counties were political "outs," mostly Mahone men and disaffected champions of agrarian interests. Their policies ranged from Mahone's proposal of 3 per cent interest to some Negroes' demands for outright repudiation.[72]

The convention set up a readjuster state committee, consisting of a three-member executive committee and a district chairman from each congressional district. General Mahone became the chairman of the executive and state committees. In an address that state Senator Harrison H. Riddleberger drafted, the assemblage condemned Royall's society, accused Governor Holliday of betraying the Conservative platform, and rejected the then-pending McCulloch bill as perpetuating the Funding Act's worst defects and adding new ones. The address specified the essentials of an acceptable debt settlement: It must release Virginia from any responsibility for the West Virginia third of the original debt. It must be compatible with the current tax rate and with liberal expenditures for government,

71. Pearson, *Readjuster Movement,* pp. 95–98.
72. *Ibid.,* pp. 98–99.

schools, and public institutions. It must not include tax-receivable coupons, tax exemption, discrimination among creditors, or funding through agencies beyond the state's control. It must be subject to ratification by a popular referendum and to modification by future legislatures.[73]

General Mahone began at once to organize the movement at the local level. In western counties, readjusters selected their officers in mass meetings, but in funder-dominated areas they operated secretly. All in all, their activity was so unobtrusive that funders hoped the movement had expired. Then, late in July, the readjusters began a spirited campaign that took the funders by surprise. The "debt-payers" counterattacked desperately. Ignoring the readjusters' demand for a Conservative state convention to determine the party's debt policy, the Conservative State Committee, on August 6, declared by a vote of thirteen to two that acceptance of the McCulloch Act was a standard of party loyalty. Read out of the Conservative organization, the readjusters became in name, as they already were in fact, the Readjuster party.[74]

State officeholders, as well as Conservative party officers, closed ranks against the insurgents. School and institutional officials helped the insecure treasury by failing to press their agencies' full claims. Auditor Taylor, for the first time since 1871, began expressing optimism about state finance. Deviant treasury employees fell victim to an administrative "reign of terror."[75] Even Attorney General Field, breaking with the readjusters, endorsed the McCulloch Act and campaigned for Conservative candidates for the legislature.[76] Governor Holliday tried to rehabilitate Bradley T. Johnson, whose indictment for defrauding the Commonwealth embarrassed the funders, by appointing him as one of the state's attorneys in the federal Supreme Court case of *Virginia* v. *Rives*. Field, humiliated by the appointment, nevertheless refused to break the administration's public unanimity.[77]

The campaign to elect members of the legislature raged from August until November. There was a contest for almost every seat, and each party's orators canvassed the other's strongholds. In many

73. *Ibid.*, pp. 99–101.
74. *Ibid.*, pp. 119–21; William Mahone to Harrison H. Riddleberger, March 13, 1879, and Mahone to Riddleberger, April 2, 1879, both in Riddleberger Papers.
75. W. N. Newman to Lewis E. Harvie, June 18, 1879, and Newman to Harvie, November 13, 1879, both in Harvie Papers; Burton, "Taxation," p. 158.
76. Moore, "Field," pp. 85–86; Petersburg *Index and Appeal*, September 11, 1879.
77. Moore, "Field," pp. 77–85.

places, speakers carried on joint debates for four or even six hours. General Mahone marshaled the Readjuster forces skillfully, while a rival railroad man, General Thomas M. Logan of the Richmond and Danville, directed the funder campaign as Conservative state chairman.[78] The funders, having most of the business and political establishment on their side, mobilized money, prominent figures, newspapers and governmental machinery for their cause. Readjusters accused their opponents, probably correctly, of bribing black voters,[79] but there was no reason to doubt that some of their own number engaged in the same practice.

The fault line that divided funders and readjusters ran athwart the old line between Conservatives and Republicans. "It is a break across the grain," the Richmond *State* later wrote, "and not a split with it."[80] The Republican State Executive Committee endorsed all Republican nominees, but both committee and candidates were divided over readjustment. Many Negroes and poor white Republicans supported the Readjusters, out of agrarian radical sympathies and revenge against the Conservative organization. Funders, however, also solicited Republicans' support, and in six counties they endorsed the Republican nominees. Both parties sought help from the federal administration, but President Hayes, motivated by fiscal orthodoxy, used his influence among Virginia Republicans to assist the Conservatives. The administration blundered in its patronage maneuvers, removing a funder postmaster whom it mistook for a Readjuster but overlooking the Readjuster collector of customs at Norfolk.[81]

L. Q. Washington, a relatively detached observer, found "the whole canvass . . . needlessly violent & excited & both sides much to blame."[82] Among the lower classes, the Readjusters carried the day. Some white farmers believed that the McCulloch Act added 3 per cent to the previous 6 per cent interest rate to make a total of nine, and some blacks thought a Conservative victory would bind them to

78. *Ibid.*, p. 89; Pearson, *Readjuster Movement*, pp. 114–15, 120–21; Thomas M. Logan to James L. Kemper, September 18, 1879, and Logan to Kemper, September 22, 1879, both in Kemper Papers, University of Virginia; and the many letters from Mahone in the Riddleberger Papers for those months.

79. Thomas T. Fauntleroy, Jr., to Lewis E. Harvie, November 11, 1879, Harvie Papers.

80. Quoted in Richmond *Whig*, October 9, 1880, clipping in Ruffin Scrapbook, I, 53.

81. Pearson, *Readjuster Movement*, pp. 127–28; De Santis, *Republicans*, pp. 94–95.

82. L. Q. Washington to Robert M. T. Hunter, December 6, 1879, Hunter-Garnett Papers.

labor for forty years to pay slaveowning Virginia's debt.[83] The Reverend J. L. M. Curry, who stumped the state for the Conservatives, thought that "Ambition for place, communism, ignorance & a little honest delusion" accounted for the Readjusters' strength. The radical labor leader Dennis Kearny, he added, "would have been applauded by some in every audience I spoke to."[84] Mahone and some other Readjuster leaders were able to use their followers' radical tendencies but nevertheless hold them in check.

Some funders, the week before the election, expected a victory so decisive that it would administer the quietus to the Readjuster movement.[85] The election returns gave them a rude surprise, for the Readjuster party elected fifty-six of the hundred delegates and twenty-four of the forty senators. About 82,000 Virginians voted for Readjuster candidates, and about 62,000, for Conservatives. Readjusters carried most of the western and the predominantly-black counties, and those in which realty values had declined most sharply. The towns and cities, and the northern Piedmont counties, upheld the funders. Funders claimed that most of the taxpayers and white voters had endorsed their position, but Readjusters argued that a majority of each race had voted for their candidates.[86]

The funders who had controlled the Conservative party could expect little co-operation from the impending legislature. They could try to detach the most moderate Readjusters individually from their caucus, as in the preceding session, or to recruit the Republicans to an anti-Readjuster coalition.[87] The new Readjuster party, though, was a cohesive organization with high morale and party discipline—a far cry from the amorphous grouping that had supported the Barbour bill. The Readjusters had not, admittedly, defined their policy farther than their Mozart Hall platform of the preceding February had stated it, and they differed on how to put

83. Hoge and Bayne, *Ego and Alter*, p. 11; Pearson, *Readjuster Movement*, pp. 128–29.

84. Jabez L. M. Curry to Wyndham Robertson, November 24, 1879, Wyndham Robertson Papers, University of Chicago.

85. Richard O. Morris to B. Johnson Barbour, October 23, 1879, B. Johnson Barbour Papers, University of Virginia; reference to Robert Beverly in Richmond *Whig*, September 20, 1880, clipping in Ruffin Scrapbook, I, 36.

86. Pearson, *Readjuster Movement*, pp. 126, 129–31; unidentified clipping [probably Richmond *Whig*, August? 1880], in Ruffin Scrapbook, I, 44–46.

87. William Mahone to Lewis E. Harvie, November 10, 1879, and Frank G. Ruffin to Harvie, November 11, 1879, both in Harvie Papers; Asa G. Rogers to William Henry Ruffner, November 23, 1879, Ruffner Papers; Jabez L. M. Curry to Wyndham Robertson, November 24, 1879, Wyndham Robertson Papers.

the platform into effect. Almost all, however, were prepared to carry out "forcible" readjustment if necessary, and to depose most of the state administrative officials, who had collaborated in the funder policies and supported the funders in the election.[88]

The election of 1879 brought to an end the era that the "new movement" had inaugurated ten years before. As an organization, the Conservative party would persist, becoming the "Democratic party" of Virginia in 1883. Nevertheless, the movement that had defeated Radicalism in 1869 and governed during the 1870's had divided into two parties, both of which had absorbed Republican elements and which presented well-defined alternative policies on the financial questions that preoccupied vocal Virginians in 1879. Politics was taking a new turn and the era of the Virginia Conservatives was passing, but many features of their politics and ideology lived on to play important roles in Virginia and other Southern states during the ensuing decades.[89]

88. Mahone to Harvie, November 10, 1879; Ruffin to Harvie, November 11, 1879; Thomas T. Fauntleroy, Jr., to Harvie, November 11, 1879; W. N. Newman to Harvie, November 13, 1879; and John E. Massey to Harvie, November 14, 1879, all in Harvie Papers.

89. For the state politics of the years 1879–85 and the subsequent history of the Virginia debt question see Pearson, *Readjuster Movement*, pp. 132–74; and Benjamin U. Ratchford, *American State Debts* (Durham: Duke University Press, 1941), pp. 227–29.

17.

The Source of the Conservative Impulse

"Good God," Pennsylvania's Senator Simon Cameron exclaimed on meeting Senator Robert E. Withers, "A Senator from Virginia who neither drinks whiskey, nor chews tobacco! Why, what's the world coming to?"[1] His temperate habits were not all that distinguished Withers from the sort of statesmen who had governed the Old Dominion before 1865. Members of the Conservative party were not all of a kind, since the party included almost all non-Republicans who participated in politics. Many were traditionalists, committed to the remains of the antebellum way of life and suspicious of innovation. Others simply lacked comprehension of the transformation taking place around them. The principal Conservative leaders, however, consciously strove to adapt their part of the world to the tendencies of the bourgeois revolution of their time and to confer on it the benefits of industrial capitalism. Some opted for adaptation as a positive good; some, as a necessary evil; and some, as an irresistible necessity. However motivated, they co-operated to bring Virginia into the mainstream of Gilded-Age America.

BUSINESSMEN AND THE INDUSTRIAL VISION

The very essence of the adaptation the Conservative leaders promoted was the economic regeneration of Virginia on Northern capitalist lines. During the late 1860's, the *Whig* sounded the keynote in calling attention to "material interests." While Europe and the North had entered the age of industry and the "dignity of labor," it stated, Southerners had contented themselves with the slow-moving agricultural economy that afforded comfort to their

1. Withers, *Autobiography*, p. 331.

[276]

dominant class. The War, destroying that system, had thrown Southerners into competition with the enterprising Yankees. The South's only hope for recovering her lost estate was "hard labor in agriculture, commerce, manufactures and the mechanic arts."[2] Virginia's resources now invited the miner, the manufacturer, and the merchant to contest with the agriculturist for mastery of the Old Dominion. Northern immigrants would displace inefficient cultivators in the Tidewater, building "a great manufacturing and commercial power" there. The *Whig*'s only advice to planters who preferred the old ways was to sell their surplus land in lots to poorer neighbors and convert from lazy, luxurious plantation agriculture to intensive cultivation of small farms.[3] They might thereby rescue agricultural pursuits, even though in a form unsuited to their tastes. During the political agitation of Reconstruction, the *Whig* popularized scores of projects for economic modernization and development.[4] The former Whig leader William L. Goggin predicted, "The plow, the loom, and the anvil; the steamship and the steam car will call into requisition the labor of hundreds of thousands of those who now stand all the day idle waiting and watching for something to turn up."[5]

When the Conservatives took office, many observers expected that Virginia would bolt headlong into the mainstream of industrial society.[6] As early as August, 1870, Conservative leaders found it necessary to rebuke followers disappointed that the anticipated economic miracle was not already manifest.[7] Governor Walker confidently predicted that Virginia would yield more mineral wealth than any other state, that it would become a great manufacturing state, that the James River and Kanawha Canal would affect world trade as profoundly as the Suez Canal, and that Norfolk would soon become the eastern point of a transcontinental railroad and one of the foremost transatlantic ports.[8]

Governor Kemper embraced the industrial gospel as ardently as did Governor Walker. Virginia's antebellum leaders, he thought,

2. Richmond *Whig and Public Advertiser*, January 18, 1867.

3. *Ibid.*, September 1, 1865; see *ibid.*, May 31, 1867.

4. See, e.g., Richmond *Daily Whig*, January 9, 11, 15, 16, 22, 27, 28, 29; February 4, 6, 7, 12, 15, 17, 26, 27, 28; March 4, 6, 18, 19, 24, 25, 30; April 8, 10, 1868.

5. Quoted in Richmond *Whig and Public Advertiser*, July 9, 1867.

6. See above, pp. 82–83; Hugh W. Sheffey to William Cabell Rives, Jr., January 7, 1870, and George Long to Rives, June 10, 1870, both in William Cabell Rives Papers, Library of Congress.

7. *Conservative Address, 1870*, pp. 4–5.

8. Governor's Message, February 8, 1870, *Senate Journal* (1869–70), pp. 41–42; Governor's Message, December 4, 1872, *Senate Journal* (1872–73), p. 22.

had unfortunately devoted their talents to constitutional theory and neglected economic development. Consequently, while Southerners had won honors as orators and statesmen, Northern entrepreneurs had taken over the nation's resources. Bleak New England had prospered, and fertile Virginia lay almost as unimproved as when the first settlers had landed. Times were changing, however. "The age of inaction, of metaphysical politics is exhausted and gone. The age of labour, of masterly activity, of practical advancement has come." Virginia, Kemper believed, presented almost limitless opportunities for capitalist development. Contemporaries, he predicted, would live to see the state dotted with furnaces and factories, railroad stations and spinning jennies. Water-power would do the work of thousands of men, and livestock and grain fields would abound. The next generation would find southwest Virginia's annual products worth four times as much as the entire Commonwealth's were in Kemper's day.[9] Governor Holliday shared his predecessors' fascination with the marvels of the new technology and chided farmers for lagging behind commerce and manufacturing in taking advantage of them.[10]

The Conservative leaders' vision of capitalist prosperity was, in part, an idealization of the Northern social institutions that had demonstrated their competitive superiority to the South's traditional institutions. It was also, however, the social utopia of the capitalist class. It was not surprising, then, that to realize that objective, business entrepreneurs became powers in Conservative politics, and Conservative politicians actively engaged in business enterprises.

One Sunday morning in September, 1870, Colonel Withers, at his southwest Virginia farm, received a telegram from the tobacco manufacturer William T. Sutherlin. Sutherlin had written, from New York: "Meet me in Richmond, business of importance to yourself." Entirely in the dark about the "business," Withers nevertheless prepared to depart at once. "Major Sutherlin," he told his astonished wife, "is a business man and would never send such a message unless it were really a matter of importance." Unable to find the

9. James L. Kemper, manuscript address at Virginia Agricultural and Mechanical College, August 8, 1876 (James Lawson Kemper Papers, Virginia Historical Society), pp. 4–12.

10. Frederick W. M. Holliday, speech to American Public Health Association, 1878, and speech to National Grange, November 21, 1878, both unidentified clippings in Holliday Scrapbook (1850–99), Part II, pp. 20, 22–23, Frederick William Mackey Holliday Papers, Duke University.

neighborhood blacksmith, Withers, for the first time in his life, shod his own horse. After a brief snack, he rode the long journey to the railroad station, took a train, and arrived in Richmond early Tuesday morning. Sutherlin there explained that he had recommended Withers to the University Publishing Company as Virginia agent for its "Southern" textbook series. That same morning, Withers took a steamer to New York, where he conferred with his new employers and signed their contract. On his return, he sold his farm, haggling over each cow's price, to move nearer to a railroad station. Two weeks after he received Sutherlin's telegram, the Colonel started to work selling textbooks.[11]

It would be difficult to imagine a Virginia statesman of antebellum days enacting this scene. Among Withers' Conservative associates, however, entrepreneurial activity was quite common. Governor Walker had been a prominent Norfolk businessman. Governor Kemper had engaged in a multitude of business projects between 1865 and 1873. Governor Holliday found it difficult to live down his legal services to the Bank of the Valley while it had been under the control of receivers acting in behalf of Northern creditors.[12] Mahone, Sutherlin, and Thomas M. Logan (who in the 1880's became one of the most powerful railroad executives in the South) were only the most prominent entrepreneurs in Conservative politics. The early members of the Conservative Central Committee included bankers Thomas and James R. Branch, merchants James R. Fisher and William Lovenstein, publisher Henry K. Ellyson, and other prominent businessmen. The other members of the Central Committee were successful Richmond lawyers and journalists, in a time when large legal fees came almost exclusively from corporations[13] and when the Richmond newspapers were "understood to be the organs of railroads & no longer independent journals."[14] The non-Richmond members of the Conservative State Committee also included a respectable proportion of businessmen.[15] Railroad promotion was a favorite pursuit of Conservative politicians.[16]

11. Withers, *Autobiography*, pp. 293–98.

12. H. L. D. Lewis to Frederick W. M. Holliday, January 13, 1877, and Holliday to Lewis (copy), January 15, 1877, both in Holliday Papers.

13. See, e.g., Jones, *Ranger Mosby*, p. 287, and Caldwell, "Walker," p. 221.

14. L. Q. Washington to Robert M. T. Hunter, December 14, 1871, Hunter-Garnett Papers, University of Virginia.

15. E.g., William Mahone, James H. Cox, James L. Kemper, John R. Kilby, William W. Watts, and George P. Tayloe.

16. See Wyatt S. Beazley to James L. Kemper, March 3, 1871; Bolivar Christian to Kemper, January 2, 1872; Jeremiah Morton to Kemper, January 13, 1873; and

Business influence, evident as a force in state government,[17] was in some areas an integral feature of the Conservative party's structure. In Norfolk, a "committee of merchants and members of the [city] executive committee of the Conservative Party" directed election campaigns.[18] Petersburg merchants made valuable business contacts in the hinterlands through political campaigns,[19] and men whose business carried them to distant cities were especially available as delegates to conventions.[20]

An indirect reflection of the business influence in politics was the urban influence. Once, Virginia statesmen had found it no disadvantage to reside on isolated country estates. Now, as Richmond's business community gave the city a life of its own, it became the nerve-center of politics. From 1867 until 1873, the Conservative Central Committee, a body of Richmond residents, effectively controlled party activities between conventions. After 1873, the resident Executive Committee still enjoyed a great deal of discretion. In 1869, the Central Committee circularized the state for campaign funds to be used exclusively in Richmond and four surrounding counties.[21] Every Conservative state convention met in Richmond. "To hold the convention elsewhere than Richmond," William D. Chesterman observed in 1873, "is to decapitate six or seven of the present members of the State Committee."[22] Just before the State Convention of 1876, party leaders expected that 484 of the 839 delegates would be present. These included all the 69 delegates from the Third Congressional District—Richmond and the surrounding counties—but only 30 of the 130 from the Ninth—southwest Virginia.[23] "I wish you were in Richmond or in some city," L. Q. Washington wrote to R. M. T. Hunter, isolated on his Essex County

---

Thomas P. Wallace to Kemper, April 24, 1873, all in James Lawson Kemper Papers, University of Virginia.

17. See above, Chapter 10.

18. W. L. Oswald to William Mahone, October 17, 1872, William Mahone Papers, Duke University.

19. Petersburg *Index and Appeal*, September 30, 1876.

20. See Thomas P. Wallace to James L. Kemper, June 20, 1872, Kemper Papers, University of Virginia.

21. Conservative State Committee Circular No. 14, May 20, 1869, copy in William Thomas Sutherlin Papers, Southern Historical Collection, University of North Carolina at Chapel Hill.

22. *Daily Petersburg Index*, April 8, 1873.

23. Richmond *Dispatch*, May 31, 1876.

estate. "I am sure it would not be long before you found a remunerative employment of some kind."[24]

Conservative leaders placed the creation of conditions conducive to business enterprise among their principal objectives. In a campaign speech in Norfolk in 1873, John W. Daniel quoted Robert W. Hughes's admission that the "wealthy and educated classes" in Virginia shunned the Republican party. Daniel proudly enumerated enterprises begun in Virginia since 1869 "by charters granted or plans formed under Conservative rule, and in nine cases out of ten, by capital furnished or introduced by Conservative gentlemen." There were able Republican industrialists, but they found themselves comfortably at home in predominantly Conservative companies and business circles. Wealth, education, and philanthropy—the magnets, Daniel said, to attract capital—resided among the Conservatives. The large majority of the Republicans were mere sans-culottes. "Ours," the speaker boasted, "is the cause that lights the engine, lays the track and speeds the plow. Ours is the cause that shelters the laborer with his homestead, secures him wages for his labor, and opens the schoolhouse to his children."[25] Conservatives took pride in their attempts to encourage business. Senator John W. Johnston, in 1881, rested his defense of the Conservatives' record almost entirely on the Commonwealth's economic progress since 1870.[26]

Considered objectively, that progress was significant. Although some agricultural pursuits—notably tobacco-raising—sagged below prewar levels of production, gains in newer activities made up for their stagnation. The volume of manufacturing in Virginia in 1880 was twice that of 1860. Richmond, Norfolk, and a few other cities enjoyed prosperity and rapid growth. Norfolk, by its railroad connections, became a major cotton port, the Norfolk-Portsmouth customs district reporting domestic exports to the value of $14,065,455 in 1880, in contrast with $479,558 in 1860. The production of pig-iron, in 1880, recovered the level it had attained before the Panic of 1873. In all these enterprises, entrepreneurs in the 1870's pre-

24. L. Q. Washington to Robert M. T. Hunter, January 14, 1871, Hunter-Garnett Papers.

25. Richmond *Daily Whig*, October 9, 1873, clipping in John Warwick Daniel Papers, University of Virginia. Daniel's reference to protecting homesteads accorded ill with Conservative judges' invalidating the homestead exemption.

26. *Cong. Record*, 47 Cong., Special Senate Sess., p. 61 (1881).

pared the ground for striking advances during the early 1880's.[27]

As of 1879, nevertheless, all this seemed a meager fulfillment of the Conservatives' original visions of industrial grandeur. In comparison with the progress of much of the North and most of the West, it was very disappointing. Conservative leaders kept their hopes up. Ten years after Appomattox, General Logan dismissed the current stagnation as a temporary effect of the disruption of the plantation system and wrote that emancipation had laid the foundations of a future, unprecedented prosperity.[28] In 1877, the Petersburg *Index* predicted that labor unrest in the North would persuade businessmen there to direct investment southward.[29] In 1879, Governor Holliday reported that he saw signs of growth and prosperity everywhere he traveled.[30] These omens nevertheless seemed to many a miserable anticlimax to fifteen years of prophecies of riches. Most Virginians received only the tiniest benefits from the United States' striking economic growth in the postwar decades. For those who had lost all in the War and struggled ever since to make ends meet, the all-important question—"When will prosperity come?"—still remained unanswered at the end of the Conservative ascendancy.[31]

Suddenly discovering the industrial revolution through the cataclysmic Northern conquest, Conservative leaders naturally overestimated the rapidity of its extension and overlooked the obstacles to immediate industrialization in their region.[32] During military Reconstruction, they blamed social unrest and Radical agitation for retarding economic progress.[33] After Conservative rule failed to bring instantaneous change, they sought other explanations for delay, each man projecting his own prejudices on the problem.[34] Governor Kemper contended that non-Virginians hesitated to invest or settle in Virginia because they feared that Virginians were

27. *Imboden Report, 1886,* pp. 78–100, 122–24, 157, 170–72, 203.

28. Morrill, *Builder of the New South,* p. 118.

29. Petersburg *Index and Appeal,* August 17, 1877.

30. Frederick W. M. Holliday, speech at Lynchburg, October 10, 1879, quoted in unidentified clipping, Holliday Scrapbook (1850–99), Part II, pp. 27–28, Holliday Papers.

31. See Richmond *Industrial South,* [n.d.], 1882, quoted in Broadus Mitchell, *The Rise of Cotton Mills in the South* ("Johns Hopkins University Studies in Historical and Political Science," XXXIX, No. 2 [Baltimore: The Johns Hopkins Press, 1921]), p. 104n.

32. See comment in Jones, "Conservative Virginian," pp. 52–53.

33. See above, p. 51; *Immigration Report, 1870,* p. 3.

34. In addition to the following, see above, p. 182.

unreconstructed "Bourbons."[35] Businessman William W. Watts thought the trouble was that the Commonwealth was "cursed with every sort of vicious legislation about our debts public & private."[36] Superintendent Ruffner argued that Virginia lacked the level of mass education a stable industrial society required.[37] All agreed, however, in *postponing* their hopes rather than abandoning them. The Conservative leaders' faith in capitalist development as an objective was unshaken.

That faith sheds a great deal of light on two other characteristics of post-Reconstruction Southern conservatives that have attracted historians' attention—the prominence of former Whigs in their counsels and the well-nigh universal leadership of former Confederate officers. In terms of the Virginia situation, both these features reflected, indirectly, the movement's tendency to adapt to postwar Yankee America.

WHIGS AND DEMOCRATS

In Virginia, the old-line Whigs of the Henry Clay school had acquired experience, before 1865, in asserting nationalist, commercial-industrial, and moderate ideas, however timidly.[38] In the election of 1865, former Whigs seized the initiative and voters confided in the party that had been most skeptical of the experiment of secession. The former Whigs in the Baldwin legislature sought reconciliation with the Union and economic rebuilding. Adjusting too slowly to satisfy Northern statesmen, these former Whigs demonstrated both their readiness and their unreadiness to sponsor the advent of a New South.

During military Reconstruction, former Whigs contributed much more than their share to the Conservatives' collective education. By conspiratorial methods, they controlled the selection of delegates to the National Union Convention in 1866 and the activities of the Committee of Nine in 1869. By more conventional means, they exerted great influence in the Conservative state conventions of 1867, 1868, and 1869. The Richmond *Whig*, still in the hands of the party's veteran journalists, spoke for the most advanced and adaptive Conservatives, and the Whigs of Richmond were among the first Conservatives to address political appeals to Negro voters.

35. Governor's Message, January 1, 1874, *Senate Journal* (1874), p. 18.
36. William W. Watts to William Mahone, March 8, 1875, Mahone Papers.
37. *School Report, 1878,* pp. 64L–64N.
38. See above, pp. 14–15.

Former Whigs, in both the Conservative party and the True Republican faction, led in forming the "new movement" that brought military Reconstruction to an end in 1869 and 1870.

Usually readier for change than former Democrats, the former Whigs counted for more than their numbers in the Conservative party's leadership. From the early 1840's until 1865, the Whig party had never won a majority in a statewide election. Of the seventy elections in Virginia to the national House of Representatives between 1850 and 1858 inclusive, the Whigs won only four—and only two in districts that remained in Virginia after 1865. In the Conservative leadership, however, the two groups were about evenly balanced. The thirty-three members of the Conservative Executive Committee in December, 1867, represented fairly well the major elements of the leadership. Former Democrats and former Whigs held an approximate parity in the committee membership, the Whigs predominating in the Central Committee:

	Central Committee	*Consulting Members*	*Full Committee*
Former Whigs	6	9	15
Former Democrats	3	14	17
Unidentified	0	1	1
TOTAL	9	24	33

The membership in 1869 differed only in that a Democrat had replaced a deceased Whig member. Some Democrats of 1860 in the committee, such as Central Committee member James R. Branch, had been Whigs before the national disintegration of the Whig party. The State Committee in later years continued to include former Democrats and former Whigs in about equal proportions, still, therefore, overrepresenting the former Whigs:

	June, 1872		
	Central Committee	*Consulting Members*	*Full Committee*
Former Whigs	3	14	17
Former Democrats	5	7	12
Unidentified	2	6	8
TOTAL	10	27	37

August, 1873

Former Whigs	9
Former Democrats	8
Unidentified	14
TOTAL	31

The numbers of identifiable former Democrats and identifiable former Whigs remained about equal in later years, but the predominance of members whose prewar affiliation defies attempts at identification renders the fact meaningless. Raleigh T. Daniel and Nathaniel B. Meade, who between them held the party chairmanship from 1867 until 1877, had both been nationalist Whigs.[39]

After 1870, the solidification of the Conservative party gradually dissolved the former political differences between former Democrats and former Whigs. The old tensions persisted for years, however. During the Walker campaign, former Whig Robert Ridgway complained that former Democrats were assisting Wells by their coolness to Walker and, in a few cases, by conversion to Republicanism. "If I did not know to the contrary, in a few instances," he wrote, "I should be tempted to swear that no man, who was ever a Democrat, can by any possibility be an honest man and a patriot. As a general thing, they are an untrustworthy, slippery and snaky generation. I hope I shall not be vexed by their presence in another world, having been sorely travailed on account of their deviltries in this."[40]

In 1870, former Democrats accused the former Whig majority of the Conservative Central Committee of showing partiality to former Whigs in filling vacancies in the party organization.[41] In 1871, a former Democrat objected that the Richmond *Whig* showed the

39. For lists of committee members, see Richmond *Whig and Public Advertiser*, December 17, 1867; Richmond *Daily Whig*, April 22, 1869, and June 29, 1872 [misprint "Kidd" for "Kilby"); *Hunter Speech, 1873*, p. 24; Richmond *Dispatch*, May 31 and June 1, 1876, and August 11, 1877. In identifying party allegiances, I have relied particularly on lists of participants in party conventions, in Richmond *Whig* and *Enquirer* for 1859 and 1860. These "base years" somewhat underestimate former Whigs' participation, since many former Union Whigs had joined the Democratic party by 1860. For our purposes, one might better define a "former Whig" as a participant in the Whig, American, Opposition, or Constitutional Union parties for a significant period between 1848 and 1861.

40. Robert Ridgway to Wyndham Robertson, May 28, 1869, Wyndham Robertson Papers, University of Chicago.

41. Abram Fulkerson to William Mahone, October 8, 1870, Mahone Papers.

same partiality in its columns.[42] "It is a very easy thing," the *Enquirer* wrote in 1872, "for our old Whig friends to accept Mr. Greeley even without a particle of salt. It is with them only a return of the old love." Speaking for former Democrats, the paper complained that it had become "the fashion" for Southern conservatives "to curse the Democracy." James Barron Hope, at the same time, feared a party split along the old lines. "Already," he noticed, "I hear men talking as *Whigs* and *Democrats*."[43]

Such expressions persisted in the middle years of the decade. In 1873, Judge Waller Staples, a former Whig, advised General Mahone that "if you have a *democratic* secessionist for Governor—your second man must be an old line Whig—if not your third also."[44] In 1874, friends of R. M. T. Hunter and "Extra Billy" Smith credited the former Whigs with influence in defeating those Democratic elder statesmen for election to the United States Senate.[45] In 1876, a crotchety former Democrat complained that every state proxy the incumbent Board of Public Works had appointed from the lower Valley had been "a warm Whig."[46] In the same year, the Richmond *Dispatch* criticized the Democratic National Convention's "two-thirds" rule. "In Virginia," the *Dispatch* argued, "almost half the Conservatives are old Whigs. They have never professed to be in love with the ante-bellum principles of the Democratic Party, and certainly not with the rules by which its national conventions have been hampered for so many years."[47] At that time, a Richmond Negro still thought that "the Whigs and Democrats cannot much longer bury their former hatred and animosity under the term 'Conservative.' "[48]

The last writer did not take account of the extent to which former

42. S. Bassett French to Mahone, n.d. [January 18, 1871?], *ibid.*

43. James Barron Hope to Mahone, June 6, 1872, *ibid.*; Richmond *Enquirer*, May 31, 1872.

44. Waller Staples to William Mahone, June 4, 1873, Mahone Papers. The Conservative state tickets of 1868, 1869, and 1873 each consisted of two Whigs and a Democrat. The 1877 ticket, after Daniel's death, consisted of three former Democrats.

45. L. Q. Washington to Robert M. T. Hunter, January 14, 1874, Hunter-Garnett Papers; Hunter to Lewis E. Harvie, January 17, 1874, Lewis Evarts Harvie Papers, Virginia State Library; William Smith to John W. Daniel, November 25, 1873, John Warwick Daniel Papers, Duke University.

46. Quoted in James L. Kemper to J. W. Ware (copy), March 27, 1876, James Lawson Kemper Executive Letter-Book (1875–77), Virginia Historical Society.

47. Richmond *Dispatch*, June 16, 1876.

48. "W.C.R." in Alexandria *People's Advocate*, May 27, 1876.

Whigs and former Democrats, by 1876, had embraced a common "Conservative" outlook and shed old party identifications.[49] Increasingly, party backgrounds ceased to correlate strongly with policy differences. The trend advanced faster with the rise to leadership of men who, because of youth or indifference, had not been active in party politics before 1861. The resulting Conservative politics showed a strong resemblance to Whiggery. Like their counterparts in other Southern states, former Whigs in Virginia helped to account for the Conservative party's refusal to adopt the name "Democratic," its moderate and probusiness policies, and its affinity to conservative Northern Republicans and longing for a middle-of-the-road national party.[50]

To suppose that the Conservatives followed those policies because many of their leaders had been Whigs would be to misinterpret the significance of "persistent Whiggery." It would be more realistic to say that former Whigs attained prominence in the Conservative party because they had already anticipated many of the policies to which other Conservatives turned only in the afterglow of the national holocaust. More important than the number of former Whigs who became Conservative leaders was the extent to which former Democrats active in Conservative politics came to espouse the sentiments which during the 1850's had characterized the Union Whigs. By 1875, former Whig Bolivar Christian could comfortably hold up Daniel Webster and William H. Seward as examples for former Democrat James Lawson Kemper.[51] The postwar roles of some former Whigs were symptoms of the Conservatives' adaptive orientation, not its cause.

THE VETERAN GENERATION

During the 1870's, the Democratic statesmen who had dominated Virginia politics during the 1850's ceased—to their surprise—to wield appreciable power. R. M. T. Hunter, Henry A. Wise, "Extra Billy" Smith, Robert L. Montague, and John Letcher were,

49. "I am by inheritance a whig," Charles M. Blackford wrote, "& antagonism to democracy was bred in my bones," but he thought the Democratic party of 1874 retained "no part of the odour of our old enemies but their name." Charles M. Blackford to Wyndham Robertson, November 1, 1874, Robertson Papers.

50. See Alexander, "Persistent Whiggery," pp. 321–29.

51. Bolivar Christian to James L. Kemper, March 29, 1875, Kemper Papers, University of Virginia.

for the most part, lost and disoriented in the politics of the Conservative period.[52] Into their places stepped a host of young Confederate officers such as John W. Daniel, Harrison H. Riddleberger, Thomas M. Logan, John S. Wise, and William L. Royall, all of whom had been teen-agers in 1860. Other Conservatives considered the newcomers' lack of antebellum political experience an asset. "He has grown up," the Chesapeake *Current* wrote of Daniel, "with the new order of things, is untrammeled by ante-war record, and would grasp the new issues that are forcing themselves on the country with a vigor that cannot reasonably be expected from those whose preconceived ideas and past political history will always raise up more or less opposition in the minds of the old politicians of the North."[53] Gilbert C. Walker considered Daniel "the true representative of those young Virginians" on whom he had always relied and on whom the state's future depended.[54] John S. Wise resented the eagerness with which his contemporaries sought to displace the politicians of his father's generation as "old fogies."[55]

After Kemper's election in 1873, a number of antebellum figures did try to return to political life, many of them hoping for election to the United States Senate during the General Assembly session of 1874. R. M. T. Hunter, carefully coached by younger friends, tried to conform to postbellum political conditions. In a campaign speech at Winchester in 1873, however, he proposed a subtle plan for federal grants which Southern states could use to compensate slaveowners for emancipation. His traditionalist lapse alienated many Conservatives, giving credence to the belief that the old politicians were incurable mossbacks.[56] The Petersburg *Index* complained that half the candidates for the Senate were "men who have just crawled out of their holes," supported by other "old fogies." Young Virginians, it recalled, had fought in the Confederate Army, led the Walker movement, and campaigned strenuously in 1873. Prewar politicians, many of whom had remained aloof from the Conserva-

52. See comment on this phenomenon in Wyndham Robertson to Lewis E. Harvie, December [n.d.], 1876, Harvie Papers.

53. Quoted in Vecellio, "Daniel," p. 122.

54. Gilbert C. Walker to John W. Daniel, January 1, 1876, Daniel Papers, Duke University.

55. Wise, *Lion's Skin*, pp. 322–23.

56. Nathaniel B. Meade to Robert M. T. Hunter, October 27, [1873]; L. Q. Washington to Hunter, November 26, 1873; Meade to Hunter, January 15, 1874, all in Hunter-Garnett Papers.

tive effort in 1869 and even in 1873, were not entitled to the fruit of the younger men's work.[57] Many legislators were afraid that to send an old politician identified with the Confederacy to Washington would inspire Northern politicians' distrust and forfeit their co-operation.[58] "Extra Billy" Smith found that "a singular combination between certain old Whigs & young Americans" opposed his candidacy because of his advanced age. To appease the young men's ambitions, Smith advanced the argument that he would probably die in a few years, creating a vacancy, and that each of the younger aspirants could use the intervening time to improve his own competitive position![59]

The Conservative caucus in the General Assembly took several weeks and seventy or eighty ballots before it finally eliminated all candidates but Hunter, Withers, and John Goode. Near the caucus location in the Capitol, Colonel Frank Ruffin, a supporter of Hunter, encountered Withers and expressed confidence that his favorite would win. Withers predicted that, on the contrary, Hunter would certainly lose, because of the rivalry between the generations; once the caucus should eliminate either Goode or Withers, the younger men would unite behind the remaining "young" candidate against Hunter's "old fogies." At that moment, someone announced that the caucus had eliminated Goode and begun its final ballot. Presently, a whoop of many voices arose, and Jubal Early, standing by, exclaimed, "Colonel, by God you have won, that was the Rebel yell." Out of the caucus-room burst a swarm of enthusiastic legislators—Major John W. Daniel, limping from his combat wound, in the lead—to celebrate Withers' nomination.[60]

Analyzing their defeat, Hunter's friends concluded that the rivalry between prewar and postwar politicians had proved their undoing. They had, Hunter admitted, underestimated the determination of the "young Virginians" to set aside the "fossils."[61] L. Q. Washington found that Hunter had suffered from his reputation as

57. Petersburg *Index and Appeal*, December 12, 1873, and February 24, 1874; see also Norfolk *Virginian*, November 8, 1873.

58. L. Q. Washington to Robert M. T. Hunter, December 11, 1873, Hunter-Garnett Papers.

59. William Smith to John W. Daniel, November 25, 1873, Daniel Papers, Duke University. So potent were the "young Americans" that Alexander H. H. Stuart later revived the argument in his own behalf. Alexander H. H. Stuart to Marshall Hanger, December 7, 1875, Alexander Hugh Holmes Stuart Papers, University of Virginia.

60. Withers, *Autobiography*, pp. 317–19.

61. Robert M. T. Hunter to Lewis E. Harvie, January 17, 1874, Harvie Papers.

"behind the times, an old politician, a Bourbon &c" and that "Withers had in his favor the army feeling & the young men."[62]

It was significant that "the army feeling" and "the rebel yell" belonged to the Confederate colonel who had been a Whig and conditional Unionist—not to the secessionist statesman who had sat in the Confederacy's Cabinet and been president pro tempore of its Senate. That fact was at the heart of the rivalry between prewar and postwar politicians. The cleavage between generations was not simply a matter of age but of education. To the young Conservatives, the antebellum world was a distant memory, dimmed by the intervening clash of arms. The Confederate Army, not the antebellum society, had been the school of their early manhood. It had exposed them to technological and logistical problems, as well as to some exercises in political manipulation. It had, by painful tugs, pulled them loose from traditional, provincial moorings, and taught them to distrust the politicians and orators of the Southern Rights viewpoint. The experience of defeat had buried their past lives, and the victory of the progressive, industrial North had given them an inspiration by which to plan new ones.[63] For Hunter and his colleagues, the Confederate experience had been the last of the Old South; for Withers and many of his comrades-in-arms, it had been the first of the New.

The Conservative veterans learned their lessons well. Their army experiences, and their subsequent sruggles to recoup their fortunes and reconstruct their state, left them indifferent or even cynical in regard to inherited traditions, especially those of Southern Rights. Pursuing those traditions, they had learned, did not pay. "One by one," the Richmond *Enquirer* wrote in 1875, "every position we took up, declaring our determination to die in its defence, has been surrendered, until now we are really at the 'last ditch'. . . . Shall we, still hugging our delusions, throw ourselves in and be buried, the quick with the dead, or shall we cut loose, take a new step forward, and endeavor to retrieve ourselves by forcing from the future, what we have in vain sought to draw from the past?"[64]

"Slavery was the material bone of contention," John W. Daniel declared in a speech at the University of Virginia in 1877, "secession

---

62. L. Q. Washington to Hunter, January 14, 1874, Hunter-Garnett Papers. Frank Ruffin sadly agreed that *"young Virginia* did the work." Frank G. Ruffin to Hunter, January 13, 1874, *ibid.*

63. See above, pp. 28–30, 31–33; see editorial in Richmond *Enquirer*, June 26, 1872.

64. Richmond *Enquirer*, March 2, 1875.

was the fiction of law adopted in pleading for its defence. The war ended, but slavery had departed forevermore, and by the arbitrament of battle secession was buried with it in a common grave. . . . The cause is dead, dead—let it rest!"[65]

Some found the veteran generation opportunistic in forsaking tradition for "practicality." Jefferson Davis could not understand Daniel's 1877 speech; the sacred cause, he felt, must still be *right*, even if impracticable.[66] When young Conservatives branded the traditionalists as "abstractionists," Robert L. Dabney replied that the highest principles of thought and conduct were abstractions and that to scorn abstraction was to reject intellect and ethics.[67] At the time of redemption the Richmond *Enquirer*, still under traditionalist control, warned that "we are in danger of swapping our Don Quixotes for Barnums and Forneys." The *Enquirer* insisted that "no matter what the war destroyed—there is still a right and a wrong in Virginia" and that the "utilitarians" who were teaching the contrary were "public malefactors" serving poison from golden vessels.[68] The Norfolk *Virginian*, too, resented the facility with which young Conservatives brushed aside time-honored traditions in the name of "progress" and dismissed their elders as "recalcitrant," "reactionary," "fogies," "obsolete," and "dead."[69]

Many Conservatives worried about the low moral tone they found among their colleagues. Frank Ruffin thought the state had been "ruined" in "character & *tone*" by the Northern conquest.[70] John Wise found his contemporaries hypocritical, lacking in integrity, and ready to compromise essential principles.[71] "The very atmosphere of politicians sickens me," Chairman Meade lamented in 1873; "all is false—hollow and unreal. They are all selfish and would betray you for less than the thirty pieces of silver."[72] "Great God," Kemper's secretary wrote when a railroad scandal erupted in 1877, "I repeat what my wife said to me Sunday *'is no one honest?'* "[73] It

65. Daniel, ed., *Daniel Speeches*, pp. 145–46.

66. Jefferson Davis to John W. Daniel, July 19, 1877, Daniel Papers, University of Virginia; Davis to Daniel, July 19, 1877, Daniel Papers, Duke University. These are separated portions of the same letter.

67. Dabney, *Discussions*, IV, 46–52.

68. Richmond *Enquirer-Examiner*, September 24, 1869.

69. Norfolk *Virginian*, January 24, 1874.

70. Frank G. Ruffin to Lewis E. Harvie, August 9, 1876, Harvie Papers.

71. Wise, *Lion's Skin*, pp. 322–23.

72. Nathaniel B. Meade to James L. Kemper, December 8, 1873, Kemper Papers, University of Virginia.

73. S. Bassett French to William Mahone, January 17, 1877, Mahone Papers.

was not for men whose faith in their ancestral principles had been crushed under the Yankee juggernaut to set examples of principled idealism.

Both "the rejuvenation of Whiggery" and "the rule of the Brigadier Generals" that writers have identified as characteristics of the post-Reconstruction Southern leadership[74] reflected the leadership's adaptive character. Both the Whig party and the Confederate officer corps served as schools that prepared those who passed through them for accommodation to the world in which Conservatives found themselves living after 1865. In neither case was the schooling designed for that end, and neither left all its pupils with the same conclusions—as the case of General Jubal Early, a former Whig, clearly attested. The later leaders of Virginia Conservatism, though, found in the Whig policies and the Confederate military experience lessons that supplemented their later education from direct experience in an industrializing nation. Colonel Withers' lack of personal vices, on which Cameron commented, assuredly did not prepare him for the environment of the United States Senate in the Grant era. He had, though, acquired useful preparation in his experience as a Union Whig in antebellum politics, as a colonel in the Army of Northern Virginia, and as sales agent for the University Publishing Company.

A REVOLUTIONARY ROLE?

One can, as James S. Allen has suggested, see the course of Reconstruction politics as the Northern middle class's search for a bloc of reliable Southern allies to insure its continued supremacy in the federal government.[75] The absence in the South of a large capitalist middle class schooled in "Yankee" ideas presented a problem. In 1865, federal officials tried to build a sympathetic Southern movement on the base of the small minority of wartime Unionists. The Republican majority in the North lost patience as governments of Unionists became governments of moderate former Confederates. Even the more flexible "Johnson governments"—such as the one in Virginia—were confused about the Northern conquerors' terms and hesitated to comply with them. In 1867, Congress instituted its own Reconstruction program, enfranchising the black

74. For these phrases, see Woodward, *Reunion and Reaction*, p. 23, and Nash K. Burger and John K. Bettersworth, *South of Appomattox* (New York: Harcourt, Brace and Company, 1959), p. 4.
75. Allen, *Reconstruction*, pp. 29–36, 79–86, 186–97.

freedmen as the basis of an allied movement in the South. The resultant Southern Republicanism fulfilled many of Congress' expectations—but its complex social composition gave birth to both tendencies to social radicalism and tendencies to incompetence and corruption—all of which repelled many propertied Northern Republicans. In addition, opposition by the propertied Conservatives called into question the Radicals' ability to guarantee public order. Tiring of their union with Southern Radicalism, conservative Northern Republicans found Southern conservatives increasingly acceptable as "junior partners" in preserving a Thermidorian *status quo*. A fast-growing business element acquired great influence in the conservative movement, which grew increasingly moderate, accepted formal equality of rights for Negroes, adjusted to the War's social effects, and conciliated Northern Republicans.

The Conservatives of Virginia played an important role in the sectional stabilization. As former Confederates, they found their state in 1865 a conquered country, under the rule of an enemy animated by the institutions and ideas of nineteenth-century democratic capitalism. Only on Northern Republicans' terms could a former Confederate state recover autonomy and representation in the federal government. Northern leaders intended that the South should, sooner or later, assume the North's social characteristics. The abolition of slavery was the first revolutionary step toward that objective. During the succeeding years, Northern statesmen advanced social change in the South by measures to give Negroes the rights of free laborers, citizens, and voters, to disfranchise some antebellum political leaders, and to readmit the seceded states to their privileges in the Union under constitutions and leaders acceptable to Northern congressmen. Commercial, social, and intellectual contacts furthered the process of Southern assimilation to Northern norms.

Responding to this situation, Conservative leaders sought for their state a future consistent with the conquerors' national objectives. Emancipation and military destruction had broken up the structure of plantation agriculture, and economic ruin combined with Negro suffrage, proscription, and the discrediting of secessionist leaders to break the planters' former political power. The planters' debacle occasioned the advance of town-based commercial elements and of small-scale farmers, who had played only secondary roles in the South before 1861. The industrializing North's resources and dynamism implanted in many Virginians an almost eschatological vision of prosperity through capitalist development. The sight of smoldering ruins about them only quickened their efforts to develop their region and to create a governmental and social environment conducive to economic progress.

The mission of Conservatives of this forward-looking stamp was, properly speaking, not innovative but adaptive. Their history would have been very different, to say the least, if emancipation had come about by an indigenous movement instead of by external intervention. Having stood by the Confederacy in the armed conflict, most of the Conservative leaders underwent a conversion to the position their enemies had maintained. Retaining their distinctiveness in some ways, they adapted to Northern terms in regard to the central issues of the conflict. In a popularly received lecture in 1866, George W. Bagby played on the adaptive qualities of "Bacon and Greens," the staples of the Virginia diet. No animal, Bagby said, had managed to survive in as many different environments as the hog, and no plant had proved as universally adaptive as the turnip. The Virginian, composed of these two components, would be able to preserve his existence in the new age—by conforming to the circumstances of that age.[76]

In Virginia, less "Southern" in some respects than the cotton states, the Conservatives adapted relatively rapidly. By 1869 progressive groups, largely businessmen, wrested control of the Conservative party from traditionalists. The Conservatives adopted a policy of universal suffrage and universal amnesty, coalition with moderate Republicans, conciliation with the Grant administration, and acceptance of a nonproscriptive version of the Radicals' Underwood constitution. Under that program the Conservatives won control of the state government in 1870, at the end of military Reconstruction.

During the 1870's, the slow rate of economic change and the persistence of traditionalist attitudes prevented the Conservative party from realizing the full progressive potential of the "new movement." The moderate, capitalist-oriented Conservatives nevertheless continued to shape party and government policy. That element consisted largely of businessmen and related urban professional men, to whom were added former Union Whigs and Confederate officers—groups schooled, each in its own way, in adaptation to postwar Northern norms. The principal Conservative leaders, for one reason or another, worked to adapt Virginia to those norms: Ameri-

76. Bagby, *Old Virginia Gentleman*, pp. 194–95.

can nationalism, industrial capitalism, Gilded-Age politics, and freedom without equality for Negroes. Traditionalists suspected these forward-looking Conservatives as bearers of alien, "Yankee" tendencies.

The Conservative administrations took a marked, albeit hesitant, step from the "Old South" to the "New." Their free public schools, however modest by twentieth-century standards, were a revolutionary innovation, an important concomitant of the nascent industrial society. Adopting a laissez-faire policy, the state ceased to support and regulate railroads and canals. It nevertheless helped first one, then another, private company in the contest by which Northern corporations ousted native ones from supremacy in the transportation network. The Commonwealth neglected the interests of impoverished farmers as conspicuously as it promoted business interests. It guaranteed to freedmen a modicum of civil rights by a juridical equality that did not imperil white supremacy in government and society. In federal politics, Conservatives abandoned the State-Rights theories of the 1850's. Officially independent of national parties, they aligned themselves in national elections with the Democratic party. Some were attracted to the Republican party—the political agent of "the Last Capitalist Revolution"— but to affiliate with the Republicans would have cost Conservatives the support of rural and traditionalist voters. The Conservative administrations recognized the Funding Act of 1871 as a binding contract with the holders—mostly Northern and foreign—of antebellum Virginia bonds. However, their repeated failure, after attempting a variety of expedients, to pay full interest on the bonds eventually made the state debt policy a controversial issue. In 1879 the controversy split the Conservative party into two mutually hostile parties, along a line roughly approximating the line that divided business-oriented and farming-oriented Conservatives. Neither of the new parties had much in common with the Southern Rights politics of the 1850's—and that fact was an impressive testimony to the effectiveness of the Conservative party's work.

During their decade of supremacy, the Virginia Conservatives did not bring their state far into the future that their most advanced leaders foresaw. Their "failure," in that sense, resulted partly from contradictions in their policies and partly from conditions beyond their control. Hoping to incorporate the Old Dominion into an industrial America, they interpreted the principal forces of their age correctly. They did not appreciate, though, how slowly those forces would operate and how persistently vestiges of Southern tradition would withstand the erosive effects of change. Nor did they recognize that, in an economic system characterized by uneven development, the South might for generations perform important functions in the national system without attaining the Northeast's level of economic and social development. Although they erred in "timing," the adaptive Conservatives anticipated much of the course of Southern progress during the ensuing century. They set out to bring to birth a New South on the ashes of the Old. It took three generations to fulfill their most ambitious visions. A century after the "new movement," their successors—the liberals of the fourth generation—still did not conceive of a progress that would go beyond the Conservatives' objective of adaptation to Yankee industrial capitalism.[77]

77. As I write these words, exactly a hundred years after the election that elevated the Conservatives to power in Virginia, I learn that a number of Southern liberals are forming a new organization called "the L. Q. C. Lamar Society." Concerned mainly to promote economic development on rational lines, they have taken the name of the Mississippi conservative leader because of his efforts for racial and sectional harmony during the Reconstruction period. [Durham] North Carolina *Anvil*, July 12, 1969. The occurrence is a reminder of the essential continuity between the more enlightened Southern conservatives of Reconstruction days and the Southern liberals of the twentieth century.

Bibliography of Sources Cited

I. PRIMARY SOURCES

A. Manuscripts

Library of Congress, Washington, D.C.
    William Cabell Rives Papers.
    John McAllister Schofield Papers.

University of Virginia, Charlottesville, Va.
    William A. Anderson Papers.
    B. Johnson Barbour Papers.
    Barbour-Ellis Papers.
    John Warwick Daniel Papers.
    Hamilton James Eckenrode Papers.
    Hunter-Garnett Papers.
    John Daniel Imboden Papers.
    James Lawson Kemper Papers.
    Alexander Hugh Holmes Stuart Papers.

Virginia Historical Society, Richmond, Va.
    George William Bagby Papers.
    James Lawson Kemper Papers.

Virginia State Library, Richmond, Va.
    Samuel Bassett French Papers.
    Lewis Evarts Harvie Papers.
    James Lawson Kemper Executive Correspondence and Letter-Books.
    Frank Gildart Ruffin Scrapbooks.
    Gilbert Carlton Walker Executive Correspondence.

College of William and Mary, Williamsburg, Va.
    James Barron Hope Papers.

[297]

Charles Triplett O'Ferrall Papers.
Harrison Holt Riddleberger Papers.
John Sergeant Wise Papers.

Historical Foundation of the Presbyterian and Reformed Churches, Montreat, N.C.
William Henry Ruffner Papers.

Duke University, Durham, N.C.
John Esten Cooke Papers.
John Warwick Daniel Papers.
Frederick William Mackey Holliday Papers.
Johnston-McMullen Papers.
William Mahone Papers.

Southern Historical Collection, University of North Carolina at Chapel Hill, Chapel Hill, N.C.
Edmund Willcox Hubard Papers.
Thomas Muldrup Logan Papers.
William Thomas Sutherlin Papers.
Tucker Family Papers.
James Alexander Walker Papers.

University of Chicago, Chicago, Ill.
Wyndham Robertson Papers.

Calais Free Library, Calais, Me.
James Shepherd Pike Diary. Examined in typescript copy in possession of Professor Robert F. Durden, Duke University.

B. Public Documents

United States Congress
Congressional Globe, 1870–73.
Congressional Record, 1873–81.
Joint Committee on Reconstruction. *Report of the Joint Committee on Reconstruction*, 39 Congress, 1 Session (1866).
Imboden, John D., "Virginia," in *Report on the Internal Commerce of the United States, December 20, 1886, Appendix: The Commercial, Industrial, Transportation, and Other Interests of the Southern States*, House Doucument 7, Part II, 49 Cong., 2 Sess. (1886).

United States Supreme Court
Wallace's Reports, Volumes 11–23, 1870–74.
United States Reports, Volumes 91–100, 1875–79.

United States Commissioner of Education
"Proceedings of the Department of Superintendence of the National Education Association at Its Meeting at Washington, D.C., February 18–20, 1880," in *Circulars of Information of the United States Commissioner of Education, 1880*, No. 2. Washington: Government Printing Office, 1880.

Virginia General Assembly
Virginia *House Journal*, 1869–79.
Virginia *Senate Journal*, 1869–79.

Virginia Supreme Court of Appeals
Grattan's Reports, Volumes 19–32, 1870–80.

Virginia Auditor of Public Accounts
Report of the Auditor of Public Accounts for the Fiscal Year ending September 30, 1871. Richmond: C. A. Schaffter, Superintendent of Public Printing, 1871.

Virginia Commissioner of Agriculture
First Annual Report of the Commissioner of Agriculture, of the State of Virginia. Richmond: James E. Goode, 1877.

Virginia Department of Public Instruction
Circular No. 89: "Public School Difficulties Removed." N.p., n.d.
First Annual Report of the [Virginia] *Superintendent of Public Instruction, for the Year ending August 31, 1871*. Richmond: C. A. Schaffter, Superintendent of Public Printing, 1871.
Second Annual Report of the Superintendent of Public Instruction, for the Year ending August 31, 1872. First Report of the Board of Visitors of the Agricultural and Mechanical College. Richmond: Richard F. Walker, Superintendent of Public Printing, 1872.
Third Annual Report of the Superintendent of Public Instruction, for the Year ending August 31, 1873; with Reports of the Virginia Agricultural and Mechanical College, and Hampton Normal and Agricultural Institute. Richmond: Richard F. Walker, Superintendent of Public Printing, 1873.
Fourth Annual Report of the Superintendent of Public Instruction, for the Year ending August 31, 1874; with Reports of the Virginia Agricultural and Mechanical College, and Hampton Normal and Agricultural Institute. Richmond: Richard F. Walker, Superintendent of Public Printing, 1874.
Fifth Annual Report of the Superintendent of Public Instruction for the Year ending July 31, 1875; with Reports of the

Virginia Agricultural and Mechanical College and Hampton Normal and Agricultural Institute. Richmond: Richard F. Walker, Superintendent of Public Printing, 1875.

Sixth Annual Report of the Superintendent of Public Instruction, for the Year ending July 31, 1876. Richmond: Richard F. Walker, Superintendent of Public Printing, 1876.

Seventh Annual Report of the Superintendent of Public Instruction, for the Year ending July 31, 1877. Richmond: Richard F. Walker, Superintendent of Public Printing, 1877.

Eighth Annual Report of the Superintendent of Public Instruction, for the Year ending July 31, 1878. Richmond: R. E. Frazier, Superintendent of Public Printing, 1878.

City of Norfolk

Message of John R. Ludlow, Mayor of the City of Norfolk, Va., to the Select and Common Councils, together with Municipal Reports, for the Fiscal Year ending December 31, 1872. Norfolk: Virginian Book and Job Print, 1873.

C. Newspapers

Alexandria *People's Advocate*, 1876.
Alexandria *Virginia Sentinel*, 1873–75.
London (Great Britain) *Index*, 1862.
Norfolk *Landmark*, 1873–77.
Norfolk *Virginian*, 1873–75.
Petersburg *Index*, 1870–73.
Petersburg *Index and Appeal*, 1873–79.
Richmond *Dispatch*, 1872, 1875–76.
Richmond *Enquirer*, 1869, 1872, 1875.
Richmond *Examiner*, 1866.
(Richmond) *Religious Herald*, 1875.
Richmond *Whig*, 1859–69, 1872, 1877.
Staunton *Vindicator*, 1877.

D. Periodical Articles

Burr, C. Chauncey. "Dialogue between a Democrat and a 'Conservative,'" *The Old Guard*, VIII (April, 1870), 257–63.

Johnson, Bradley T. "Can States Be Compelled to Pay Their Debts?" *The American Law Review*, XII (July, 1878), 625–59.

"Personnel of the General Assembly," *The Old Dominion*, IV (May 15, 1870), 297–301.

Pollard, Edward A. "The Negro in the South," *Lippincott's Magazine*, V (April, 1870), 383–91.

————. "New Virginia," *Old and New*, V (March, 1872), 279–90.

Riddleberger, Harrison H. "Bourbonism in Virginia," *The North American Review*, CXXXIV (April, 1882), 416–30.

Ruffner, William Henry. "The Co-education of the White and Colored Races," *Scribner's Monthly*, VIII (May, 1874), 86–90.

"Some Recent Observations in Virginia," *The Nation*, XXV (September 13, 1877), 163–65.

Young, H. H. "Democrats and 'Conservatives,' " *The Old Guard*, V (July, 1867), 543–45.

E. Pamphlets and Broadsides

[Bagby, George W.]. *John Brown and Wm. Mahone (1860–1880): An Historical Parallel, Foreshadowing Civil Trouble*. Richmond: C. F. Johnston, 1880.

Cameron, William E. *Some Interior Phases of Reconstruction: How Virginia Got Back into the Union; Glimpses of Great Men North and South*. Broadside, n.p., n.d. Copy in Harrison Holt Riddleberger Papers, College of William and Mary.

Campbell, John A. *Reminiscences and Documents Relating to the Civil War during the Year 1865*. Baltimore: John Murphy and Company, 1887.

The Case of the Foreign Bondholders and the Atlantic, Mississippi & Ohio R. R. Co.: The Answer of the Company and Accompanying Documents; Correspondence between General William Mahone, President, and John Collinson, Agent of the Company; also General Mahone's Letter to Captain Tyler, Who Presided over the Meeting of Foreign Bondholders in London, &c., &c. Richmond: n.p., 1876.

[Edmunds, John R.]. *Speech of John R. Edmunds of Halifax before the State Conservative Convention, April 28th, 1869*. N.p., [1869].

[Educational Association of Virginia]. *Minutes of the Educational Association of Virginia Assembled in University Hall, Charlottesville, Virginia, Tuesday, July 17th, 1866*. Richmond: C. H. Wynne, 1866.

————. *Minutes of the Educational Association of Virginia. Fourth Annual Session, held in Lexington, Virginia, July 13–16, 1869*. Lynchburg: Schaffter and Bryant, 1870.

————. *Minutes of the Educational Association of Virginia, July 12–15, 1870*. Richmond: Educational Journal Print, 1870.

Hoge, Peyton H. and Howard R. Bayne. *The Travels of Ego and Alter: An Epistolary Narrative of a Tramp through the Old Dominion*. Richmond: West, Johnston, and Co., 1879.

[Holliday, Frederick William Mackey]. *Inaugural Address of Gov. Fred. W.M. Holliday, delivered in Richmond, Va., Jan. 1, 1878*. N.p., [1878].

Horace Greeley's Views on Virginia. N.p., [1872].

[Kemper, James L.]. *Letter from Governor Kemper: The Petersburg Charter; The Political Situation Considered; The Principles and*

Aims of the Conservative Party; Our Relations with the Federal Government. N.p., [1874].

Letters of Col. Mosby and John Tyler, Jr. N.p., [1876].

[Mahone, William]. *The Express Question: Correspondence between a Committee of Business Men of Richmond, and Wm. Mahone, President, Atlantic, Mississippi & Ohio R. R. Co., with an Appendix.* N.p., [1874].

_____. *General Mahone against Convict Labour in Competition with Honest Labour and Private Enterprise.* N.p., [1877].

Mosby, Charles L., *Congressional Test Act Examined in Two Letters in Which Are Considered, First the Constitutionality of the Act, and Second, Its Proper Construction and Application.* Lynchburg: *Virginian* Power-Press Printing Office, 1865.

[Ould, Robert]. *Speech of Judge Robt. Ould before the Senate Committee on Roads and Internal Navigation, on the Application of Mr. Reuben Ragland for an Amendment to the Charter of the Petersburg Railroad Company. Delivered February 15, 1873.* Richmond: Clemitt and Jones, 1873.

Plan of Organization of the Conservative Party of Va., June 27th, 1872. N.p. [1872].

Report of the Rector of the University of Virginia in Reference to the "Congressional Grant of Lands for Agricultural and Technical Schools." N.p., [1870].

[Ruffner, William Henry]. *The Proper Educationial Policy for the Colored People: Extract from an Address delivered by W. H. Ruffner at the Hampton Institute, June 11 [, 1873].* N.p., n.d.

_____. *The Public Free School System: Dr. Dabney Answered by Mr. Ruffner.* N.p., [1876].

Second Reunion of Mahone's Brigade, Held on the Anniversary of the Battle of the Crater, in the Opera House, Norfolk, July 31, 1876. Norfolk: Landmark Book and Job Company, 1876.

[Segar, Joseph]. *Letter of the Hon. Joseph Segar, on the Late Elections in Virginia.* N.p., [1869].

Shall Virginia Be Represented at the Philadelphia Industrial Exhibition? And, If So, How? N.p., n.d.

Speech of Hon. R. M. T. Hunter, delivered at Richmond, Aug. 22, 1873; Biographical Sketches of Gen. James L. Kemper, Col. Robert E. Withers and Hon. Raleigh T. Daniel, Conservative Nominees; Platform and Resolutions, Plan of Organization, State and Executive Committees. N.p., [1873].

Virginia Conservative Address and Organization, 1870. N.p., [1870].

[Virginia State Agricultural Society]. *Journal of the Proceedings of a General Meeting of the Virginia State Agricultural Society and Convention of Virginia Farmers, Held in Richmond on the 20th, 21st, and 22nd, Nov., 1866, Pursuant to a Call by Hon. Willoughby Newton, President Va. State Ag. Society.* Richmond: Charles H. Wynne, 1866.

————. *Memorial of the Virginia State Agricultural Society on Immigration, Presented to the General Assembly of Virginia, January 10th, 1872.* N.p., [1872].

[Walker, Gilbert C.]. *Address of Gov. Gilbert C. Walker, Delivered at the Commencement of the Agricultural and Mechanical College, at Blasksburg, Montgomery County, Virginia, July 9th, 1873.* N.p., [1873].

F. Books

American Annual Cyclopaedia and Register of Important Events, Volumes IX–XVIII, 1869–78. New York: D. Appleton and Company, published annually.

Bledsoe, Albert Taylor, *Is Davis a Traitor[?]; or Was Secession a Constitutional Right Previous to the War of 1861?* Baltimore: Innes and Company, 1866.

Bruce, Philip Alexander, *The Plantation Negro as a Freeman: Observations on His Character, Condition, and Prospects in Virginia.* New York and London: G. P. Putnam's Sons, 1889.

[Democratic Party]. *Official Proceedings of the National Democratic Convention Heild at New York, July 4–9, 1868.* Boston: Rockwell and Rollins, 1868.

————. *Official Proceedings of the National Democratic Convention Held in St. Louis, Mo., June 27th, 28th, and 29th, 1876.* St. Louis: Woodward, Tiernan and Hale, 1876.

Olmsted, Frederick Law. *The Cotton Kingdom: A Traveller's Observations on Cotton and Slavery in the American Slave States, Based upon Three Former Volumes of Journeys and Investigations by the Same Author.* Edited, with an introduction, by Arthur M. Schlesinger. New York: Alfred A. Knopf, 1953.

[Peabody Education Fund]. *Proceedings of the Trustees of the Peabody Education Fund, 1874–1881.* Volume II of *Proceedings.* Boston: University Press: John Wilson and Son, 1881.

Pollard, Edward A. *The Key to the Ku-Klux.* Lynchburg: n.p., 1872.

————. *The Lost Cause: A New Southern History of the War of the Confederates.* New York: E. B. Treat and Company, 1866.

————. *The Lost Cause Regained.* New York: G. W. Carleton and Company, 1868.

Ruffin, Edmund. *Anticipations of the Future, To Serve as Lessons for the Present Time, in the Form of Extracts of Letters from an English Resident in the United States, to the London Times, from 1864 to 1870, with an Appendix, on the Causes and Consequences of the Independence of the South.* Richmond: J. W. Randolph, 1860.

Somers, Robert. *The Southern States since the War, 1870–1.* London and New York: Macmillan and Company, 1871.

Trowbridge, John Townsend. *The South: A Tour of Its Battle-Fields and Ruined Cities, A Journey through the Desolated States and Talks with the People....* Hartford, Conn.: L. Stebbins, 1866.

G. *Collections of Documents and Other Data*

Abbott, Martin, ed. "A Southerner Views the South, 1865: Letters of Harvey M. Watterson," *Virginia Magazine of History and Biography*, LXVIII (October, 1960), 478–89.

Bagby, George W. *The Old Virginia Gentleman and Other Sketches.* Edited by Ellen M. Bagby. Fourth Edition. Richmond: Dietz Press, 1943.

Bear, James A., Jr., ed. "Henry A. Wise and the Campaign of 1873: Some Letters from the Papers of James Lawson Kemper," *Virginia Magazine of History and Biography*, LXII (July, 1954), 320–42.

Dabney, Robert Lewis. *Discussions by Robert L. Dabney, D.D., LL.D., Recently Professor of Moral Philosophy in the University of Texas, and for Many Years Professor of Theology in Union Theological Seminary in Virginia.* 4 volumes. Edited by Clement Read Vaughn. Mexico, Mo.: Crescent Book House, 1897.

Daniel, Edward M., ed., *Speeches and Orations of John Warwick Daniel.* Lynchburg: J. B. Bell Company, 1911.

Dumond, Dwight L., ed., *Southern Editorials on Secession.* New York and London: Century Company for American Historical Association, 1931.

Fleming, Walter Lynwood, ed. *Documentary History of Reconstruction: Political, Military, Social, Religious, Educational & Industrial—1865 to the Present Time*, 2 volumes. Cleveland: A. H. Clark Company, 1906–7.

Hope, James Barron. *A Wreath of Virginia Bay Leaves: Poems of James Barron Hope.* Edited by Janey Hope Marr. Richmond: West, Johnston, and Company, 1895.

Jones, Wilbur D., ed. "A British Report on Postwar Virginia," *Virginia Magazine of History and Biography*, LXIX (July, 1961), 346–52.

Lanier, Sidney. *The Works of Sidney Lanier.* Edited by Charles B. Anderson and Aubrey H. Starke. Centennial Edition, 10 volumes. Baltimore: The Johns Hopkins Press, 1945.

Ruchames, Louis, ed. *A John Brown Reader.* London and New York: Abelard-Schuman, 1959.

Thorpe, Francis Newton, ed. *The Federal and State Constitutions, Colonial Charters and Other Organic Laws of the States, Territories, and Colonies Now or Hereafter Forming the United States of America, Compiled and Edited under Act of Congress of June 30, 1906.* 7 volumes. *House Document No. 357, 59 Cong., 1 Sess.* Washington: Government Printing Office, 1909.

United States Bureau of the Census. *Historical Statistics of the United*

States, Colonial Times to 1957. Washington: Government Printing Office, 1960.

H. *Autobiographies and Recollections*

[Allan-Olney, Mary]. *The New Virginians.* 2 volumes. Edinburgh and London: William Blackwood and Sons, 1880.

Avary, Myrta Lockett. *Dixie after the War: An Exposition of Social Conditions Existing in the South, during the Twelve Years Succeeding the Fall of Richmond.* New York: Doubleday, Page and Company, 1906.

Bradley, A. G. *Other Days: Recollections of Rural England and Old Virginia, 1860–1880.* London: Constable and Company, 1913.

Claiborne, John Herbert. *Seventy-Five Years in Old Virginia: with Some Account of the Life of the Author and Some History of the People among Whom His Lot Was Cast—Their Character, Their Condition, and Their Conduct before the War, during the War and after the War.* New York and Washington: Neale Publishing Company, 1904.

Johnston, Joseph E. *Narrative of Military Operations Directed during the Late War between the States.* New York: D. Appleton and Company, 1874.

Massey, John E. *Autobiography of John E. Massey.* Edited by Elizabeth Hazelwood Hancock. New York and Washington: Neale Publishing Company, 1909.

O'Ferrall, Charles Triplett. *Forty Years of Active Service: Being Some History of the War between the Confederacy and the Union and of the Events Leading up to It, with Reminiscences of the Struggle and Accounts of the Author's Experiences of Four Years from Private to Lieutenant-Colonel and Acting Colonel in the Cavalry of the Army of Northern Virginia; also, Much of the History of Virginia and the Nation in Which the Author Took Part for Many Years in Political Conventions and on the Hustings and as Lawyer, Member of the Legislature of Virginia, Judge, Member of the House of Representatives of the United States and Governor of Virginia.* New York and Washington: Neale Publishing Company, 1904.

Royall, William L. *History of the Virginia Debt Controversy: The Negro's Vicious Influence in Politics.* Richmond: George M. West, 1897.

————. *Some Reminiscences.* New York and Washington: Neale Publishing Company, 1909.

Schofield, John McAllister. *Forty-Six Years in the Army.* New York: Century Company, 1897.

Wise, John S. *The End of an Era.* Boston and New York: Houghton, Mifflin and Company, 1899.

————. *The Lion's Skin: A Historical Novel and a Novel History.* New York: Doubleday, Page and Company, 1905.

Withers, Robert E. *The Autobiography of an Octogenarian.* Roanoke, Va.: Stone Printing and Manufacturing Company, 1907.

II. SECONDARY WORKS

A. Books and Pamphlets

Alderman, Edwin A., and Armistead C. Gordon. *J. L. M. Curry: A Biography.* New York: Macmillan Company, 1911.

Allen, James S. *Reconstruction: The Battle for Democracy, 1865–1877.* New York: International Publishers, 1937.

Ambler, Charles H. *Francis H. Pierpont: Union War Governor of Virginia and Father of West Virginia.* Chapel Hill: University of North Carolina Press, 1937.

_____. *Sectionalism in Virginia from 1776 to 1861.* Chicago: University of Chicago Press, 1910.

Arnold, Benjamin W., Jr., *History of the Tobacco Industry in Virginia from 1860 to 1894.* ("Johns Hopkins University Studies in Historical and Political Science," XV, Nos. 1–2.) Baltimore: The Johns Hopkins Press, 1897.

Bell, John W. *Memoirs of Governor William Smith of Virginia: His Political, Military, and Personal History.* New York: Moss Engraving Company, 1891.

Benét, Stephen Vincent. *John Brown's Body,* New York: Rinehart and Company, 1928.

Blake, Nelson M. *William Mahone of Virginia: Soldier and Political Insurgent.* Richmond: Garrett and Massie, 1935.

Bond, Horace Mann, *Negro Education in Alabama: A Study in Cotton and Steel.* Washington: Associated Publishers, 1939.

Boney, F. N. *John Letcher of Virginia: The Story of Virginia's Civil War Governor.* University, Ala.: University of Alabama Press, 1966.

Bruce, Kathleen. *Virginia Iron Manufacture in the Slave Era.* New York and London: Century Company for American Historical Association, 1931.

Bruce, Philip Alexander. *History of the University of Virginia, 1819–1919: The Lengthened Shadow of One Man.* 5 volumes. New York: Macmillan Company, 1920–22.

Carrington, Wirt Johnson. *A History of Halifax County (Virginia).* Richmond: Appeals Press, 1924.

Christian, William Asbury. *Richmond: Her Past and Present.* Richmond: L. H. Jenkins, 1912.

Cooper, William J., Jr., *The Conservative Regime: South Carolina, 1877–1890.* ("Johns Hopkins University Studies in Historical and Political Science," 86th Series, No. 1.) Baltimore: The Johns Hopkins Press, 1968.

Coulter, E. Merton. *The Confederate States of America, 1861–1865.* Baton Rouge: Louisiana State University Press, 1950.

———. *The South during Reconstruction, 1865–1877.* Baton Rouge: Louisiana State University Press, 1947.

Craven, Avery O. *Soil Exhaustion as a Factor in the Agricultural History of Virginia and Maryland, 1606–1860.* ("University of Illinois Studies in the Social Sciences," XIII, No. 1.) Urbana: University of Illinois, 1925.

Curry, Jabez L. M. *A Brief Sketch of George Peabody and a History of the Peabody Education Fund through Thirty Years.* Cambridge, Mass.: University Press: John Wilson and Son, 1898.

Curry, Richard Orr. *A House Divided: A Study of Statehood Politics and the Copperhead Movement in West Virginia.* Pittsburgh: University of Pittsburgh Press, 1964.

De Santis, Vincent P. *Republicans Face the Southern Question: The New Departure Years, 1877–1897.* ("Johns Hopkins University Studies in Historical and Political Science," LXXVII, No. 1.) Baltimore: The Johns Hopkins Press, 1959.

Eaton, Clement. *Freedom of Thought in the Old South.* Durham: Duke University Press, 1940.

———. *The Mind of the Old South.* Rev. ed. Baton Rouge: Louisiana State University Press, 1967.

Eckenrode, Hamilton James. *The Political History of Virginia during the Reconstruction.* ("Johns Hopkins University Studies in Historical and Political Science," XXII, Nos. 6–8.) Baltimore: The Johns Hopkins Press, 1904.

Freeman, Douglas Southall. *R. E. Lee: A Biography.* 4 volumes. New York and London: Charles Scribner's Sons, 1934.

Genovese, Eugene D. *The Political Economy of Slavery: Studies in the Economy and Society of the Slave South.* New York: Pantheon Books, 1965.

Heatwole, Cornelius J. *A History of Education in Virginia.* New York: Macmillan Company, 1916.

Jackson, Luther Porter. *Negro Office-Holders in Virginia, 1865–1895.* Norfolk: Guide Quality Press, 1945.

Johnston, Angus James, II. *Virginia Railroads in the Civil War.* Chapel Hill: University of North Carolina Press for Virginia Historical Society, 1959.

Jones, Virgil Carrington. *Ranger Mosby.* Chapel Hill: University of North Carolina Press, 1944.

McConnell, John Preston. *Negroes and Their Treatment in Virginia from 1865 to 1867.* Pulaski, Va.: B. D. Smith and Brothers, 1910.

McKitrick, Eric L. *Andrew Johnson and Reconstruction.* Chicago: University of Chicago Press, 1960.

May, Henry F. *The Protestant Churches and Industrial America.* New York: Harper, 1949.

Mitchell, Broadus. *The Rise of Cotton Mills in the South.* ("Johns Hopkins University Studies in Historical and Political Science," XXXIX, No. 2.) Baltimore: The Johns Hopkins Press, 1921.

Morrill, Lily Logan. *A Builder of the New South: Notes on the Career of Thomas M. Logan.* Boston: The Christopher Publishing House, 1940.

Nevins, Allan. *The Emergence of Lincoln.* 2 volumes. New York: Charles Scribner's Sons, 1950.

Nicholls, William H. *Southern Tradition and Regional Progress.* Chapel Hill: University of North Carolina Press, 1960.

Overdyke, W. Darrell. *The Know-Nothing Party in the South.* Baton Rouge: Louisiana State University Press, 1950.

Owsley, Frank Laurence. *State Rights in the Confederacy.* Chicago: University of Chicago Press, 1925.

Pearson, Charles C. *The Readjuster Movement in Virginia.* New Haven: Yale University Press, 1917.

Pendleton, William C. *Political History of Appalachian Virginia, 1776–1927.* Dayton, Va.: Shenandoah Press, 1927.

Phillips, Ulrich B. *Life and Labor in the Old South.* Boston: Little, Brown, and Company, 1929.

Ratchford, Benjamin U. *American State Debts.* Durham: Duke University Press, 1941.

Robertson, Alexander F. *Alexander Hugh Holmes Stuart, 1807–1891: A Biography.* Richmond: William Byrd Press, 1925.

Rogers, George W. *Officers of the Senate of Virginia, 1776–1956.* Richmond: Garrett and Massie, 1959.

Scott, William Wallace. *A History of Orange County, Virginia, from Its Formation in 1734 (O. S.) to the End of Reconstruction in 1870; Compiled Mainly from Original Records, with a Brief Sketch of the Beginnings of Virginia, a Summary of Local Events to 1907, and a Map.* Richmond: Everett Waddey Company, 1907.

Sefton, James E., Jr., *The United States Army and Reconstruction, 1865–1877.* Baton Rouge: Louisiana State University Press, 1967.

Shanks, Henry T. *The Secession Movement in Virginia, 1847–1861.* Richmond: Garrett and Massie, 1934.

Stover, John F. *The Railroads of the South, 1865–1900: A Study in Finance and Control.* Chapel Hill: University of North Carolina Press, 1955.

Talbot, Edith A. *Samuel Chapman Armstrong: A Biographical Study.* New York: Doubleday, Page and Company, 1904.

Taylor, Alrutheus A. *The Negro in the Reconstruction of Virginia.*

Washington: Association for the Study of Negro Life and History, 1926.

Tyler, Lyon G., ed. *Encyclopedia of Virginia Biography*. 5 volumes. New York: Lewis Historical Publishing Company, 1915.

Wade, Richard C., *Slavery in the Cities: The South, 1820–1860*. New York: Oxford University Press, 1964.

Waddell, Joseph A. *Annals of Augusta County, Virginia, with Reminiscences Illustrative of the Vicissitudes of Its Pioneer Settlers; Biographical Sketches of Citizens Locally Prominent, and of Those Who Have Founded Families in the Southern and Western States; a Diary of the War, 1861–'5, and a Chapter on Reconstruction*. Richmond: William Ellis Jones, 1886.

Wayland, John W. *A History of Rockingham County, Virginia*. Dayton, Va.: Raebush-Elkins Company, 1912.

Williamson, Chilton, *American Suffrage from Property to Democracy, 1760–1860*. Princeton: Princeton University Press, 1960.

Wise, Barton Haxall, *The Life of Henry A. Wise of Virginia, 1806–1876*. New York: Macmillan Company, 1899.

Woodward, C. Vann. *Origins of the New South, 1877–1913*. Baton Rouge: Louisiana State University Press, 1951.

————. *Reunion and Reaction: The Compromise of 1877 and the End of Reconstruction*. New York: Little, Brown and Company, 1951.

Wooster, Ralph A. *The Secession Conventions of the South*. Princeton: Princeton University Press, 1962.

Wiley, Bell I. *The Life of Johnny Reb: The Common Soldier of the Confederacy*. Indianapolis and New York: Bobbs-Merrill Company, 1943.

Wynes, Charles E. *Race Relations in Virginia, 1870–1902*. Charlottesville: University of Virginia Press, 1961.

Yearns, W. B. *The Confederate Congress*. Athens: University of Georgia Press, 1960.

B. Articles

Alexander, Thomas Benjamin. "Persistent Whiggery in the Confederate South 1861–1877," *Journal of Southern History*, XXVII (August, 1961), 305–29.

Bean, William G. "John Letcher and the Slavery Issue in Virginia's Gubernatorial Contest of 1858–1859," *Journal of Southern History*, XX (February, 1954), 22–49.

————. "The Ruffner Pamphlet of 1847: An Antislavery Aspect of Virginia Sectionalism," *Virginia Magazine of History and Biography*, LXI (July, 1953), 259–82.

Cappon, Lester J. "The Evolution of County Government in Virginia." in Historical Records Survey Division of the Division of the Women's and Professional Projects, Works Progress Administration, *Inventory of the County Archives of Virginia*, No. 21: *Chesterfield County*. Charlottesville: University of Virginia Press, 1938.

Goodrich, Carter. "The Virginia System of Mixed Enterprise: A Study of State Planning of Internal Improvements," *Political Science Quarterly*, LXIV (September, 1949), 355–87.

Halsell, Willie D. "The Bourbon Period in Mississippi Politics, 1875–1890," *Journal of Southern History*, XI (November, 1945), 519–37.

Hesseltine, William B. "Economic Factors in the Abandonment of Reconstruction," *Mississippi Valley Historical Review*, XXII (September, 1935), 191–210.

Hickin, Patricia. "John C. Underwood and the Antislavery Movement in Virginia, 1847–1860," *Virginia Magazine of History and Biography*, LXXIII (April, 1965), 156–68.

Knight, Edgar W. "Reconstruction and Education in Virginia," *South Atlantic Quarterly*, XV (January, 1916), 25–40, and (April, 1916), 157–74.

Mayo, Amory D. "Education in Southwestern Virginia," in *Report of the* [United States] *Commissioner of Education, 1890–1891*, pp. 881–921. Washington: Government Printing Office, 1891.

Moger, Allen W. "Railroad Practices and Policies in Virginia after the Civil War," *Virginia Magazine of History and Biography*, LIX (October, 1951), 423–57.

Pearson, Charles C. "William Henry Ruffner: Reconstruction Statesman of Virginia," *South Atlantic Quarterly*, XX (January, 1921), 25–32, and (April, 1921), 137–51.

Ruffner, William Henry. "The History of Washington College, Now Washington and Lee University, during the First Half of the Nineteenth Century: A Continuation of the 'Early History of Washington College, by Rev. Henry Ruffner, D.D., LL.D.,'" *Washington College Historical Papers*, IV (1893), 3–165; V (1895), 3–31; VI (1904), 1–110.

Sellers, Charles Grier, Jr. "Who Were the Southern Whigs?" *American Historical Review*, LIX (January, 1954), 335–46.

Shanks, Henry T. "Conservative Constitutional Tendencies of the Virginia Secession Convention," in Fletcher M. Green, ed., *Essays in Southern History Presented to Joseph Gregoire de Roulhac Hamilton, Ph.D., LL.D., by His Former Students at the University of North Carolina*. ("The James Sprunt Studies in History and Political Science," XXXI, 29–48.) Chapel Hill: University of North Carolina Press, 1949.

Smith, George Winston. "Ante-Bellum Attempts of Northern Business Interests to 'Redeem' the Upper South," *Journal of Southern History*, XI (May, 1945), 177–213.

Stuart, Meriwether. "Colonel Ulric Dahlgren and Richmond's Union Underground, April, 1864," *Virginia Magazine of History and Biography*, LXXII (April, 1964), 152–204.

Trexler, Harrison A. "The Davis Administration and the Richmond Press," *Journal of Southern History*, XVI (May, 1950), 178–91.

Vandiver, Frank E. "The Confederacy and the American Tradition," *Journal of Southern History*, XXVIII (August, 1962), 277–86.

C. Unpublished Works

Burton, Robert C. "The History of Taxation in Virginia, 1870–1901." Ph.D. dissertation, University of Virginia, 1962.

Cahill, Audrey Marie. "Gilbert Carleton [*sic*] Walker, Virginia's Redeemer Governor." M.A. thesis, University of Virginia, 1956.

Caldwell, Willie Walker. "Life of General James A. Walker." Typescript in James Alexander Walker Papers, Southern Historical Collection, University of North Carolina at Chapel Hill.

Cole, Howson White. "Harrison Holt Riddleberger, Readjuster." M.A. thesis, University of Virginia, 1952.

Eckenrode, Hamilton James. "History of Virginia since 1865." Typescript in Hamilton James Eckenrode Papers, University of Virginia.

Fahrner, Alvin Arthur. "The Public Career of 'Extra Billy' Smith." Ph.D. dissertation, University of North Carolina, 1955.

Fields, Emmett B. "The Agricultural Population of Virginia, 1850–1860." Ph.D. dissertation, Vanderbilt University, 1953.

Hickin, Patricia P. "Antislavery in Virginia, 1831–1861." Ph.D. dissertation, University of Virginia, 1968.

Jones, Robert R. "Conservative Virginian: The Post-War Career of Governor James Lawson Kemper." Ph.D. dissertation, University of Virginia, 1964.

Lowe, Richard G. "Republicans, Rebellion, and Reconstruction: The Republican Party in Virginia, 1856–1870." Ph.D. dissertation, University of Virginia, 1968.

McFarland, George M. "The Extension of Democracy in Virginia, 1850–1895." Ph.D. dissertation, Princeton University, 1925.

Moore, John Hammond. "The Life of James Gaven Field, Virginia Populist (1826–1902)." M.A. thesis, University of Virginia, 1953.

Ours, Robert Maurice. "Virginia's First Redeemer Legislature." M.A. thesis, University of Virginia, 1966.

Smith, James Douglas. "Virginia during Reconstruction, 1865–1870: A Political, Economic, and Social Study." Ph.D. dissertation, University of Virginia, 1955.

Vecellio, Sylvia D. "John Warwick Daniel: Lame Lion of Lynchburg: Youth, Soldier, and Rising Politician, 1842–1885." M.A. thesis, University of Virginia, 1956.

Index

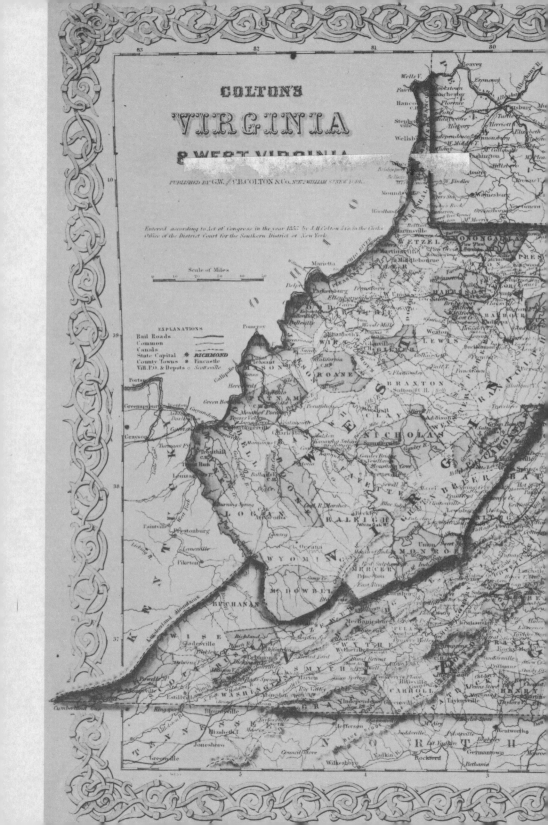